C000197995

True Colours

International Football Kits

The Illustrated Guide

An Exploration of the Kit Designs of the Major National Teams

John Devlin

This book is dedicated with love to my wonderful daughter Amelie – my reason for everything.

BLOOMSBURY SPORT

Bloomsbury Publishing Plc

50 Bedford Square, London, WC1B 3DP, UK

BLOOMSBURY, BLOOMSBURY SPORT and the Diana logo are trademarks of Bloomsbury Publishing Plc

First published in Great Britain 2018

A catalogue record for this book is available from the British Library

Library of Congress Cataloguing-in-Publication data has been applied for

ISBN: PB: 978-1-4729-5629-3; eBook: 978-1-4729-5627-9

2 4 6 8 10 9 7 5 3 1

Typeset in Helvetica Neue and Lato
Designed and typeset by John Devlin

Printed and bound in India by Replika Press Pvt. Ltd.

True Colours

International Football Kits

The Illustrated Guide

An Exploration of the Kit Designs of the Major National Teams

John Devlin

BLOOMSBURY SPORT
LONDON • OXFORD • NEW YORK • NEW DELHI • SYDNEY

The 1990 World Cup final – West Germany in their iconic 1988–91 home kit and Argentina sporting their 1990–91 blue change strip (both adidas).

CONTENTS

NOTES ON THE ILLUSTRATIONS

The kit histories for each team start from the 1966 World Cup, but in many cases the designs were also worn prior to that date. Additional 'change' shorts, socks or other minor anomalies are included in the pull-out round boxes. Where a shirt is worn with the away shorts or socks for some games this will be referred to in the text. If there is a wholesale change with alternative shorts or socks then this is included in the pull-out round boxes.

Major tournaments in which the kit appeared are noted on the right-hand side of each kit and if the design was worn in the finals by the winners of a major trophy a small star is also included. ★

The Netherlands, clad in their famous adidas 1988 strip, take on the USSR in their away kit of white in the final of Euro 88.

The extraordinary Spanish away kit from Euro 2016 – the design was inspired by a heat map based on Fernando Torres' famous goal in Euro 2012 – in action against a Puma-clad Italy.

INTRODUCTION

England's Bobby Charlton swaps shirts with an Argentinian player after their clash in the 1966 World Cup finals.

Any football kit designer will claim that there is no difference between creating an international shirt and a domestic team jersey, but it can't be denied that there is something extra-special about a kit destined for exposure on the biggest stages in world football.

Yes, there is the most obvious difference that there is no need to accommodate a shirt sponsor (and no, the Soviet Union's famous CCCP moniker from the '60s, '70s and '80s doesn't count). More important, though is the deeper brief to reflect the country's national identity and also, arguably, to forge a deeper emotional connection with the team kit.

There are so many iconic strips in world football: the Netherlands' omnipresent orange, the workmanlike white and black of Germany, Argentina's sky blue and white stripes, Brazil's classic yellow/blue/white combo . . . the list goes on. Thousands of memories feature these instantly recognisable colours, displayed at the very pinnacle of the sport.

The more casual football supporter must wonder why the sides don't just sport kits in their national colours, with the country's flag replicated as an integral part of the design. Some – such as Denmark, Sweden and Brazil – do take their colours from their national identity. Others – including Germany, the Netherlands, Italy and even to some extent England – opt for a different colour scheme, emerging from long-standing historical reasons, some geographic and some political.

Thanks to the massive media interest around the World Cup and other major international tournaments, sportswear companies now use these events as shop windows to launch and show off their next range of styles. Most teams will be wearing a brand new kit whenever these feasts of football kick off, and versions of the designs will then be rolled out domestically the following season.

The modern game, with its fast turnaround of strips, has led to increased pressure for new and more daring designs that push the boundaries of tradition and, in the opinion of some purists, good taste. Designs have proved challenging at times for supporters: the more familiar away colour schemes have been discarded, often in favour of 'disruptive' designs, before the return of a traditional interpretation of the team kit – and a national sigh of relief.

One of the main reasons for the attraction and interest in international kit colours must surely come from the fact that they're exotic, glamorous and, well, just plain different. International kits bring in all manner of colour combinations, reflecting differences in cultural expectations, with the result that colours that otherwise clash are often seen together. Before the powerful mechanics of world football kicked into gear, the teams of smaller nations at a World Cup (so small that many fans would struggle to identify them on a globe, let alone a pitch) wore outfits that seemed several years out of date. Or occasionally they were emblazoned with curious and bizarre badges and text: Zaire in 1974 featured a large circular motif in the centre of the shirt, and in 1982, Algeria played the second half of their World Cup games in a slightly different shirt. On at least one occasion, this included a completely different rendering of the team name. Provided sportswear firms don't completely homogenise the game, international football shirts give us supporters a chance to glance into the very culture of a nation through the lens of a football match. They provide us with visual flavours different from those we experience in our usual domestic fixtures.

For those football kit connoisseurs who subscribe to the notion of the modern-day football shirt acting as the simulacra for the colourful military uniforms of centuries past, the power and importance of each team's strip takes on extra impetus – especially when there is historical relevance between the countries on the pitch. Viewed in these terms, the customary swapping of shirts between players can be interpreted as claiming a trophy of war (though this now generally takes place in the tunnel to avoid upsetting technical kit suppliers who have paid millions for their logo to be seen on the team jerseys).

Governing body rules about apparel are also stricter than those generally applied in club football. Since the advent of television the two kits of the competing teams must contrast – one team sporting a light kit, the other a dark kit. Originally this was to ensure differentiation for those watching on black and white televisions, but today it assists referees in making decisions on the pitch. Naturally this places a restriction on colour choices and has led to some federations and sportswear companies erroneously interpreting this to mean that each team must wear a single monochromatic strip. FIFA rules also state that no more than four colours can be used in a kit, and striped or chequered outfits must balance colours equally.

As well as strict rules over the integration of flags and additional logo placement, the international stage has also led the way in terms of additional identification on the pitch. As far back as 1974 the standard numbers on the back of shirts were accompanied by additional smaller versions on the front of the shorts. In 1992 at the European Championships these squad numbers were included in the centre of the front of the shirts and were joined by players' surnames on the reverse. Soon these additional adornments found their way into club level football.

An international football kit must not only capture the identity of the team; it also needs to represent the identity of the nation. That's a tall order, creating a massive responsibility for the companies behind the strips: the greatest teams in the world should have the greatest kits. Via ever more daring and effective design ideas, they need to reflect the tradition of the nation's football heritage within a contemporary retelling of the country's character.

The kits must create a cohesive and strong footballing brand that can inspire the millions of supporters cheering on their heroes as they do battle on the world's biggest football stages.

John Devlin, 2018

ARGENTINA

Argentina are one of those international sides with a unique and iconic kit design. Take sky blue and white stripes, add black shorts, and you have an instantly recognisable strip that translates around the world.

Interestingly, the kits of La Albiceleste (the white and sky blue) didn't settle into a consistent style until the early '90s. Until then, the basic format of the kit remained the same, but a plethora of tiny tweaks, anomalies and design foibles meant that the strip seldom appeared exactly the same twice.

To document every single variation of Argentina kits would take a book twice this size, so this is an attempt to present a cohesive story that guides you through the main strips.

For away kits, royal blue – or, more recently, navy blue – is by far the preferred choice, although white does pop up from time to time as a third choice.

Given the team's highly individual colours, however, away outfits are seldom needed – even when playing teams who sport a similar palette, such as the nation's South American neighbours Uruguay. For many years, Argentina away kits only really appeared in force at major tournaments and in low-key friendlies against domestic club sides, for which the Argentine Football Association (AFA) forbade the side to wear their cherished sky blue and white stripes.

Throughout the 1980s it was Le Coq Sportif that supplied a series of great Argentinian sides – most notably the 1986 World Cup champions.

Since 1990 though, adidas has been the long-term technical partner of La Albiceleste. It also kitted out the side for a brief period in the 1970s. In fact, Argentina were wearing adidas when they claimed their first World Cup title in 1978.

SPECIAL THANKS TO RICHARD JOHNSON

Argentina's exquisite Le Coq Sportif home kit worn as the team line up before the 1986 World Cup Final against West Germany.

HOME 1966–75

Design: Sportlandia

Juan Carlos Lorenzo's Argentina took part in their first World Cup in 1966 sporting this fetching collared shirt, quite unlike any other kit in the tournament. The shirt, which was worn in both long and short versions, was paired with black shorts and two designs of grey socks.

Worn in: A 0–0 draw with eventual World Cup runners up West Germany. Later worn in the 1–0 quarter-final defeat by England.
Worn by: Jorge Solari, Luis Artime.

HOME 1966–70

Design: Sportlandia

An alternative short-sleeved shirt was worn in a few games in 1966 through to 1970. The jersey featured an open neck/collar combination in a style also favoured by Brazil and Portugal at the time. Argentina's socks varied throughout the '60s with many different versions worn.

Worn in: A 3–0 defeat by Italy in a friendly prior to the 1966 World Cup.
Worn by: Oscar Mas, Daniel Onega.

AWAY 1966–68

Design: Sportlandia

Although not required in the World Cup itself, Argentina's regular away strip at the time was a muted shade of blue, fashioned into a standard long sleeved, crew neck shirt which was worn with the home shorts and socks. The Argentina kits at the time were produced by a local brand, Sportlandia.

HOME 1968–75

Design: Sportlandia

A familiar '60s-style version of the famous blue and white stripes did appear in 1968 and was worn as the primary long sleeved option until the arrival of adidas in 1974. A short sleeved version was also produced that featured a central white stripe rather than blue.

Worn in: A 3–1 win over Paraguay in a 1973 qualifier for the 1974 World Cup.
Worn by: Carlos Guerin.

HOME 1966–74

Design: Sportlandia

Since the mid '50s and well into the '70s Argentina occasionally donned various short sleeved v-neck versions of their kit. It must be remembered that through this period there was no consistent Argentina kit and a wide variety of styles were worn.

Worn in: The 1969 2–2 draw with Peru that meant Argentina would miss out on the 1970 World Cup finals.
Worn by: Rafael Albrecht, Alberto Rendo.

AWAY 1968–74

Design: Unknown

A darker blue away shirt with self-coloured crew neck and cuffs also appeared towards the end of the '60s and was worn with light blue shorts and rather striking hooped socks. The shorts were also worn with the home kit at times. Given the rarity of Argentina needing an away kit at this time it can be assumed this outfit was seldom worn. The legendary César Luis Menotti was appointed head coach in 1974.

HOME 1974–76

Design: adidas

Argentina took to the field in the 1974 World Cup wearing adidas, with whom they were to later sign up. Their first outfit for Vladislao Cap's team was the company's regular v-necked shirt of the time, minus the three stripes on the shoulders and sleeves but plus an adidas logo.

Worn in: A 1–1 draw with Italy in the first group stage of the 1974 World Cup, also the 2–1 defeat by Brazil in the second stage.
Worn by: Agustin Balbuena, Hector Yazalde.

AWAY 1974–76

Design: adidas

The updated adidas design for Argentina's away kit worked beautifully – especially with its non-contrasting v-neck and cuffs. The shirt was worn with the regular home shorts and (presumably) non-adidas socks.

Worn in: The 1–1 draw with East Germany in the second group stage of the 1974 World Cup. Curiously, in the match Rene Houseman's shirt had a white v-neck and cuffs!
Worn by: Roberto Telch, Ruben Ayala.

HOME 1976

Design: adidas

The familiar long-sleeved, crew-neck home shirt was updated with branded adidas shorts and white socks in 1976. Given the relative fluidity of kit contracts in the mid '70s, it is highly likely that this was a non-adidas long-sleeved shirt from the first part of the decade.

Worn in: Friendly wins over the USSR (1–0) and Poland (2–1).
Worn by: Marcelo Trobbiani, Ricardo Bochini.

HOME 1976

Design: Uribarri

The AFA switched to a local supplier, Uribarri, for a short period in 1976. Their kit was available in both long and short sleeved versions and featured a smart collar with open crew neck and the introduction of a team crest for the first time. The shorts and socks were plain with no branding evidence.

Worn in: A 3–1 victory over Peru in a friendly.
Worn by: Enzo Trossero, Raul Francisco Aguero.

HOME 1977–78

Design: adidas

1977 saw the previous Uribarri strip re-branded by adidas – the design remained the same apart from the addition of a small adidas logo on the shirt and shorts (in a 'landscape' format) and three-stripe trim on the shorts and socks. Again, this design was worn in both long and short sleeved versions.

Worn in: Consecutive 1–1 friendly draws against England and Scotland in 1977.
Worn by: Pedro Alexis Gonzalez, Ricardo Villa.

AWAY 1977

Design: adidas

This stunning strip comprised of one of adidas' regular long sleeved templates of the time, complete with wrapover neck, in a heroic all-white, trimmed elegantly with the familiar Argentinian light blue. As in the first part of the decade, change kits were seldom worn by the side, with the famous stripes the most common kit.

HOME 1977

Design: adidas

The trend of fluctuating kit designs continued throughout the '70s – even with the mighty adidas on board. An alternative long sleeved jersey was favoured that included a rather dated collar with loop neck and a slightly darker shade of (wider) blue stripes. Adidas' branding remained throughout the rest of the ensemble.

Worn in: A 3–1 friendly defeat against West Germany.
Worn by: Vicente Pernia, Omar Larrosa.

AWAY 1977

Design: adidas (assumed)

An all-white away strip in the new (or was it 'old'?) long sleeved shirt design, although unlike the home version this strip featured no adidas branding whatsoever which suggests it may have been supplied by a local company.

Worn in: A close 1–0 win over Boca Juniors in the 1977 Gold Cup.
Worn by: René Houseman, Jorge Carrascosa.

1978 FIFA WORLD CUP
1979 COPA AMERICA

HOME 1978–80

Design: adidas

As the AFA prepared to host the 1978 World Cup some consistency was finally introduced to the kitbag with the launch of this standard, adidas template, worn in both long and short sleeved versions (long sleeves favoured throughout the World Cup).

Worn in: Argentina's first World Cup trophy thanks to the 3–1 win over the Netherlands in the 1978 final.
Worn by: Osvaldo Ardiles, Oscar Alberto Ortiz.

1978 FIFA WORLD CUP
1979 COPA AMERICA

AWAY 1978–80

Design: adidas

Royal blue was firmly reinstated as first choice away colour for the tournament, although in the end the outfit wasn't called into action. Available in both long and short sleeved incarnations in the familiar adidas 'Worldcup Dress' template, the jersey was normally worn with the home kit's shorts and socks.

Worn in: A 2–0 friendly over Argentinian club side Club Cipolletti in 1978.
Worn by: Víctor Bottaniz, Daniel Killer.

THIRD 1978–80

Design: adidas

Another beautiful white kit was used as third choice strip option towards the end of the decade. Following the same Worldcup Dress design as the away shirt, the kit was trimmed throughout with royal blue, therefore also creating alternative shorts and socks for the away strip if necessary.

Worn in: A 2–1 victory over local domestic team Liga de Corrientes.
Worn by: Miguel Oviedo, Claudio Bravo.

HOME 1980–86

Design: Le Coq Sportif

French sportswear legends Le Coq Sportif took over the AFA contract in 1980 and dressed Menotti's team in a long sleeved shirt featuring a high wrapover crew neck – very similar to that produced by adidas. The Le Coq Sportif logo varied in style during the shirt's life and the new AFA badge began to appear from 1985.

Worn in: A 5–1 win over Austria, part of a series of 1980 friendly matches.
Worn by: Leopoldo Luque, José Van Tuyne.

HOME 1980–83

Design: Le Coq Sportif

Le Coq Sportif's standard Argentina short sleeved shirt incorporated a wide, curved v-neck that at times almost resembled a crew design. The Le Coq Sportif logo would appear on either leg of the shorts depending on whether a squad number was included. Logo positioning on the shirt also varied.

Worn in: A superb 1–0 win over Brazil in the 1983 Copa America.
Worn by: José Daniel Ponce, Oscar Garré.

AWAY 1980–86

Design: Le Coq Sportif

La Albiceleste's royal blue away strip also followed the basic kit design agenda as introduced by Le Coq Sportif. The long sleeved shirt included a high wrapover crew neck and was worn with the home shorts and socks.

Worn in: A 1–0 win over Portuguese club side Benfica in 1981 as part of Argentina's series of friendlies against domestic teams during which the side never donned their iconic stripes.
Worn by: Américo Gallego, Diego Maradona.

AWAY 1980–82

Design: Le Coq Sportif

The short sleeved blue away shirt mirrored the stylings of the home version including the wide, v-neck. Argentina's kits throughout the '70s included a wide variation of designs and the '80s were no different.

Worn in: A 1–0 win against Spanish club side Valencia in 1981.
Worn by: Alberto Tarantini, Luis Galván.

THIRD 1980–86

Design: Le Coq Sportif

A white away kit completed the trilogy of Le Coq Sportif's standard outfits for Argentina. The long sleeved jersey included the same neck as its home and away partners but was now paired with the white home change shorts and the standard white away socks.

Worn in: A 1981 3–2 friendly win against Argentinian club side Combinado de Salta.
Worn by: José Daniel Valencia, Patricio Hernández.

THIRD 1980–86

Design: Le Coq Sportif

The same short sleeved, wide v-neck design featured on this version of the white strip. These third kits – complete with the older style badge – were in use until 1986, unlike their home and away counterparts which had their badges updated.

Worn in: A 1–0 defeat in a friendly against Spanish legends Barcelona in 1981.
Worn by: Jorge Olguín, Santiago Santamaría.

HOME 1982–84

Design: Le Coq Sportif

A new Argentina crest was launched in 1982 and appeared on this shirt that was worn throughout the 1982 World Cup in Spain. The Le Coq Sportif logo was also changed to a marque-only version. Throughout this era there was very little consistency with the team strip.

Worn in: Consecutive defeats to Italy (2–1) and Brazil (3–1) that meant World Cup elimination for Menotti's team.
Worn by: Ramon Diaz, Juan Barbas.

1982 FIFA WORLD CUP

AWAY 1982–86

Design: Le Coq Sportif

The new badge and Le Coq Sportif logo was also updated on the blue away kit, that now tended to be paired with matching plain blue shorts and socks. This fetching affair was packed and ready for the 1982 World Cup but not required, Argentina playing all their matches in their regular home strip.

Worn in: A pre-World Cup warm-up against Spanish side Villajoyosa – Argentina won 15–0.
Worn by: Daniel Bertoni, Roberto Osvaldo Diaz.

HOME 1984

Design: Le Coq Sportif

A rather curious one-off short sleeved crew-necked shirt appeared for at least one game in 1984. The stripes on the jersey were placed off centre causing the Le Coq Sportif logo and team crest to be positioned in an unsightly and unbalanced fashion.

Worn in: A 1-1 friendly with Mexico – during the game some players wore this shirt, and others the side's v-necked jersey.
Worn by: Ricardo Gareca.

HOME 1984–85

Design: Le Coq Sportif

A slightly more standard v-neck was introduced to the now cuffless home shirt in 1984 (a long sleeved incarnation was also worn). A variant of the design included a central white stripe, rather than the usual blue. The Le Coq Sportif logo was included in three slightly different versions during this shirt's lifespan.

Worn in: A close 3–2 victory over Venezuela in a 1985 qualifier for the 1986 World Cup.
Worn by: Nestor Clausen, Miguel Angel Russo.

1986 FIFA WORLD CUP

★

HOME 1986

Design: Le Coq Sportif

Crew necks were back in fashion just in time for the 1986 World Cup. However, the central stripe on this new airtex fabric jersey was now white and the shirt was cuffless. The trim on the shadow striped shorts was moved to the hem and the socks were given an additional stripe on the turnover.

Worn in: The thrilling 3–2 triumph over West Germany in the 1986 World Cup final.
Worn by: Julio Olarticoechea, Ricardo Giusti.

1986 FIFA WORLD CUP
1989 COPA AMERICA

AWAY 1986–89

Design: Le Coq Sportif

The team's regular away shirt for the World Cup retained the v-neck but removed the cuffs (although white cuffs did reappear in 1989). However, during the strip's one appearance players complained that the cotton fabric was too uncomfortable in the fierce Mexican heat, prompting the AFA to source an alternative.

Worn in: The 1986 World Cup 1–0 victory over neighbours Uruguay.
Worn by: Pedro Pasculli, Jorge Valdano.

1986 FIFA WORLD CUP

AWAY 1986

Design: Le Coq Sportif

This second blue change kit worn at the 1986 World Cup has entered Argentina legend. Players complained that the previous blue shirt was too hot to wear in the Mexican sun, so AFA staff purchased this smart shadow striped alternative in Mexico City which they promptly badged up (with the previous design).

Worn in: The infamous semi-final win over England with help from the 'Hand of God'.
Worn by: Hector Enrique, José Luis Brown.

1986 FIFA WORLD CUP

THIRD 1986

Design: Le Coq Sportif

Although not required in the World Cup, this new white third version of the latest Argentina outfit was match-prepared and apparently used in some low-key friendlies against club sides prior to the tournament. The design reversed the design of the away strip and, like that outfit, was worn with the home white socks.

1987 COPA AMERICA
1989 COPA AMERICA

HOME 1986–89

Design: Le Coq Sportif

For the rest of the decade Argentina opted for this cuffless, wrapover crew-necked shirt as their primary home outfit (although of course a v-neck was occasionally worn). Introduced after the 1986 World Cup, the kit was available in both short and long sleeves and with the central stripe varying between blue and white.

Worn in: The 3–0 win over Ecuador in the 1987 Copa America.
Worn by: José Luis Cuciuffo, Roque Alfaro.

AWAY 1986-89

Design: Le Coq Sportif

The team's long sleeved version of its blue away kit was updated in 1986 to include the new badge and more low-slung wrapover crew neck. The shirt was also worn with short sleeves.

Worn in: The 1987 Copa America 1–0 defeat against Uruguay – Argentina ended the tournament in fourth place.
Worn by: Carlos Daniel Tapia, Juan Gilberto Funes.

THIRD 1986

Design: Le Coq Sportif

Argentina embarked on a series of low-key friendlies prior to the 1986 South American games and instead of reaching for their regular white third kit, for some reason they opted for this long sleeved jersey based on their standard training wear design.

SPECIAL 1986

Design: Le Coq Sportif

One of the more unusual examples in the Argentina historic kitbag was this blue and white shirt, worn for just a couple of matches in 1986. The AFA has a tradition of not wearing its famous blue and white stripes while playing friendlies against club sides, meaning the odd kit anomaly, such as this, pop up.

Worn in: A 1986 0–0 friendly with Colombian club side Atletico Junior, based in Barranquilla.
Worn by: Daniel Passarella, Claudio Borghi.

HOME 1988

Design: Le Coq Sportif

A special long-sleeved jersey was worn throughout the 1988 Bicentennial Gold Cup in Australia. Featuring a wrapover crew neck, the most striking feature about the shirt was its use of much thinner stripes than would usually be found on an Argentina kit.

Worn in: A 2–0 win over Saudi Arabia and a shock 4–1 humiliation at the hands of Australia in the Bicenntenial Gold Cup.
Worn by: Oscar Garre, Hernan Diaz.

THIRD 1989

Design: adidas

This rather Uruguay-like outfit made just one appearance in 1989, against Brazil in the Copa America. It was a rather superfluous kit given the range of outfits already in the kitbag and the fact that playing Brazil doesn't traditionally constitute a clash. Perhaps its selection for the game was due to its airtex fabric?

Worn in: A 2–0 defeat against Brazil in the Copa America.
Worn by: José Luis Brown, Pedro Troglio.

HOME 1990

Design: adidas

After a decade with Le Coq Sportif, the AFA signed a new deal with its technical suppliers in the '70s: adidas. For a run of friendly matches prior to the 1990 World Cup an often overlooked, stop-gap shirt was introduced. Featuring a solid arrangement of stripes, the shirt incorporated a simple white v-neck and three-stripe trim on the sleeves.

Worn in: A 2–1 win over Israel.
Worn by: Sergio Batista, José Basualdo.

AWAY 1990

Design: adidas

A real rarity in the Argentina kit history was this one-off change kit. It followed the geometric patterned template made popular by the Netherlands in Euro 88, fashioned in a gradated royal blue and topped with a collar.

Worn in: A friendly 1–0 win against Northern Irish side Linfield, prior to the 1990 World Cup in Italy.
Worn by: Nestor Lorenzo, Gabriel Calderon.

HOME 1990-91

Design: adidas

After a brief run with the previous kit, a new shirt appeared just in time for the 1990 World Cup. Featuring a simple display of three light blue stripes, white sleeves and a trimmed v-neck, the shirt was breathable and made from cooling airtex fabric. Later versions included an updated badge and a standard fabric.

Worn in: The 4–3 penalties victory over Italy in the 1990 World Cup semi-final.
Worn by: Sergio Goycoechea, Jorge Burruchaga.

1990 FIFA WORLD CUP

AWAY 1990–91

Design: adidas

A simple but fit for purpose royal blue away strip was also worn by Carlos Bilardo's team in the Italian World Cup. Unlike its home equivalent, this change jersey featured a wrapover v-neck and trimmed cuffs. The fabric, though, remained the mesh-like airtex. Also worn with the black shorts of the home kit.

Worn in: The below par 1–0 defeat by West Germany in the final of the 1990 World Cup.
Worn by: Gustavo Dezotti, José Serrizuela.

1991 COPA AMERICA
1992 FIFA CONFEDERATIONS CUP

HOME 1991–93

Design: adidas

By the time the 1991 Copa America kicked off Argentina were sporting an updated version of their kit, very similar to the previous one, The differences were a v-neck, dual colour trimmed shorts and light blue trim on the socks.

Worn in: The 1991 Copa America final triumph over Colombia. Also worn in the 1992 King Fahd (Confederations) Cup 3–1 final win over Saudi Arabia.
Worn by: Ricardo Altamirano, Sergio Vazquez.

1991 COPA AMERICA

AWAY 1991–92

Design: adidas

The Italia 90 away kit went through a similar refresh to the home outfit with the addition of a plain, untrimmed v-neck and the removal of the cuffs. The triumphant 1991 Copa America was the first tournament the side played in under new manager Alfio Basile.

Worn in: A 1–0 win over the USA in a 1991 friendly match.
Worn by: Dario Franco, Sergio Berti.

1993 COPA AMERICA

AWAY 1992–93

Design: adidas

The charismatic new strip featured a collar and an athletic combination of white stripes on each side of the shirt. It was paired with light blue shorts and socks. Although packed and ready for the 1993 Copa America it wasn't required during the tournament and it's unclear whether it ever saw action with the first team.

1993 COPA AMERICA

HOME 1993–94

Design: adidas

Again, rather than bringing in wholesale changes, the La Albiceleste's home shirt saw just minor changes in 1993, with the introduction of a new, trimmed snub v-neck.

Worn in: Argentina's second consecutive Copa America victory thanks to a great 2–1 win over Mexico in the final. Also worn that year in the horrendous 5–0 defeat against Colombia that threatened to derail World Cup qualification.
Worn by: Gustavo Zapata, Ramon Bello.

AWAY 1993–94

Design: adidas

In a move that was to set a trend for Argentina away kits for years to come, navy blue was introduced as the side's new change colour. Honed into a standard adidas template, the shirt featured stylish light blue and white stripes on each sleeve and was paired with the home black shorts. As with the previous blue change kit, it's uncertain whether this strip was required by the first team (although it was worn by junior sides).

1994 FIFA WORLD CUP

HOME 1994–96

Design: adidas

The stripe quota was upped on this shirt that was introduced for the 1994 World Cup. A decent button-up collar was included along with simple white sleeves to create an attractive design.

Worn in: The 3–2 defeat by Romania in the knock-out stage of the 1994 World Cup that eliminated an Argentina side still reeling from Maradona's expulsion from the tournament.
Worn by: Roberto Sensini, Fernando Redondo.

1994 FIFA WORLD CUP
1997 COPA AMERICA

AWAY 1994–97

Design: adidas

Along with the 1986 change blue shirt this must be one of the most famous Argentina kits – thanks to its role in the team's controversial 1994 World Cup. A dynamic combination of diamonds in a three-stripe arrangement decorated the left hand side of the shirt.

Worn in: The 4–0 thrashing of Greece in the 1994 World Cup and the infamous Maradona TV goal celebration that followed.
Worn by: Oscar Ruggeri, Claudio Caniggia.

HOME 1996–97

Design: adidas

After the simplicity of the previous shirt adidas employed a 'more is more' ethos with this design. The shirt featured a series of dynamic shards on each sleeve complemented by asymmetrical shorts that were available in either white or black (initially the white change shorts from the away kit were also worn).

Worn in: The 2–1 defeat against Peru that eliminated Argentina from the Copa America.
Worn by: Rodolfo Esteban Cardoso.

THIRD 1997

Design: adidas

This sublime adidas template was rolled out through much of their roster in the late '90s, and also found a home in the Argentina kitbag, albeit as a third kit option. With its splendid arching panels of light and navy blue, subtly blended, it was a suitable Argentina kit, yet it appears it never saw first team action.

HOME 1998

Design: adidas

It was a confident Argentina side who approached the France World Cup in 1998. A new and strong design was launched, ample in its fit, with raglan sleeves and a multitude of fine trim, including gold piping and a much increased use of black.

Worn in: The 5–0 group win over Jamaica in the 1998 World Cup, followed by the last minute 2–1 defeat by the Netherlands in the semi-final.
Worn by: Roberto Sensini, Abel Balbo.

AWAY 1998

Design: adidas

Arguably an even better design than the home strip was this all navy blue ensemble. It featured a simple, trimmed v-neck and white and light blue panels under the arms and down each side of the jersey. Curiously, the shirt and shorts were paired with the same multi-logoed black socks from the home strip.

Worn in: The thrilling penalties victory over England in the 1998 World Cup quarter-finals.
Worn by: Gabriel Batistuta, José Chamot.

HOME 1999–2000

Design: Reebok

When Marcelo Bielsa's team stepped out against Venezuela in February 1999 it was the first time in almost 20 years they had not worn adidas kit. The AFA had signed with Reebok who provided La Albiceleste with a simple all blue, baggy shirt with four white stripes paired with navy, not black, shorts.

Worn in: The 2–1 defeat against Brazil in the 1999 Copa America quarter-final.
Worn by: Kily Gonzalez, Diego Cagna.

AWAY 1999–2001

Design: Reebok

If the home Reebok strip was perhaps not the most exciting design, the away more than made up for it. A classy affair of navy blue, decorated with two light blue hoops across the chest that housed an AFA monogram. Paired with light blue shorts and navy socks it was a fine outfit.

Worn in: A 1–0 friendly defeat against the USA in 1999.
Worn by: Anders Guglielminpietro, Hugo Benjamin Ibarra.

HOME 2000–01

Design: Reebok

Reebok squeezed one last home design in before its short contract with Argentina ended and opted for a modern twist on the famous light blue and white stripes. Black was still a no-go though, with navy blue providing a key contrast colour. Also worn with the socks from the previous home kit.

Worn in: An impressive 2002 World Cup campaign including a 2–0 win over Chile.
Worn by: Claudio Daniel Husain, Nelson Vivas.

HOME 2001–02

Design: adidas

After the brief sojourn with Reebok the AFA re-signed with previous long-term kit partners adidas and launched a new strip in November 2001. It was a solid, functional and attractive design, with a simple arrangement of two stripes, joined by white under arm and side panels. It also resurrected the traditional black shorts.

Worn in: A 2–0 victory over Peru in a 2001 qualifier for the 2002 World Cup.
Worn by: Claudio Javier Lopez, Julio Cruz.

AWAY 2001–02

Design: adidas

The first away strip in the new adidas contract followed the design of the home, in the now familiar navy blue, creating a pragmatic design. Light blue panels decorated the sides of the shirt which was complemented by simple white shorts and socks. Both this and its home equivalent lasted for a period of just four games.

Worn in: The 1–1 draw with Uruguay in a 2002 World Cup qualifier (2001).
Worn by: Ariel Ortega, Pablo Aimar.

2002 FIFA WORLD CUP

HOME 2002–03

Design: adidas

Adidas launched a new range in 2002 designed to improve the wicking of sweat and regulate body temperature: dual layered shirts with side mesh panels that allowed the inner layer to be visible. In essence this kit, released just five months after the last, minimised the striped theme but worked brilliantly.

Worn in: The 1–0 defeat against England in the group stages of the 2002 World Cup.
Worn by: Mauricio Pochettino, Diego Simeone.

2002 FIFA WORLD CUP

AWAY 2002–03

Design: adidas

The inner layer of the new navy away Climacool kit was light blue, which when viewed through the side mesh panels gave a mesmerising moiré colour effect. Replicas were single layered though and merely replicated this effect through sublimation. Also worn with the home kit shorts and socks.

Worn in: Two 2002 World Cup games: a 1–0 win over Nigeria and a 1–1 draw with Sweden.
Worn by: Juan Sebastian Veron, Walter Samuel.

2002 FIFA WORLD CUP

THIRD 2002–03

Design: adidas

Following the design of the away strip, this white third Climacool outfit was given extra sparkle thanks to the inner light blue layer. One key difference between this and its home and away partners was the contrasting v-neck. Truncated three-stripe trim featured on the shorts. The kit was taken to the disappointing World Cup but not required.

2004 COPA AMERICA
2005 FIFA CONFEDERATIONS CUP

HOME 2004–05

Design: adidas

A striped shirt will always throw up problems for the designer in terms of how to create something new and exciting that retains the integrity of the tradition. Adidas achieved this wonderfully with this home kit that coupled light blue sleeves with a gradated and fading effect on the three blue stripes.

Worn in: The crushing 4–1 defeat against Brazil in the Confederations Cup final.
Worn by: César Delgado, Luciano Figueroa.

2004 COPA AMERICA
2005 FIFA CONFEDERATIONS CUP

AWAY 2004–05

Design: adidas

The last of adidas' run of dual-layered Climacool shirts emerged in 2004, with a more subtle visual appearance than the previous versions. This was a solid and functional design, with striking light blue panels on each sleeve, pointed three-stripe trim and the addition of a small Argentina flag.

Worn in: A 4–2 victory over Uruguay in the 2004 Copa America.
Worn by: Roberto Ayala, Lucho Gonzalez.

2004 COPA AMERICA
2005 FIFA CONFEDERATIONS CUP

THIRD 2004–05

Design: adidas

To date, this beautiful all-white strip is the last Argentina third kit produced. The design replicated that of the standard away, including the dual layer construction and two-colour trim, creating a solid kitbag of mix and match elements across all three strips. On this range of dual-layered shirts, the coloured panels on the sleeve were also included on the reverse.

2006 FIFA WORLD CUP
2007 COPA AMERICA

HOME 2005–07

Design: adidas

Aesthetic experimentation continued with this next strip. A minimalist neck was accompanied by a gold trimmed, curved mesh strip that reached across the chest and down each side of the shirt. The adidas logo was now placed on the reverse of the shorts for 360° branding.

Worn in: A 2–1 victory over Mexico in the World Cup and the superb 2007 Copa America that ended in a 3–0 defeat by Brazil in the final.
Worn by: Lionel Scaloni, Juan Pablo Sorin.

2006 FIFA WORLD CUP
2007 COPA AMERICA

AWAY 2005-07

Design: adidas

This extravagant change kit was premiered in a friendly against Croatia in 2006 and featured curved panels of light blue and white alongside dual colour three-stripe trim and gold piping. adidas' 'Teamgeist' symbol featured on the left sleeve. Worn twice in the 2010 World Cup with the home black shorts.

Worn in: The 4-2 penalties defeat by Germany in the quarter-finals of the 2006 World Cup.
Worn by: Hernan Crespo, Maxi Rodriguez.

HOME 2007-09

Design: adidas

After the design flamboyance of the previous home strips it was a back to basics approach for La Albiceleste in 2007. A simple round-necked design was added to broader stripes while breathable Climacool fabric helped regulate players' temperatures. Replica versions of the shirt appeared to have the black three-stripes reaching to the cuffs.

Worn in: A 3-0 win vs Bolivia in 2007.
Worn by: Juan Roman Riquelme, German Denis.

AWAY 2007-09

Design: adidas

There was a touch of restrained elegance about this VERY dark navy blue away kit that featured attractive light blue curved piping on either side and a dual colour three-stripe trim on the sleeves that were now truncated to allow for tournament patches. Alfio Basile had been appointed manager in 2006.

Worn in: A 2-1 win over Uruguay in a 2008 qualifier for the 2010 World Cup.
Worn by: Carlos Tevez, Esteban Cambiasso.

2010 FIFA WORLD CUP

HOME 2009-11

Design: adidas

The white crew neck of this Climacool strip (available in either a Techfit compression style or a looser Formotion fit) was a nod to the 1986 World Cup shirt. Slightly thinner stripes were joined by a royal blue outline. Oddly, the away kit's blue-trimmed white socks were favoured in the 2010 World Cup.

Worn in: A 4-0 loss to Germany in the 2010 World Cup quarter-finals.
Worn by: Martin Demichelis, Gabriel Heinze.

2010 FIFA WORLD CUP

AWAY 2009-11

Design: adidas

First worn against Jamaica in February 2010, the nostalgic influence for this kit was clear to all Argentinians: the legendary 1986 World Cup away strip. A beautiful shade of royal blue was trimmed simply with white and reversed seams and decorated with shadow stripes. Also worn with blue change shorts and socks.

Worn in: The 2-0 victory for Maradona's team over Greece at the 2010 World Cup.
Worn by: Martin Palermo, Diego Milito.

2011 COPA AMERICA

HOME 2011-13

Design: adidas

Adidas simplified the basic look of this kit (which was one of the longest serving outfits in recent years), issuing, in essence, a rich sky blue shirt with two vertical white stripes. Again, the shirt was available in either Techfit or Formotion fittings. The crest was housed within a black shield and a delicate gold was used as trim.

Worn in: A good 3-0 triumph over Costa Rica in the 2011 Copa America.
Worn by: Fernando Gago, Nicolas Burdisso.

2011 COPA AMERICA

AWAY 2011-13

Design: adidas

The team's away kit was given a shake-up in time for the 2011 Copa America, with the now navy blue Techfit/Formotion jersey adorned with just a dash of gold (taken from the team crest) and a broad chest panel of fading light blue and white bands. Heavily trimmed white shorts and socks finished off the design.

Worn in: The 5-4 penalties defeat against Uruguay in the 2011 Copa America final.
Worn by: Javier Zanetti, Sergio Agüero.

2014 FIFA WORLD CUP

HOME 2013-14

Design: adidas

2014 saw a continuation of the trend for single colour kits in the international world, a trend that was extended to Argentina with the launch of this kit that featured controversial white shorts (although black change pairs were available). The shirt was trimmed with black and adorned with a faint diagonal pattern.

Worn in: The 4-2 penalties win over the Netherlands in the 2014 World Cup semi-final.
Worn by: Enzo Perez, Javier Mascherano.

AWAY 2013–14

Design: adidas

Adidas kits in the 2014 World Cup were known for their excitement and imagination and traditional themes were given a highly creative twist. Argentina's away kit combined navy and royal blue, decorated with fine diagonal stripes and trimmed beautifully with gold.

Worn in: The disappointing 1–0 defeat against Germany for Alejandro Sabella's team in the 2014 World Cup final.
Worn by: Lionel Messi, Martin Demichelis.

HOME 2015

Design: adidas

There was a much lighter feel to the Argentina kit that was introduced in preparation for the 2015 Copa America. Crafted from Climacool fabric, the shirt introduced light blue sleeves and shoulder panels. White shorts were still preferred, in the main, although more traditional black change pairs were also worn.

Worn in: The penalties defeat against Chile in the 2015 Copa America final.
Worn by: Pablo Zabaleta, Angel Di Maria.

AWAY 2015–17

Design: adidas

A more muted tone of navy blue was selected for this kit, launched at the start of the year. A simple design, it paired a self-coloured v-neck with darker cuffs and a broad hem trim of white and light blue. At the bottom corner of both this and the home shirt was a tonal emblem with the text: 'We are all Argentina'.

Worn in: The storming 4–0 win over the USA in the semi-final of the 2016 Copa America.
Worn by: Ezequiel Lavezzi, Marcos Rojo.

HOME 2015–17

Design: adidas

A special 'Copa America Centenario' was announced for 2016 that was to include CONCACAF teams. It meant a new home kit for Martino's Argentina that was first worn in the last game of 2015 and saw black return as a key accent colour. Black or white shorts and socks completed the kit.

Worn in: Another penalties defeat against Chile in the Copa America final (2016).
Worn by: Gonzalo Higuain, Ever Banega.

HOME 2017–18

Design: adidas

Adidas' grand unveiling of their 2018 World Cup kits included this subtly superb new Argentina home kit. Not as heavily retro-influenced as the majority of adidas' outfits for the World Cup, the design was simply balanced, with the most striking aspect the block of gradated shades of blue that made up the stripes. White socks returned and dual trim was introduced to the shorts.

Lionel Messi and Gonzalo Higuain wearing adidas during a 2014 World Cup qualifier against Chile in October 2011.

Diego Maradona in the 1986 World Cup quarter-final against England – Argentina sourced a last-minute lightweight away shirt for the match.

1966 FIFA WORLD CUP

France, wearing their deep, v-necked home strip, take on Mexico in their maroon/navy change outfit in a Group One match. The tournament saw a wide variety of short- and long-sleeved shirts.

1966 FIFA WORLD CUP

Hungary sporting the archetypal mid-'60s long-sleeved, crew-neck jersey whereas their opponents Brazil opt for a short-sleeved, collared style that was preferred by South American sides.

BELGIUM

With a colour palette as rich and striking as Belgium's red, yellow and black kit, designers have it easy. Complement that with a white away kit, and you'll always end up with a fine set of strips.

Even from their earliest days, there has always been something special about the Belgian kit, and there has been remarkable consistency in the application of the colours over the years to create a splendid canon of outfits that capture the country's identity perfectly.

The side have been kitted out by a handful of firms over the years: from Umbro in the early 1970s, through adidas, Admiral, Diadora, Burrda and then back to adidas again.

It is adidas that have arguably dressed the side with the most panache over the years. The 'casual' look of the early '80s, which bravely managed to incorporate a diamond Argyle pattern into the design, successfully competes in the style stakes with the superb set of kits produced for Euro 2016, when Belgium's iconic sky blue cycling jersey design was reappropriated for the beautiful game.

The fact that the Argyle motif has been brought back for their new 2017–18 home strip as part of adidas' glorious retro-inspired range of outfits shows the high regard for the design.

As well as the traditional white for away kits, which are generally beautifully trimmed with the national colours, black and yellow have also appeared in the kitbag from time to time.

The Red Devils are lucky that their away strips, though mainly white, retain their national identity thanks to the unique colour scheme.

The Belgium team wearing their beautiful adidas 1986-90 away kit before a match in the 1986 FIFA World Cup finals.

HOME 1966–67

Design: Unknown

The Belgium kit had remained pretty consistent for decades as the '60s gathered pace. A red long-sleeved shirt, trimmed liberally with black, yellow and red, combined to replicate the national flag. Blacks shorts and red socks completed the outfit and could be interchanged with the away pairs with ease. The team failed to qualify for the 1966 World Cup.

Worn in: A 1–0 win over Switzerland in 1966.
Worn by: Roger Claessen, Jef Jurion.

AWAY 1966–67

Design: Unknown

The Belgians got it spot on right from the start when it came to kit design. Their change strip was a simple, classic white and featured the same Belgium flag-style trim throughout. It was a wonderful ensemble that managed to provide a suitable colour clash option yet still retain the national identity.

Worn in: A 3–0 win over France in a 1967 qualifier for Euro 1968 (worn with black shorts).
Worn by: Jacques Stockman, Johnny Thio.

HOME 1967–75

Design: Umbro

Collars were distinctly old-fashioned as the decade ended and in 1967 Belgium switched to a neat, modern v-neck design, still decorated with the national colours. Interestingly, research indicates that long-sleeved shirts were always worn. If it was warm, players simply rolled up their sleeves!

Worn in: A good 3–0 win over El Salvador in Belgium's first game in the 1970 World Cup.
Worn by: León Smelling, Raoul Lambert.

AWAY 1967–75

Design: Umbro

Naturally, modernity also fashioned the away kit as Raymond Goethals' side prepared for the 1970 World Cup. Clad in this magnificent outfit, which curiously switched the colour order of the trim used on the home strip, the team were known as the 'White Devils' in Mexico. A white cuffed version of the shirt was also worn.

Worn in: A 2–1 win vs Hungary to clinch third place for Belgium in Euro 1972.
Worn by: Paul van Himst, Jan Verheyen.

HOME 1975–80

Design: adidas

adidas began to dominate kit design in the mid-'70s and in 1975 arrived in Belgium with a new interpretation of the national strip. The rich design incorporated a dual-coloured adidas three-stripe trim and added yellow socks in to the tricolour mix.

Worn in: A 1–0 win over the Netherlands in a 1982 World Cup qualifier (1980).
Worn by: Wilfried Van Moer, Jos Heyligen.

AWAY 1975–80

Design: adidas

Curiously this white away kit must have been a real favourite with Guy Thys' team as it was also often worn at home during its lifespan as well as just when a change forced it. A beautiful black, yellow and red trim offset the shirt.

Worn in: A 2–0 triumph in Northern Ireland (1976) in a qualifier for the 1978 World Cup.
Worn by: Roger Van Gool, Paul Courant.

HOME 1975–80

Design: adidas

A standard adidas short sleeved v-neck jersey was worn in warmer weather by the Belgians. The shirt included the same dual-coloured three-stripe trim as the long sleeved version and featured the familiar low positioning of the team crest as so many adidas strips of the era favoured.

Worn in: The qualifying campaign for the 1978 World Cup finals.
Worn by: Guy Dardenne, Jean Janssens.

AWAY 1975–80

Design: adidas

Naturally an all-white version of the short sleeved, warmer weather kit was also produced and, like its home partner, included non-contrasting v-neck and cuffs and was paired with the familiar shorts and socks from the home outfit. Traditionally, however, long sleeves were preferred by the Belgians at this time.

Worn in: The qualifying campaign for the 1978 World Cup finals.
Worn by: Ludovic Coeck, Eddy Voordeckers.

1980 UEFA EUROPEAN CHAMPIONSHIP

HOME 1980

Design: adidas

In the last year of its deal with the Royal Belgian Football Association, adidas also updated the short sleeved version of its kits (presumably in preparation for Euro 80). The shirt now featured a simple red collar and cuffs with the rest of the outfit remaining the same.

Worn in: The 2–1 defeat against West Germany in the Euro 80 final.
Worn by: René Vandereycken, Julien Cools.

1980 UEFA EUROPEAN CHAMPIONSHIP

AWAY 1980

Design: adidas

The white change outfit mirrored the updated design of the home, including the collar and exquisite tricolour trim. During Euro 80 UEFA rules meant the adidas logo had to be covered with tape on both kits.

Worn in: A stunning 2–1 win over Spain in a magnificent Euro 80 tournament for the Belgian side.
Worn by: Jan Ceulemans, François van der Elst.

1980 UEFA EUROPEAN CHAMPIONSHIP

HOME 1980

Design: adidas

Quite possibly the most curious shirt in Belgium's kit history. For just one game in Euro 80 the side sported a dual-colour pinstriped version of their home kit. The reasons why are unclear but the pinstripes were at least one year ahead of their time.

Worn in: A 0–0 draw with Italy in Euro 80 – good enough for Belgium to go through to the second stage.
Worn by: Walter Meeuws, Raymond Mommens.

HOME 1981–83

Design: Admiral

Surprisingly given its financial difficulties at the time, English kit legends Admiral took over the Belgium contract in 1981. It produced one of its classic 'tramline' style strips that was given extra sparkle with the addition of small Admiral logos in the tramlines. The long sleeved version featured a collar.

Worn in: A vital 1–0 win over the Republic of Ireland in a 1981 World Cup qualifier.
Worn by: Albert Cluytens, Eric Gerets.

1982 FIFA WORLD CUP

HOME 1981–83

Design: Admiral

The short sleeved version of this fine Admiral ensemble was more commonly worn than its long sleeved cousin and suited the modern design better in many ways. Belgium qualified for their first World Cup in 12 years. The red shirts were also worn with the away kit shorts on occasion.

Worn in: A 1–0 triumph over reigning champions Argentina in the 1982 World Cup.
Worn by: Frankie Vercauteren, Marc Baecke.

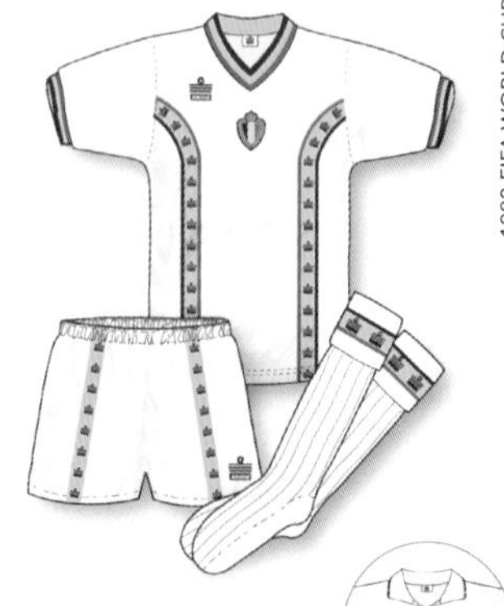

1982 FIFA WORLD CUP

AWAY 1981–83

Design: Admiral

The short sleeved away shirt reflected the design of the home. Although in the kitbag the strip was not required in the 1982 World Cup. This period in Belgian football history is regarded as a golden age for the nation. As with the home shirt, the long sleeved version featured a different collar and cuffs design.

Worn in: A 2–0 defeat against Spain in a 1981 friendly match.
Worn by: Willy Geurts, Luc Millecamps.

1984 UEFA EUROPEAN CHAMPIONSHIP

HOME 1983–86

Design: adidas

After two and a half years with Admiral, adidas returned to the Belgian fold, bringing with them arguably two of the greatest football shirt designs ever. The home featured a broad white panel that housed a lavish 'Argyle' diamond pattern of red, yellow and black.

Worn in: A humiliating 5–0 defeat by France in Euro 84 – proof perhaps that a great looking kit doesn't always inspire a great performance!
Worn by: Nico Claesen, Michel de Wolf.

1984 UEFA EUROPEAN CHAMPIONSHIP

AWAY 1983–86

Design: adidas

Again it seems the away kit outshone the home! Having the Argyle pattern sitting directly on to the main colour base of the shirt worked so well on this away kit. The badge was placed centrally in the middle of the pattern that had a real 'casual' fashion feel. Totally unique.

Worn in: A 2–0 win over Yugoslavia in what ultimately turned out to be a disappointing European Championship for Belgium.
Worn by: Walter de Greef, Georges Grun.

1986 FIFA WORLD CUP

HOME 1986–90

Design: adidas

In preparation for the Mexico World Cup in 1986 a new Red Devils strip was launched. Simpler in look then the previous two home outfits it featured a non-contrasting collar and beautiful yellow and black three-stripe trim. Adidas' familiar diagonal 'brickwork' shadow pattern decorated the fabric.

Worn in: The nail-biting and dramatic 4–3 win over the USSR in the 1986 World Cup.
Worn by: Enzo Scifo, Leo van der Elst.

1986 FIFA WORLD CUP

AWAY 1986–90

Design: adidas

A plain white away version of the new dynamic yet elegant adidas strip made a couple of appearances in the Mexico World Cup, including a game against the hosts where it was worn with the red shorts of the home kit. The Belgian tricolor still featured on the socks.

Worn in: The amazing 5–4 penalties win over Spain in the 1986 World Cup quarter-finals.
Worn by: Danny Veyt, Patrick Vervoort.

1990 FIFA WORLD CUP

HOME 1990–91

Design: adidas

Design continuity was preserved with this kit that was very similar to that worn in the 1986 World Cup. A simple shadow pinstripe, trim on the collar and a slight tweak in adidas three-stripe colours provided the differences. Also of course the unexplained switching over in positions of adidas logo and team crest.

Worn in: The unlucky 1–0 defeat by England in the second round of the 1990 World Cup.
Worn by: Bruno Versavel, Stefan Demol.

1990 FIFA WORLD CUP

AWAY 1990–91

Design: adidas

Another fine white version of the home kit (both launched in May 1990) made a couple of appearances in Italia 90 with long term boss Guy Thys back in charge after a brief spell with Walter Meeuws as manager. This was to be the last of adidas' kits for The Red Devils...for now.

Worn in: A 2–0 win over the Korea Republic in Belgium's first game in the 1990 World Cup followed later by a 2–1 defeat against Spain.
Worn by: Philippe Albert, Marc Emmers.

HOME 1991–93

Design: Diadora

Italian firm Diadora took over from adidas in 1991. Their first set of strips introduced a slightly different design for the long and short sleeved versions. The long-sleeved featured a typically early '90s collar with short button-up placket trimmed delicately with yellow and black.

Worn in: 1994 World Cup qualifier wins over Wales (2–0) and Cyprus (3–0).
Worn by: Marc Degryse, Dirk Medved.

HOME 1991–93

Design: Diadora

The short-sleeved version of Diadora's first home kit retained the same fading abstract shadow print as the home but topped it off with a v-neck style collar. These outfits were worn as Belgium, led by Paul Van Himst, failed to qualify for Euro 92.

Worn in: A 2–0 win over Luxembourg (1991) in a Euro 92 qualifier.
Worn by: Lorenzo Staelens, Roby Langers.

AWAY 1991–93

Design: Diadora

A new shadow fabric pattern comprising small geometric shapes was introduced on to the long-sleeved version of the next Red Devils away shirt. The red collar and cuffs from the first choice jersey remained. Diadora's logo was included on the socks of all their Belgian strips at this time.

Worn in: A 2–0 friendly win over Hungary in 1991.
Worn by: Francis Severeyns, Marc Wilmots.

AWAY 1991–93

Design: Diadora

The white short-sleeved strip included the same geometric shadow pattern as the home with the shirt replicating the open v-neck collar of the home short sleeved incarnation. The fit was noticeably larger on these Diadora kits compared to the previous adidas uniforms.

Worn in: An 2–1 victory over Czechoslovakia in a 1994 World Cup qualifier (1992). Also worn that year in an exciting 3–3 draw with France.
Worn by: Johan Walem, Franky van der Elst.

HOME 1994–96

Design: Diadora

Belgium's 1994 World Cup shirt had a touch of glamour not seen since the days of adidas in 1983. An abstract sleeve trim in white with red, black and yellow details decorated each arm, providing a strong focal point for the kit. Subtle shadow stripes finished off the design.

Worn in: The superb 1994 World Cup 1–0 win over the Netherlands, followed by the tight 3–2 defeat against Germany in the knockout stage.
Worn by: Alexandre Czerniatynski, Luc Nilis.

AWAY 1994–96

Design: Diadora

No surprises with the next Belgium change shirt – once again, a straightforward copy of the home kit in the traditional white. The collar and cuffs remained red and Belgian national colours provided an elegant trim. The Diadora logo on both kits was updated to a new design towards the end of the strips' lifetime.

Worn in: A 1–0 win over Morocco in the Red Devils' first game in the USA World Cup.
Worn by: Josip Weber, Lorenzo Staelens.

HOME 1996–98

Design: Diadora

There was a distinctly minimalist and classy look to this next Belgium kit, introduced for the last game of 1996 – a vast move on from the flamboyant nature of the previous design. A tidy, collar and wrapover neck design was joined by truncated Belgian flag trim on the cuffs and hem of the shorts along with a large shadow print of the team crest.

Worn in: A 6–0 thrashing of San Marino (1997).
Worn by: Emile Mpenza, Eric Van Meir.

AWAY 1996–98

Design: Diadora

The away version of this strip proved to be another Diadora success with the swish simplicity of the white combining well with the richness of Belgium's national colours. The small coloured inset within the wrapover neck element of the collar added a nice touch to the outfit.

Worn in: An important 2–1 triumph in Wales in a 1997 qualifier for the 1998 World Cup.
Worn by: Bart De Roover, Dominique Lemoine.

HOME 1998–99

Design: Diadora

Modernity hit the Belgium kitbag with the final Diadora home strip. A smart button-up neck (reminiscent of a cycling jersey) combined with a fine ribbed fabric, a shadow rendering of the badge and yellow piping to create this beautiful strip. First worn in the World Cup itself.

Worn in: A 2–2 draw with Mexico – this wonderful outfit's only appearance in the 1998 World Cup.
Worn by: Luis Oliveira, Eric Deflandre.

AWAY 1998–99

Design: Diadora

The Belgian kits for the 1998 World Cup were arguably the best in the tournament. The change version was just as good as the home, with the yellow piping replaced by red and the Belgian flag cleverly replicated throughout.

Worn in: Two draws in the World Cup group stage: 0–0 with the Netherlands and 1–1 with the Korea Republic meaning an early exit for Georges Leekens' team.
Worn by: Philippe Clement, Vital Borkelmans.

HOME 1999–2000

Design: Nike

After eight years with Diadora, Belgium switched to Nike for their apparel. Their hi-tech Dri-FIT fabric was joined by an elegant collar and black and yellow panels on each sleeve. This fine, kit was only ever worn in friendlies as Belgium were co-hosts of the forthcoming Euro 2000, thereby avoiding a qualifying campaign.

Worn in: A 3–1 win against Italy in a 1999 friendly match.
Worn by: Branko Strupar, Bart Goor.

AWAY 1999–2000

Design: Nike

In the mid to late '90s, Nike were gaining a reputation for breathing new life into international team kits, yet still retaining the nation's traditions. And this is exactly what it managed with this gorgeous outfit. By downplaying yellow it forged a whole new look for a Belgian change kit.

Worn in: The astonishing 5–5 draw with near neighbours the Netherlands in a 1999 friendly.
Worn by: Jacky Peeters, Yves Vanderhaeghe.

HOME 2000–96

Design: Nike

As Robert Waseige's side prepared to co-host the 2000 European Championship they were accompanied by a new, minimalist strip. A simple black and yellow crew neck provided the only real main focus of colour contrast on the shirt. Breathable fabric panels ran down each side of the shirt.

Worn in: A 2–1 win over Sweden in Euro 2000 – Belgium's only victory in the tournament.
Worn by: Joos Valgaeren, Nico Van Kerckhoven.

2000 UEFA EUROPEAN CHAMPIONSHIP

AWAY 2000–02

Design: Nike

Black's appeal as a change colour had been growing rapidly through the '90s so perhaps it was no surprise to see it make an appearance for Belgium where it worked incredibly well – providing a suitable mean and moody canvas for the red and yellow trim to shine. Although packed, the strip wasn't required in Euro 2000.

Worn in: A 2–2 friendly draw with Denmark (2000).
Worn by: Gert Verheyen, Philippe Leonard.

HOME 2002–04

Design: Nike

Nike's offering at the 2002 World Cup was dominated by all teams sporting this basic template featuring bold angular panels on each side of the jersey and a dual-layer construction (to aid sweat wicking and regulate heat). Curiously, the core red colour was also a more fluorescent shade that veered towards orange.

Worn in: A great 3–2 win over Russia in the 2002 World Cup.
Worn by: Johan Walem, Wesley Sonck.

AWAY 2002–04

Design: Nike

Following the success of the previous black strip the colour remained the change hue of choice as Belgium prepared for the World Cup. The design followed the standard Nike dual-layered template but with the addition of a collar. The strip was not required in the tournament itself.

Worn in: The friendly 3–1 win over Algeria in 2003.
Worn by: Wesley Sonck, Emile Mpenza.

HOME 2004–05

Design: Nike

Boundaries continued to be pushed by Nike as its next strip featured no yellow at all and focused solely on its new shade of red and black. It was a standard 'Total 90' template with black piping adorning each side and a large Nike swoosh logo on the left sleeve hem.

Worn in: A great 2005 4–1 triumph over Bosnia and Herzegovina in a 2006 World Cup qualifier.
Worn by: Thomas Buffel, Koen Daerden.

AWAY 2004–05

Design: Nike

Red and black remained the sole colour palette for the next away kit in a design that simply reversed that of the home ensemble. The Total 90 template was rolled out across all of Nike's roster and featured a large contrasting panel on the back of the shirt in which to house the player name.

Worn in: A 2–0 defeat against Spain in a 2004 qualifier for the 2006 World Cup.
Worn by: Tristan Peersman, Vincent Kompany.

HOME 2006–07

Design: Nike

After what could arguably be called a series of disruptive kits, Belgium were back in a familiar shade of red AND with '70s style black shorts and yellow socks. It was a practical design from Nike, the main talking point being the return of the old favourite colours bringing a sense of real identity back to the strip.

Worn in: A 3–0 victory against Armenia in a 2007 qualifier for Euro 2008.
Worn by: Moussa Dembélé, Timmy Simons.

AWAY 2006–07

Design: Nike

A white, fresh new away strip arrived in 2006, replacing the somewhat 'heavy' black and red stylings of the past six years. The design was the same as that of the home paired with red shorts. The kits coincided with a dismal era for Belgium who didn't qualify for the 2006 World Cup – the first they were to miss since 1978.

Worn in: An all-white 4–0 defeat by Portugal in 2006 (2008 European Championship qualifier).
Worn by: Marouane Fellaini, Gaby Mudingayi.

HOME 2008–10

Design: Nike

With both parties deciding not to renew the kit contract this was to be the last Nike home shirt for Belgium. The result was a functional but unremarkable design that retained the traditional shirt/shorts/socks colourway and added some flashes of yellow on the sides of the shirt for good measure.

Worn in: The 2008 3–2 win over Estonia in a 2010 World Cup qualifier.
Worn by: Steven Defour, Kevin Mirallas.

AWAY 2008–10

Design: Nike

The away version of the home kit followed the same design (including the 'outlined' v-neck), but with a more muted amber providing the trim accompaniment rather than yellow. As with the home shirt, no black was present.

Worn in: Consecutive 2010 World Cup qualifier defeats to Spain (5–0) and Armenia (2–1), both played in 2009.
Worn by: Eden Hazard, Daniel Van Buyten.

HOME 2010–11

Design: Burrda

Qatar-based company Burrda who were yet to make an impact in the international kit world took over the Belgium contract. Their first strip was premiered in September 2010 and went for a single colour look, in a more muted shade of red, topped with black and yellow trim. Large Burrda logos featured on each shoulder.

Worn in: The 2010 4–4 goalfest against Austria in a 2012 European Championship qualifier.
Worn by: Marvin Ogunjimi, Jelle Vossen.

AWAY 2010–11

Design: Burrda

The careful combination of the red, black and yellow trim helped create this great looking change kit. A crew neck replaced the collar of the home and yellow piping accentuated the side panels. It was a good start for Burrda and their relationship with the KBVB and Georges Leekens' team, although unfortunately this smart strip was never worn in action.

HOME 2011–12

Design: Burrda

After the smart but relatively sober start to its deal with Belgium, Burrda went for a dynamic, bold approach to its next home kit. A large curved panel sat across the chest and sleeves with an asymmetric approach to the shorts. The large shadow print team badge on the fabric made a reappearance.

Worn in: A great 4–1 triumph over Kazakhstan in a Euro 2012 qualifier (2011).
Worn by: Nacer Chadli, Jan Vertonghen.

AWAY 2011–12

Design: Burrda

Black returned as the away colour of choice for Belgium in the form of this complex, extravagant outfit. Curved panels in a muted yellow combined with piping and modernist red neck to really make a statement on the pitch. Shorts and socks were straight reversals of the home pairs.

Worn in: The 2–0 win over Austria in 2011 qualifier for Euro 2012.
Worn by: Axel Witsel, Kevin Mirallas.

HOME 2012–13

Design: Burrda

Arguably Burrda's best design to date was sported by Marc Wilmots' team as they aimed for 2014 World Cup qualification. Aggressive shoulder panels were complemented by a black and yellow wave across the front of the shirt and a large offset, shadow print badge, all accentuated by a careful use of yellow trim.

Worn in: A 2–0 triumph over Scotland (2012) in a 2014 World Cup qualifier.
Worn by: Christian Benteke, Dries Mertens.

AWAY 2012–13

Design: Burrda

The Red Devils' new black change outfit was another classic, modernistic design. It took an asymmetric approach to panelling, piping and colour but brought consistency with the home outfit by retaining the distinctive dual colour wave across the chest.

Worn in: An impressive 2–1 win in Croatia in 2013 (2014 World Cup qualifier).
Worn by: Romelu Lukaku, Toby Alderweireld.

2014 FIFA WORLD CUP

HOME 2014

Design: Burrda

As Belgium readied themselves for battle in the 2014 World Cup, Burrda's last set of kits were unveiled to great acclaim. The designs dispensed with some of the more flamboyant, asymmetrical elements of the previous outfits and opted for a solid, simple and strong look that was unmistakably Belgian.

Worn in: The 2–1 win over the USA in the second round of the World Cup.
Worn by: Divock Origi, Kevin De Bruyne.

2014 FIFA WORLD CUP

AWAY 2014

Design: Burrda

Sashes were THE kit fashion statement of the 2000s and Belgium played their own part with this attractive black outfit. The basic shirt construction was the same as the home kit but the muted sash added a real touch of glamour to the kit. The Belgian flag was replicated on the shorts' hem of all three kits this year.

Worn in: The 1–0 victory over South Korea in the 2014 World Cup group stages.
Worn by: Adnan Januzaj, Nicolas Lombaerts.

2014 FIFA WORLD CUP

THIRD 2014

Design: Burrda

For the first time ever, an official third kit was launched to help complete a fabulous set of strips, with one in each of the Belgian national colours. The design followed that of the home with the trimmed crew neck and cuffs, the striking chest detailing and large watermarked team crest. Belgium enjoyed a good tournament, making it to the quarter-finals. This kit was never worn, however.

HOME 2014–15

Design: adidas

With the four-year deal with Burrda due to expire the day after the World Cup final, Belgium signed a new deal with previous suppliers, adidas – back for the third stint with the country. It kitted the team out in its Condivo 14 template in a rather un-Belgian-like red and white.

Worn in: A 5–0 thrashing of Cyprus (2015) en route to Euro 2016.
Worn by: Yannick Carrasco, Michy Batshuayi.

AWAY 2014–15

Design: adidas

adidas' Torque 13 template was brought into use as Belgium's new change outfit. The bold design pulled no punches and was crafted in simple black and white. Both shirts utilised adidas' adizero fabric, designed to effectively wick sweat from the body.

Worn in: A solid 2015 4–1 victory against Andorra – part of the side's successful qualifying campaign for Euro 2016.
Worn by: Zakaria Bakkali, Laurent Depoitre.

2016 UEFA EUROPEAN CHAMPIONSHIP

HOME 2015–17

Design: adidas

If the first kits of adidas' return were criticised in some quarters for not being distinctive enough, amends were certainly made in late 2015 with the launch of this superb home kit. This formidable design saw the shirt divided between black and white with a fluorescent yellow trim for highlights.

Worn in: An important 3–0 triumph over the Republic of Ireland in Euro 2016.
Worn by: Laurent Ciman, Jason Denayer.

2016 UEFA EUROPEAN CHAMPIONSHIP

AWAY 2015–17

Design: adidas

Without doubt one of the greatest kits on show at the 2016 European Championship was this fine outfit. In something completely new for the side, the jersey took its inspiration from the iconic Belgian cycling jersey. A broad representation of the national flag dominated the design. Also worn with sky blue shorts.

Worn in: A fine 4–0 thrashing of Hungary in Euro 2016 followed by a 3–1 loss to Wales.
Worn by: Thomas Meunier, Thomas Vermaelen.

2018 FIFA WORLD CUP

HOME 2017–18

Design: adidas

Retro was all the rage with the array of kits adidas launched for the 2018 World Cup. In Belgium's case the design took clear influence from the 1983–86 'Argyle' patterned shirts, bringing the style up to date with more muted and subtle shades. It was an exquisite design, and one that arguably was even greater than the original kit that inspired it.

1970 FIFA WORLD CUP

England's Bobby Moore holds off Brazil's Carlos Alberto in the epic Group Three clash. Coping with the intense Mexican heat was vital in the tournament. Here, an all-white England are wearing special short-sleeved, Umbro airtex shirts.

1970 FIFA WORLD CUP

Italy, in their resplendent away strip, against Israel, in their light blue home kit, during a Group Two match. The game ended goalless.

BRAZIL

When it comes to colours that encapsulate excellence and glamour in football, the palette of yellow, green, blue and white – the colours of Brazil – is often the first to spring to mind.

Such is the admiration for the Brazilian national side that the colour scheme has entered the world psyche and its influence can be seen far and wide.

But these iconic colours were not Brazil's first choice, and were chosen only in 1954. The team had worn a white and blue strip until that point, but a crushing defeat by Uruguay in the 1950 World Cup prompted calls for a fresh start.

A competition to design a new Brazil kit was announced by the newspaper *Correio da Manhã* in 1953, with the only requirement that the kit needed to reflect the national colours of the Brazilian flag.

The winner was 18-year-old illustrator Aldyr Garcia Schlee. Focusing on balance and harmony, he concocted the famous combination recognised by the whole of football today.

Away colours focus primarily on a royal blue shirt, paired with white shorts, although third kits of white, black and dark green have also been unveiled – but it is doubtful whether these ever saw active duty.

Until the arrival of adidas in 1977, local sportswear companies supplied the team strip, and throughout the 1980s it was Topper that kitted out the side with a series of functional but slightly anachronistic outfits. Umbro took over the contract in 1991 and brought the famous yellow, green, blue and white firmly up to date.

In 1997 Nike partnered with the Brazilian Football Confederation (CBF) for consistently striking and inventive designs – all designed to capture the power and beauty of the Brazilian game.

Brazil line up in their crew necked Topper kits, before the 4–0 thrashing of New Zealand in the 1982 FIFA World Cup.

HOME 1966–69

Design: Athleta

Brazil played their unique brand of football in the mid-'60s in this standard issue international-style shirt. It featured a wide collar that led down to an open neck design and was available in both long and short sleeved versions. The shorts were pale blue and trimmed with a single stripe on each leg.

Worn in: Two surprising 3–1 defeats to both Hungary and Portugal in the 1966 World Cup.
Worn by: Ulrik Le Fevre, Kresten Bjerre.

AWAY 1966–69

Design: Athleta

The design of the home shirt worked equally well in the familiar Brazil away colour of blue. The kit was generally worn with the same socks as the home outfit. Legend has it that the 1966 World Cup found 15 out of the 16 teams in Umbro strips. However, the truth is that most sides had a kit supplied by a local company as well as being provided with an Umbro kit.

HOME 1968

Design: Athleta

One of the more mysterious kits in the Brazil canon was this yellow-trimmed crew-necked shirt that was worn at least once, in an unofficial match against a FIFA XI. The shirt, which featured two stars to symbolise the country's two World Cup crowns, was worn with darker blue shorts.

Worn in: The unofficial friendly against a FIFA XI that ended in a 2–1 Brazil win.
Worn by: Rivelino, Tostão.

HOME 1969–71

Design: Athleta

1969 gave birth to THE iconic Brazil kit – short sleeves, crew neck (apparently requested by Pelé himself), royal blue shorts with single white trim and white socks with green and yellow turnover. The team twice wore versions by both Athleta and Umbro in the 1970 World Cup. Grey socks were sported in two games.

Worn in: The incredible 4–1 victory over Italy in the 1970 World Cup final.
Worn by: Pelé, Gérson.

AWAY 1969–71

Design: Athleta

A royal blue away kit in this pragmatically simple style also appeared as the '60s drew to a close, although it wasn't required in the 1970 World Cup itself. The shorts reversed the style of the home pair, and the home white socks with green and yellow turnovers completed this strip.

HOME 1971–76

Design: Athleta

Following the impressive World Cup final result in 1970 Mário Zagallo's team added three stars above the team crest, to symbolise the side's three World Cup wins. The badge itself was slightly condensed in width but otherwise the kit remained the same. Also worn with plain white socks.

Worn in: A 1–0 win over East Germany in the second stage of the 1974 World Cup.
Worn by: Jairzinho, Valdomiro.

AWAY 1971–76

Design: Athleta

As with the home strip, Brazil's blue away didn't alter from the 1970 version, with the exception of the three stars above the tweaked badge design.

Worn in: The 2–1 win over Argentina in the 1974 World Cup second stage. Also worn in the later 2–0 defeat by an impressive Netherlands side that saw Brazil eliminated.
Worn by: Marinho Peres, Marinho Chagas.

HOME 1977

Design: adidas

The Samba Boys signed with sportswear giants adidas in 1977, although the first kits, worn throughout the year, didn't feature any logos. The only sign of adidas branding was the inclusion of its famous three-stripe trim on the shorts.

Worn in: A fantastic 8–0 triumph over Bolivia in a qualifier for the 1978 World Cup.
Worn by: José Rodrigues Neto, Reinaldo.

AWAY 1977

Design: adidas

The blue away kit also received the new shorts design this year. Adidas was keen to break more into football apparel in the mid-'70s and was rapidly expanding its roster. Their shirts from this era are now quite rightly regarded as fine examples of the genre.

Worn in: A 6–0 thrashing of Colombia on the way to qualification for the 1978 World Cup.
Worn by: Rivellino, Paulo Cézar Caju.

1979 COPA AMERICA

HOME 1978–80

Design: adidas

The biggest change to a Brazil kit since 1969 occurred in 1978 when adidas expanded its branding on to the sacred yellow and green shirt, including its three-stripe trim and iconic trefoil logo for the first time. A nice touch was the dual-colour trim on the socks that also existed in a more streamlined style.

Worn in: A 2–1 win over Argentina in the 1979 Copa America.
Worn by: Carpegiani, Pedrinho, Zenon.

1979 COPA AMERICA

AWAY 1978–80

Design: adidas

The adidas touch arguably worked even better on the away kit than it did the home. The design was the same as the home, with the shorts a straightforward reversal. The socks remained identical to those of the home outfit.

THIRD 1978–80

Design: adidas

This white shirt proves a bit of a curiosity in the Brazil kitbag. It featured in numerous team photos during the adidas era and was worn by coaching staff. The long sleeved 'Worldcup Dress' style shirt was in essence a reversal of the standard long sleeved away jersey of the time. This beautiful white shirt was never worn by the team.

1978 FIFA WORLD CUP

HOME 1978–80

Design: adidas

A long sleeved version of the adidas kit, a classic design catalogued as Worldcup Dress, was also worn by Claudio Coutinho's team. During the 1978 World Cup the kits omitted the adidas logo, although it did return for subsequent matches as the decade ended.

Worn in: The 1978 World Cup third place play-off that ended in a 2–1 triumph for Brazil.
Worn by: Nelinho, Amaral, Gil.

1978 FIFA WORLD CUP

AWAY 1978–80

Design: adidas

Naturally a blue version of the Worldcup Dress kit was also produced and made one appearance in the World Cup, although the shorts 'guested' with the home kit in the 0–0 draw with Spain.

Worn in: The commanding 3–0 victory over fellow South Americans Peru in the second round of the 1978 World Cup.
Worn by: Dirceu, Jorge Mendonca, Batista.

HOME 1980–81

Design: Topper

South American sportswear company Topper, whose head office was in Brazil, took over the team kit in 1980. Its first kit for Brazil went for a silky, shiny fabric and featured its logo on the left sleeve. In 1981 a new logo featured on the shirt – that of Café de Brasil – in surely one of the first international sponsorship deals.

Worn in: Friendly wins over West Germany (2–1), France (3–1) and England (1–0) in 1981.
Worn by: Toninho Cerezo, Paulo Isidoro.

AWAY 1980–81

Design: Topper

After the decorated adidas kits, Topper opted for a basic approach, recreating those beautiful but simple Brazil shirts of the early '70s. The shorts on both kits now featured a thin lighter blue stripe sitting between two white ones. The team badge was changed to the acronym 'CBF' (Confederacao Brasileira de Futebol) rather than the previous CBD.

1982 FIFA WORLD CUP

HOME 1982

Design: Topper

A new badge design appeared in 1982 featuring the original World Cup – the Jules Rimet trophy – with a tiny Café de Brasil logo alongside the more prominent version on the right hand side of the shirt (which was removed during the 1982 World Cup). The Topper logo remained tucked away on the sleeve.

Worn in: The 3–2 defeat by Italy – regarded as one of the all-time great World Cup games.
Worn by: Falcao, Zico, Oscar.

1982 FIFA WORLD CUP

AWAY 1982

Design: Topper

A neat and trim blue and white version of this latest home kit naturally appeared as well, and featured the same logo arrangement as the home version. Again, the socks remained the same as the home pairs. This kit was not required in what proved to be a disappointing World Cup for Telê Santana's team despite a wonderful array of players.

1983 COPA AMERICA

HOME 1983–85

Design: Topper

By 1983 the additional Cafe de Brasil logo was removed (although it remained on the badge) and the Topper marque now earned pride of place on the front of the shirt. The same iconic Brazil crew-neck kit design was the same apart from a simpler trim on the socks.

Worn in: The 1983 Copa America that Brazil lost over two legs to Uruguay.
Worn by: Roberto Dinamite, China, Júnior.

1983 COPA AMERICA

AWAY 1983–85

Design: Topper

In 1983 the strip was updated in line with the home kit but retained the same shorts and socks as the 1982 incarnation.

Worn in: An impressive 5–0 drubbing of Ecuador in the 1983 Copa America.
Worn by: Milton Tita, Leandro, Eder.

1986 FIFA WORLD CUP / 1987 COPA AMERICA
1989 COPA AMERICA

HOME 1986–89

Design: Topper

Brazil's first match of 1986 – against West Germany – saw the side take to the pitch in a brand new strip, the first major change since Topper's arrival in 1980. The favoured crew neck was gone, replaced by a '70s-style collar.

Worn in: The penalties defeat against France in the 1986 World Cup quarter-final. Also worn in the 1–0 win over Uruguay in the 1989 Copa America final, breaking Brazil's 40 year duck!
Worn by: Careca, Socrates, Mauro Galvao.

1986 FIFA WORLD CUP / 1987 COPA AMERICA
1989 COPA AMERICA

AWAY 1986–89

Design: Topper

Primed and ready for the Mexico World Cup, the next Brazil away kit reflected the design of the home but in the familiar change colours blue and white. The kit ended up not being used in the tournament, although the shorts made an appearance with the home shirt on one occasion.

Worn in: A 2–0 victory over Australia in the 1988 Australian Bicentennial Gold Cup.
Worn by: Romario, Muller, Nelsinho.

1990 FIFA WORLD CUP
1991 COPA AMERICA

HOME 1989–91

Design: Topper

Clearly resistant to wholesale change, Topper updated the Brazil shirt midway through 1989 by removing the v-neck element of the collar and replacing it with a self-coloured inset. In many ways it was another rather old fashioned style but thanks to the Brazil magic it worked.

Worn in: A 1–0 defeat against Argentina in the 1990 World Cup. Also worn in the 2–0 win vs Chile in the 1991 Copa America.
Worn by: Dunga, Valdo, Branco.

1990 FIFA WORLD CUP
1991 COPA AMERICA

AWAY 1989–91

Design: Topper

Topper took a simple approach overall to their last away kit for the Samba Boys. The shirt, naturally, copied the design of the home, but the shorts and socks were plain, with no additional trim. The kit was not required in the 1990 World Cup. Paulo Roberto Falcao took over as coach from Sebastião Lazaroni in 1990.

Worn in: A 2–0 defeat against Colombia in the 1991 Copa America.
Worn by: Mazinho, Renato Gaucho, Marcio.

HOME 1991-93

Design: Umbro

In October 1991 Brazil stepped out in a radically different strip (although, of course, in their traditional colours!) courtesy of UK brand, Umbro. A deeper shade of blue on the shorts was joined by a large, button-up collar and an asymmetrical flash on the right sleeve. By 1993 a different sock design was worn.

Worn in: A 3-0 victory against Paraguay in the 1993 Copa America.
Worn by: Palhinha II, Boiadeiro, Valber.

AWAY 1991-93

Design: Umbro

After an entire decade sporting kits that were, arguably, out of time with contemporary fashion, Umbro brought Brazil bang up to date with asymmetrical flourishes and a complex shadow pattern featuring large CBF initials. This first batch of Umbro kits also saw the reintroduction of the classic '70s team badge.

Worn in: A 0-0 draw with Ecuador in a 1993 qualifier for the 1994 World Cup.
Worn by: Rai, Luiz Henrique, Careca.

HOME 1994-96

Design: Umbro

Umbro's next home kit for Carlos Alberto Parreira's team had something of an '80s feel to it, primarily thanks to its neat collar. The fabric was dominated by a large print of three team crests (one for each of Brazil's past World Cup titles). The shirt was updated later to include four crests following events in the USA!

Worn in: The 3-2 penalties triumph over Italy in the 1994 World Cup final.
Worn by: Romário, Aldair, Marcio Santos.

AWAY 1994

Design: Umbro

Curiously, Brazil opted to retain the 1991 away kit for the 1994 World Cup – with some minor adjustments: the shorts were now plain, the team crest and a white turnover with blue stripe were added to the socks and the Umbro logo was updated throughout.

Worn in: The classic 3-2 win vs the Netherlands in the 1994 World Cup quarter-final.
Worn by: Bebeto and co for his famous 'baby' goal celebration.

AWAY 1995-96

Design: Umbro

The final away kit from Umbro was designed to celebrate the magnificent fourth World Cup title by replicating the updated 1994 home shirt (in blue and white of course) and including the four shadow crests, in an attractive composition on the front.

Worn in: A narrow 1-0 win over Sweden in 1995's Umbro Cup.
Worn by: César Sampaio, Jorginho.

HOME 1997-98

Design: Nike

In 1996 Nike signed a £100m deal with the CBF – the largest kit deal ever at the time for a national side. It immediately made its mark with a design featuring a similar collar to the last Umbro shirt, accompanied by a single green stripe on each sleeve.

Worn in: The 3-1 victory over Bolivia in the Copa America final and the 6-0 thrashing of Australia in the final of the Confederations Cup.
Worn by: Edmundo, Roberto Carlos.

AWAY 1997-98

Design: Nike

Nike played safe with its first change strip for Mario Jorge Lobo Zagallo's team with a traditional blue and white interpretation of the home strip. With both these outfits, green featured on the shorts for the first time. As usual with Brazilian strips, the shorts and socks could be interchanged between the outfits.

Worn in: A 2-0 win over Colombia in the 1997 Copa America.
Worn by: Leonardo, Mauro Silva.

HOME 1998-2000

Design: Nike

With less than three months until the World Cup the second Nike kit was unveiled. With its now iconic sleeve trim it was, in many ways, a natural move on from the first, with a trimmed crew neck replacing the collar.

Worn in: The incident-packed 3-0 defeat against France in the 1998 World Cup final. Also worn in the 3-0 win over Uruguay in the 1999 Copa America final.
Worn by: Márcio Amoroso, Flavio Conceicao.

1998 CONCACAF GOLD CUP / 1998 FIFA WORLD CUP
1999 COPA AMERICA / 1999 FIFA CONFEDERATIONS CUP

AWAY 1998–2000

Design: Nike

Although packed and ready for the 1998 World Cup this blue incarnation of the latest home design wasn't required in the tournament (although the shorts did see some action against Morocco). Unlike most Samba Boys change strips, the crew neck was self-coloured, rather than contrasting.

Worn in: The 1–0 defeat against the USA in the semi-finals of the 1998 Gold Cup.
Worn by: Zinho, Sergio Manoel, Ze Maria.

THIRD 1998–2000

Design: Nike

An all-white third kit emerged during this period that comprised elements from both the home and away strips and paired them with a smart white shirt that essentially reversed the change jersey. This rather nice kit was never worn by the first team. The design team at Nike had to convince the CBF that the time was right to bring back the classic Brazil crew neck with this set of kits.

2001 COPA AMERICA
2001 FIFA CONFEDERATIONS CUP

HOME 2000–02

Design: Nike

The next Brazil outfit embraced the basic themes of the 1998 kit, but refined and simplified them further with this Dri-FIT outfit, leaving a pure but beautifully crafted strip with a clean, fresh look that echoed the glory days of 1970. The shorts and socks were free of any additional trim.

Worn in: The shock 2–0 defeat by Honduras in the quarter-finals of the 2001 Copa America.
Worn by: Denílson, Guilherme, Alex de Sousa.

2001 COPA AMERICA
2001 FIFA CONFEDERATIONS CUP

AWAY 2000–02

Design: Nike

Breathable and lightweight Dri-FIT fabric was also used to construct this strip that followed the plain, pragmatic aesthetic of the home kit. One difference with this jersey, however, was the addition of a blue trim on the white crew neck.

Worn in: A 1–0 defeat against Ecuador in a 2001 qualifier for the 2002 World Cup.
Worn by: Vampeta, Juliano Belletti.

2002 FIFA WORLD CUP
2003 FIFA CONFEDERATIONS CUP

★

HOME 2002–03

Design: Nike

A bright lemon shade of yellow was selected for this strip that was constructed with 'Cool Motion' dual layers in an attempt to wick sweat away from players' bodies. Aesthetically the template was worn across Nike's entire roster and featured intimidating mesh panels that allowed the inner layer to be seen.

Worn in: The masterful 2–0 victory over Germany in the 2002 World Cup final.
Worn by: Ronaldo – two-goal hero in the final.

2002 FIFA WORLD CUP
2003 FIFA CONFEDERATIONS CUP

AWAY 2002–03

Design: Nike

The 'Cool Motion' dual layer approach was also utilised on this blue away kit, although a collar was featured rather than the minimal neck of the home. Nike wanted a uniform approach to the visual appearance of its strips, with a focus on innovation and fabric technology.

Worn in: The 2–1 triumph over England in the 2002 World Cup quarter-final featuring a wonder goal from Ronaldinho.
Worn by: Cafu, Roque Junior.

SPECIAL 2004

Design: Nike

To celebrate FIFA's centenary a special commemorative match was organised between Brazil, as World Cup holders, and France, as European champions. To add extra interest both teams turned out in replicas of their shirts from the era. In Brazil's case this meant an exquisite lace-up white shirt with bold cuff trim.

Worn in: The 0–0 draw with France in the above match.
Worn by: Luisão, Cris.

2004 COPA AMERICA
2005 FIFA CONFEDERATIONS CUP

★★

HOME 2004–06

Design: Nike

Carlos Alberto Parreira's team sported another set of generic Nike templates, named 'Total 90', for their next strips. Visually, the shirts were dominated by the centrally placed badge (now with additional 'World Cup' star) and squad number housed within a large key lined circle

Worn in: Victories over Argentina: the penalties win in the 2004 Copa America final and the 4–1 win in the 2005 Confederations Cup final.
Worn by: Adriano, Kleberson.

AWAY 2004–06

Design: Nike

As was becoming the norm, the same template was used with the away kit including the physique-enhancing arched piping. The only exception came with a different neck design, in this case a more curved approach rather than the slick v-neck of the home jersey. The reverses of the Total 90 jerseys featured broad white panels across the shoulders in which sat the player's name. Like several Brazil away kits, this strip was never required on the pitch.

SPECIAL 2005

Design: Nike

A courageous initiative designed to combat racism in football, 'Stand Up, Speak Up' was launched by Nike in 2005. Its roster of international teams ditched their traditional colours and donned a half black/half white strip for a single match in a powerful gesture of unity. However, the Brazilian team never sported their own version.

HOME 2006–08

Design: Nike

As the 2006 World Cup loomed Nike moved away from its recent more generic designs and instead brought in bespoke outfits for its roster. The emphasis with this Brazil kit, with its neat mandarin-style collar and shield around the badge, was on simplicity and strength.

Worn in: The 1–0 defeat against France in the World Cup quarter-final and the 3–0 victory over Argentina in the 2007 Copa America final.
Worn by: Juninho, Ze Roberto.

AWAY 2006–08

Design: Nike

With influence gained from the classic Brazilian away strips of the '70s, Nike's next away kit saw the return of a nice and simple crew neck. This outfit was never actually required in the 2006 World Cup, although the shorts and socks were occasionally paired with the home shirt.

Worn in: A 1–0 win over Ecuador in the 2007 Copa America under manager Dunga who had been appointed following the 2007 World Cup.
Worn by: Robinho, Mineiro.

HOME 2008–10

Design: Nike

The team's new kit for the 2010 World Cup qualifying campaign saw the fripperies stripped back even further with raglan sleeves complemented by a minimalist neck design and hemline accents that were echoed on the shorts. Green made a prominent return to the socks as part of the turnover.

Worn in: The 3–2 win over USA in the final of the 2009 Confederations Cup.
Worn by: Luís Fabiano, Lucio.

AWAY 2008–10

Design: Nike

Although at first glance the side's next away kit appeared identical in structure to the home outfit, it did in fact include a different, sleek v-neck. The introduction of yellow trim on the shorts and socks brought extra freshness to the design. It was not required for the 2009 Confederations Cup tournament.

Worn in: A 2009 1–1 draw with Ecuador in the 2010 World Cup qualifying campaign.
Worn by: Júlio Baptista, Elano.

HOME 2010–11

Design: Nike

The 2010 World Cup in South Africa saw Brazil sporting this fine jersey, that once again sought inspiration from the side's iconic early '70s period. Launched at a lavish London event, the shirt featured a silicon stripe down each sleeve and on the seams of the shorts.

Worn in: Wins over North Korea, Ivory Coast and Chile in the 2010 World Cup finals.
Worn by: An 18-year-old Neymar who made his debut (and scored) against the USA in 2010.

AWAY 2010–11

Design: Nike

In essence this shirt again mirrored the design of the home kit (including the smart layered crew neck) with the notable exception of a sparkling yellow dot pattern throughout the main body of the shirt. Nike kits were now 100% recycled, made entirely from up to eight recycled plastic bottles.

Worn in: Another disappointing World Cup quarter-final exit – a 2–1 defeat by Holland.
Worn by: Dani Alves, Kaká.

2011 COPA AMERICA

2011 COPA AMERICA

THIRD 2010-11

Design: Nike

Another all-white third kit exists from this period, although the outfit was never worn by the first team. The shirt featured a clipped crew neck with the only adornments coming from the Nike swoosh logo and Brazil team crest.

HOME 2011-12

Design: Nike

The previous home kit lasted for just one year to allow a new design to be worn in the 2011 Copa America. In a radical shake-up, the new shirt featured no contrasting trim; the only decoration a bold green panel inspired by the stripe that Brazilian natives painted across their body before going to war in days gone by.

Worn in: The 2-0 win over Argentina in the 2011 Superclasico de las Americas 2nd leg.
Worn by: Alexandro Pato, Ganso.

AWAY 2011-12

Design: Nike

The Brazilian warrior stripe also found its way on to the 2011 away kit where it formed part of a strip that incorporated a much more muted and controversial blue/turquoise tone, helping create a brand new look for Mano Menezes' team. Sadly there was never a need for this fine strip to be worn as the home kit was selected for all matches during its lifespan.

THIRD 2011-12

Design: Nike

One of the more mysterious kits in the Brazil canon was this black affair. Officially marketed as a third kit as part of the Nike Brazil Pitch Black Collection, it was strictly speaking more of a training/leisure top as the shirt was never worn by the team – Brazil's tradition is that only the colours of the country's flag should form part of a kit. An all-black version featuring tonal appliqués was also launched.

2013 FIFA CONFEDERATIONS CUP

2013 FIFA CONFEDERATIONS CUP

HOME 2012-13

Design: Nike

After a decidedly rocky patch on the pitch, Nike decided to make the strip itself a source of inspiration. Clean and elegant, with the merest touch of green on the v-neck, the extra large green cuffs could be rolled back to reveal the nation's rallying cry 'Nascido Para Jogar Futebol' ('Born to Play Football') in a graffiti style.

Worn in: An aggregate 2012 win over Argentina in the Superclasico de las Americas.
Worn by: Thiago Neves, Fred.

AWAY 2012-13

Design: Nike

As host nations for the 2014 World Cup and with therefore no qualification campaign to battle through, it was a time of consolidation for the team. In keeping with the ethos behind the home strip, Brazil's next away kit returned to the nation's classic royal blue. The design reflected that of the home shirt (including laser-cut ventilation holes on each side).

Worn in: A solid 3-0 win over Sweden in 2012.
Worn by: Leandro Damiao, Paulinho.

HOME 2013-14

Design: Nike

Nike went back to the '70s for inspiration for the next Brazil home kit with the shirt featuring the introduction of a design ubiquitous with that decade: a collar/insert combination (although ironically the Samba Boys favoured a simple crew neck during that era!)

Worn in: The superb 3-0 win for Luiz Felipe Scolari's men against Spain in the 2013 Confederations Cup final.
Worn by: David Luiz, Hulk.

AWAY 2013-14

Design: Nike

This away strip opted for a completely fresh design that moved away from the trappings of the home. A self-coloured crew neck and cuffs was accompanied by a single white stripe on each arm. Simple yet highly effective, but, due to Brazil's reluctance to change strip unless a colour clash made it absolutely necessary, the strip never saw active duty.

HOME 2014–15

Design: Nike

Another sublime design as the Samba Boys prepared to host the 2014 World Cup – it was slimmer in fit than in previous years and included a low slung v-neck collar alongside the laser-cut breathable holes. The socks sported nothing more than the Nike swoosh logo.

Worn in: A match all of Brazil wants to forget – the 7–1 humiliation at the hands of Germany in the World Cup semi-finals.
Worn by: Bernard, Maicon.

AWAY 2014–15

Design: Nike

In a design that harked back to the dots of the 2010 shirt, the side's new away jersey was adorned with complex, yet effective, dotted tonal hoops. Although the shirt wasn't required in the World Cup, the shorts were paired with the home jersey on four occasions.

Worn in: The second half of a 2014 friendly against South Africa (the home kit was worn in the first 45 minutes!)
Worn by: Alexandro Pato, Marcelo.

THIRD 2014–15

Design: Nike

A new entry to the archives of 'never to be worn Brazil third kits' was this fine outfit, rendered in a very dark green that, according to Nike, paid 'tribute to the dynamic and diverse country' of Brazil. Although the jersey was relatively simple, the shorts included a mouthwatering series of graduated and multi-coloured thin stripes that were inspired by surf shorts, even to the extent that the cut was a little longer than usual.

HOME 2016–17

Design: Nike

A new shirt was due in 2015 but was apparently cancelled due to poor sales of the 2014 replicas. Instead fans had to wait until 2016 and the launch of Nike's Vapor template. Unlike Nike's other teams, though, the familiar team colours (named as Varsity Maize and Pine Green) were left unaltered.

Worn in: The 2017 win over Paraguay (3–0) that sealed World Cup 2018 qualification.
Worn by: Renato Augusto, Casemiro.

AWAY 2016–17

Design: Nike

The Vapor design, with its strong focus on performance (thanks to its Aeroswift fabric that was lighter and wicked sweat faster than previous shirts) rather than aesthetic niceties, appeared with the next away kit. Two tones of blue were used on the shirt, with a third lighter blue dominating the socks.

Worn in: A 0–0 draw with Ecuador in the 2016 Copa America.
Worn by: Willian, Gabriel Jesus.

THIRD 2017

Design: Nike

'Seaweed Green' was the official colour of this Brazil third kit that, although it passed the CBF's requirement that all kit must be formed from colours found in the national flag, is unlikely ever to be worn in a game. Trimmed with dark green and gold and featuring again the Vapor template, it is a gorgeous design.

Mazinho, Bebeto and Romario, wearing Umbro away kits, and their famous 'rocking baby' goal celebration in the 1994 World Cup against the Netherlands.

Ronaldo celebrates scoring in Nike's dual-layered 2002–03 home strip during the 2002 World Cup Group C match against Turkey.

DENMARK

Their colours of red and white, taken of course from their national flag, are far from rare in the football world, but there is always a little something extra about the Denmark kit, which gives it a unique quality.

It could be the varied and often very creative application of white throughout the design, or even the exquisitely crafted DBU shirt crest with its art nouveau sensibilities. But in all probability it's the team's long relationship with Hummel, their supplier, and fellow countrymen, that has made the difference.

Hummel have never lost faith in their unique chevron trim as the uniform's USP.

Such loyalty is relatively unusual in the football strip market, and a brand that also hails from the same country as the team does add something.

Since the Danes moved up to professional football in 1979 and signed with Hummel, the company have kitted them out in a variety of consistently wondrous designs that constantly create and reinforce a strong visual identity for the team. occasionally stopping to reinvent and rethink the strips along the way.

From the multi-pinstriped kits of the early '80s, via the iconic 'half and half' shirts of Mexico 1986 and up to the kit of 2000 inspired by cycling, Hummel have always ensured the Danes looked magnificent.

Away strips have traditionally simply been straightforward reversals of the home kits, although the odd third kit has been thrown in to break up the colour palette from time to time.

It was a big surprise to many when the team switched to adidas for their kit in 2004. The German kit masters supplied the team with some solid ideas, but 12 years later Denmark returned to their spiritual home: Hummel.

SPECIAL THANKS TO MORTEN GARBERG

The legendary Denmark Hummel 1986 away kit as worn by Michael Laudrup against Scotland in a 1986 World Cup Group E game.

HOME 1966–72

Design: Unknown

The Danish side played their football in the '60s like so many other teams, in a simple but functional long-sleeved, crew neck shirt which, in the Danes' case, featured non-contrasting neck and cuffs. Denmark, managed by Erik Hansen and Ernst Netuka at the time, were still operating under a strict 'amateurs only' rule.

Worn in: The legendary 14–2 humiliation of Iceland in 1967.
Worn by: Ulrik Le Fevre, Kresten Bjerre.

AWAY 1966–72

Design: Unknown

A simple reversal of the home kit provided an adequate change strip for the Danes – a kit philosophy that has stood them in good stead for many years. The team crest at the time was a shield with 'DBU' (Dansk Boldspils-Union) placed centrally. The side's 'amateur only' rule was eventually lifted in 1971.

Worn in: A close 3–2 defeat against the mighty Brazil in a 1966 friendly.
Worn by: Finn Laudrup, Erik Dyreborg.

HOME 1967

Design: Unknown

A one-off set of v-necked long sleeved shirts were also worn briefly in 1972. The rest of the strip was identical to the regular crew neck designs, including plain white shorts and red socks with white turnover. Denmark failed to qualify for the 1968 European Championship finals with Henry From replacing Netuka as joint manager with Erik Hansen in 1968.

AWAY 1967

Design: Unknown

A v-necked version of the team's away kit at this period was worn on at least one occasion. Until 1979 Denmark had no official kit contract and obtained strips from a variety of sources which could explain this design anomaly.

Worn in: A superb 5–0 victory over Norway in a 1967 friendly.
Worn by: John Steen Olsen, John Worbye.

HOME 1972–76

Design: Unknown

In 1972, to coincide with the inclusion of professional players into the national side, a new Denmark Football Association or Dansk Boldspils-Union (DBU) crest was introduced to the team shirt. It was a beautifully crafted crest with an exquisite art nouveau-style typeface and has remained virtually unchanged ever since. Also worn with plain white socks.

Worn in: A 1–0 friendly win vs Norway (1973).
Worn by: Kristen Nygaard, Helge Vonsyld.

AWAY 1972–76

Design: Unknown

Like the home, the Danish away kit for the first half of the '70s remained unchanged from the '60s version, except for the addition of the new DBU crest. This kit was worn during Rudi Strittich's team's unsuccessful qualification for the 1974 World Cup and Euro 76.

Worn in: A 3–1 defeat by Scotland in a 1975 qualifier for Euro 76.
Worn by: Jens Kolding, Lars Bastrup.

HOME 1976–79

Design: Umbro

A tiny tweak took place with the home kit that was to accompany the final years of Denmark's amateur status. The shirt and shorts remained the same but now dual stripes were added to the white turnover of the socks. A short sleeved version of the shirt made at least one appearance, in a 1976 friendly vs France.

Worn in: A thrilling 4–3 defeat against England in a 1978 qualifier for Euro 80.
Worn by: Henning Munk-Jensen, Allan Hansen II.

AWAY 1976–79

Design: Umbro

Black shorts now became first choice for the away kit. The socks also now switched to all-white and carried the same dual stripe trim on the turnovers as the home pair.

Worn in: A 1–0 defeat by Portugal in a 1978 World Cup qualifier (1976) and a 2–1 loss to Northern Ireland in 1978 while attempting to qualify for Euro 80.
Worn by: Henning Jensen III, Lars Larsen.

HOME 1976–79

Design: Umbro

The first visibly branded Denmark shirt emerged in 1976. Worn only in a short sleeved incarnation, this standard Umbro red jersey featured a white inset collar and cuffs but otherwise was free from any additional trim.

Worn in: A 2–1 defeat against Poland in a 1978 World Cup qualifier played in 1977. Kurt 'Nikkelaj' Nielsen's Danish side ultimately failed to qualify for the tournament.
Worn by: Flemming Lund, Ole Bjornmose.

AWAY 1976–79

Design: Umbro

The last 'short term' kit before the DBU made the final switch from amateur to professional and signed a contract with Hummel was this plain and simple white short sleeved shirt. It followed the design of the home but opted instead for a self-coloured inset collar and cuffs. Worn with either black or royal blue shorts.

Worn in: The good 2–1 win over Norway in a 1978 friendly match.
Worn by: Benny Nielsen, Birger Jensen.

HOME 1979–82

Design: Hummel

The Danish Football Association allowed professional teams into the league for the first time in 1978. A sponsorship deal with Carlsberg was signed and was followed in 1979 with the national team's first official apparel contract with local company Hummel. Later versions of this shirt featured raglan sleeves.

Worn in: The superb 3–1 win over Italy in a 1981 qualifier for the 1982 World Cup.
Worn by: Ole Rasmussen, Per Rontved.

AWAY 1979–82

Design: Hummel

The start of the Hummel deal brought an instant and highly contemporary visual identity to the Danish national side. Hummel's first kits followed the same design and employed its trademark chevron trim on the sleeves and sides of the shirt. Like the home kit, raglan sleeves were used later in the shirt's tenure.

Worn in: An impressive 1981 2–1 victory in Luxembourg (1982 World Cup qualifier).
Worn by: John Eriksen, Morten Olsen.

THIRD 1979–82

Design: Hummel

A third kit also emerged at this time in a dark, bottle green colour. The design reflected that of the red home and white away, including the collar and v-neck combination, and dual chevron motifs on the socks turnover. It is not clear, however, whether this kit was actually worn during its lifespan.

HOME 1982–83

Design: Hummel

Pinstripes were everywhere in the early '80s – including this Denmark kit. A modern v-neck was introduced to the raglan sleeved jersey. Unusually for the time, the pinstripes continued on the shorts. The socks remained identical to those on the previous kit.

Worn in: A 1–0 win over Greece in a 1983 qualifying match for Euro 84.
Worn by: Jesper Olsen, Ole Madsen II.

AWAY 1982–83

Design: Hummel

It's interesting to note how Hummel's strips for the Danish side were, in many ways, so ahead of their time. The away kit mirrored the design of the home strip and, as usual, provided the necessary elements to mix and match with the home outfit if necessary.

Worn in: A 2–1 defeat by Norway in the 1981 Nordic Championships.
Worn by: Jens Jorn Bertelsen, Steen Hansen.

THIRD 1982–83

Design: Hummel

Blue was introduced as a third kit colour at this time and followed the style of its home and away companions. Like the green strip from the previous set of outfits, it's uncertain, however, whether this fine looking kit ever saw any action on the pitch.

HOME 1983-84

Design: Hummel

Sophistication oozed from this next set of strips – thanks no doubt to the non-contrasting v-neck and cuffs and the always slick shadow stripes, a much more subtle form of decoration than the pinstripes of the very early '80s. As with the first Hummel kits, the chevron taping also ran down the sides of the shirt.

Worn in: A good 1-0 win over England in a 1983 qualifier for Euro 84.
Worn by: Allan Simonsen, Klaus Berggreen.

AWAY 1983-84

Design: Hummel

Once again, the away outfit simply replicated the design of the home, with the colours reversed, providing options for different combinations of shorts and socks. Thanks to some strong results in this set of kits the Danes achieved qualification for Euro 84.

Worn in: A 1-0 defeat by Hungary in a Euro 84 qualifier (1983). Also worn in a horrific 6-0 defeat by the Netherlands in a 1984 friendly.
Worn by: John Lauridsen, Ivan Nielsen.

1992 UEFA EUROPEAN CHAMPIONSHIP

HOME 1984-86

Design: Hummel

Denmark entered their first major tournament – the 1984 European Championship – wearing a brand new kit design. The shirt in essence was similar to the previous one but now introduced a contrasting v-neck and white raglan sleeves to accompany the side chevron trim.

Worn in: A superb 5-0 drubbing of Yugoslavia in Euro 84 followed by a 3-2 win over Belgium – both in the group stage.
Worn by: Henrik Andersen, Per Frimann.

1992 UEFA EUROPEAN CHAMPIONSHIP

AWAY 1984-85

Design: Hummel

The away kit for Euro 84 flipped the colours of the home as was the tradition, although as ever, elements could be switched over between the two kits if a colour clash still occurred. The tournament was a great success for Sepp Piontek and his 'Danish Dynamite' team.

Worn in: The disappointing penalties defeat against Spain in the semi-final of Euro 84 after a 1-1 draw (Denmark playing in all white).
Worn by: Kenneth Brylle, John Sivebaek.

AWAY 1985-86

Design: Hummel

Fans of English team Tottenham Hotspur will recognise this away design which was introduced for the second year of Hummel's fourth set of kits. All white, the shirt featured a wrapover v-neck and chest decoration of fine diagonal pinstripes bordered with chevron trim. It was a superb and confident creation.

Worn in: An incredible 5-1 triumph vs Norway in a 1985 qualifier for the 1986 World Cup.
Worn by: Soren Busk, Jan Molby.

1986 FIFA WORLD CUP

HOME 1986-88

Design: Hummel

In 1986 Hummel launched a new Danish strip as the side prepared for their first ever World Cup and unveiled this iconic design that has entered football kit legend. Half and half, with thin stripes throughout, it was a groundbreaking design. Originally unveiled with matching halved shorts, although these were quickly ditched.

Worn in: Amazing wins over Uruguay (6-1) and West Germany (2-0) in the 1996 World Cup.
Worn by: Michael Laudrup, Preben Elkjær Larsen.

1986 FIFA WORLD CUP

AWAY 1986-88

Design: Hummel

An all-white version of this incredible design formed the Danes' next away kit. However, with thin red stripes still present it arguably didn't differ that much from the superb home design.

Worn in: The 1-0 victory over Scotland at the 1986 World Cup. Also worn in the second stage 5-1 defeat by Spain – it was a memorable tournament for Sepp Piontek's Danes.
Worn by: Soren Lerby, Frank Arnesen.

THIRD 1986-88

Design: Hummel

A green third strip version of this fabulous design (officially, and rather appropriately, named 'Mexico') also exists. Whether this was ever actually worn in action is unclear, however. The halved design found its way around the world, and appeared in the UK with teams like Southampton, Aston Villa and Coventry.

1988 UEFA EUROPEAN CHAMPIONSHIP

HOME 1988–90

Design: Hummel

The Danes' impressive form on the pitch continued and they donned this equally impressive kit at Euro 88. The strip was an ingenious blend of modernity and retro with its combination of hoops joined by a '70s-style inset collar. Blue was incorporated as an additional trim colour for the first time.

Worn in: 2–0 defeats by West Germany and Italy in an incredibly tough Euro 88 group.
Worn by: Flemming Povlsen, Lars Olsen.

1988 UEFA EUROPEAN CHAMPIONSHIP

AWAY 1988–90

Design: Hummel

A straight reversal of the home strip again became the Danish change kit of choice. The Hummel chevron trim on these designs was toned back and restricted to just two pairs on the shoulders and sleeves. A nice touch was the placement of the Hummel 'bee' logo within the inset of the collar.

Worn in: Another 'all white' defeat against Spain, this time 3–2 in Euro 88.
Worn by: John Helt.

HOME 1990–92

Design: Hummel

A sleek modern design was unveiled as the next Danish kit. Broad white bands adorned each sleeve, which were far baggier than in recent years. Two slightly different designs of shorts were worn. Denmark failed to qualify for Italia 90 leading to the resignation of long term manager Sepp Piontek.

Worn in: A 3–1 victory over Austria in a Euro 92 qualifier.
Worn by: John Jensen, Lars Elstrup.

AWAY 1990–92

Design: Hummel

After the excitement and success of the '80s, results at this time seemed to indicate that Denmark's fortunes were faltering. Still, one consolation was that they still dressed well! This next set of Denmark outfits introduced a geometric shadow pattern to the shirt and broad contrasting side panels to the shorts.

Worn in: A 2–1 defeat by Italy in the 1991 Scania 100 Tournament.
Worn by: Kim Vilfort, Bent Christensen.

1992 UEFA EUROPEAN CHAMPIONSHIP

★

HOME 1992–94

Design: Hummel

1992 has to go down as one of the most extraordinary years in Danish football. Late qualifiers to Euro 92 thanks to the political upheaval in Yugoslavia, the side sported this bold design featuring an array of sleeve stripes and angular patterns. A shadow pattern of 'Danish Dynamite' featured on the fabric.

Worn in: The unforgettable 2–0 triumph over West Germany in the Euro 92 final!
Worn by: Torben Piechnik, Kim Christofte.

1992 UEFA EUROPEAN CHAMPIONSHIP

AWAY 1992–94

Design: Hummel

Richard Møller Nielsen had taken over as manager in 1990 and led the side to Euro 92 glory. The change kit at the time was a reversal of the home kit, as was the norm, and included the blue-trimmed collar and dual chevron trim on each shoulder. The shorts featured a sharp block trim on each leg and across the hem.

Worn in: A penalties win over the Netherlands in the Euro 92 semi-final.
Worn by: Henrik Larsen, Brian Laudrup.

1995 FIFA CONFEDERATIONS CUP

★

HOME 1994–96

Design: Hummel

There was a distinctly different look about the next Denmark home kit. Predominantly red, the visual focus was taken up by a large oblique abstract pattern that reached down the right hand side of the shirt. The previous shirt's 'Danish Dynamite' shadow pattern was incorporated into the fabric yet again.

Worn in: The 2–0 win over Argentina in the final of the 1995 Confederations Cup.
Worn by: Jakob Friis-Hansen, Peter Rasmussen.

1995 FIFA CONFEDERATIONS CUP

AWAY 1994–96

Design: Hummel

The white version of the 1994 kit replicated and reversed the abstracted shirt pattern but also added a gradated red sleeve for good measure. The shorts were far more sober than in recent years with just dual chevron trim for decoration. An alternative collar design featuring pairs of chevrons was also worn.

Worn in: A 3–0 defeat against Spain in a 1994 qualifying match for Euro 96.
Worn by: Mark Strudal, Thomas Helveg.

HOME 1996–97

Design: Hummel

After the experimentation of the 1994–96 kits it must have been a relief to Danish supporters to see their team in a more typical Hummel design. White sleeves joined the red shirt and a squared trimline ran across the shoulders. The shorts and socks stayed exactly the same (except for the positioning of the Hummel logo).

Worn in: A 3–0 defeat by Croatia followed by a win by the same score over Turkey at Euro 96.
Worn by: Marc Rieper, Michael Schjonberg.

AWAY 1996–97

Design: Hummel

A flipped version of the home kit was launched as the official away kit for 1996. However, it appears this version of the away kit was never worn and an all-white strip preferred in its place. Bo Johansson took over the managerial role in 1996.

THIRD 1996–97

Design: Hummel

A stunning blue version of the latest Hummel strips was launched and unlike previous designs, this did see some match action. The outfit replicated the design of the home – including the contrasting white sleeves. All Denmark jerseys at this time included an abstract, painterly shadow pattern.

Worn in: The 1–1 draw with Croatia in a 1997 qualifier for the 1998 World Cup.
Worn by: Mikkel Beck, Jes Hogh.

AWAY 1996–97

Design: Hummel

Despite the existence of a reversal of the home kit as the Danes' change outfit for Euro 96, an all-white away strip was worn after concerns were raised about how much contrast to the home outfit the original kit gave. The basic design was the same as the original away – minus the red sleeves.

Worn in: A 1–1 draw with Portugal in the Danes' first game of Euro 96.
Worn by: Claus Thomsen, Jens Risager.

HOME 1998–2000

Design: Hummel

Rather than the traditional launch of a new Danish kit just prior to a major tournament, this strip instead appeared in the first game of 1998 against Scotland. A functional design, it included a trimmed collar, white shoulder panels, sleeve trim piping and a watermark of the DBU crest on the fabric.

Worn in: The desperately unlucky 3–2 defeat by Brazil in the 1998 World Cup quarter-final.
Worn by: Martin Jorgensen, Allan Nielsen.

AWAY 1998–2000

Design: Hummel

The new strip worked beautifully in white with all elements reversed from the home. As well as the DBU crest watermark a fine ribbed effect was noticeable on the fabric. As before, the shorts and socks could be combined with the home shirt.

Worn in: An impressive 4–1 triumph over Nigeria in the 1998 World Cup second round (Denmark in all white).
Worn by: Peter Moller, Ebbe Sand.

THIRD 1998–2000

Design: Hummel

Supposedly in the kitbag for the 1998 World Cup was this outrageous third kit that bizarrely appeared completely at odds with its equivalent home and away outfits. The futuristic, abstract body print was in fact taken from the side's current goalkeeper jersey topped off by the same trim and collar style of the regular home and away kits. It seems the strip was never worn.

HOME 2000–02

Design: Hummel

Quite possibly one of the best recent Danish kits, this shirt featured a tidy neck design combined with a zip-effect placket giving the overall feel of a cycling jersey. A DBU crest watermark appeared again, coupled with a horizontal, striped pattern. Sadly, performances on the pitch didn't match the quality of the kit.

Worn in: The 3–0 defeat against France in the Danes' first game at Euro 2000.
Worn by: Stig Tofting, Morten Bisgaard.

2000 UEFA EUROPEAN CHAMPIONSHIP

AWAY 2000-02

Design: Hummel

It was another great Danish away kit that was on display at Euro 2000 and, as was customary, the design mirrored that of the fine home strip. Bo Johansson's side had qualified for Euro 2000 by the skin of their teeth, thanks to a play-off against Israel.

Worn in: Defeats to the Netherlands (3-0) and Czech Republic (2-0) in a poor Euro 2000.
Worn by: Jesper Gronkjaer, Jon Dahl Tomasson.

THIRD 2001

Design: Hummel

This curious design was worn in 2001 for at least one game although quite why a third strip should be the same core colour as the away is a mystery. The design featured a new colourway of white, black and just a dash of a reflective silver on the Hummel chevron trim.

Worn in: A 0-0 draw with the Czech Republic in a 2001 qualifier for the 2002 World Cup.
Worn by: Dennis Rommedahl, Rene Henriksen.

THIRD 2001-02

Design: Hummel

Another blue Danish strip emerged during this period, although again it's unclear if it was ever worn by the first team. The long-sleeved design also appeared slightly at odds with the current strips due to an older style neck design. It can be assumed it would have been paired with blue shorts and socks should it have been needed.

2002 FIFA WORLD CUP

HOME 2002-03

Design: Hummel

Morten Olsen was appointed manager in 2000 and to accompany his team was this beautifully simple strip, free of all the design excesses of previous kits. It featured a crew neck with a retro chevron trim. The lower half of the shirt included a curious twin peaked lighter area.

Worn in: The wonderful 2-0 win over France and the 3-0 defeat at the hands of England in the 2006 World Cup.
Worn by: Christian Poulsen, Niclas Jensen.

2002 FIFA WORLD CUP

AWAY 2002-03

Design: Hummel

The classic simplicity of this next set of Hummel kits extended to the away kit which was a plain white jersey, featuring the same trim and neck/cuff design of the home. It was a stunning kit that brought some breathing space after the liveliness of earlier designs. Sadly, it never featured in the 2002 World Cup.

Worn in: A 2-2 draw with Norway in a Euro 2004 qualifier (2002).
Worn by: Claus Jensen, Morten Wieghorst.

2002 FIFA WORLD CUP

THIRD 2002-03

Design: Hummel

With shades of the team's 1979-82 third kit, a new strip in bottle green was launched prior to the 2002 World Cup. It replicated the design of its home and away kit companions including the simple crew neck.

Worn in: A 2-1 friendly win over Tunisia in 2002 – the only time this strip was worn.
Worn by: Thomas Gravesen, Jan Heintze.

2004 UEFA EUROPEAN CHAMPIONSHIP

HOME 2003-04

Design: Hummel

This next batch of kits – which would prove, to be Hummel's last for the team – were very much stylistically a natural follow-on from the previous outfits: a simple composition that saw breathable fabric panels joined by a minimalist neck and truncated chevron sleeve taping.

Worn in: The 2-2 draw with rivals Sweden in Euro 2004 followed by the crushing 3-0 defeat against the Czech Republic in the quarter-finals.
Worn by: Peter Lovenkrands, Brian Priske.

2004 UEFA EUROPEAN CHAMPIONSHIP

AWAY 2003-04

Design: Hummel

The Danes had qualified for Euro 2004 and armed themselves with another sublime set of outfits. This kit, a reversal of the home design, was not required in the tournament, however, and in fact was only worn once, when it was paired with the home shorts.

Worn in: A 2-0 defeat against Spain in a 2004 friendly match – the only time this kit was ever worn.
Worn by: Peter Madsen, Daniel Jensen.

THIRD 2003-04

Design: Hummel

A grey/silver version of the last batch of Hummel kits also exists, alongside black shorts and grey/silver socks. No surprises with the design as it replicated the other strips but, again, it seems this was never worn.

HOME 2004-05

Design: adidas

After what felt like a lifetime with Hummel, Denmark signed a deal in 2004 with adidas. It was going to take a while for fans to get used to not seeing their team kitted out in chevrons. adidas' first strip introduced distinctive white mesh bands on each side of the chest and under the arms of the jersey.

Worn in: The 3–0 victory over Kazakhstan in a 2005 qualifier for the 2006 World Cup.
Worn by: Soren Larsen, Per Nielsen.

AWAY 2004-06

Design: adidas

The first adidas away strip for Morten Olsen's team followed the same design as the home but chose not to include contrasting colour for the side bands. On both shirts, the bottom of the reverse was constructed from a white mesh panel. The kits were worn during the side's unsuccessful 2006 World Cup qualifiers.

Worn in: A 2004 2–0 win in Albania (with white shorts) in a 2006 World Cup qualifier.
Worn by: Henrik Pedersen, Peter Skov-Jensen.

HOME 2006-07

Design: adidas

2006 brought with it a new elegant and flamboyant range of strips across adidas' roster of teams. Graceful, wavy panels decorated each side of the shirt with the ability to colour block particular areas – a style that suited the Danish strip perfectly. The adidas logo on the shorts was moved to the reverse.

Worn in: A 1–0 win over Germany in a 2007 friendly match.
Worn by: Rasmus Würtz, Morten Nordstrand.

AWAY 2006-07

Design: adidas

A straightforward reversal of the home outfit – complete with coloured side 'waves' and additional flashes on the shorts – formed this away kit. There was more disappointment for the Danes, though, as they missed out on 2008 European Championship qualification.

Worn in: A 2–1 defeat in Spain in a Euro 2008 qualifier (2007).
Worn by: Michael Gravgaard, Dennis Sorensen.

HOME 2007-09

Design: adidas

First worn in the Euro 2008 qualifier against Iceland, this shirt was more slim-fitting than in recent years. It employed a basic initial look but introduced a compelling array of fine white stripes on the lower sides of the jersey.

Worn in: Two memorable 1–0 triumphs over rivals Sweden in qualifiers for the 2010 World Cup (both in 2009).
Worn by: Thomas Kahlenberg, Jakob Poulsen.

AWAY 2008-09

Design: adidas

A exciting display of pinstripes that splayed out at the top of the shirt formed the primary aesthetic focus of this shirt. As with the home kit, the adidas logo was placed centrally to allow for a squad number on the right-hand side. The shorts and socks reversed the design of the home pairs.

Worn in: A superb 3–1 win in Portugal in a 2008 qualifier for the 2010 World Cup.
Worn by: Martin Retov, Leon Andreasen.

THIRD 2008-09

Design: adidas

Adidas' first-ever third shirt for the Danes saw it reintroduce a rich royal blue as its core colour. It featured a different template (using Formotion fabric) to the home and away shirts and included white applications on each side. During the only game it which it was worn, it was paired up with the red home socks.

Worn in: A 1–1 draw with Poland in a 2008 friendly match.
Worn by: Martin Vingaard, Tommy Kristensen.

2010 FIFA WORLD CUP

HOME 2009–11

Design: adidas

Unveiled towards the end of 2009 but primarily prepared for the 2010 World Cup, this home shirt with its 11 dotted lines across the torso was intended to pay tribute to past Danish football players and their coming together to represent the country. adidas' three stripes were broken to leave space for sleeve patches.

Worn in: A sad 3–1 defeat against Japan in the group stage of the 2010 World Cup.
Worn by: Daniel Agger, Simon Busk Poulsen.

2010 FIFA WORLD CUP

AWAY 2010–11

Design: adidas

Denmark had done well to qualify from a tough group for the 2010 World Cup and, as they prepared, this Climacool away kit was launched. A relatively plain ensemble, the most striking feature was the curved piping that reached over the shoulders from the slick neck design.

Worn in: A 2–0 defeat against the Netherlands, followed by an all-white 2–1 victory over Cameroon in the 2010 World Cup.
Worn by: Simon Kjær, Lars Jacobsen.

2012 UEFA EUROPEAN CHAMPIONSHIP

HOME 2011–13

Design: adidas

Arguably one of the best adidas designs for the Danish Dynamite was this shirt. Thanks to the collar, shoulder panels and navy trim, it managed to conjure the essence of the iconic Denmark kit from Euro 92, to which it paid tribute, with an inner graphic panel. And was that a hint of a chevron in the shadow pattern?!

Worn in: A thrilling 3–2 defeat against Portugal in Euro 2012 with Denmark in all red.
Worn by: Nicklas Bendtner, Niki Zimling.

2012 UEFA EUROPEAN CHAMPIONSHIP

AWAY 2012–13

Design: adidas

This kit made use of the same basic template design as the home outfit – with the exception of the inclusion of a minimalist crew neck. Both this and the home shirt were also available in tight fitting 'Techfit' versions that featured compression webbing and were designed to enhance performance.

Worn in: A shock 1–0 win over the Netherlands in the side's first Euro 2012 match.
Worn by: Michael Krohn-Delhi, William Kvist.

HOME 2013–15

Design: adidas

This was another cleverly understated jersey. Essentially crafted from the Condivo 14 template, the slim-fitting shirt included additional shadow stripes that subtly recreated the Danish flag. The reverse of the Climacool design featured a standard adidas single stripe across the shoulder blades to symbolise 'unity'.

Worn in: A 2–0 win over Serbia – from the disappointing Euro 2016 qualifying campaign.
Worn by: Pierre-Emile Højbjerg, Simon Kjær.

AWAY 2014–15

Design: adidas

A very different design philosophy was clearly employed with the creation of this fine Climacool away kit. The strip dispensed with the traditional red and instead opted for a white and navy concoction, trimmed sparingly with royal blue. Worn with either blue or white shorts.

Worn in: A 1–0 defeat against Portugal in a 2015 qualifier for Euro 2016.
Worn by: Michael Krohn-Delhi, Emil Berggreen.

HOME 2015–16

Design: adidas

There were distinct shades of Hummel's classic half and half Euro 86 shirt in this final home kit from adidas which was launched, rather prematurely as it turned out, as the Danes' Euro 2016 shirt. A no-frills design saw the addition of white crew neck and cuffs and adidas three-stripe trim on the sides of this two-tone jersey.

Worn in: The crushing 4–3 defeat by Sweden over two legs in the Euro 2016 qualifier.
Worn by: Yussuf Poulsen, Jannik Vestergaard.

AWAY 2015–16

Design: adidas

adidas' last away kit for Denmark was very much a progression from the previous one and featured a simple white and black design, with just a touch of red, and horizontal tonal mesh stripes. Printed on the reverse of the necks of both kits this year was the DBU slogan 'Part of Something Bigger'.

Worn in: A 2–2 draw with Bosnia and Herzegovina in the Kirin Cup (2016).
Worn by: Christian Eriksen.

SPECIAL 2016

Design: Hummel

Much to the excitement of Denmark supporters, the DBU re-signed with previous long-term kit partner Hummel in 2016 in a new eight-year deal. Under the banner of 'A New Beginning' a special one-off all-white strip, representing the 'blank canvas' needed to write new football tales, was launched.

Worn in: A 5–0 thrashing of Liechtenstein in the Danes' first game back in Hummel kit.
Worn by: Andreas Cornelius, Viktor Fischer.

HOME 2016–17

Design: Hummel

The first new Hummel Danish kit in 12 years was a classic – simple and strong, complete with truncated chevron trim and a modern neck design. A shadow print of legendary Danish viking warrior Holger Danske was included on the shirt, designed to inspire Age Fridtjof Hareide's side to new football glory.

Worn in: A 2018 World Cup qualifier 4–0 triumph against Poland in 2017.
Worn by: Nicolai Jorgensen, Andreas Bjelland.

AWAY 2016–17

Design: Hummel

This strip made a bold statement of nationalistic pride with a rendering of the Danish flag on the right-hand side of the shirt with the DBU crest sitting at the centre of the cross. The shorts and socks reflected the design of the home pairs, apart from an additional stripe on the socks.

Worn in: The all-white 4–1 win over Armenia in a 2018 World Cup qualifier (2017).
Worn by: Thomas Delaney, Pione Sisto.

SPECIAL 2017

Design: Hummel

6 June 2017 marked the 25th anniversary of Denmark's famous Euro 1992 win and to commemorate the occasion this special shirt was worn in the match played on that date. The design took influence from the Hummel kit of 1992 with the addition of a gold outline around the DBU crest.

Worn in: The above-mentioned friendly match against Germany that ended in a 1–1 draw.
Worn by: Martin Braithwaite, Riza Durmisi.

Denmark line up in their Hummel 1992–94 home kit prior to the Euro 92 match against England that ended in a 0–0 draw. The team went on to win the tournament wearing this strip.

1974 FIFA WORLD CUP

Scotland's Joe Jordan (in typical early '70s Umbro strip, complete with sock tags) heads past Buhanga in Zaire's formidable adidas home kit.

1974 FIFA WORLD CUP

Adidas began their dominance of world football apparel in the 1974 FIFA World Cup, where the Netherlands sported the famous stripes.

ENGLAND

England are one of those few fortunate sides who look equally at home in their traditional away kit of red as they do in their first choice, white.

Of course, the reasons behind this kit ambidexterity can be traced to the country's sole World Cup success in 1966. Then they famously wore red against West Germany (having lost the coin toss), ensuring the colour's immortality in English football culture. The home kit at the time was simply white and navy, and red has become a vital third component in the palette since then.

As well as red outfits, blue has also made the odd appearance in the England away kit bag: several sky blue third strips were launched in the '80s and '90s and even a couple of navy shirts a couple of decades later.

The side has worn a plethora of wonderful designs. Some were minimalist and clean, sticking firmly to traditional kit values. Others introduced colour in a brave and inventive way, such as Admiral's revolutionary outfits from the '70s, which boldly rewrote the football apparel rule book.

England's 2009 all-white home shirt also did exactly that. Amid the noise of ever-convoluted designs featuring all manner of excessive decoration, it bucked the trend and called for silence with its clean simplicity and focus on great tailoring. This subsequently created a whole new kit trend just on its own. The magic of this strip emerged from Umbro, long-term technical partners of the England side until the Manchester company split with then owners Nike, who subsequently took on the contract themselves.

The England team may disappoint and underachieve on occasion, but their strips seldom do, ensuring there is always great anticipation to see the next new design for the English team.

Jubilant England players celebrate winning the 1966 World Cup Final against West Germany in their classic red away Umbro 'Aztec' shirts.

HOME 1966–74

Design: Umbro

Something about the simplicity of England's '60s strips still resonates with fans and this white shirt – long-sleeved (although short sleeves were also sometimes worn) and crew-necked – is often regarded as the definitive England outfit and was worn during the nation's most successful footballing period.

Worn in: 2–0 wins over Mexico and France in the group stages of the 1966 World Cup.
Worn by: Bobby and Jack Charlton.

AWAY 1966–74

Design: Umbro

Surely the most iconic England outfit ever?! This long sleeved, crew neck jersey, paired with plain white shorts and red socks, has entered English folklore as the strip worn when England were world champions. Since then, the design has been an influence for many subsequent England change shirts. Also worn short sleeved.

Worn in: That thrilling 4–2 triumph over Germany in the 1966 World Cup final.
Worn by: Geoff Hurst, Bobby Moore.

HOME 1970, 1973–74

Design: Umbro

With the oppressive Mexican heat in the forefront of the England camp's minds a new lightweight shirt was launched in 1970 and created from breathable airtex fabric. Worn short sleeved and with white shorts and socks it created a heroic look for Sir Alf's team. The shirt also made appearances in 1973 and 1974.

Worn in: The nailbiting 1–0 defeat against Brazil in the 1970 World Cup group stage.
Worn by: Alan Ball, Francis Lee.

AWAY 1970

Design: Umbro

A delicate pale blue was selected as a more suitable colour to combat the fierce temperatures in the World Cup. Constructed from the same airtex fabric as the home shirt, the outfit caused problems for black and white TV viewers as in its only outing against a white-clad Czech side the teams proved hard to distinguish for those watching at home.

Worn in: The 1-0 win over Czechoslovakia.
Worn by: Jeff Astle, Colin Bell.

THIRD 1970, AWAY 1974

Design: Umbro

Although officially relegated to England's third choice for Mexico, the traditional red change strip did make an appearance in all its airtex glory in the country's final game of the tournament, thanks to the TV problems encountered in the Czechoslovakia game. Also worn for two games in 1974 when red.

Worn in: A 3–2 defeat against West Germany in the 1970 World Cup quarter-finals.
Worn by: Alan Mullery, Martin Peters.

THIRD 1973

Design: Umbro

Umbro opted for another pale hue for England's change kit for the unsuccessful 1973 European friendly tour – yellow. It was a move away from traditional England colours and only lasted for a brief period before red was back full time. New navy shorts complemented the airtex shirt.

Worn in: A 1–1 draw with Czechoslovakia and two 2–0 defeats against Italy and Poland.
Worn by: Allan Clarke – the only player to score for England in this shirt.

HOME 1974–80

Design: Admiral

England's traditional plain and simple kit underwent a radical overhaul in 1974 thanks to the FA and new manager Don Revie's lucrative deal with Admiral, who were busy reinventing the football kit world. Out went the navy and in came royal blue alongside trim on the sleeves and shorts.

Worn in: A 5–1 thrashing of Scotland in the 1975 Home Internationals.
Worn by: Trevor Francis, Steve Coppell.

AWAY 1974–81

Design: Admiral

Naturally the adventurous new design was implemented on the red away kit, with the white and blue trim creating a very stylish effect. The shorts and socks were mixed and matched with the home versions. These Admiral kits coincided with a downturn in English football that led to Don Revie's demise.

Worn in: A 1–1 draw with Brazil in a 1978 Wembley friendly.
Worn by: Kevin Keegan, Trevor Brooking.

ENGLAND

1976 – 1986

THIRD 1976

Design: Admiral

Yellow made a surprising return to the England kit palette in 1976 thanks to England's participation in the American Bicentennial Tournament that year. This was actually the very first Admiral change kit worn by England, as the team had always sported their first choice home strip up until that point.

Worn in: The 3–1 win over 'Team America' in a match not recognised as a full international.
Worn by: Gerry Francis, Trevor Cherry.

1980 FIFA WORLD CUP
1982 UEFA EUROPEAN CHAMPIONSHIP

HOME 1980–83

Design: Admiral

Admiral all but disappeared from the football world in 1980 due to financial problems but somehow clung on to the valuable England contract. With its large colourful chest panels this shirt was regarded as controversial at the time, but today it is regarded as a classic.

Worn in: A 2–1 win over Spain in the 1980 European Championship during which the kit was worn without manufacturer's logos.
Worn by: Kenny Sansom, Mick Mills.

1982 FIFA WORLD CUP
1982 UEFA EUROPEAN CHAMPIONSHIP

AWAY 1981–83

Design: Admiral

Launched a year after the unveiling of Admiral's second home kit, this new outfit again reflected the design of its white equivalent. Two versions of the shirt were worn: the second with a thicker white band at the bottom of the chest panel in which the thinner blue line was then situated.

Worn in: A 3–1 triumph over France in the 1982 World Cup finals.
Worn by: Ray Wilkins, Phil Thompson.

HOME 1984–87

Design: Umbro

After the bold and bright colours of the Admiral era, a prodigal Umbro brought back a more sober and classy England palette. A multi-trimmed v-neck, shoulder piping and thin shadow pinstripes brought a touch of elegance back to England football apparel.

Worn in: The classic 2–0 win over Brazil at the Maracana in 1984.
Worn by: John Barnes – scorer of a wonder goal in that match.

AWAY 1984–88

Design: Umbro

Umbro's new sophisticated approach to the England kit continued with this fine new away ensemble, including the silky, shadow pinstriped fabric. This set of kits are also notable for including the England badge on the shorts for the first time. Bobby Robson took over as manager in 1982, replacing Ron Greenwood.

Worn in: 5–0 wins over Finland (1984) and Turkey (1985), bizarrely both at home!
Worn by: Bryan Robson, Mark Hateley.

1986 FIFA WORLD CUP

HOME 1986

Design: Umbro

With shades of 1970, England and Umbro again considered their options to compensate for the Mexican heat as the World Cup loomed. Once again airtex was the answer. The tweaked shirt abandoned cuffs (another cooling technique) and introduced thin shadow stripes.

Worn in: A 3–0 win over Poland en route to the infamous 'Hand of God' defeat against Argentina where the shirt was worn with blue shorts/socks.
Worn by: Gary Lineker, Mark Wright.

1986 FIFA WORLD CUP

AWAY 1986

Design: Umbro

Although not required for the Mexico World Cup finals, a red version in the new lightweight, airtex style was produced and featured the same modifications that had been implemented with the home strip. Replica versions were heavily marketed prior to the tournament's commencement in June. These three kits were only temporary; once the World Cup was over the team reverted to the standard designs.

1986 FIFA WORLD CUP

THIRD 1986

Design: Umbro

Again taking influence from 1970, a new pale blue third kit was launched for the tournament – the first time an England third kit had been produced and marketed for replica sale. Umbro's new design worked beautifully in this colour scheme with the shirt utilising exactly the same neck design as the home. Sadly the strip was never worn, although the shorts and socks did see some action in the ill-fated quarter-final match against Argentina.

HOME 1987–89

Design: Umbro

New advances in fabric technology led to Umbro, in conjunction with ICI, developing a new moisture-controlling material, Tactel, which was used in this kit. The design (officially named 'International') featured a triangular-based shadow pattern and a button-up crew neck.

Worn in: Three losses in Euro 88: 1–0 to the Republic of Ireland and 3–1 to the USSR and the Netherlands.
Worn by: Tony Adams, Glenn Hoddle.

AWAY 1988–89

Design: Umbro

The previous red kit lasted a little longer than the home, meaning that this seldom-worn strip did not arrive until 1988. The shirt, as usual, mirrored the design of the home, therefore providing the option to interchange the shorts and socks with the white outfit. The famous 'three lions' graphic appeared on the socks.

Worn in: A 2–1 win over Greece in a 1989 friendly – the only victory earned in this strip.
Worn by: Peter Beardsley, Terry Butcher.

THIRD 1988–89

Design: Umbro

England once again launched an official all pale blue third strip and once again it was never worn in action. Modelled with natural grace and poise by Peter Beardsley in promotional photos, the kit followed the same style of the home and away strips. Unlike the previous pale blue third outfit, however, the traditional England red was ditched as a trim in favour of a pale blue/navy/white approach.

HOME 1990–92

Design: Umbro

Other than the red of 1966, this jersey is possibly one of the most iconic England shirts ever and was worn during the Gazza-inspired heroics of Italia 90. Aptly the shirt design was officially named 'World Cup'. The baggy fitting jersey saw the return of a collar which was teamed up with a diamond embossed pattern.

Worn in: A last-minute 1–0 win over Belgium in the 1990 World Cup.
Worn by: David Platt, Stuart Pearce.

AWAY 1990–93

Design: Umbro

Rather than featuring a non-contrasting neck/collar as all previous Umbro England away kits had done, this next outfit opted for a navy design. A new complex shadow pattern was utilised throughout the fabric. The strip was taken to both the 1990 World Cup and the 1992 Euro Championship, but used in neither.

Worn in: A 2–2 draw with Argentina in the 1991 England Challenge Cup.
Worn by: Paul Gascoigne, Des Walker.

THIRD 1990–92

Design: Umbro

Pale blue was retained for the next England third kit that was also in the kitbag for the 1990 World Cup but, once again, was not called into active service for the tournament. In fact, this shirt (with its diamond-based 'Copa Mondial' two-tone shadow pattern) was only ever worn once.

Worn in: A 1991 1–0 win over Turkey in a Euro 92 qualifier.
Worn by: Gary Pallister, Lee Dixon.

THIRD 1992–93

Design: Umbro

This last Umbro third kit produced for the side was launched in time for the Euro 92 finals. The all pale blue strip now incorporated a bold design based around the three lions – who seemed to have been given a slightly cartoon-like makeover. The socks were retained from the previous outfit.

Worn in: A 2–2 draw with Czechoslovakia in a 1992 friendly.
Worn by: David Batty, Gary Mabbutt.

HOME 1993–94

Design: Umbro

Any shirt that followed the splendour of the Italia 90 effort had a lot to live up to. Premiered in the first fixture of 1993 (a 6–0 win over San Marino), this kit had one of the shortest reigns of any England home strip and was worn in the dismal 1994 World Cup qualifiers. The shirt's collar included a second, miniature team crest.

Worn in: A 2–2 draw with the Netherlands in a 1993 World Cup qualifier.
Worn by: Alan Shearer, Graeme Le Saux.

AWAY 1994–95

Design: Umbro

An all-red design was launched in 1994 with Terry Venables now England manager following the resignation of Graham Taylor. It was another short-lived strip and was created from a much deeper hue (officially described as 'wine') than had been worn previously. Like many kits of the era, it also included long, loose-fitting shorts.

Worn in: The 5–0 rout of Greece in a home friendly (1994).
Worn by: Gary Neville, Matthew Le Tissier.

1996 UEFA EUROPEAN CHAMPIONSHIP

HOME 1995–96

Design: Umbro

The mid-'90s found Umbro experimenting with unorthodox colour schemes. In England's case, red was discarded and replaced by turquoise – giving a totally fresh look. The badge and new text-only Umbro logo were placed centrally, and a new, cleverly constructed collar introduced.

Worn in: The jaw-dropping 4–1 victory over the Dutch during the memorable Euro 96 tournament, hosted in England.
Worn by: Teddy Sheringham, Jamie Redknapp.

1996 UEFA EUROPEAN CHAMPIONSHIP

AWAY 1996–97

Design: Umbro

This controversial new change kit was the first non-red England primary change outfit for many years. With the popularity of replica jerseys at an all-time high, the 'indigo blue' shirt was one of the first to be designed as a leisure item ('to look good with jeans!') as well as a piece of functional football apparel.

Worn in: The emotional penalties defeat against Germany in the semi-finals of Euro 96.
Worn by: Steve Stone, Steve McManaman.

HOME 1997–99

Design: Umbro

New coach Glenn Hoddle masterminded the side's qualification for the France 98 World Cup finals in this strong strip which saw a welcome return of red to the England palette. Similar in style to many of Umbro's kits at the time, the design blended large panels with a bulky collar.

Worn in: The defeat on penalties with old foes Argentina in the second stage of the 1998 World Cup after a David Beckham sending off.
Worn by: Michael Owen, Paul Scholes.

1998 FIFA WORLD CUP

AWAY 1997–99

Design: Umbro

It was a return to red although the shade again appeared much deeper – partly due to the shadow striped 'St George's flag' motif. Unlike the previous kit, these shorts and socks could be interchanged with the home pairs. The three lions on the FA crest were changed from navy to sky blue.

Worn in: A 2–0 victory over Colombia in the 1998 World Cup finals.
Worn by: Sol Campbell, Martin Keown.

2000 UEFA EUROPEAN CHAMPIONSHIP

HOME 1999–2001

Design: Umbro

A far more restrained England kit emerged in 1999 alongside a new manager in Kevin Keegan. The strip, launched on St George's Day, exuded sophistication. It reverted to two colours for the first time since the early '70s, and featured a tonal version of Umbro's resurrected sleeve taping.

Worn in: Poor 3–2 defeats to Portugal and Romania in Euro 2000.
Worn by: David Beckham, Robbie Fowler.

2000 UEFA EUROPEAN CHAMPIONSHIP

AWAY 1999–2001

Design: Umbro

Traditional kit values were firmly back in vogue in the late '90s. The jersey featured an old-fashioned navy collar with a dashing white and navy button-up placket. Incredibly, in the seven matches this strip was worn, only one was actually played away from home.

Worn in: The last ever game in the old Wembley – a 0–0 defeat against Germany.
Worn by: Kieron Dyer, Nick Barmby.

HOME 2001–03

Design: Umbro

The February 2001 match vs Spain saw the debut not only of this alluring new outfit but also of new manager Sven Goran Eriksson. Red returned with a vengeance via a single vertical stripe – the influence of the national flag looming large – and for the first time a unique pair of white change shorts were produced.

Worn in: The unforgettable 5–1 humiliation of Germany in a 2002 World Cup qualifier (2001)
Worn by: Steven Gerrard, Emile Heskey.

2002 FIFA WORLD CUP

AWAY 2002–04

Design: Umbro

Premiered at Wembley in a 2002 friendly defeat against Italy, this shirt saw the side return to a much more contemporary away design. The jersey featured reversed blue stitching along with breathable fabric panels. The replica version also made a bit of England kit history by being the side's first-ever reversible shirt.

Worn in: The fantastic 1–0 win over Argentina in the Japan/Korea 2002 World Cup finals.
Worn by: Ashley Cole, Rio Ferdinand.

2004 EUROPEAN CHAMPIONSHIP

HOME 2003–05

Design: Umbro

Umbro's next home ensemble followed very much in the vein of the previous, with red still playing a prominent role in the strip. The colour was incorporated into a tapered sleeve design that culminated with a tiny gold star on the left sleeve to mark the country's World Cup winning triumph of 1966.

Worn in: The 2–2 draw with hosts Portugal that saw England eliminated from Euro 2004.
Worn by: Wayne Rooney, Darius Vassell.

2004 EUROPEAN CHAMPIONSHIP

AWAY 2004–06

Design: Umbro

Although Umbro's influence in the domestic league had waned somewhat, their ground-breaking kits for England were still big successes. This next outfit was crafted from Umbro's 'X-Static' heat-regulating fabric and featured two cleverly constructed red crosses sitting on white backgrounds.

Worn in: The wonderful 4–2 win over Croatia in the Portugal Euro 2004 finals.
Worn by: Frank Lampard, John Terry.

2006 FIFA WORLD CUP

HOME 2005–06

Design: Umbro

Again, the St George's cross was an integral element to the next England outfit and formed a dynamic flash of red on the right shoulder. Intricately constructed from state-of-the-art lightweight fabric, the shirt also featured additional sparks of red trim on the left sleeve.

Worn in: The heartbreaking defeat against Portugal on penalties (again!) in the 2006 World Cup quarter-finals.
Worn by: Owen Hargreaves, Peter Crouch.

2006 FIFA WORLD CUP

AWAY 2006–07

Design: Umbro

40 years on, a modern-day interpretation of the 1966 World Cup winning jersey was introduced in 2006, although on first inspection the kit was very similar to the previous design. The St George's Cross featured again as a subtle hint on the right shoulder and a rich gold trim was employed with restraint throughout the design.

Worn in: The 2–2 draw with Sweden in England's poor 2006 World Cup campaign.
Worn by: Jamie Carragher.

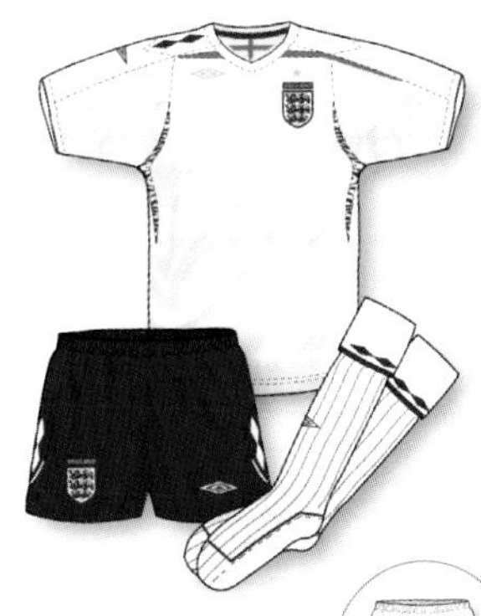

HOME 2007–09

Design: Umbro

As the 2000s progressed, Umbro's kits became ever more complex and intricate. This new kit featured an asymmetrical arrangement of truncated diamond taping and red spear with abstracted underarm flashes. Formed from 'Trilogy' fabric, designed to regulate temperature and moisture more effectively.

Worn in: A superb 4–1 triumph in Croatia in a 2008 qualifier for the 2010 World Cup.
Worn by: Joe Cole, Gareth Barry.

AWAY 2007–08

Design: Umbro

With its home partner, these shirts are perhaps often overlooked due to England's failure to qualify for Euro 2008. This change jersey featured a navy chest panel as its main visual focal point with a centrally placed badge amid a pot pourri of complicated Umbro embellishments.

Worn in: A fine 2–1 friendly victory over Germany in 2008.
Worn by: Jermain Defoe, Shaun Wright-Phillips.

2010 FIFA WORLD CUP

HOME 2009–10

Design: Umbro

In a football kit world growing ever more distracting and complex, Umbro bucked the trend and raised the bar with this simply beautiful, new, Mexico 1970-inspired all white England strip. Naturally, with any brave design controversy follows, but soon everyone was following the 'Tailored by Umbro' lead.

Worn in: Disappointing draws against the USA and Algeria in the 2010 World Cup.
Worn by: Glen Johnson, Aaron Lennon.

AWAY 2010

Design: Umbro

Designer Aitor Throup was creative consultant for Umbro (now Nike-owned) on this fine change shirt. Carefully constructed to fit with a player's physique on the pitch, it focused primarily on performance. A neat touch came from the self-coloured crew neck combined with white cuffs.

Worn in: The 4–1 thrashing by Germany that knocked Capello's men out of the World Cup.
Worn by: Matthew Upson, James Milner.

HOME 2010–11

Design: Umbro

Another outside designer, the legendary Peter Saville, was brought in to work on the follow-up shirt to the glorious 2009 home strip. He introduced a sequence of tiny, multi-coloured crosses on the shoulders to symbolise the multi-cultural nature of modern England. Blue returned to play a major role in the strip.

Worn in: A 4–0 victory over Bulgaria in the Euro 2012 qualifying campaign (2010).
Worn by: Theo Walcott, Phil Jagielka.

AWAY 2011–12

Design: Umbro

Never afraid to break the mould and try something new, Umbro unveiled this 'Galaxy Blue' away shirt with the help of boxing champion David Haye. Although it garnered a mixed response from the England faithful, with its sophisticated collar and pale blue trim it created a distinctive, if untraditional, look.

Worn in: A close 3–2 win over Sweden in the group stage of Euro 2012.
Worn by: Andy Carroll, Scott Parker.

HOME 2012–13

Design: Umbro

With Nike's sale of Umbro imminent this all-white ensemble would prove to be the last kit made by the company for the England side. Along with a confident button-up neck, multi-tonal red trim provided the only real aesthetic attraction on this functional outfit. Blue was dispensed with altogether.

Worn in: A penalties defeat against Italy in the Euro 2012 quarter-finals.
Worn by: Danny Welbeck, Joleon Lescott.

HOME 2013–14

Design: Nike

Nike held on to the England deal after selling Umbro and wasted no time in bringing out its first home strip. Simple, clean and traditional, the shirt featured the specially designed gold-trimmed badge that marked 150 years of the FA. Some fans commented that the blue was too dark, making the kit look like a German one!

Worn in: A 3–2 win over Scotland in a Wembley friendly (2013).
Worn by: Adam Lallana, Rickie Lambert.

AWAY 2013–14

Design: Nike

Tradition was key to Nike's strategy for the first England kits – and supporters were delighted to see red back as the team's change colour. The basic construction of the shirt was similar to the 2011 blue strip, with a tidy collar and placket. Badges were tonal gold throughout. The strip was only worn twice with England drawing both games.

Worn in: A 2–2 with Brazil in a 2013 friendly.
Worn by: Gary Cahill, Alex Oxlade-Chamberlain.

HOME 2014–15

Design: Nike

After what was in some respects a stop-gap set of kits, Nike set to work with the next strips for Roy Hodgson's team. The home Dri-FIT outfit reverted to all white and featured silver strips on the shoulders, a smart wrapover neck design and fine shadow pinstripes.

Worn in: The awful 2014 World Cup campaign: defeats to Italy and Uruguay (both 2–1) and a 0–0 draw with Costa Rica.
Worn by: Raheem Sterling, Daniel Sturridge.

AWAY 2014–15

Design: Nike

Memories of 1966 came flooding back with this slick strip that managed to blend tradition and history with contemporary design perfectly. Minimalist in appearance, a fine crew neck was accompanied by thin tonal stripes that formed a very subtle St George's Cross. The kit was taken to the 2014 World Cup but not used.

Worn in: A 3–2 win over Slovenia in 2015, a qualifier for Euro 2016.
Worn by: Jack Wilshere, Jordan Henderson.

HOME 2016–17

Design: Nike

2016 saw Nike issue all of its roster with the same Vapor template – all teams in the same basic design with only colourways separating them. The template featured raglan sleeves and intriguing navy underarm panels that revealed flashes of red when the fabric was stretched.

Worn in: The 2–1 win over Wales at Euro 2016, followed by the bitterly disappointing 2–1 loss to Iceland.
Worn by: Harry Kane, Eric Dier.

AWAY 2016–17

Design: Nike

The Vapor design extended of course to the away kit, with the two-tone jersey accompanied by blue trim. As with most of these strips, the shirts and shorts matched in colour, with the socks contrasting to create a 'flicker effect' when a player ran, therefore helping teammates identify them.

Worn in: The fortunate 2–2 draw with Scotland in a 2018 World Cup qualifier (2017).
Worn by: Jamie Vardy, Kyle Walker.

AWAY 2017

Design: Nike

Navy blue returned to the England kitbag in the shape of this strip (officially 'Midnight Navy'), that again followed the basic Vapor template. Darker blue sleeves were joined by a gorgeous sky blue shade as trim. All three elements of the kit were now a uniform colour – with no red visible whatsoever.

Worn in: A 4–0 win over Malta in a 2017 qualifier for the 2018 World Cup.
Worn by: Jake Livermore, Ryan Bertrand.

HOME 2018

Design: Nike

Much to the relief of the traditionalists, a more familiar colour combination of white and navy formed the core of the next England home kit – launched in February in preparation for the World Cup. A subtle tonal weave and hi-tech breathable Vapor fabric helped ensure that players would stay cool during matches. An exquisite flash of red adorned the sleek neck and a lighter blue tonal badge was included on the shorts.

AWAY 2018

Design: Nike

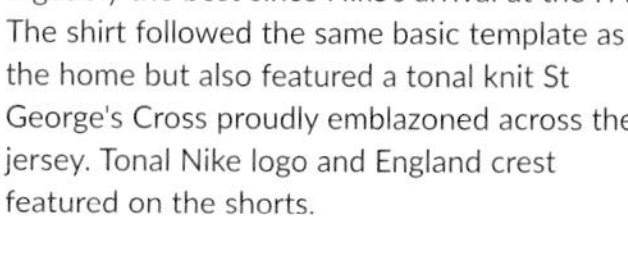

Red returned in glory to the England away kitbag and completed a fine set of strips – arguably the best since Nike's arrival at the FA. The shirt followed the same basic template as the home but also featured a tonal knit St George's Cross proudly emblazoned across the jersey. Tonal Nike logo and England crest featured on the shorts.

In a break from tradition England adopted an Umbro 'indigo blue' away kit in 1996 – here they line up before the Euro 96 semi-final against Germany.

1978 FIFA WORLD CUP

France's Michel Platini wearing the green and white striped jersey the French were forced to borrow from local side Club Atlético Kimberley in their Group One match against Hungary.

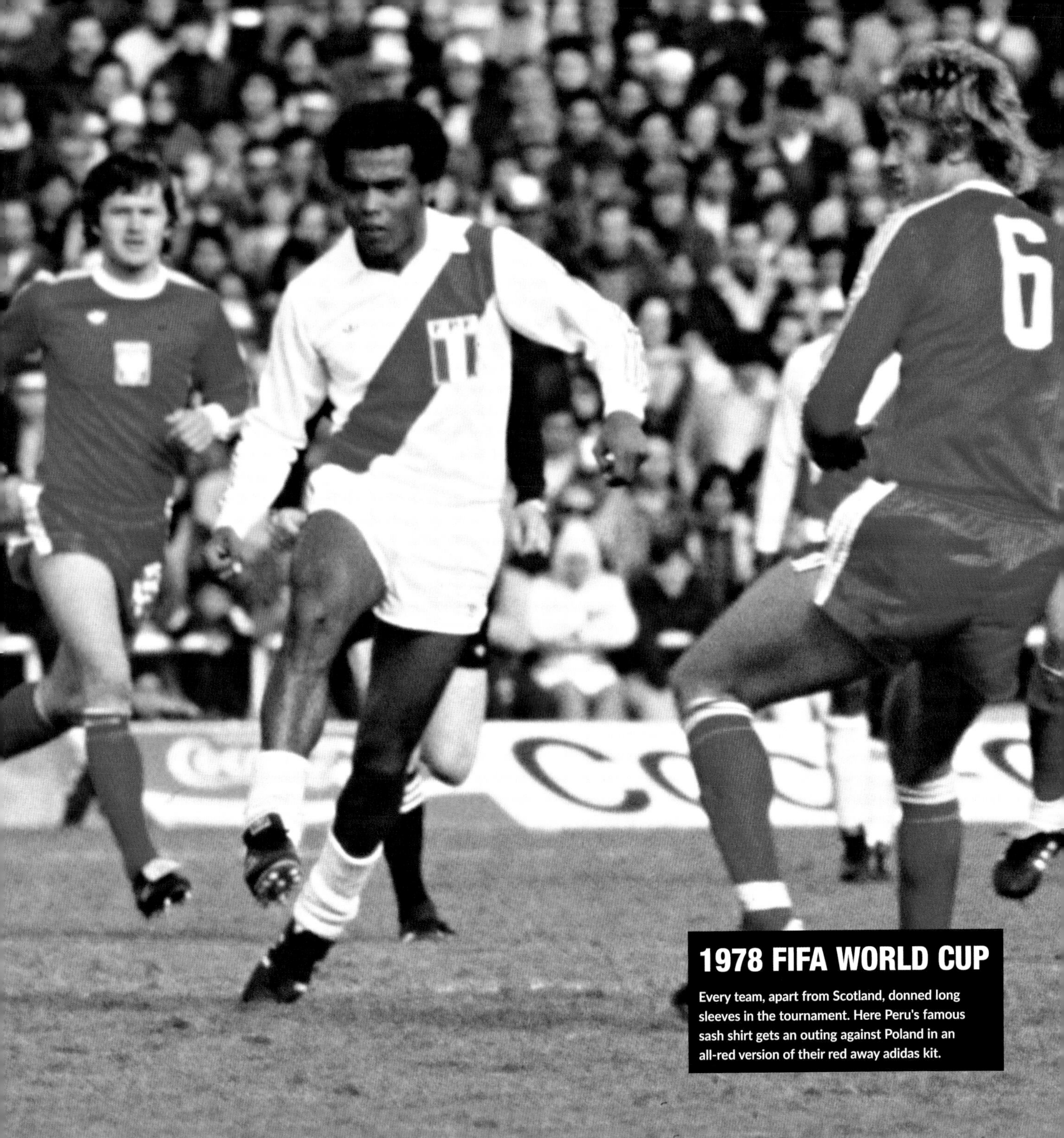

1978 FIFA WORLD CUP

Every team, apart from Scotland, donned long sleeves in the tournament. Here Peru's famous sash shirt gets an outing against Poland in an all-red version of their red away adidas kit.

FRANCE

The French kit is one kit that football strip fanatics look forward to seeing at every major tournament. There's something special about the way colour works on their kit, creating consistent outfits of real style, panache and national identity.

Traditionally the French home colours have comprised a blue shirt, white shorts and red socks, with away outfits switching the shirt and short colours and pairing up with either red or white socks.

adidas took over the French Football Federation contract in 1972, and introduced a stroke of genius by including red within their trademark three-stripe trim, thereby recreating the French national flag – the tricolore – on pretty much every France kit they subsequently produced. Adidas also created a trademark French look in 1984 with the introduction of a simple red chest band, a design motif that has subsequently appeared on numerous France strips.

When Nike took over the contract for Les Bleus in 2011, eyebrows were raised, so intrinsic was the FFF's bond with adidas. However, the American sportswear giant has breathed new life and identity into the French kit, dressing them in imaginative, traditional and brave outfits of glamour and beauty. Nike has never been afraid to challenge familiar expectations when it comes to the French kit and has created designs reflecting national pride.

The attention to detail paid by the French to their kit is also apparent with their badge, the Gallic Rooster. This has been beautifully designed throughout all of its numerous incarnations and provides the perfect accompaniment to the blue, white and red of France.

SPECIAL THANKS TO JÉ FRANCIS HANDLEY

The French team during the national anthem wearing the 1998–99 home kit, prior to the 1998 World Cup final against Brazil.

HOME 1966–69

Design: Kopa

France sported a relatively sober kit in the second half of the '60s which, it can be assumed, was produced by Kopa. The shirt featured non-contrasting deep v-neck and cuffs and featured a cockerel badge (although badgeless shirts were also occasionally worn).

Worn in: A 1967 3–1 triumph for Louis Dugauguez's team over Luxembourg in a Euro 68 qualifying match.
Worn by: Jean Baeza, Bernard Bosquier.

AWAY 1966–69

Design: Kopa

An all white v-necked shirt and shorts formed Les Bleus' away kit of choice at this time. The kit was worn either with blue socks with red turnover, the plain red socks of the home or, for one game against the USSR in 1966, a startling red and blue hooped concoction.

Worn in: An awful 5–1 thrashing at the hands of Yugoslavia in 1968 in a Euro 68 qualifier.
Worn by: Fleury Di Nallo, Claude Quittet.

1966 FIFA WORLD CUP

HOME 1966

Design: Le Coq Sportif

France celebrated qualification for the 1966 World Cup by sporting a special one-off set of Le Coq Sportif kits just for the tournament. The short sleeved shirt featured a plunging v-neck, cleverly trimmed with the red, white and blue of the French flag in what was to become a recurring theme for French outfits.

Worn in: A 1–1 draw with Mexico and a 2–0 defeat against England in the 1966 World Cup.
Worn by: Joseph Bonnel, Jacques Simon.

1966 FIFA WORLD CUP

AWAY 1966

Design: Le Coq Sportif

A simple change of shirt was all that was required to provide an alternative colour option to the home kit for the World Cup in 1966. Text under the badge read 'Coupe du Monde 1966' or in English 'World Cup 1966' – a very early example of adding commemorative tournament embroidery to a shirt.

Worn in: The 2–1 defeat against Uruguay in the 1966 World Cup finals.
Worn by: Yves Herbet, Hector de Bourgoing.

HOME 1967–69

Design: Kopa

The long sleeved French kit of the late '60s continued the minimalist appeal of its short sleeved partner. The jersey featured a wrapover crew neck and the familiar team crest. Kopa was a local French sportswear firm, founded by ex-player Raymond Kopa, and its logo appeared occasionally on the shorts.

Worn in: A solid 3–0 triumph over Sweden in a 1970 World Cup qualifier (1969).
Worn by: José Broissart, Andre Guy.

HOME 1967–72

Design: Le Coq Sportif

A new range of alternative short sleeved shirts was introduced in 1967, again from Le Coq Sportif. In an era before exclusive kit deals, they were worn simultaneously with the plainer v-necked designs. Taking the nod from the 1966 World Cup kits, the tricolore trim was now extended to the cuffs.

Worn in: The astonishing 4–3 win over Argentina in a 1971 friendly.
Worn by: Jean-Noël Huck, Gilbert Gress.

AWAY 1967–69

Design: Kopa

As Louis Dugauguez's side prepared for the qualifying campaigns to Euro 68 and the 1970 World Cup, they wore this simple white away version of the home kit which was paired with plain blue shorts. Commemorative match embroidery was occasionally included on these shirts.

Worn in: A 3–1 defeat against Spain in a 1968 friendly match.
Worn by: Robert Herbin, Robert Szczepaniak.

AWAY 1967–72

Design: Le Coq Sportif

The away shirt simply reflected the design of the home equivalent, as was the custom at the time, and was paired with Le Coq Sportif branded blue shorts along with the same red socks as the home kit. A new rendering of the Gallic rooster team badge was introduced.

Worn in: A 3–1 win in Norway in a Euro 72 qualifier (1971).
Worn by: Jacques Vergnes, Georges Carnus.

THIRD 1967–72

Design: Le Coq Sportif

A fantastic range of strips was completed by this stunning red shirt complete with the plunging v-neck and tricolore trim that featured on its home and away partners. The same red socks were sported across all three designs.

Worn in: The 2–0 win over an Africa Select in the Independence Cup, held in Brazil in 1972 – the only time this shirt was worn.
Worn by: Jean-Pierre Adams, Bernard Blanchet.

HOME 1970–71

Design: Le Coq Sportif

A new year, a new decade and a new kit. It seems Le Coq Sportif took over the long sleeved contract from Kopa and immediately made its mark by introducing its favoured red, white and blue trim on the smart neck and cuffs. A single red and blue stripe adorned each side of the shorts.

Worn in: A 3–1 victory over Norway in a 1970 Euro 72 qualifier.
Worn by: Louis Floch, Jean-Michel Larque.

AWAY 1970–71

Design: Le Coq Sportif

Le Coq Sportif added its tricolore sparkle to the white change kit, reversing the shorts and pairing them with the same red socks of the home outfit. As with all French kits at this time, match embroidery was added to the team crest on the jerseys.

Worn in: A 2–1 defeat against Switzerland in a 1970 friendly match.
Worn by: Jacques Novi, Jean Djorkaeff.

HOME 1971–72

Design: Le Coq Sportif

There was a minor adjustment to Georges Boulogne's team kit in 1971 with the trim removed from the shorts and on the long sleeved shirt, a continuation of the French tricolore flag on the cuffs.

Worn in: A 2–1 win over Bulgaria in a 1971 qualifier for Euro 72.
Worn by: Georges Lech, Charly Loubet.

AWAY 1971–72

Design: Le Coq Sportif

The away kit went through the same design tweak as the home with the broader trim on the cuffs and neck creating an attractive counterpoint to the pure white shirt. Match details were incorporated within the team crest.

Worn in: A thrilling 2–2 draw with Spain in a 1971 friendly.
Worn by: Georges Bereta, Michel Mezy.

HOME 1972

Design: adidas

1972 saw the FFF begin a breakaway from Le Coq Sportif and sign up with adidas who were just beginning to make inroads into football apparel. This beautiful and distinctive shirt included match details within the badge. The shirt was worn with the shorts and socks from the last Le Coq Sportif kit.

Worn in: The friendly 3–1 win over Greece in September 1972.
Worn by: Hervé Revelli, Henri Michel.

HOME 1972–77

Design: adidas

The adidas era really kicked off properly with the introduction of one of its iconic '70s long sleeved jerseys, topped off with a self-coloured, high, wrapover crew neck and low-slung team badge (early versions omitted the adidas logo). For at least two 1972 matches numbers were also worn on the front of these shirts.

Worn in: A 2–0 victory over the Republic of Ireland en route to the 1978 World Cup.
Worn by: Dominique Bathenay, Olivier Rouyer.

AWAY 1972–77

Design: adidas

The next long sleeved away shirt followed the design of the home, but in all white, trimmed beautifully with adidas' three stripes, cleverly rendered in a reproduction of the French tricolore flag – a design trademark that was to remain for virtually every subsequent strip adidas produced for Les Bleus.

Worn in: A 1–0 win over the USSR in France's disappointing 1974 World Cup qualifiers.
Worn by: Jean-Paul Rostagni, Serge Chiesa.

THIRD 1972–77

Design: adidas

This sumptuous red version of the long sleeved design was also produced and retained the non-contrasting neck and cuffs approach of the home and away strips, along with the new Gallic rooster team crest design. However, it is uncertain as to whether this design was ever worn by the first team. adidas' strong relationship with the FFF was born during this period and was to last until 2010.

HOME 1974–79

Design: adidas

After almost solely wearing long sleeves throughout 1972–73, this alternative, and often overlooked, adidas shirt began to be worn. Characterised by non-contrasting v-neck and cuffs, it was often minus the adidas logo. Despite being superseded in 1978 by a new design, this shirt also popped up again in 1979.

Worn in: A 2–0 victory over Poland in a 1974 friendly.
Worn by: Christian Coste, François Bracci.

AWAY 1974–78

Design: adidas

Although Michel Hidalgo's side clearly preferred long sleeved jerseys throughout the '70s, they were able to fall back on some strong short sleeved incarnations if desired. This strip reversed the qualities of the home, but retained the red socks. As with most adidas kits of the era, the trefoil logo on white fabric was black.

Worn in: A 1976 1–1 friendly draw with Denmark.
Worn by: Jean-Pierre Adams, Marius Trésor.

1978 FIFA WORLD CUP

HOME 1977–80

Design: adidas

Towards the end of 1977 the iconic long sleeved jersey was updated with contrasting neck and cuffs replacing the previous self-coloured versions. Although just a tiny tweak, it managed to change the entire look of the strip.

Worn in: A 2–1 defeat against hosts Argentina in the 1978 World Cup. Although France wore three strips in the tournament, ironically the only game they won was in a borrowed outfit!
Worn by: Michel Platini, Didier Six.

1978 FIFA WORLD CUP

AWAY 1978–80

Design: adidas

The white change strip was also updated with a contrasting wrapover neck and cuffs in time for the Argentina World Cup. As with most France kits, the shorts could be swapped between the home and away strips with ease if a clash occurred.

Worn in: A 2–1 defeat in the opening game for the French against Italy in the 1978 World Cup.
Worn by: Bernard Lacombe, Maxime Bossis.

1978 FIFA WORLD CUP

SPECIAL 1978

Design: Unknown

One of the most bizarre strips ever worn by Les Tricolores was this green and white striped jersey that made one appearance in the 1978 World Cup against Hungary. Due to a kitbag mix-up, the French had only brought a white shirt that clashed with that of their opponents, and so were forced to borrow this jersey from local Argentian side Club Atlético Kimberley.

Worn in: A 3–1 triumph over the Hungarians.
Worn by: Christian Lopez, Marc Berdoll.

THIRD 1978–80

Design: adidas

An attractive red version of this second set of long sleeved adidas jerseys was also produced at the time, but like its crimson predecessor, it appears the design was never worn by the first team. Red was the standard French away kit between the '30s and '50s, but had since fallen out of favour to be replaced by the now familiar white change outfits.

HOME 1978–80

Design: adidas

For warmer weather a new short sleeved, cuffless home shirt was produced that featured a tidy white collar and v-neck combination. Given that the designs of the long and short sleeved jerseys differed in this period the entire team had to ensure they were consistent with their shirt choice during a match.

Worn in: A good 3–1 away win in Sweden in a 1979 qualifier for Euro 80.
Worn by: Patrick Battiston, Christian Lopez.

AWAY 1978–80

Design: adidas

Naturally a reversed white version of the cuffless and collared short sleeved shirt also emerged in 1978. adidas' cuffless jerseys were something of a continental style and certainly didn't become popular in the English domestic game until the mid-'80s.

Worn in: A 7–0 humiliation of minnows Cyprus in an away 1980 qualifier for the 1982 World Cup.
Worn by: Leonard Specht, Jacques Zimako.

HOME 1980–84

Design: adidas

Modernity hit the French strip with a bang in 1980 with the introduction of this splendid new outfit. The long sleeved shirt featured red and white pinstripes and a similarly decorated collar, complete with large white inset panel. Initially worn with the previous red socks, a sophisticated pinstriped pair later appeared.

Worn in: The vital 1981 2–0 win over the Netherlands in a 1982 World Cup qualifier.
Worn by: Dominique Rocheteau.

HOME 1980–84

Design: adidas

The short sleeved version of the latest Bleus home shirt opted for a slightly different design to that of the long sleeved incarnation. First called into action in 1981 and worn throughout the 1982 World Cup qualifying campaign, a slick white v-neck was introduced in place of the collar.

Worn in: The cracking 3–2 win over Belgium in a 1981 qualifier for the 1982 World Cup.
Worn by: Gerard Soler, Alain Giresse.

AWAY 1980–84

Design: adidas

The long sleeved design (officially known as 'Santiago' in the adidas teamwear catalogue) was also produced in this white, reversed, away version as France aimed to make up for the disappointment of not reaching the Euro 80 finals by focusing on qualification for the 1982 World Cup.

Worn in: The 1981 3–2 defeat by the Republic of Ireland in a 1982 World Cup qualifier.
Worn by: Bruno Baronchelli.

AWAY 1980–84

Design: adidas

A v-necked, short sleeved version of the white away kit was also worn during this period in a template known as 'La Paz' in the adidas catalogue. The red home socks continued to be the preferred choice across all of France's kits at the time. Michel Hidalgo's team were beginning to flourish as the '80s dawned.

Worn in: The 1982 World Cup qualifier against Belgium that ended in a 2–0 defeat for France.
Worn by: Patrick Hiard, Alain Moizan.

1982 FIFA WORLD CUP

HOME 1982

Design: adidas

Les Bleus wore a special set of strips just for the 1982 World Cup in Spain. The dual-coloured pinstripe theme of the regular jerseys remained but was extended on to the neck of the newly introduced collar and also the shorts.

Worn in: The penalties defeat against West Germany in the 1982 World Cup semi-finals – regarded as one of THE all-time great matches in World Cup history.
Worn by: Bernard Genghini, Manuel Amoros.

1982 FIFA WORLD CUP

AWAY 1982

Design: adidas

Pinstripes were in abundance at the Spain World Cup with several teams wearing variants of this adidas design. Curiously, the 'adidas' wordmarque was added to the trefoil logo on these special France kits yet failed to appear on the regular outfits. Worn with the same red socks as the home strip.

Worn in: A storming 4–1 triumph over Kuwait in the group stage of the 1982 World Cup.
Worn by: Réne Girard, Gérard Janvion.

1984 UEFA EUROPEAN CHAMPIONSHIP

★

HOME 1984–86

Design: adidas

A great design becomes even greater if the team perform well while wearing it; if it's worn in a major tournament win, it becomes legendary. Such is the case with this home design that set a benchmark for French kits for years to come. Also worn with the red pinstriped socks from the previous strip.

Worn in: The glorious 2–0 win over Spain in the Euro 84 final – France's first major honour.
Worn by: Yvon Le Roux, Luis Fernandez.

AWAY 1984–86

Design: adidas

The dual-coloured arrangements of hoops that adidas introduced in 1984 created a home and away set of shirts that simply exuded style. The kits included athletic-style shorts with trimmed hems. Also worn with alternative tricolore adorned socks.

Worn in: The jaw-dropping 5–0 thrashing of neighbours Belgium (complete with a Platini hat-trick) en route to the Euro 84 final.
Worn by: Jean Tigana, Bruno Bellone.

HOME 1986–89

Design: adidas

One great kit leads to another – as a confident France prepared for Mexico 86, this distinctive home outfit was unveiled. As well as the regular three-stripe trim a second set of stripes reached up each sleeve and over the chest.

Worn in: A great World Cup including the stunning penalties win over Brazil in the quarter-final followed by a 2–0 defeat against West Germany in the semis.
Worn by: Jean-Marc Ferreri, Michel Bibard.

AWAY 1986–89

Design: adidas

This iconic design translated well into the familiar white change version. As with all French kits at the time, it was available in both long and short sleeves. The kits again featured a graphic-only trefoil logo, minus 'adidas' text. The shorts included a fashionable waistband.

Worn in: An impressive 2–0 win over the current World and European Champions Italy in the 1986 World Cup.
Worn by: Jean-Pierre Papin, William Ayache.

AWAY 1986

Design: adidas

A real rarity in the France historical kitbag was this white, long sleeved jersey that was worn once against Iceland. The shirt was actually regularly sported by the U21 side, who traditionally have often worn different strips to the first team. The reasons for its one-off selection are shrouded in Icelandic mist.

Worn in: A 0–0 draw with Iceland in a Euro 88 qualifying match.
Worn by: Yannick Stopyra, Philippe Vercruysse.

HOME 1989–91

Design: adidas

adidas employed a 'more is more' philosophy with this design that, it appears, was a totally bespoke strip. A perplexing arrangement of panels, bands and colours adorned the top half of the shirt with dainty shadow pinstripes decorating the shorts.

Worn in: The impressive Euro 92 qualifying campaign that included victories over Iceland (3–1) and Czechoslovakia (2–1).
Worn by: Didier Deschamps, Frank Sauzée.

AWAY 1989–91

Design: adidas

France were enduring a low period in the late '80s. After missing out on Euro 88 and the 1990 World Cup, the side, now under manager Michel Platini, embarked on an impressive Euro 92 qualifying campaign during which they sported this white change strip.

Worn in: An astonishing 19-match unbeaten stretch prior to Euro 92 including an all-white 2–1 win over Spain.
Worn by: Jocelyn Angloma, Bernard Casoni.

HOME 1992–94

Design: adidas

The bold approach of the new adidas equipment brand hit France in 1992. The result was this great looking strip with large slabs of red and white on each shoulder dominating the design. Towards the end of its tenure a new adidas text-only logo was included.

Worn in: The 2–1 defeat vs Bulgaria in 1993 that meant Gerard Houliler's side would miss the USA World Cup. Also worn in Euro 92.
Worn by: David Ginola, Eric Cantona.

HOME 1992–94

Design: adidas

A straightforward reversal of the newly branded adidas equipment home strip formed the new away outfit. As with the home kit, a text-only adidas logo arrived in 1993 bringing with it a return of the three stripes on the socks. The kit was taken to the ultimately disappointing for the French Euro 92 tournament, but not required.

Worn in: The all-white 4–0 triumph over Israel in a 1994 World Cup qualifier (1993).
Worn by: Alain Roche, Bixente Lizarazu.

HOME 1994–95

Design: adidas

France was still reeling from not qualifying for the USA World Cup when its next set of strips were launched. Again, they were crafted from a standard adidas template that featured a series of dual-colour diamonds in a three-stripe arrangement on the right-hand side, that was then echoed on the left side of the shorts.

Worn in: The amazing 10–0 thrashing of Azerbaijan in a 1995 qualifier for Euro 96.
Worn by: Vincent Guérin, Christophe Dugarry.

AWAY 1994–95

Design: adidas

The charismatic new design was also used for the side's next white change kit with colours reversed throughout. Although predominantly worn with the same white shorts as the home kit, on occasion it was paired with the blue change pair that the first choice strip also made use of. Aimé Jacquet was now team manager.

Worn in: A 0–0 draw with Slovakia (1994) in the Euro 96 qualifying campaign.
Worn by: Paul Le Guen, Reynald Pedros.

1996 UEFA EUROPEAN CHAMPIONSHIP

HOME 1996–97

Design: adidas

The first game of 1996 saw France emerge in one of its most extravagant strips to date. Large striped panels of red, white and blue pointed sharply on either side of the shirt and were joined by a rich shadow 'cockerel' pattern and an old-fashioned lace-up collar. Also worn with the previous kit's home socks.

Worn in: Wins over Romania (1–0) and Hungary (3–1) in Euro 96.
Worn by: Marcel Desailly, Laurent Blanc.

1996 UEFA EUROPEAN CHAMPIONSHIP

AWAY 1996–97

Design: adidas

This flamboyant outfit was launched for Euro 96 and included a stub v-neck and arching coloured shoulder panels. It was primarily worn with the white shorts from the home kit although a blue change pair were available.

Worn in: The penalties victory over the Netherlands in the quarter-final of Euro 96 followed by the penalties defeat against the Czech Republic in the semis.
Worn by: Lilian Thuram.

1998 FIFA WORLD CUP

HOME 1998–99

Design: adidas

As Aimé Jacquet's team prepared to host the 1998 World Cup, this full-on new strip was unveiled. It included a myriad of white and red piping and stripes, that brought back memories of the jersey from Euro 84 (also hosted in France). Also worn with the blue away shorts, most notably against Croatia in the World Cup.

Worn in: The simply glorious 3–0 win over a rattled Brazil side in the 1998 World Cup Final!
Worn by: Zinedine Zidane, Emmanuel Petit.

1998 FIFA WORLD CUP

AWAY 1998–99

Design: adidas

adidas kept it simple with this away strip, by just reversing the home design, including the FFF sock crest. Match details were incorporated into the badge design. As often occurs in major tournaments, the shirt was frequently worn with the home white shorts. Roger Lemerre was appointed manager after the World Cup.

Worn in: The all-white penalties win over Italy in the 1998 World Cup quarter-final.
Worn by: Christian Karembeu, Youri Djorkaeff.

2000 UEFA EUROPEAN CHAMPIONSHIP
2001 FIFA CONFEDERATIONS CUP

HOME 2000–01

Design: adidas

The red chest band theme that had featured on the previous home shirt (and of course the Euro 84 strip) appeared again on this shirt, alongside a collar with elongated neck. As before, replicas featured 'FFF' on the team crest with players' versions including match details.

Worn in: The nerve-wracking 2–1 win over Italy in the Euro 2000 final – France were now World Champions AND European Champions!
Worn by: Sylvain Wiltord, David Trezeguet.

2000 UEFA EUROPEAN CHAMPIONSHIP
2001 FIFA CONFEDERATIONS CUP

AWAY 2000–01

Design: adidas

After the excesses of recent change strips, the simple purity of this outfit acted as a palate cleanser. A trimmed collar was joined by side panels of breathable fabric and, as with the home shirt, the external sleeve stripe curved round to form the cuff trim. The shorts and socks were mixed and matched with the away kit.

Worn in: The 1–0 triumph over Japan in the 2001 Confederations Cup final.
Worn by: Nicolas Anelka, Thierry Henry.

2002 FIFA WORLD CUP
2003 FIFA CONFEDERATIONS CUP

HOME 2002–03

Design: adidas

Ever developing new kit innovations, adidas launched dual-layered shirts across its roster in 2002. They were designed to wick sweat more effectively and keep players cool. Mesh panels on either side of the jersey allowed the red inner layer to peek through, creating an intriguing colour effect.

Worn in: The 1–0 win over Cameroon (aet) in the 2003 Confederations Cup final.
Worn by: Frank Leboeuf, Djibril Cissé.

2002 FIFA WORLD CUP
2003 FIFA CONFEDERATIONS CUP

AWAY 2002–03

Design: adidas

Although in essence the same design as the home, the away shirt included longer side mesh panels. Replica shirts were single-layered and only featured a printed representation of the visual effect the dual layer/mesh panels created. Shorts and socks could be interchanged between these kits.

Worn in: The 2002 World Cup 2–0 defeat by Denmark that saw the French eliminated.
Worn by: Patrick Vieira, Claude Makélélé.

SPECIAL 2004

Design: adidas

FIFA celebrated its centenary in 2004 with a special match between current World Champions, Brazil, and European Champions, France. To add extra spice, both teams turned out in retro versions of their kits. The French full button-up shirt was pure class and was joined by pale cream shorts, complete with belt!

Worn in: The FIFA Centenary match against Brazil that ended in a 0–0 draw.
Worn by: Bernard Mendy, William Gallas.

2004 UEFA EUROPEAN CHAMPIONSHIP

HOME 2003–05

Design: adidas

Dual layers remained with this home kit, although now much more subtly as the inner layer was the same colour as the outer and only just visible through the lower mesh panels. The familiar red band stretched across the chest in a new gradated style. Worn by Jacques Santini's team with two different sock designs.

Worn in: A surprising 1–0 defeat against Greece in the knockout stage of Euro 2004.
Worn by: Olivier Dacourt, Louis Saha.

2004 UEFA EUROPEAN CHAMPIONSHIP

AWAY 2003–05

Design: adidas

The same dual-layered construction of the home shirt naturally also found a home with the white away strip that was first worn in a November 2003 friendly against Germany (the home kit was not worn until the first game of 2004). The backs of these shirts included large contrasting panels on the sleeves.

Worn in: A 3–1 win over Switzerland in the Euro 2004 group stages.
Worn by: Mikael Silvestre, Robert Pires.

2006 FIFA WORLD CUP

HOME 2005–07

Design: adidas

adidas' 2006 shirts were some of the most flamboyant the company had produced for some time and incorporated large ribbon-like waves of colour on each side. Two styles of badge were featured; one with match details replacing the 'FFF' initials. The shorts of this and the away kit were, as ever, interchangeable.

Worn in: A 2–0 win over Togo in the group stages of the 2006 World Cup.
Worn by: Franck Ribéry, Florent Malouda.

2006 FIFA WORLD CUP

AWAY 2005–07

Design: adidas

The away strip mirrored the design of the home but added for good measure an attractive, gradated red and blue curved panel across the body. Both strips were constructed using adidas' Formotion technology which combined a variety of fabrics.

Worn in: The 2006 World Cup quarter-final, semi-final and final that eventually ended in a penalties defeat by Italy (France in all white).
Worn by: Alou Diarra, Eric Abidal.

2008 UEFA EUROPEAN CHAMPIONSHIP

HOME 2007–08

Design: adidas

Premiered in a November 2007 friendly against the Ukraine, adidas went for a dramatic arching arrangement of red and light blue waves on the front of this jersey. Match details were included within the new badge design. Worn throughout Euro 2008 by Raymond Domenech's team with the away kit's blue shorts and socks.

Worn in: An awful Euro 2008 tournament including a 4–1 defeat against the Netherlands.
Worn by: Patrice Evra, Willy Sagnol.

AWAY 2007-09

Design: adidas

For the first time since the third kits of the '70s, red formed the core colour of a France away shirt rather than the traditional white. This unorthodox jersey featured a different construction to that of the home, and alongside breathable fabric panels an alternative wave embellishment was included.

Worn in: A 1-0 friendly defeat against Spain (who were also wearing their away kit) in 2008.
Worn by: Lassana Diarra, Jeremy Toulalan.

HOME 2008-09

Design: adidas

Surprisingly, a new kit was launched immediately following the disappointment of Euro 2008. It was unlike any other previous French shirt and incorporated two shades of blue – and no red. In 2008 the FFF announced a seven-year deal with Nike, to start in 2011.

Worn in: The 2009 friendly against Nigeria in which the players' names were printed on the back of the shirts in Braille dots.
Worn by: Karim Benzema, Loïc Rémy.

HOME 2009-10

Design: adidas

After the controversial two-colour approach of the previous shirt, adidas returned to a classic French tricolore look for their last home kit for the side. Dynamic red and white flashes decorated each side of the shirt, which was available in either a Techfit compression style or the more relaxed Formotion fitting.

Worn in: Defeats by Mexico (2-0) and South Africa (2-1) in the unsettled 2010 World Cup.
Worn by: André-Pierre Gignac, Gaël Clichy.

AWAY 2009-10

Design: adidas

The memorable France kits of the early '80s provided suitable inspiration for this final adidas change outfit. Dual-colour pinstripes were the main decorative feature of this jersey, which, like the home, was available in the two standard fitting styles, Techfit or Formotion.

Worn in: The 0-0 draw with Uruguay (France wearing white shorts) in a 2010 World Cup hit by internal disputes in the French camp.
Worn by: Sidney Govou, Bakary Sagna.

HOME 2011-12

Design: Nike

A carefully selected shade of blue, trimmed with a navy collar, monochromatic badge and optional folded red cuffs came together beautifully in the first, eagerly anticipated, Nike French strip. On the inside of the shirt, behind the badge, was the slogan 'our differences unite us', that addressed issues of diversity and race.

Worn in: The strip's debut: a 1-0 win for Laurent Blanc's team in an all-Nike friendly with Brazil.
Worn by: Yann M'Vila, Jeremy Menez.

AWAY 2011-12

Design: Nike

Memories of adidas faded fast with the launch of this away kit, which, along with the home strip, forged a magnificent start to the Nike era. A courageous Dri-FIT fabric design brought the traditional 'Marinière' jersey (worn by French seamen) into the football world. Also worn with the change blue shorts from the home kit.

Worn in: A 2-1 victory against Albania in a 2011 qualifier for Euro 2012.
Worn by: Karim Benzema, Samir Nasri.

HOME 2012-13

Design: Nike

Inspired by French military uniforms this kit was a bold departure from previous outfits and combined two-tone blue hoops with a lighter 'Pacific' blue alongside a gold-trimmed high neck. The military theme was extended to the sleeve hem epaulets as each contained a tonal gold hexagon, symbolising France.

Worn in: The Euro 2012 2-0 victory over the Ukraine in the group stages.
Worn by: Yohan Cabaye, Mathieu Debuchy.

AWAY 2012-13

Design: Nike

2012 saw Nike proudly announcing that its shirts were now made from 96% recycled polyester and were even lighter than any previous Nike jersey. The away was a heroic plain white that introduced elements of the 'Marinière' on the cuff trim.

Worn in: A dismal 2-0 defeat against Spain that saw Laurent Blanc's side eliminated with a whimper from Euro 2012.
Worn by: Olivier Giroud, Anthony Réveillére.

AWAY 2013–14

Design: Nike

The traditional French tricolore made a welcome return as chic trim on this pale blue strip that was unveiled in February 2013, giving a totally fresh look to Les Bleus. The jersey, which was similar in style to the previous away outfit, was constructed from Nike's Dri-FIT fabric and featured laser-cut ventilation holes on each side.

Worn in: A 0–0 draw with Belgium in 2013.
Worn by: Laurent Koscielny, Dimitri Payet.

2014 FIFA WORLD CUP

HOME 2013–15

Design: Nike

Another simply exquisite home shirt – this time in an elegant navy shade – was unveiled in preparation for the World Cup. With a svelte, curved collar, plunging placket, new badge and denim-style finish (in tribute to France's claim as the birthplace of the fabric) it was a work of art. Red socks helped create the tricolore look.

Worn in: A 1–0 defeat by Germany in the 2014 World Cup quarter-finals (with blue shorts).
Worn by: Antoine Griezmann, Mamadou Sakho.

2014 FIFA WORLD CUP

AWAY 2014–15

Design: Nike

The 'Marinière' style was back with this change strip – albeit in a more subtle way than the 2011 version with the hoops now a pale grey. A 'grandad' neck topped off the beautifully fitted shirt that, like the home kit, also incorporated laser-cut ventilation side holes.

Worn in: The tremendous 5–2 victory over Switzerland for Didier Deschamps' team in the 2014 World Cup.
Worn by: Blaise Matuidi, Moussa Sissoko.

AWAY 2015

Design: Nike

A year after the World Cup change kit came another white away outfit that continued the pale hooped theme but complemented it with a new v-neck and dashing red stripes down the sides of the shirt and shorts (although it was also worn with the white home shorts). Swanky hooped socks finished off the design.

Worn in: A 2–1 friendly win over Denmark.
Worn by: Anthony Martial, Raphaël Varane.

2016 UEFA EUROPEAN CHAMPIONSHIP

HOME 2016–17

Design: Nike

The uniform Vapor template was issued to virtually all of Nike's roster in 2016 with a general ethos that jerseys and shorts colours matched, whereas the socks featured a contrasting hue. The body of this shirt returned to a classic blue (now named 'Hyper-cobalt').

Worn in: The 2–0 triumph over Germany in the semi-final of Euro 2016 followed by the 1–0 defeat against Portugal in the final.
Worn by: Paul Pogba, Samuel Umtiti.

2016 UEFA EUROPEAN CHAMPIONSHIP

AWAY 2016–17

Design: Nike

Who was to foresee that the red and blue sleeve colours on the white version of the Vapor shirt would cause so many problems when it was due to be worn against Switzerland in Euro 2016? UEFA banned the jersey as it contravened the rule that says the two sleeve colours must be consistent on a team kit.

Worn in: A 1–0 win over the Netherlands in a 2016 qualifier for the 2018 World Cup.
Worn by: Kévin Gameiro, Layvin Kurzawa.

2016 UEFA EUROPEAN CHAMPIONSHIP

THIRD 2016

Design: Nike

With the regular away kit unable to be worn against the Swiss at Euro 2016, a special alternative shirt was produced that knocked back the tint of the sleeves to create a shirt that at a glance appeared virtually all white. Problem solved! The shirt was paired with navy shorts and white socks.

Worn in: The infamous 0–0 draw with Switzerland in Euro 2016.
Worn by: Kingsley Coman, André-Pierre Gignac.

THIRD 2017

Design: Nike

This chic all-black outfit was unveiled in March 2017 and was designed to complement the two existing French kits. Minimal in visual styling, its only aesthetic focus other than the Nike swoosh was a turquoise rendering of the French crest.

GERMANY / WEST GERMANY

The simplicity and strength of the Germany kit lies in its colour combination of white shirts, black shorts and white socks – perfectly reflecting the essence and effectiveness of the team's football.

For years this simple approach stood the team in good stead, but in the mid '80s manager Franz Beckenbauer suggested that the team strip be enriched with the addition of the red and yellow from the national flag, and the German kit was elevated to a new level of beauty. It featured a representation of the German flag emblazoned confidently across the chest – and was one of the most celebrated kits in modern times. The strip was so popular (and so good!) that it lasted for two major tournaments: Euro 88 and Italia 90.

Since then, most of the team's kits have found a way to incorporate the national colours alongside the familiar white and black.

German away strips have traditionally been green, a very popular footballing colour in the country, in various shades and tones, but more recently black, red and even grey have also been used to great effect.

One of the longest lasting and successful kit supply relationships exists between the Deutscher Fußball-Bund (DFB) and their fellow countrymen adidas.

West Germany line up before the Group 1 match against East Germany in the 1974 World Cup.

Lothar Matthaus and Rudi Voeller celebrate in one of the most famous kits of all time during the 1990 World Cup final against Argentina.

GERMANY / WEST GERMANY

HOME 1966–76 1

Design: Umbro (66–74) Erima (74–76)

This simple crew-neck, long sleeved shirt is arguably one of the most iconic in German football. Also sported in a short sleeved version and occasionally worn with black socks and the away kit's white shorts, the shirt featured in three major tournaments.

Worn in: The fantastic 1974 2–1 World Cup final win against the Netherlands. Also worn in the 3–0 over the USSR in the Euro 72 final.
Worn by: Franz Beckenbauer, Gerd Müller.

HOME 1966–76 2

Design: Umbro (66–74) Erima (74–76)

For warmer weather a v-neck short sleeved version of the home kit was favoured. For the 1970 Mexico World Cup airtex shirts were worn that featured a breathable 'teabag' fabric designed to keep players cool in the fierce heat. Also worn with the away kit's white shorts.

Worn in: The 4–3 defeat against Italy in the semi-final of the 1970 World Cup – a match billed as 'the game of the century'.
Worn by: Raoul Lambert, Uwe Seeler,

AWAY 1966–73 3

Design: Umbro

West Germany's regular away strip from the mid-1960s to 1971 saw their established green change colour (green of course being the colour of the Deutscher Fußball-Bund) fashioned into the long sleeved, crew-neck style of the era. Green change shorts and socks were also worn. The kit wasn't needed at the 1966 World Cup.

Worn in: A 2–1 win over Belgium in the 1972 European Championship semi-final.
Worn by: Wolfgang Overath, Willi Schulz.

AWAY 1969–73

Design: Umbro

As with the home kit, long-term manager Helmut Schön's side also sported a short sleeved v-neck version of the away kit. Early versions of the shirt had the badge applied via a sewn-on square patch but towards the end of its life it was applied straight to the fabric. Also worn with green change socks.

Worn in: A 3–1 victory over Peru in the group stages of the 1970 World Cup finals.
Worn by: Hannes Löhr, Reinhard Libuda.

AWAY 1974–76

Design: Erima

When Erima took over the West German contract in 1974 it retained the basic style of away kit that had been worn for the last decade. The only difference came from the adoption of green socks as first choice.

Worn in: Wins over Australia (3–0) and Sweden (4–2) in the 1974 World Cup.
Worn by: Erwin Kostedde, Karl-Heinz Korbel.

HOME 1976–78

Design: Erima

The first changes to the West German kit for over 10 years came in 1976 with Erima's new strip. Gone was the familiar crew neck, replaced by a sleek wrapover design, a style still at odds with the collared strips of the time. Towards the middle of 1977 the Erima logo began to be included on the jersey.

Worn in: The Euro 1976 final vs Czechoslovakia who emerged winners 5–3 on penalties.
Worn by: Bernd Holzenbein, Dieter Müller.

AWAY 1976–78

Design: Erima

As usual, a green change version of the West German shirt emerged that mirrored the design of the home – including the three-stripe trim on the socks, a symbol of Erima's close links to adidas. As with the home kit an Erima logo only appeared on the shirt in the latter years of its life. The kit was not required in Euro 1976.

Worn in: A 3–1 triumph over Argentina in a 1977 friendly.
Worn by: Erich Beer, Klaus Fischer.

HOME 1978–80 4

Design: Erima

What better time than a World Cup to launch a new strip? Erima unveiled a new set of West German kits that now featured a white collar (trimmed with black) and black piping. The shorts now included a permanent Erima logo.

Worn in: All of the Germans' matches in the 1978 World Cup finals, including a 6–0 drubbing of Mexico (wearing green socks) and a 3–2 defeat against Austria in the second round.
Worn by: Berti Vogts, Rainer Bonhof.

AWAY 1978–80

Design: Erima

The traditional German green away kit worked beautifully in the new Erima style. As usual it followed the design of the home – the only difference coming with the lack of trim on the white collar. Although in the kitbag for the tournament, the outfit wasn't required in the 1978 World Cup.

Worn in: A 3–1 defeat against Sweden in a 1978 friendly game.
Worn by: Hansi Müller, Rolf Rüssmann.

HOME 1980–84 5

Design: adidas/Erima

Although Erima had kitted out the team during Euro 80, by the time the side reached the final, parent company adidas (who were to take over the German contract later that year) decided that the team should wear their brand new shirt for the match. For the rest of the kit's four-year life Erima shorts were still worn.

Worn in: The thrilling 2–1 victory over Belgium in the 1980 European Championship final.
Worn by: Horst Hrubesch, Uli Stielike.

AWAY 1980–82

Design: adidas/Erima

With the adidas deal now well underway the new away kit appeared. Copying the design of the home, it included raglan sleeves and innovative side piping alongside white Erima shorts. The kit, which was only worn once, saw the team revert to their favoured white socks.

Worn in: An impressive 4–0 win over Finland in a 1981 World Cup qualifying match.
Worn by: Paul Breitner, Felix Magath, Klaus Fischer, Hans Peter Briegel.

AWAY 1981–84 6

Design: adidas/Erima

One of adidas' all-time kit design gems was adopted in German green in 1981 – midway through the nation's World Cup qualifying campaign. The style, which was only available in long sleeves, was also worn by France and Czechoslovakia and incorporated fashionable pinstripes and a large white inset collar panel.

Worn in: A 3–1 win away in Austria in a 1981 World Cup qualifier.
Worn by: Ronald Borchers, Wilfried Hannes.

HOME 1982 7

Design: adidas/Erima

Adidas kitted out Jupp Derwall's team with a special new strip especially for the 1982 Spain World Cup. Not a million miles away from their regular strip, the main differences came from traditional sleeves, a new black collar design and lack of piping.

Worn in: Every single game in the tournament including the disappointing 3–1 defeat against Italy in the final itself.
Worn by: Manfred Kaltz, Karl-Heinz Rummenigge.

AWAY 1982–84

Design: adidas/Erima

The pinstripes were retained for the short sleeved version of the early '80s German away kit although the flamboyant collar and inset panel were replaced by a rather more pedestrian v-neck. The Erima shorts remained although an adidas-branded green pair were also worn.

Worn in: A 1983 3–0 win in Turkey in a Euro 84 qualifier.
Worn by: Pierre Littbarski, Stefan Engels.

HOME 1984–86 8

Design: adidas

The German kit underwent a modernist overhaul in time for Euro 84 with the adoption of adidas' 'Aberdeen' template. The collar was replaced by a trimmed, wrapover v-neck and horizontal shadow stripes decorated the fabric. Adidas shorts were also worn to create, for the first time, a cohesively branded ensemble.

Worn in: A disappointing Euro 84 – the side only mustering one win, 2–1 vs Romania.
Worn by: Klaus Augenthaler, Uwe Rahn.

AWAY 1984–86 9

Design: adidas

This fine German kit, which opted for a powerful all-green version of the shadow striped home outfit was unfortunately only used once and wasn't required in Euro 84 or the subsequent World Cup qualifying campaign under the new leadership of the legendary Franz Beckenbauer.

Worn in: A 3–1 friendly defeat for Franz Beckenbauer's side by Argentina in Dusseldorf.
Worn by: Ralf Falkenmayer, Dietmar Jakobs.

AWAY 1985

Design: adidas

With West Germany taking part in the Azteca 2000 tournament in Mexico they once again opted for special airtex breathable fabric shirts to help them cope with the high temperatures. The cuffless shirt was basic but functional with just a simple v-neck design.

Worn in: Defeats to England (3–0) and Mexico (2–0) – the new shirts not enough to help the side as they endured a dismal tournament.
Worn by: Frank Mill, Ludwig Kogl.

HOME 1986 1

Design: adidas

An optimistic German side headed for Mexico with a special new strip in the kitbag. Once again dealing with the stifling heat was a concern and like the previous year's one-off design this new set of kits were constructed from cooling Climalite fabric. The colours of the national flag were included on the shirt.

Worn in: The tight 2–0 win over France in the 1986 World Cup semi-finals.
Worn by: Norbert Eder, Karlheinz Förster.

AWAY 1986 2

Design: adidas

The World Cup Climalite shirt reflected the design of the home including the neat wrapover crew neck and cuffless sleeves and was worn with either white or green socks. The adidas logo appeared on the opposite leg than that on the home shorts

Worn in: A 1–1 draw with Uruguay in the Germans' opening match in Group E and the thrilling 3–2 defeat by Argentina in the final.
Worn by: Lothar Matthäus, Thomas Berthold.

HOME 1986–87

Design: adidas

The all-singing, all-dancing version of the new German kit appeared following the World Cup and displayed a new enigmatic diagonal shadow pattern and trimmed cuffs. The side embarked on a series of friendlies in preparation for Euro 88 – as hosts they didn't need to qualify. Interestingly adidas' three-stripe trim was still omitted from the shorts.

Worn in: A 2–0 win against Denmark in 1986.
Worn by: Jürgen Kohler, Matthias Herget.

AWAY 1986–87

Design: adidas

As expected adidas' next away kit for the Germans again followed the design of the new home, including the diagonal shadow pattern, although curiously this version ditched the cuffs. Worn with white or green socks.

Worn in: A 4–1 thrashing at the hands of neighbours Austria (1986) followed a year later by a 1–0 defeat against Argentina.
Worn by: Olaf Thon, Wolfgang Rolff.

HOME 1987

Design: adidas

For just a handful of games towards the end of 1987 West Germany switched to a slightly different version of their latest strip. To the kit novice it appeared the same, but the neck was in fact a simple crew design rather than wrapover (although it retained the German flag colours) and the shadow pattern was omitted.

Worn in: Wins over France (2–1) and England (3–1).
Worn by: Klaus Allofs, Hans Dorfner.

HOME 1988–91 3

Design: adidas

Germany had the good fortune to wear two of the most iconic kit designs ever. This home design has gone into football legend thanks to its confident interpretation of the German flag emblazoned across the chest (an idea inspired by manager Franz Beckenbauer).

Worn in: The 1–0 win over Argentina in the 1990 World Cup final. Also worn that year in the first unified German match against Sweden.
Worn by: Karl-Heinz Riedle, Jürgen Klinsmann.

AWAY 1988–91 4

Design: adidas

Although this famous geometric pattern shirt design is more commonly associated with the orange of Holland, other countries also sported it – including Germany. Like the home, the design, in a new more teal-like shade of green, lasted for two major tournaments and saw the arrival of new coach Berti Vogts.

Worn in: The 4–3 victory (on penalties) against England in the 1990 World Cup semi-finals.
Worn by: Andreas Brehme, Rudi Völler.

AWAY 1988–91

Design: adidas

Long sleeved versions of the iconic adidas design that West Germany wore as their away kit in this period added a small collar to the wrapover v-neck of the shirt – other than that the design was identical to that of its short sleeved equivalent.

Worn in: A 1–0 win over Argentina in the 1988 Four Nations Tournament in Berlin.
Worn by: Ulrich Borowka, Dieter Eckstein.

AWAY 1991 5

Design: adidas

The friendly match against England in 1991 produced this fine long-sleeved shirt that copied the classic design of the home jersey and crafted it in traditional German away green. The colours shouldn't really have worked together as a design –but they did, and it was a shame the shirt was worn only once.

Worn in: The friendly match vs England in 1991 – Germany coming out 1–0 winners.
Worn by: Guido Buchwald, Thomas Häßler.

HOME 1992–93 6

Design: adidas

1991 saw adidas in a period of change with a re-brand of their performance sportswear as 'adidas equipment' complete with new logo. This featured on the German shirt alongside a modern wide v-neck and national flag colours on each sleeve.

Worn in: The tense Euro 92 semi-final 3–2 win over Sweden followed by the shock 2–0 defeat against Denmark in the final.
Worn by: Matthias Sammer, Stefan Effenberg.

AWAY 1992–93 7

Design: adidas

A green reversal of the home strip became the Germans' next away outfit as they prepared for Euro 92. Red, yellow and black trimmed the collar and, as with the home design, shadow stripes in sets of three adorned the fabric. Adidas equipment logos were included on the socks. Not used in Euro 92.

Worn in: A 1–0 win over Turkey in a 1992 friendly game.
Worn by: Manfred Binz, Andreas Möller.

HOME 1994–96 8

Design: adidas

The start of the year brought a new flamboyant and confident 'batwing' (i.e. without separate sleeves) kit design. Coloured diamonds fanned out over the shoulders in a gradated style to form a feather-like pattern. The adidas three-stripe sock trim now echoed the German flag.

Worn in: The 3–2 victory over Belgium in the 1994 World Cup followed by the shock quarter-final 2–1 defeat against Bulgaria.
Worn by: Martin Wagner, Stefan Kuntz

AWAY 1994–96

Design: adidas

The home shirt's design was replicated on the seemingly slightly darker green change shirt including the dainty DFB logo on each side of the neck and on each sleeve. However the shadow pattern present on the home kit was not included. The kit was not required in the USA 94 World Cup.

Worn in: Another defeat against Bulgaria – this time 3–2 in a 1995 qualifier for Euro 96.
Worn by: Thomas Strunz, Heiko Herrlich.

HOME 1996–97 9

Design: adidas

It was a radically different looking German side that stepped out to play Denmark in March 1996. Gone were the colourful excesses of the past eight years – replaced by a calm, stylish and beautiful white and black design with the national colours restricted just to trim.

Worn in: The glorious Euro 96 final 2–1 triumph against the Czech Republic thanks to a Golden Goal from Oliver Bierhoff.
Worn by: Stefan Reuter, Christian Ziege.

AWAY 1996–97

Design: adidas

The next German away outfit surprisingly didn't simply follow the design of the home but went for a completely different design (albeit a standard adidas template of the era) that featured three large swooping colour panels reaching down from each shoulder. The three 'World Cup' winning stars were rendered in the German national colours.

Worn in: A 2–0 1996 win against Poland.
Worn by: Oliver Bierhoff, Dieter Eilts.

1
2
3
4
5
6
7
8
9

GERMANY / WEST GERMANY

HOME 1998–99 1

Design: adidas

A relatively sedate new strip was unveiled at the start of 1998, ready for the World Cup in France later that year. A simple black v-neck and side/under arm panels was joined by a restrained three-stripe chest design in Germany's national colours. White side panels featured on the shorts.

Worn in: The 3–0 defeat against Croatia in the quarter-finals of the 1994 World Cup.
Worn by: Jens Jeremies, Dietmar Hamann.

AWAY 1998–99 2

Design: adidas

Yet again, Die Mannschaft managed to go through an entire major tournament without wearing their away kit! Which is a pity, as this new modern looking outfit, with its centrally placed white stripe-was rather nice. Worn with either green or white shorts. Berti Vogts was replaced as manager by Erich Ribbeck.

Worn in: A 2–0 win over New Zealand in the 1999 Confederations Cup.
Worn by: Olaf Marschall, Christian Worns.

HOME 2000–02 3

Design: adidas

There was a menacing feel about the adidas kit that Germany unveiled in 2000 thanks to the new dark green sleeve panels that were introduced (and also featured on the shorts) Red and yellow was reduced to just collar trim and the turnovers on the socks. Made from adidas' Climalite fabric.

Worn in: An awful 3–0 defeat by Portugal at Euro 2000 that meant elimination for Germany.
Worn by: Marco Bode, Michael Ballack.

AWAY 2000–02

Design: adidas

The green became even darker on this strip but due to its inclusion on the home kit for the first time brought a real sense of cohesion to the outfits. White curved panels decorated each side of the shirt which was worn with green or white shorts. Rudi Völler took over as manager following a dismal showing at Euro 2000.

Worn in: The 1–0 defeat against England in Euro 2000.
Worn by: Carsten Jancker, Mehmet Scholl.

HOME 2002–03 4

Design: adidas

Völler's team regrouped after the disappointing 2000 European Championship and in 2002 took to the pitch in the simplest German shirt since the mid '80s with a palette reduced to a plain black and white. However the shirt's construction was complex with dual Climacool layers and mesh panels down each side.

Worn in: An 8–0 thrashing of Saudi Arabia and the 2002 World Cup final 2–0 defeat by Brazil.
Worn by: Miroslav Klose, Carsten Ramelow.

AWAY 2002–03 5

Design: adidas

In a curious move all green was banished from this next set of German kits and instead two tones of grey were introduced in a simple design featuring a broad chest panel that housed the adidas logo and team crest. The kit didn't see any action in the 2002 World Cup.

Worn in: A 1–0 friendly defeat against Argentina in 2002 – the kit's sole outing.
Worn by: Torsten Frings, Jens Nowotny.

HOME 2004–05

Design: adidas

The solid white of the German shirt was refreshed with the addition of black sleeves complemented by red and yellow flashes that were echoed on the shorts. A small flag graphic was included on the left sleeve of this dual- layer shirt (standard replicas were single-layered however).

Worn in: The 2–1 defeat by the Czech Republic that knocked Germany out of Euro 2004.
Worn by: Bastian Schweinsteiger, Philipp Lahm.

AWAY 2003–05

Design: adidas

This black change shirt appeared late in 2003 and worked incredibly well. It featured the same design as the 2004 home kit, with a neat coloured collar and dual-layer construction – the red inner layer just visible through the side mesh panels. Jürgen Klinsmann was appointed manager in 2004.

Worn in: A 1–0 friendly victory over Croatia in 2004.
Worn by: Kevin Kurányi, Paul Freier.

THIRD 2004–05 6

Design: adidas

Germany's first ever third kit completed a fine and cohesive set of strips for Euro 2004 (although both the black away and this red third jersey were not needed in the tournament). The design mirrored that of Germany's other kits at the time.

Worn in: A 2–2 draw with Argentina in the 2005 Confederations Cup.
Worn by: Thomas Hitzlsperger, Lukas Podolski.

HOME 2005–07 7

Design: adidas

A bold and fearless template emerged in 2005. The design featured a sequence of curved colour panels on each side of the shirt which, when rendered in Germany's national colours, resembled a fluttering flag. A minimalist neck and flashes on the shorts completed the design.

Worn in: A penalties win over Argentina in a 2006 World Cup quarter-final. Also worn in the semi-final defeat against Italy.
Worn by: Sebastian Kehl, Mike Hanke.

AWAY 2005–07

Design: adidas

Red remained as the Die Mannschaft away colour with this next set of Climacool outfits. The big, flamboyant design followed the same template as the home but with an asymmetrical black right-hand side. The adidas logo on both the home and away kits was now placed on the reverse. This strip was not required in the 2006 World Cup.

Worn in: A 4–1 friendly win vs Italy in 2006.
Worn by: David Odonkor, Manuel Friedrich.

HOME 2007–09 8

Design: adidas

First worn in a November 2007 fixture against Cyprus this jersey was dominated visually by a striking black chest band (highlighted with red and yellow) that neatly housed the team crest. The overall design was simple, but functional with a variety of breathable fabric panels

Worn in: The 3–2 triumph over Turkey in the Euro 2008 semi-final, followed by the 1–0 defeat against Spain in the final.
Worn by: Arne Friedrich.

AWAY 2007–09

Design: adidas

Another impressive red and black change kit was adopted for the Euro 2008 tournament (although it was never called into action). Trimmed with gold, a broad black vertical stripe ran down the centre of the shirt with side panels in a breathable fabric. Joachim Löw was now team manager.

Worn in: A 3–3 draw with Finland (2010 World Cup qualifier) in 2008.
Worn by: Piotr Trochowski, Simon Rolfes.

HOME 2009–11

Design: adidas

This exquisite design oozed sophistication and elegance with a sequence of red, yellow and black lines drawing the eye to the team crest that sat within a black shield. This shirt was available in either a Techfit version (worn tight with compression taping) or a more relaxed Formotion fit.

Worn in: The 1–0 defeat against Spain in the semi-final of the 2010 World Cup.
Worn by: Piotr Trochowski, Mesut Özil.

AWAY 2010–11 9

Design: adidas

Following a few months after the launch of the home kit, this shirt was inspired by Germany's first unofficial match (known as the 'Ur match') in 1898 in which the side wore black against the White Rovers Club. The jersey was trimmed with gold and asymmetrical red piping. Also worn with the home kit's black shorts.

Worn in: The 3–2 victory over Uruguay in the 2010 World Cup third place play-off.
Worn by: Cacau, Per Mertesacker.

HOME 2011–13

Design: adidas

Essentially another classic white and black German strip, this design was lifted by the memorable three diagonal pinstripes in Germany's national colours. The colours were also incorporated into the sock designs.

Worn in: The 4–2 triumph over Greece in the Euro 2012 second round, followed by the poor 2–1 defeat against Italy in the semi-final.
Worn by: Mario Gómez, Sami Khedira.

1
2
3
4
5
6
7
8
9

GERMANY / WEST GERMANY

AWAY 2012–13 1

Design: adidas

Incredibly it had been 10 years since Germany last wore their once traditional away colour of green so it was long overdue a revival. This gorgeous kit hinted at the 'Aberdeen' adidas template of the early '80s with its horizontal shadow stripes. Unfortunately not needed in Euro 2012.

Worn in: An astonishing 5–3 friendly defeat to Switzerland in 2012.
Worn by: André Schürrle, Mats Hummels.

HOME 2013–15 2

Design: adidas

Quite possibly one of the more controversial German home kits, this design, first worn in November 2013, followed the single-colour trend that was within football at the time. The lack of black shorts did not please all fans however. An exciting chevron in muted colours provided the main focal point for the shirt.

Worn in: The glorious 1–0 victory over Argentina in the 2014 World Cup final!
Worn by: Thomas Müller, Christoph Kramer.

AWAY 2014–15 3

Design: adidas

Red and black were the order of the day with the away kit prepared for the 2014 World Cup. The shirts featured hoops, a button-up 'grandad' neck design and silver trim throughout. The shorts and socks replicated the designs of the home outfit.

Worn in: A unforgettable, and quite astonishing, 7–1 demolition of hosts Brazil in the 2014 World Cup semi-final.
Worn by: Toni Kroos, Benedikt Höwedes.

HOME 2015–16 4

Design: adidas

This understated design provided a perfect antidote for those who don't care for the more extravagant Die Mannschaft kits. Formed from simple black and white, the inclusion of the national colours on the cuffs only was a real touch of class. Adidas' three stripes were included on the sides of the shirt.

Worn in: A 2–0 defeat against France in the Euro 2016 semi-final.
Worn by: Joshua Kimmich, Julian Draxler.

AWAY 2015–17 5

Design: adidas

The Euro 2016 away kit blended two tones of hooped grey with muted green sleeves to create a new spin on the Germany change outfit. Inspired by street football, replica versions were reversible, with a neon green inner layer designed to be worn as an adidas-branded bib.

Worn in: A 3–2 friendly defeat against England (also in their away kit) in March 2016.
Worn by: Marco Reus, Emre Can.

HOME 2016–17 6

Design: adidas

Just a year after the launch of the previous home shirt a sedate new design was unveiled that attempted to blend both old influences and modern fabrics. The jersey featured a subtle and rather elegant shadow recreation of the famous adidas geometric pattern of the 1990 away kit.

Worn in: The superb 1–0 win over Chile in the final of the 2017 Confederations Cup.
Worn by: Lars Stindl, Timo Werner.

HOME 2017–18 7

Design: adidas

Adidas' retro influence continued with the shirt that the Germans will wear at the 2018 World Cup – although now, arguably the greatest ever Germany shirt, the 1988–91 home shirt was the inspiration. FIFA rules on colour usage saw the famous chestband reproduced monochromatically to create a beautiful kit.

Worn in: A 0–0 friendly draw with England on the kit's debut.
Worn by: Leroy Sané, İlkay Gündogan.

Paul Breitner scores West Germany's goal in the 3–1 defeat against Italy in the 1982 World Cup Final wearing the tournament's unique adidas/Erima kit.

1
2
3
4
5
6
7

ITALY

Arguably no national team kit encapsulates the style and character of the team itself more than Italy's.

The team are known as Azzurri (Blues) and traditionally wear Savoy Blue, a shade associated with the Italian royal dynasty that unified the nation in 1861. Thanks to guidelines as to what can, and can't, be included on the team strip, its history is one of simplicity, style and sheer class. Blue and white dominate the palette – with just the odd splash of Italy's traditional colours adding patriotic sparkle. Initially, the team wore white shirts with each player sporting the shorts of his club side, but by the third game the famous blue shirts were first choice.

For much of their life the Italian Football Federation (FIGC) have eschewed additional visual decoration, preferring a pure approach that meant even necks, collars and cuffs have often been the same colour.

In the 1980s, under Le Coq Sportif, the team adopted a basic set of four kits: blue home and white away, each in both long- and short-sleeved incarnations. When Diadora took over in 1984 the designs remained essentially the same, ensuring a consistent kit approach for the entire decade. Incredibly, all strips at the time were also worn on the pitch without manufacturers' logos (although these were included on replicas). Only the Italian crest was permitted – an admirable show of integrity that ensured national identity always came first.

By 1999, however, the ruling was rescinded and the distinctive marque of Kappa, the team's new supplier, featured on the outfits. Kappa later set the standard for innovative and classy designs, their tight-fitting Kombat shirts ensuring that yet again, Italy were on the tips of fashion tongues around the world.

Azzurri have enjoyed a fruitful relationship with Puma since 2003.

That World Cup winning moment – the Italians, in an all-blue version of their 2005–06 Puma kit, race towards match-winning goal scorer Fabio Grosso in the final of the 1996 World Cup against France.

1966 FIFA WORLD CUP

HOME 1966–74

Design: Unknown

Incredibly this kit – for many the epitome of Italian football apparel – was sported for 14 years! The design was simple but solid with the only visual decoration other than the badge being the dual white stripes on the socks. Also worn with away black shorts against North Korea and USSR in 1966.

Worn in: The shock 1–0 defeat against North Korea in the 1966 World Cup.
Worn by: Giacomo Bulgarelli, Gianni Rivera.

1966 FIFA WORLD CUP

HOME 1966–68

Design: Unknown

For a short period in the mid-'60s a short sleeved v-neck shirt was worn (although long sleeves were the preference). As with the more familiar home shirt, the neck and cuffs were non-contrasting. The iconic Italian shield design, featuring the colours of the flag, provided a strong visual focus for the shirt.

Worn in: A solitary win for in the 1966 World Cup – 2–0 against Chile.
Worn by: Sandro Mazzola, Paolo Barison.

AWAY 1966–74

Design: Unknown

This white shirt with blue chest band was such a distinctive design that it's a pity in a way ALL Italian away kits don't carry this feature! The ensemble featured the FIGC's preferred combination of white shirt, white shorts and blue socks.

Worn in: A 0–0 draw for Edmondo Fabbri's team against France in 1966.
Worn by: Mario Corso, Luigi Riva.

1966 FIFA WORLD CUP

AWAY 1966–70

Design: Unknown

The short sleeved version of the standard '60s away kit was in the kitbag for the 1966 World Cup but not used (although its shorts were called into action twice). Curiously, unlike its long sleeved partner, the placement of the Italian badge sat above the chest band.

Worn in: A 2–0 win over Cyprus in a 1968 European Championship qualifier (1967).
Worn by: Angelo Domenghini, Giacinto Facchetti.

1968 UEFA EUROPEAN CHAMPIONSHIP
1970 FIFA WORLD CUP

★

HOME 1966–74

Design: Unknown

The standard short sleeved version of the high-necked home strip began to be preferred as the '60s progressed.

Worn in: The 2–0 replay win over Yugoslavia in the final of Euro 68 – the Italians' first major trophy for 30 years! Also worn in the famous 4–3 win over West Germany in the 1970 World Cup semi-final, followed by the sad 4–1 defeat against Brazil in the final.
Worn by: Tarcisio Burgnich, Pietro Anastasi.

1968 UEFA EUROPEAN CHAMPIONSHIP
1970 FIFA WORLD CUP

AWAY 1970–74

Design: Unknown

Navy blue shorts appeared in the Italian kit repertoire in time for the 1970 World Cup, replacing the previous black pairs. The shirt was worn with the same blue socks as the home outfit. Ferruccio Valcareggi's side enjoyed a golden spell in these fine strips as the '70s dawned.

Worn in: A 0–0 draw with Israel in the last group stage game of the 1970 World Cup.
Worn by: Roberto Rosato, Mario Bertini.

1974 FIFA WORLD CUP

HOME 1974

Design: Unknown

Despite their sartorial stability a small change occurred in 1974 as Azzurri prepared for another World Cup. Thanks to the inclusion of three stripes on the socks, it's commonly believed it was adidas who produced this strip but in fact it was a local company.

Worn in: The surprising 2–1 defeat against Poland in the group stages that saw an early exit for Italy.
Worn by: Fabio Capello, Luciano Spinosi.

1974 FIFA WORLD CUP

AWAY 1974

Design: Unknown

This mighty all-white kit was selected as the change option for the World Cup, with white socks topped with a blue turnover now first choice. Local supplier, Baila, took over the contract later in 1974.

Worn in: Italy's opening match in the 1974 World Cup – a 3–1 victory over Haiti.
Worn by: Romeo Benetti, Giorgio Chinaglia.

HOME 1974–79

Design: Baila/Landoni

Local firm Baila took over the kit supply deal for Italy under new manager Fulvio Bernardini. The slim-fitting strip remained the same as that worn since the mid-'60s. A long sleeved version featured in the 1978 World Cup. Also worn with change blue shorts and white socks.

Worn in: The disappointing 2–1 defeat by the Netherlands at the 1978 World Cup that denied Italy a place in the final.
Worn by: Franco Causio, Renato Zaccarelli.

AWAY 1974–79

Design: Baila/Landoni

Sadly the unique blue chest band disappeared from the Italian away kits after the 1974 World Cup. Instead the jersey was now plain white with the confident swagger of the self-coloured crew neck and cuffs of the previous strip gone. The kit was available in long and short sleeves.

Worn in: A 3–0 defeat against Czechoslovakia in a 1978 friendly match.
Worn by: Gaetano Scirea, Mauro Bellugi.

HOME 1980–81

Design: Le Coq Sportif

After remaining virtually unchanged since 1966, the home outfit now incorporated plain blue socks – brought in by new kit suppliers Le Coq Sportif. Worn with both long and short sleeves and, on occasion, with white change socks.

Worn in: A 1–0 early win over England in Euro 80, followed later by the third place play-off defeat on penalties to Czechoslovakia.
Worn by: Giuseppe Baresi, Giampiero Marini.

AWAY 1980–81

Design: Le Coq Sportif

Although not required for active duty during this period it is a fair assumption that this was the Italian away kit ready and waiting in the kit cupboard should a colour clash occur. If it had been required, this would have been the change strip for the 1980 European Championship. No manufacturer's logo appeared on the shirts due to a special request by the Italian Football Federation.

HOME 1981–82

Design: Le Coq Sportif

In the second year of Le Coq Sportif's tenure, they introduced a kit design philosophy for Azzurri that was to last until 1993. The first element: a long sleeved shirt with a self-coloured collar/crew neck combination. The trim featured the colours of the national flag and provided a splash of colour to the outfit.

Worn in: A 1–0 win against Luxembourg in a 1981 World Cup qualifying match.
Worn by: Roberto Pruzzo, Francesco Graziani.

HOME 1981–82

Design: Le Coq Sportif

For warmer weather a new short-sleeved jersey was released. This also featured a tricolour trimmed collar but included a v-neck rather than a crew as in the long sleeved version. Plain white shorts and blue socks completed the outfit – an outfit that was to win the World Cup.

Worn in: The unforgettable 3–1 victory over West Germany in the 1982 World Cup Final – equalling Brazil's record of three final wins.
Worn by: Paolo Rossi, Giuseppe Bergomi.

AWAY 1981–82

Design: Le Coq Sportif

In addition to the two different home kits, two away strips in the traditional white were also produced. They simply reflected the design of the home outfits, with the neck element of the collar in white. The regular home shorts and socks were used to complete the kit.

Worn in: A 1–1 draw with Yugoslavia (1981) in a qualifier for the 1982 World Cup.
Worn by: Giuseppe Dossena, Roberto Bettega.

AWAY 1981–82

Design: Le Coq Sportif

The last of the four basic kit designs that Italy were to sport throughout the decade was the away version of the short-sleeved, collared jersey. Blue change shorts and white change socks could be called on should a clash exist.

Worn in: A 1–1 draw with Cameroon in the group stages of the 1982 World Cup – a magnificent tournament for Enzo Bearzot's team.
Worn by: Gaetano Scirea, Giancarlo Antognoni.

HOME 1983–84

Design: Le Coq Sportif

For Le Coq Sportif's last hurrah they retained pretty much the same set of strips as previously worn. The only difference came with the introduction of a new team crest shield that now featured three stars to symbolise the nation's three World Cup Final wins.

Worn in: An impressive 5–0 thrashing of Mexico in a 1984 friendly.
Worn by: Salvatore Bagni, Franco Baresi.

HOME 1983–84

Design: Le Coq Sportif

As with the long sleeved shirt, the short sleeved strip was updated with the new crest. Although replicas of these strips featured the Le Coq Sportif logo, these never appeared on the matchworn versions due to the FIGC's insistence that the shirt be branding-free.

Worn in: A 2–0 defeat against Sweden in 1983 – another disappointing result in Italy's dreadful Euro 84 qualifying campaign.
Worn by: Francesco Graziani, Marco Tardelli.

AWAY 1983–84

Design: Le Coq Sportif

The next set of away kits followed, as expected, the design of the home and replicated the now familiar white shirt, white shorts, blue socks combination which, given the fact that only the shirt was different to the home kit, provided a surprisingly effective change option.

Worn in: A 1–1 draw with Cyprus (1983) in a Euro 84 qualifier.
Worn by: Fulvio Collovati, Claudio Gentile.

AWAY 1983–84

Design: Le Coq Sportif

To complete this final set of Le Coq Sportif Italy strips was the de rigueur white version of the short sleeved shirt, although it appears it was never needed on the pitch as the only two times Italy needed to change kits during this period saw them opt for long sleeves. Surprisingly, Enzo Bearzot's side failed to qualify for the 1984 European Championship.

1988 UEFA EUROPEAN CHAMPIONSHIP
1986 FIFA WORLD CUP / 1990 FIFA WORLD CUP

1988 UEFA EUROPEAN CHAMPIONSHIP
1986 FIFA WORLD CUP / 1990 FIFA WORLD CUP

HOME 1984–90

Design: Diadora

Probably one of the most frequently worn Italy shirts since the '70s was this long sleeved home shirt – the first produced for Azzurri by new kit suppliers, local firm Diadora, who followed the established apparel policy. A new circular badge design and Italian flag colour trim on the socks was introduced.

Worn in: A 3–2 win vs Switzerland in a Euro 88 qualifying match in 1986.
Worn by: Dario Bonetti, Antonio Cabrini.

HOME 1984–90

Design: Diadora

The short sleeved home shirt followed the established basic Italy design, although the v-neck was slightly narrower than Le Coq Sportif's and it included the new badge with italicised text and the three 'World Cup' stars.

Worn in: Two major tournament semi-final defeats: 2–0 vs USSR in Euro 88 and then two years later to Argentina on penalties in the 1990 World Cup finals – hosted in Italy.
Worn by: Paolo Maldini, Toto Schillaci.

AWAY 1984–90

Design: Diadora

There were a couple of changes with Diadora's first cold weather, long sleeved change outfit compared to the previous (apart from the new crest of course). First, a blue rather than white round neck was included and, secondly, the sock turnovers were now blue and included the elegant Italian flag trim. Azeglio Vicini was appointed manager in 1986.

Worn in: A 1988 1–1 draw with Yugoslavia.
Worn by: Riccardo Ferri, Roberto Donadoni.

AWAY 1984–90

Design: Diadora

The classic integrity of the team strip was retained by Diadora under guidance from the Italian Football Federation with this set of outfits that, incredibly, lasted for three major tournaments. As with the Le Coq Sportif kits, although replicas featured the manufacturer's logos, these silky players' versions were blank.

Worn in: A 3–2 win over South Korea in the 1986 World Cup group stage.
Worn by: Alessandro Altobelli, Bruno Conti.

HOME 1991–93

Design: Diadora

The kit world entered a massively creative phase in the early '90s, yet still the traditional Italian kit style remained, albeit in a more fashionable baggy fit. A complex coloured trim featuring a combination of triangles and lines was included on the collar alongside another new badge design.

Worn in: The superb 3–1 victory against Portugal in a 1994 World Cup qualifier (1993).
Worn by: Roberto Mancini, Attilio Lombardo.

HOME 1991–93

Design: Diadora

The short sleeved version of the silky new home shirt extended the new trim to the cuffs and included the new logo of the FIGC which featured an additional circle above the main shield. The shorts and socks had remained unchanged since 1984 – symbolic of Italy's simple but stylish kit approach.

Worn in: A cracking 3–2 win against the Netherlands in a 1992 friendly.
Worn by: Alberto Di Chiara, Moreno Mannini.

AWAY 1991–93

Design: Diadora

There were no surprises with Diadora's next set of away kits – the last (for now) to feature differing designs for the long and short sleeved versions. The long sleeved option retained the collar/crew neck combination, although now the neck element reverted to white. Blue shorts were worn with the kit rather than white.

Worn in: A 1992 0–0 draw in Scotland in a qualifier for the 1994 World Cup.
Worn by: Stefano Eranio, Gianluigi Lentini.

AWAY 1991–93

Design: Diadora

This short sleeved away strip followed the tried and tested kit formula that had accompanied Italy's adventures on the pitch for the past 10 years. Despite leading Italy through two impressive major tournaments, Azeglio Vicini saw his side miss out on qualification for the European Championship in 1992.

Worn in: A 2–0 win over the Republic of Ireland in the 1992 US Cup.
Worn by: Giuseppe Signori, Roberto Galia.

1994 FIFA WORLD CUP

HOME 1993–94

Design: Diadora

Diadora's last set of kits for Azzurri were the first for a decade to feature identical designs for both the long and short sleeved versions – apart from the absence of the all-over shadow print that featured the Italian team crest and that was only incorporated into the fabric of the short sleeved shirts.

Worn in: The 1994 World Cup Final defeat on penalties to Brazil (the game ended 0–0).
Worn by: Roberto Baggio, Daniele Massaro.

1994 FIFA WORLD CUP

AWAY 1993–94

Design: Diadora

Worn during Italy's qualifiers for the 1994 World Cup, this next away strip followed the design lead of the home, including a neat button-up collar and the trusty triangular trim first introduced for the 1991 strips. The basic designs were only a gentle progression from the previous outfits and still unbranded.

Worn in: A nervous 2–1 triumph over Nigeria in the second round of USA 94 (Italy in all-white).
Worn by: Gianfranco Zola, Nicola Berti.

HOME 1995–96

Design: Nike

US sportswear giants Nike took over the Italian contract in 1995 and launched a kit featuring arguably the biggest ever leap in style to date for an Italian outfit. A contrasting white collar featuring gold trim was introduced and gold piping reached down each arm and the side of the shorts. A 'three star' motif appeared on each cuff.

Worn in: A 4–1 triumph vs Estonia in 1995.
Worn by: Fabrizio Ravanelli, Paolo Negro.

AWAY 1995–96

Design: Nike

Nike's first Italy away shirt was only worn once and, as in the past, was paired with the home shorts and socks. Both strips featured a large and complex shadow pattern with a crest that featured a subtle Nike logo. However, that was the only place the 'swoosh' was to be found, as the players shirts remained unbranded.

Worn in: The 2–0 win in Ukraine (1995) in a qualifier for Euro 96 – its only outing.
Worn by: Lorenzo Minotti, Demetrio Albertini.

1996 UEFA EUROPEAN CHAMPIONSHIP

HOME 1996–98

Design: Nike

Introduced for the second game of 1996, this new Italy shirt encapsulated Nike's switch in focus, with the shadow-printed fabric of their previous kits replaced by a material more designed for athletic performance rather than visual appeal. Gold was retained on the new strip and two large collar trims were added.

Worn in: The 2–1 victory over Russia and a 0–0 draw with Germany in Euro 96.
Worn by: Pierluigi Casiraghi, Roberto Mussi.

1996 UEFA EUROPEAN CHAMPIONSHIP

AWAY 1996–98

Design: Nike

Arrigo Sacchi and his team had qualified for Euro 96, and in readiness for the tournament unveiled this next set of kits. The away was a straightforward reversal of the home and, like the home, was produced using Nike's Dri-FIT fabric, designed to wick sweat and keep the wearer cool and comfortable.

Worn in: A 3–1 win over Moldova (1996) in a 1998 World Cup qualifier.
Worn by: Roberto Di Matteo, Moreno Torricelli.

1998 FIFA WORLD CUP

HOME 1998

Design: Nike

Nike's final Italy kits were simpler aesthetically than their previous offerings, and also appeared slightly looser, baggier and shinier. The Dri-FIT shirts, which reverted to a dual colour palette, retained a collar, trimmed with restraint in white, and introduced a white stripe under each arm and on the side of the shirts.

Worn in: A quarter-final penalties defeat by France in the 1998 World Cup (Italy in all blue).
Worn by: Alessandro Del Piero, Dino Baggio.

1998 FIFA WORLD CUP

AWAY 1998

Design: Nike

Another straightforward reversal of the home design was sported as Cesare Maldini's team prepared for the 1998 World Cup in France. The clean simplicity of these designs led themselves perfectly to mixing and matching. It's astonishing to realise that as late as 1998 Italy were still wearing a visually unbranded kit!

Worn in: The 2–2 draw with Chile in Italy's first match in the 1998 World Cup.
Worn by: Christian Vieri, Luigi Di Biagio.

HOME 1999–2000

Design: Kappa

A brave new kit world dawned for Italy with the start of a deal with fellow countrymen Kappa, and, for the first time, the inclusion of a manufacturer's logo! Kappa's first long sleeved home outfit made reference to the classic Italian kits of the '60s and '70s with its crew neck and minimal visual stylings.

Worn in: A 1–0 win over Sweden in a 2000 friendly match.
Worn by: Gianluca Pessotto, Alessio Tacchinardi.

HOME 1999–2000

Design: Kappa

Unlike the previous Nike strips, the first short sleeved Kappa shirts brought in a slightly different design by adding a smart v-neck. The rest of the strip was simple, yet strong, and pleased traditionalists by reintroducing the traditional old tricolour Italian shield as the team badge.

Worn by: A 4–0 thrashing of Wales in a 1999 qualifier for Euro 2000.
Worn by: Angelo Di Livio, Antonio Conte.

AWAY 1999–2000

Design: Kappa

Kappa wore their influences on their sleeves (and chests) with their first set of kits for Dino Zoff's team. The blue band from the iconic Italy change kits from earlier decades made a welcome return to this superb looking outfit. As with the home jersey, the World Cup three stars were placed on the right shoulder.

Worn by: An important 2–1 win in Denmark in a Euro 2000 qualifier (1999).
Worn by: Eusebio Di Francesco, Enrico Chiesa.

AWAY 1999–2000

Design: Kappa

The first set of Kappa strips was completed by a white v-necked short sleeved shirt which, like the long sleeved version, brought in contrasting colour panels on the neck and cuffs that balanced out the chest band nicely. Although in the Azzurri kitbag, this particular version of the away kit was never worn.

HOME 2000–02

Design: Kappa

Every now and then a kit turns up that is so innovative and different from the norm it creates a massive impact in the football world. Italy's 2000 figure-hugging fit jersey (officially named the Kombat 2000) with its paler shade of blue was such a kit and created quite a stir in that year's European Championship.

Worn in: The semi-final 3–1 penalties win over the Netherlands in Euro 2000.
Worn by: Vincenzo Montella, Ciro Ferrara.

AWAY 2000–02

Design: Kappa

Designed to thwart shirt-pulling, the Kombat range, with its blend of polyester and spandex, was renowned for its tight fit. However, most Italian players opted to wear the shirt a size or two too large. It also featured a Kappa logo on each sleeve which helped recreate the classic Italian look. Dino Zoff was now team manager.

Worn in: The heartbreaking 2–1 defeat by old rivals France in the final of Euro 2000.
Worn by: Francesco Totti/.

HOME 2002

Design: Kappa

The Kombat 2002 range took the basic design ethos behind the previous Kappa strips a stage further with an even tighter and more hi-tech fabric. The aesthetic of these kits, which were a natural successor to the Kombat 2000 outfits, was simplicity and uniformity, with the focus more on performance.

Worn in: The controversial World Cup defeat by the Korean Republic (2–1) that eliminated Italy.
Worn by: Cristiano Zanetti, Mark Iuliano.

AWAY 2002

Design: Kappa

In many respects Kappa's Kombat ranges were the predecessors of some of today's templated strips, dominated by lightweight fabrics. The visual appearance of this second set of strips was not much of a progression from the first, with a different neck construction and reversed stitching patterns providing the main changes.

Worn in: A tense 1–1 draw with Mexico in the 2002 World Cup.
Worn by: Alessandro Nesta, Christian Panucci.

HOME 2003–04

Design: Puma

After four fruitful years with Kappa the FIGC signed a new technical sponsor deal with German sportswear legend, Puma. Its first kit (in a more familiar savoy blue) stuck to the Italian ethos of simplicity and tradition, interpreted within a modern design. The Italian crest appeared on the shorts (and socks) for the first time.

Worn in: A 2-0 win over Finland in 2003.
Worn by: Marco Delvecchio, Fabrizio Miccoli.

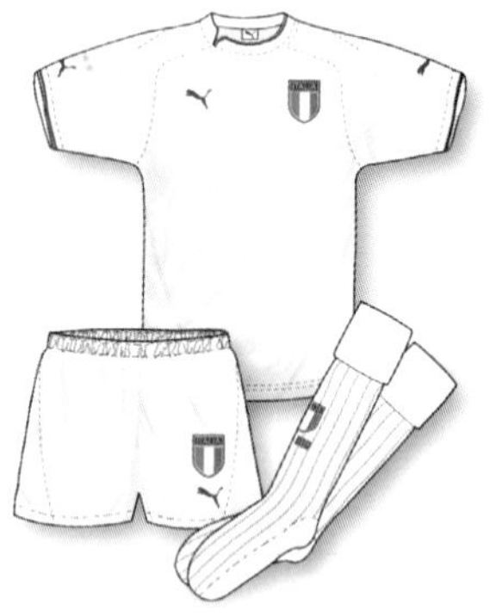

AWAY 2003–04

Design: Puma

A reversal of the home kit was selected as the next change strip for Giovanni Trapattoni's team. Alongside the asymmetrical neck design and reversed stitching (for extra comfort), additional Puma logos were included on each sleeve. The shirt was only worn once, where it was joined by the home kit's white shorts.

Worn in: A 1–1 draw with Serbia and Montenegro in 2003.
Worn by: Bernardo Corradi, Filippo Inzaghi.

HOME 2004–05

Design: Puma

With its non-contrasting crew neck and plain design appliqués, this strip brought back memories of the classic '70s Italian outfit at a glance. However, the centrally placed badge, gold Puma logos and breathable fabric panels gave the shirt a unique feel.

Worn in: A 1–1 draw with Sweden followed by a last-minute 2–1 triumph over Bulgaria; not enough to see the Italians progress in Euro 2004.
Worn by: Stefano Fiore.

AWAY 2004–05

Design: Puma

Italy's high hopes for Euro 2004 were dashed after a disappointing group stage with Trapattoni replaced soon after by Marcello Lippi. The team's away kit for the tournament, launched in Spring 2004, reflected the design of the home. The three World Cup stars were now placed above the team shield

Worn in: A 0–0 draw with Denmark in the Italians' opening game in Euro 2004.
Worn by: Fabio Cannavaro, Gennaro Gattuso.

HOME 2005-06

Design: Puma

Puma's next home jersey (reported to be the lightest of any used in the tournament) retained the overall appearance of a classic Italian shirt but added a touch of intrigue with arching navy panels. The team seemed to prefer wearing an all-blue version of this strip for several games during their glorious World Cup.

Worn in: The triumphant 5–3 penalties win over France in the 2006 World Cup final!
Worn by: Luca Toni, Marco Materazzi.

AWAY 2005-06

Design: Puma

There was a real swagger about this distinctive Azzurri away kit that, along with the home, was unveiled midway through the 2006 World Cup qualifiers. Rather than just simply copying the first choice shirt, Puma introduced a plunging v-neck revealing a 'fake' inner blue crew neck design that housed the newly designed crest.

Worn in: A good 3–1 friendly win for Marcello Lippi's men against the Netherlands in 2005.
Worn by: Alberto Gilardino, Mauro Camoranesi.

HOME 2007-09

Design: Puma

With its gold v-neck and trim, this shirt created a contrast to the previous kit. The construction was simple but effective with the Italian tricolour featuring on the socks. Although launched with white shorts, teams were encouraged at this time to sport single-colour strips and the team switched between blue and white pairs.

Worn in: A 1–1 draw with Romania and a 3–0 defeat by the Netherlands in Euro 2008.
Worn by: Andrea Pirlo.

AWAY 2007-09

Design: Puma

This stylish white strip brought a new spin to the traditional Italian change outfit, thanks to its introduction of gold and navy as secondary colours. Like the home kit, the original navy shorts were often discarded in favour of a white pair to create a single-colour ensemble.

Worn in: A good 2–0 win over France in the group stage of Euro 2008 followed by another quarter-final penalties defeat, this time to Spain.
Worn by: Antonio Cassano, Simone Perrotta.

HOME 2009

Design: Puma

Thanks to their 2006 World Cup win (Italy's fourth), the side took part in the 2009 FIFA Confederations Cup. To mark the event this stunning strip resurrected the light blue wearing '30s World Cup winning side (back then, however, Italy actually wore black shorts). The team reverted to the standard home kit after the tournament.

Worn in: A 3–1 win over the USA.
Worn by: Vincenzo Iaquinta, Giuseppe Rossi.

HOME 2010-11

Design: Puma

2010 brought with it the South African World Cup. Italy's strip for the tournament again employed the all-blue route. The shirt, whose intricate neck design cleverly featured the Italian flag colours, incorporated a shadow print depicting torso muscles to create a design that exuded confidence, possibly too much confidence!

Worn in: An awful World Cup in which Marcello Lippi's team failed to win a game.
Worn by: Simone Pepe, Fabio Cannavaro.

AWAY 2010-11

Design: Puma

The new white away kit featured the same shorts and socks design as the home (enabling them to be mixed and matched with ease), but the shirt featured an array of colour panels. A nice touch saw the Italian flag sitting in a patch at the centre of the shorts waistband. The kit was not required in the World Cup.

Worn in: A 0–0 draw with Northern Ireland (worn with the home blue shorts).
Worn by: Stefano Mauri, Giorgio Chiellini.

HOME 2011-13

Design: Puma

A white collar returned with this kit that was first worn in the last game of 2011. The collar was high-fitting and elegantly trimmed with the colours of the Italian flag. A geometric shadow pattern decorated the shirt. Often worn with the blue shorts of the away kit.

Worn in: The 2–1 win over Germany in the semi-final of Euro 2012 followed by the 4–0 defeat against Spain in the final.
Worn by: Mario Balotelli, Riccardo Montolivo.

AWAY 2011–13

Design: Puma

To the joy of the traditionalists Italy's most famous away kit design – the blue chest band – returned in style with this superb strip. It was topped with a lightly trimmed v-neck and paired with blue shorts. It was just a pity the kit wasn't needed in Euro 2012.

Worn in: The 3–2 win on penalties over Uruguay in the 2013 Confederations Cup that clinched third place for Italy.
Worn by: Davide Astori, Alessandro Diamanti.

HOME 2013

Design: Puma

Thanks to Spain winning both the recent World Cup and European Championship, Italy, as runners-up in the latter, were invited again to compete in the Confederations Cup and once more a special kit was unveiled. Originally launched with white shorts, blue pairs were actually sported in the two matches in which it was worn during the tournament.

Worn in: A cracking 4–3 win against Japan.
Worn by: Antonio Candreva, Alberto Aquilani.

HOME 2014–15

Design: Puma

There was nowhere to hide if you were carrying a few extra pounds with Puma's next Italian offering. This wondrous kit was worn skin tight and featured a neat button-up collar with a long placket and white flashes on either side of the shirt. Italian flag trim sat on each cuff.

Worn in: A disappointing World Cup – Italy's only victory coming against England (2–1). Italy wore blue shorts in all three of their matches.
Worn by: Marco Verratti, Matteo Darmian.

AWAY 2014–15

Design: Puma

This pinstriped beauty completed a fine set of outfits, all primed and ready for Cesare Prandelli's side to do battle in the 2014 World Cup (although sadly it was never required in the tournament). Green and red side flashes completed this slick ensemble. Shorts and socks were reversals of the home versions.

Worn in: A home 1–0 win over Malta in a Euro 2016 qualifier (2015).
Worn by: Manolo Gabbiadini, Graziano Pelle.

HOME 2015–17

Design: Puma

This exquisite outfit was premiered in November 2015 and immediately entered the lexicon of classic Italy kits. There was a really traditional feel to this fine jersey, which was trimmed sensitively with gold piping down each arm and adorned with shadow pinstripes.

Worn in: The superb all-blue 2–0 win vs Spain in the knockout stage of Euro 2016 followed by the quarter-final defeat against Germany.
Worn by: Stefano Sturaro, Alessandro Florenzi.

AWAY 2015–16

Design: Puma

There was a retro-continental fashion look to this outfit, due in the main to the racing stripes in Italy's national colours running down the front of the shirt. The badge was placed centrally to allow the squad number to sit over the heart. The shorts and socks were able to be worn with the home kit when necessary.

Worn in: A great 2–0 victory over Belgium in Antonio Conte's Italy's first game of Euro 2016.
Worn by: Matteo Darmian.

AWAY 2016–17

Design: Puma

Launched with a 3D street art event just two months after Euro 2006, this popular kit paid tribute to the World Cup winning Italian side of 2006. Ironically the kit that inspired it was never actually worn in that tournament! The strip featured a monochromatic badge and was also worn with bespoke white change shorts.

Worn in: A 3–1 win in Israel in a World Cup qualifier (2016).
Worn by: Eder, Marco Parolo.

HOME 2017–18

Design: Puma

Italy launched another all blue outfit that will forever be remembered as the kit that didn't make it to the World Cup as, shockingly, Gian Piero Ventura's Italy failed to qualify. This great strip featured many classic elements from recent Italy kits, including tricolour trim, navy accents and an impressive shadow pattern.

An emotional Marco Tardelli with Antonio Cabrini celebrate winning the 1982 World Cup Final against West Germany in the Le Coq Sportif home strip that exuded elegance and simplicity.

1982 FIFA WORLD CUP

Bernd Krauss in Austria's red away Puma strip alongside Algeria's Lakhdar Belloumi. Algeria wore a slightly different shirt with alternative printed text in the second half of their group games.

1982 FIFA WORLD CUP

1982 brought a blend of modern v-necks and traditional collars – here Steve Coppell in fan favourite Admiral England kit beats Puma-wearing Waleed Jasem of Kuwait.

MEXICO

Mexico's football history is blessed with one of the most beloved shirts in the sport's canon: the 1996–98 home shirt resplendent with a large, all-over Aztec-inspired print.

It's a jersey that regularly features in polls for the 'greatest kit ever'. Unlike many similarly daring designs of the era, this one works beautifully because it had real meaning, drawing heavily on the country's cultural heritage. In fact, so successful was the design that the Aztec theme reoccurs frequently in the Mexican wardrobe.

Mexico's colour scheme of green, white and red (typically three colours that can be difficult to mould into an effective strip design) is taken from the country's tricolour flag. However, until the mid '50s, the team took to the pitch in maroon shirts paired with black or navy shorts, a colour scheme that has since been used as an away strip.

A wide variety of brands have manufactured Mexico kits throughout the years including Umbro, Nike, Pony and fellow countrymen ABA Sport and Atletica. One of the most memorable sets of Mexico kits appeared in 1978, courtesy of US leisurewear giants Levi Strauss. In a rare outing into the football market, it produced superb home and away kits for that year's World Cup. The Levi Strauss away kit is especially lauded for its bold green and red vertical stripes and red shorts.

Today the team kit is produced by adidas, in their third stint with the side. In 2010, adidas introduced a black away kit so popular that the colour scheme was promoted to first choice home kit in 2015. It was a brave move, though one that ruffled feathers among the team's more traditional supporters. A year later a more familiar tricolour strip returned, and it is this favourite green/white/red colour combination that the side will wear in the 2018 Russian World Cup.

Mexico wearing their iconic ABA Sport kit as they line up before the Group E clash against South Korea in the 1998 World Cup.

1966 FIFA WORLD CUP

HOME 1966–68

Design: Unknown

Like many teams, Mexico used two standard shirt designs throughout the 1960s: long sleeved and short-sleeved. The long-sleeved version included a neat tricolour trim on the crew neck and cuffs that replicated the Mexican flag.

Worn in: Mexico's last game of the 1966 World Cup – a goalless draw against Uruguay.
Worn by: Aaron Padilla, Salvador Reyes.

1967 CONCACAF CHAMPIONSHIP

HOME 1966–68

Design: Unknown

A smart v-neck short-sleeved green shirt was the second basic design the side wore in the mid-late '60s. The tricolour trim worked well with the v-neck and it was this strip that the side sported in the 1966 World Cup.

Worn in: Good wins over Trinidad and Tobago (4–0) and Honduras (1–0) in the 1967 CONCACAF Championship – Mexico ended runners-up.
Worn by: Vicente Pereda Mier, Luis Estrada.

1966 FIFA WORLD CUP

AWAY 1966–68

Design: Unknown

Mexico had actually worn maroon and navy as their first choice kit colour until the 1950s so the colour scheme made a natural choice for the team's change kit following the switch to green. Bereft of superfluous trim, the shirt featured non-contrasting crew neck and cuffs.

Worn in: A 1–1 draw against France and a 2–0 defeat against hosts England in the 1966 World Cup.
Worn by: Jesús Del Muro, Enrique Borja.

1967 CONCACAF CHAMPIONSHIP

AWAY 1966–68

Design: Unknown

As with the home outfit, a second short-sleeved strip was also found in the Mexican kt cupboard for games in warmer weather. Like the long-sleeved crew-neck version, the v-neck and cuffs were self coloured. Mexico's need for an away strip is not great, however, and it is unclear whether this design was ever worn.

HOME 1968–76

Design: Unknown

The home strip went through a slight modification in 1968. A newly designed team crest was introduced and, unusually for the era, placed centrally on the shirt. The green and red-trimmed shorts that had appeared in the 1966 World Cup now became full time first choice.

Worn in: A 2–1 friendly win over Brazil at the Maracanã in 1968.
Worn by: Isidoro Diaz Mejia, Antonio Munguia.

1970 FIFA WORLD CUP
1971, 1973 CONCACAF CHAMPIONSHIP

★

HOME 1968–76

Design: Unknown

The new badge was also added to the short-sleeved shirt but remained on the traditional left-hand side of the jersey. The jersey was paired with the new green and red-trimmed shorts and plain green socks.

Worn in: A crushing 4-0 win over debutants El Salvador at the 1970 World Cup. Also worn in the 2–1 victory over Honduras that sealed the 1971 CONCACAF Championship for El Tri.
Worn by: Javier Fragoso, Javier Valdivia.

AWAY 1968–76

Design: Unknown

Mexico's change strip remained unaltered apart from the new team crest, that on the long-sleeved version at least, remained in centre place. Following the 1970 World Cup, Mexico suffered the disappointment of failing to qualify for the 1974 tournament under the guidance of Javier de la Torre.

1970 FIFA WORLD CUP
1971, 1973 CONCACAF CHAMPIONSHIP

AWAY 1968–76

Design: Unknown

The team's regular short-sleeved shirt was also updated with the new crest as Raúl Cardenas' team prepared to host the 1970 World Cup.

Worn in: A 1–0 win over Belgium in Mexico's last group stage game of the 1970 World Cup. Also worn in the 4–1 defeat by Italy in the second round that eliminated the Mexicans from the tournament.
Worn by: Gustavo Pena Velasco, Hector Pulido.

HOME 1977–78

Design: adidas

For a brief period in 1977 José Antonio Roca's side sported their own version of adidas' classic 'Worldcup Dress' long-sleeved home template. The shirt featured contrasting white crew neck and cuffs and of course the iconic three-stripe trim. Also worn in early 1978 but with the adidas logo blocked out.

Worn in: A 4–1 win over Haiti in a qualifier for the 1978 World Cup.
Worn by: Cristóbal Ortega, Carlos Gomez.

HOME 1977–78

Design: adidas

A short-sleeved version of the team's adidas home kit was also worn. It featured a standard v-neck and alternative three-stripe trim that incorporated both red and white. The rest of the kit remained the same including the newly introduced white socks.

Worn in: An impressive 8–1 win over Suriname en route to claiming the team's third CONCACAF Championship title.
Worn by: Manuel Nájera, Eduardo Ramos.

HOME 1978–79

Design: Levi's/adidas

Possibly the most renowned era of Mexico's kit history was the strips the side sported in the 1978 World Cup. Universally assumed to be produced by Levi's (due in no small part to the inclusion of their logo on the kit!) the strip was actually produced and licensed by adidas. The strip featured exquisite dual-colour trim.

Worn in: The 2-1 defeat that rounded off Mexico's disappointing 1978 World Cup.
Worn by: Victor Rangel, Leonardo Cuéllar.

AWAY 1978–79

Design: Levi's/adidas

Completing the duo of iconic Mexico kits was this stunning away strip. Using a core colour of white, rather than the more traditional maroon, the crew-neck shirt was dominated by a broad green and red vertical stripe. Interestingly the Levi's logo also appeared on sock tags.

Worn in: Tunisia's 3-1 win over Mexico in 1978 – the first time an African side had ever won a World Cup match.
Worn by: Vázquez Ayala, Antonio de la Torre.

HOME 1979–80

Design: Pony

After the short-lived Levi's era the side signed with US sportswear firm Pony in a deal rumoured to be brokered by adidas head honcho Horst Dassler. This cracker of a kit featured red chevron trim (not to be confused with Hummel's trademark form of decoration of course) and an innovative combination of Pony logo and badge on the left-hand side.

Worn in: A 1980 2–0 friendly win vs Hungary.
Worn by: Alfredo Tena, Ramón de la Torre.

HOME 1979–81

Design: Pony

Although differences between long and short-sleeved shirts were not uncommon pre-1990, it was unusual for the changes to be quite as notable as can be seen here between the long-sleeved version of Mexico's Pony shirt and the short-sleeved. A contrasting crew neck was joined by white chevron trim and plainer shorts.

Worn in: A 1–1 draw with Canada in a 1980 qualifier for the 1982 World Cup.
Worn by: Vinicio Bravo, Ricardo Castro.

HOME 1980–81

Design: Pony

A second Pony (whose name was an acronym for Product of New York) short-sleeved shirt emerged in 1980. Much more in line with its long-sleeved partner, the jersey featured a contrasting v-neck and new white chevron trim. Two versions of the shirt were worn, the other with more conventional logo placement.

Worn in: A 5-1 victory over the United States in an early qualifier for the 1982 World Cup.
Worn by: Adrian Camacho, José Luiz Gonzalez.

AWAY 1979–81

Design: Pony

Pony's Mexican change strip retained the basic white theme of the Levi's kit but simplified the design, adding only a green v-neck and chevron trim. The shirt was worn with the left-hand combination of Pony logo and team crest. Given the relative lack of green-clad teams, Mexico away kits were scarcely required.

Worn in: A 3–1 friendly defeat by Spain in 1981.
Worn by: Francisco Castrejon, Agustini Manzo.

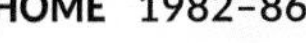
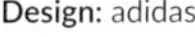

HOME 1982–86

Design: adidas

Adidas reclaimed the Mexican kit contract in 1982 and supplied the side with a functional v-neck short-sleeved home strip. Red interspersed the white adidas three-stripe trim on the sleeves. An early version of the shirt omitted the text around the crest and featured green in between the white three-stripe trim.

Worn in: An impressive 5–0 friendly win over Poland in 1985.
Worn by: Felix Cruz Barbosa, Miguel Espana.

AWAY 1982–86

Design: adidas

Dispensing with the white change kits that had been favoured in recent years, the FMF and adidas dressed Bora Milutinović's team in a maroon and navy recreation of the side's early strips – pre-green. The white trim across the two colours helped create a stunning outfit. As with all El Tri's jerseys at the time, large 'Mexico' text was displayed on the backs.

HOME 1984–86

Design: adidas

The team's home kit was modernised in 1984 to include that most iconic of all '80s kit decoration – pinstripes. The red trim on the sleeves was removed but the rest of the kit remained identical to before, including the unfamiliar design of adidas socks. It seems, however, that the standard plainer design of jersey was still retained during this period.

Worn in: A 1–1 draw with Sweden in 1984.
Worn by: Javier Aguirre.

HOME 1986–87

Design: adidas

Given that the country was hosting the 1986 World Cup the national team was well prepared for battle in the fierce summer heat. Adidas kitted Bora Milutinovic's Mexican side out in their very latest fabric technology 'Climalite' designed to wick sweat and keep players cool.

Worn in: The heartbreaking defeat on penalties to West Germany in the quarter-finals of the 1986 World Cup.
Worn by: Hugo Sánchez, Fernando Quirarte.

AWAY 1986–87

Design: adidas

The simple visual approach of the Mexican hi-tech Climalite shirts continued with the white away strip that was a straightforward reversal of the home design. The shirt was also worn with the white shorts of the home outfit. Both the home and away jerseys had 'Mexico' emblazoned across the backs.

Worn in: An all-white 2–0 victory over Bulgaria in the 1986 World Cup second round.
Worn by: Raul Servin, Tomas Juan Boy.

HOME 1987–89

Design: adidas

In one of their more unique 1980s outfits, adidas supplied Mario Velarde's team with a smart all-green home shirt with red adidas trefoil logo and just the three-stripe trim providing visual stand-out. An elegant diagonal shadow stripe pattern added a nice touch, although unusually it ran downwards rather than the more familiar up.

Worn in: An 1988 8–0 thrashing of El Salvador.
Worn by: Constantino, Javier Hernandez.

HOME 1989–90

Design: adidas

Two years after the launch of the diagonal shadow-striped home shirt the jersey went through a slight modification: the adidas logo was switched to white (and text added to the trefoil logo) and the diagonal pattern flipped to a more traditional upwards stroke. White trim and an adidas logo were added to the socks.

Worn in: A 2–0 friendly win over Argentina in 1990.
Worn by: Carlos Munoz, Gonzalo Farfan Infante.

AWAY 1987–91

Design: adidas

Adidas' last away kit of the 1980s recaptured the essence of the late 1970s Pony away kit. The non-contrasting collar and cuffs ensured the green three-stripe trim had maximum stand-out. The shadow stripes on this white jersey ran upwards. Although this strip was sported by a junior side it is unclear whether the first team ever wore it. The side were banned from the 1990 World Cup due to fielding illegitimate players.

HOME 1990–91

Design: adidas

This distinctive and challenging design made appearances in the 1990 World Cup thanks to Russia and Czechoslovakia. Mexico's version of the somewhat abstract combination of white and grey triangles sadly was not seen at the tournament due. The team crest was placed very low on the shirt.

Worn in: Two consecutive 1–0 friendly wins over Chile in 1991.
Worn by: Misael Espinoza, Hugo Pineda.

1991 CONCACAF GOLD CUP

HOME 1991

Design: Umbro

After 10 years with adidas the FMF signed with Umbro just in time for the 1991 Gold Cup. Umbro's first home kit brought a fresh and unconventional look to the strip by opting for a primarily white shirt with a large central green panel. Standard issue chequerboard red socks were also introduced.

Worn in: A convincing 4-1 win over Jamaica in the 1991 Gold Cup.
Worn by: Benjamin Galindo, Carlos Hermosillo.

1993 COPA AMERICA / 1993 CONCACAF GOLD CUP

HOME 1991–94

Design: Umbro

November 1991 saw a more traditional Mexican kit emerge from the Umbro designers. A classy white shirt featured a repeated shadow pattern, red piping and a button-up white collar. Red trim adorned the shorts' hem. The previous short-lived kit's red socks were retained for this outfit.

Worn in: The 1993 Gold Cup final, in which Mexico beat their co-hosts, USA, 4-0.
Worn by: Luis Roberto Alves, Ignacio Ambríz.

1993 COPA AMERICA / 1993 CONCACAF GOLD CUP

AWAY 1991–94

Design: Umbro

To complement the new more refined all-green jersey came this magnificent away strip that replicated in red and green Aztec feather iconography. The shorts reversed the white home pairs and the sock introduced the Mexican tricolour flag on the turnover. Incredibly this strip was never required during its three years of service. César Luis Menotti was appointed manager in 1991.

1994 FIFA WORLD CUP

HOME 1994

Design: Umbro

After missing out on the 1990 World Cup Miguel Mejía Barón's side were chomping at the bit to take part in the 1994 tournament – especially as it was close to home. Rather than producing a new kit, Umbro simply updated the existing design with a new logo and revised shorts trim.

Worn in: The unfortunate defeat on penalties to Bulgaria in the 1994 World Cup.
Worn by: Marcelino Bernal, Ignacio Ambríz.

1994 FIFA WORLD CUP

AWAY 1994

Design: Umbro

The away kit went through the same minor revisions that the home strip experienced with a new logo and a new design of shorts, featuring an asymmetrical triangular trim.

Worn in: A 1-1 draw with Italy in the group stages of the 1994 World Cup.
Worn by: Carlos Hermosillo, Claudio Suárez.

1995 COPA AMERICA
1995 FIFA CONFEDERATIONS CUP

HOME 1995

Design: ABA Sport

New year brought a new kit courtesy of local sportswear company ABA Sport. The design was dominated by a large curved 'M' across the jersey. The 'M' was actually similar to that of team sponsor Mexlub, although the FMF insisted that the initial stood for 'Mexico'!

Worn in: The 1-1 draw (won 5-4 on penalties) that clinched third place in the 1995 Confederations Cup against Nigeria.
Worn by: Jorge Rodriguez, Raul Gutierrez.

1995 COPA AMERICA
1995 FIFA CONFEDERATIONS CUP

AWAY 1995

Design: ABA Sport

The first ABA Sport away strip simply reversed the design of the home kit in time-honoured football kit tradition. Interestingly the away version was arguably more effective than the home. This first set of ABA kits included a repeated logo shadow pattern and interchangeable shorts and socks.

Worn in: A 2–1 win over Nigeria in the 1995 US Cup for Miguel Mejia Baron's team.
Worn by: Joaguin del Olmo, Perales.

HOME 1996

Design: ABA Sport

As the 1996 Gold Cup dawned in January 1996 Mexico unveiled a new kit – one that was to prove one of the most imaginative and popular outfits the side have worn. The green fabric was engulfed in a large tonal print depicting the Aztec calendar that perfectly encapsulated Mexican culture.

Worn in: A superb 2–0 win vs Brazil in the 1996 Gold Cup final.
Worn by: Raul Gutierrez, Raul Rodrigo Lara.

AWAY 1996–98

Design: ABA Sport

This wonderful all-white strip joined the Aztec inspired Mexico kit cupboard. The style reflected that of the home design and also featured the large all-over print style. The same white shorts as the home kit were favoured and two designs of socks were worn during it's lifespan.

Worn in: A 3-1 loss to Bolivia in the semi-finals of the 1997 Copa America.
Worn by: Alberto García Aspe, Ricardo Pelaez.

HOME 1997–98

Design: ABA Sport

After a year the home kit was updated with new socks and a switch to red trim on the shorts, creating a more interesting visual balance. The green-trimmed white shorts were a much better match with the away strip. From 1996 to 2000 'Mexico' text appeared in the centre of the shirt.

Worn in: The 1–0 win over Peru that sealed third place in the 1997 Copa America.
Worn by: Roberto Medina, Ramón Ramírez.

THIRD 1996–98

Design: ABA Sport

This eye-watering third shirt incorporated a deep red and green rendering of the all-over Aztec pattern. It was a bold, uncompromising design that managed to cohesively blend two colours that traditionally are not always good bedfellows.

Worn in: A 3–1 victory over Ecuador in a 1997 friendly – this kit's only first team outing.
Worn by: Eustacio Rizo, Damian Alvarez.

HOME 1998

Design: ABA Sport

The Aztec calendar kit went through one final incarnation before being retired and again the change came from updating the shorts, which now featured an angular green and red trim, although now the trim on the collar and cuffs was also enhanced.

Worn in: The glorious 1-0 win over bitter rivals, the United States, in the final of the 1998 Gold Cup.
Worn by: Luis Hernandez, Francisco Palencia.

AWAY 1998

Design: ABA Sport

With the introduction of the new shorts to the away kit red began to play a more prominent colour role in the away design. Essentially the shirt was the same, except for updated collar and cuff trim. The shorts and socks could be mixed and matched with the home pairs.

Worn in: 2–2 draws with Belgium and the Netherlands in the group stages of the 1998 World Cup.
Worn by: German Villa, Joel Sanchez.

HOME 1999–2000

Design: Garcis

Mexican iconography blended with the FMF crest in the all-over print introduced by new Mexico kit supplier Garcis on their strip for the national side. The original design on the shirt featured the official eagle of Mexico but had to be withdrawn for copyright reasons.

Worn in: The thrilling 4-3 win on home soil in the final of the 1999 Confederations Cup against Brazil.
Worn by: Miguel Zepeda, José Manuel Abundis.

AWAY 1999–2000

Design: Garcis

Taking the same approach as ABA Sport, Garcis decided to also include the identical shirt print as the home kit on their white away option for the national side. Bereft of red, the shirt plumped for a dual-colour approach. As with the shorts, socks could be interchanged with the home pairs if necessary.

Worn in: An all-white 2–0 win over Egypt in the 1999 Korea Cup.
Worn by: Adolfo Rios, Salvador Carmona.

HOME 2000–01

Design: Atletica

Mexican company Atletica signed with the FMF in 2000 and brought a modern approach to the team kit. Gone was the Aztec imagery and in its place a broad white chest/sleeve panel. Red was used on the shirt cuffs and formed the main trim on the very long and baggy shorts.

Worn in: An incredible 7–0 thrashing of Trinidad and Tobago in a 2000 qualifier for the 2002 World Cup.
Worn by: Cuauhtemoc Blanco, Duilio Davino.

AWAY 2000–01

Design: Atletica

Signing with a new company provides a fine opportunity to freshen up a team's kit palette and this is exactly what occurred with El Tri when this surprisingly white and black outfit became the team's new away kit. The more traditional green and red were reduced to just trim on the collar and cuffs.

Worn in: A 2–2 draw with the Republic of Ireland in the 2000 US Nike Cup.
Worn by: Daniel Osorno, Horacio Sanchez.

THIRD 2000–01

Design: Atletica

A more traditional colourway option was also produced as Mexico's third kit in 2000. The design reflected that of the home and away jerseys but was now rendered in white and red with green trim and piping providing visual highlights.

Worn in: A 4–0 loss to France in the opening round of a poor 2001 Confederations Cup for Enrique Meza Enriquez's team.
Worn by: Victor Ruiz, Antonio De Nigris.

HOME 2001–02

Design: Atletica

Atletica's second set of Mexico outfits took a very different approach to their first. The shirts were much more sedate and modest, preferring a solid green base with just the merest touch of red and white trim. Dark green side panels and a red hem trim also featured in this fine looking strip. Also worn with the third kit's white socks.

Worn in: The disappointing 1–0 defeat against Colombia in the 2001 Copa America final.
Worn by: Sigifredo Mercado, Jesús Arellano.

AWAY 2001–02

Design: Atletica

For the first time since the mid 1980s the Mexico players turned out in the maroon and navy colour combination that was originally used as their home style, prior to the introduction of green. The design, including raglan sleeves, piping and athletic cut shorts mirrored that of the home. Javier Aguirre became Mexico manager in 2001.

Worn in: A 4–0 friendly win vs Albania (2002).
Worn by: Adolfo Bautista, Manuel Vidrio.

THIRD 2001–02

Design: Atletica

The retaining of the side navy panels, now trimmed with maroon, gave a very different look to a Mexico change kit. The design was the same as the home and regular away versions and included a neat tricolour flash on the right sleeve and small 'Mexico' text on the left.

Worn in: A 1-0 victory over El Salvador in the group stage of the 2002 Gold Cup.
Worn by: Juan Pablo Garcia, Carlos Ochoa.

HOME 2002

Design: Atletica

As was so often the case with Mexico's strips over the years the last set of Atletica outfits went through minor modifications during their lifespan. The crew neck of the first version was updated with a red v-neck and it was this style that was used in the 2002 World Cup where it was also worn with the third kit's white socks.

Worn in: A 2-1 win over Ecuador in the group stage of the 2002 World Cup.
Worn by: Ramón Morales, Braulio Luna.

AWAY 2002

Design: Atletica

As with the home shirt, the maroon and navy change kit also replaced the crew neck with a more accommodating v-neck design. The rest of the design remained the same. The strip was packed in the side's World Cup kitbag but not required.

2002 FIFA WORLD CUP

THIRD 2002

Design: Atletica

In line with the home and away strips, the heroic all-white outfit was modified to include a v-neck. Although the strip was match prepared for the World Cup (to provide a suitable 'light' colour option to complement the darker home and away jerseys) it was not used in the tournament.

HOME 2003

Design: Nike

US sportswear giants Nike took over the FMF contract in 2003 and introduced what appears to be an interim kit that lasted for just four games. It featured a much darker, almost olive green shade and included white piping that curved around the arm. It was worn with white shorts and either white or red socks.

Worn in: A 1-0 friendly defeat by Argentina in the first game of 2003.
Worn by: Diego Martinez, Pavel Pardo.

2003 CONCACAF GOLD CUP

HOME 2003-04

Design: Nike

After the short-lived darker green kit Nike issued Mexico with one of their standard dual-layered shirts in a much more familiar shade. The shirts were designed to wick sweat more effectively therefore keeping players cooler. Dynamic, angular colour patterns provided a menacing visual appearance.

Worn in: A 1-0 win over Brazil after sudden death extra time in the 2003 Gold Cup final.
Worn by: Rafael Garcia, Juan Pablo Rodríguez.

2003 CONCACAF GOLD CUP

AWAY 2002-04

Design: Nike

A basic reversal of the home kit provided an effective change option for the Mexican side with red flourishes adding highlights to the predominantly white and green strip. The shorts and socks of this kit could be mixed and matched with the home kit if required.

Worn in: A 2-0 win over Costa Rica in the semi-finals of the 2003 Gold Cup.
Worn by: Fernando Salazar, Octavio Valdez.

2004 COPA AMERICA / 2005 CONCACAF GOLD CUP
2005 FIFA CONFEDERATIONS CUP

HOME 2004-06

Design: Nike

Nike's Total 90 (named after the concept of the kits performing for the full term of a match) provided the essence of their second set of kits for Ricardo La Volpe's team. Swish red piping curved down each side of the shirt and an enlarged Nike swoosh provided asymmetrical, abstract trim on the left sleeve.

Worn in: A 4-0 win over Guatemala in the first round of the 2005 Gold Cup.
Worn by: Jared Borgetti, Gerardo Galindo.

2004 COPA AMERICA / 2005 CONCACAF GOLD CUP
2005 FIFA CONFEDERATIONS CUP

AWAY 2004-06

Design: Nike

As expected, the team's 2004 change kit reversed the colours of the home with the exception of a complete lack of red, Nike preferring a simpler two colour only strip. Nike's Total 90 range was easily recognisable thanks to the large circle that housed the squad number on the front of matchday shirts.

Worn in: A 2-1 victory over Japan in the first round of the 2005 Confederations Cup.
Worn by: Sinha, Jaime Lozano.

2006 FIFA WORLD CUP

HOME 2006-07

Design: Nike

Nike's final set of strips for the Mexican Football Federation opted for a slightly darker green decorated with a bold white chevron that housed the Nike logo and Mexico team crest. The style, that featured a considered use of red on the neck and cuffs, was later available as Nike's 'Victory' teamwear template.

Worn in: Worn in: A 2-1 defeat after extra time by Argentina in the 2006 World Cup.
Worn by: Rafael Márquez, Francisco Fonseca.

2006 FIFA WORLD CUP

AWAY 2006-07

Design: Nike

A standard white and green version of the 'Victory' chevron design became El Tri's change strip for the 2006 World Cup. Chevrons became the football kit fashion 'must have' in the mid 2000s.

Worn in: A disappointing goalless draw in the opening round of the 2006 World Cup against Angola.
Worn by: Omar Bravo, Jesus Arellano.

HOME 2007–08

Design: adidas

Adidas returned to the FMF in 2007, bringing with them a contemporary, multi-panelled strip. Graceful red curves adorned each side of the shirt accompanied by tonal breathable fabric. The adidas logo was placed centrally, allowing space for a squad number on the right.

Worn in: The 2–1 defeat by the US in the Gold Cup final. Also, in the 6-0 win over Paraguay in the 2007 Copa America quarter-finals.
Worn by: Fausto Pinto, Juan Carlos Cacho.

AWAY 2007–08

Design: adidas

As had become the norm in recent years, the away strip replicated the design of the home kit but in a reversed colour combination. Like the home outfit, the shirt featured a minimalist neck design including a small insert panel in the centre. The adidas logo on the shorts was moved to the reverse.

Worn in: The 1–0 triumph over Guadeloupe in the semi-finals of the 2007 Gold Cup.
Worn by: Pavel Pardo, Jared Borguetti.

HOME 2008–10

Design: adidas

One of the more unusual of adidas' kit experiments over the years were the three-quarter length sleeved shirts they supplied to several of their roster in 2008. The Mexico version was superb, thanks to the inclusion of a large shadow Aztec-style pattern. Sven-Göran Eriksson took over as manager in 2008.

Worn in: The resounding 5-0 win over the US in the 2009 Gold Cup final.
Worn by: Guillermo Franco, Miguel Sabah.

AWAY 2008–10

Design: adidas

A white reversal of the home kit became El Tri's next change kit. In traditional Mexico away style, green shorts and white socks completed the outfit which, of course, featured the unorthodox three-quarter length sleeves that were included on the home shirt. Javier Aguirre was appointed manager in 2009.

Worn in: A 4-0 win over Haiti in the quarter-finals of the 2009 Gold Cup.
Worn by: Alberto Medina, Ismael Rodríguez.

HOME 2010–11

Design: adidas

Adidas began producing their match shirts in two different fit styles in 2010: Techfit, a tight fitting style that featured compression 'power web' or a more relaxed Formotion construction. Both were available on Mexico's World Cup home shirt that also featured predominantly red applications and reversed stitching.

Worn in: The 2-0 win over France in the first round of the 2010 World Cup.
Worn by: Cuauhtémoc Blanco, Pablo Barrera.

AWAY 2010–11

Design: adidas

Mexico's first ever black kit was unveiled in preparation for the World Cup. The design, including the repeated shadow pattern, replicated that of the home strip. The shirt was available to players in either Techfit or Formotion fitting styles.

Worn in: The opening game of the 2010 World Cup – a 1–1 draw against hosts South Africa.
Worn by: Carlos Salcido, Ricardo Osorio.

THIRD 2010–12

Design: adidas

A special white third kit was produced by adidas in 2010 to commemorate Mexico's bicentenary of their independence from Spanish rule. The strip followed the design of the home and away strip in a Formotion style, with the addition of a special patch on the right sleeve.

Worn in: A 2–1 friendly defeat by Ecuador in 2010.
Worn by: Elias Hernández, Leobardo Lopez.

AWAY 2011–12

Design: adidas

The team's popular away black strip was updated in time for 2011. The shirt in essence was a close relative of its predecessor but with opulent gold applications and piping replacing the green trim of the 2010–11 kit.

Worn in: The incredible 4-2 win for José Manuel de la Torre's team over the United States to clinch the 2011 Gold Cup.
Worn by: Pablo Barrera, Israel Castro.

2011, 2013 CONCACAF GOLD CUP
2011 COPA AMERICA / 2013 FIFA CONFDERATIONS CUP

HOME 2011-13

Design: adidas

After just one season a new design was produced in time for the 2011 Gold Cup. A solid enough, if unremarkable kit, the shirt featured curved gold piping on each sleeve and top of the shorts along with a minimalist crew-neck design with red central panel. Incredibly the kit lasted for four major tournaments.

Worn in: A 5–0 win over El Salvador in the first round of the 2011 Gold Cup.
Worn by: Aldo de Nigris, Israel Castro.

2013 FIFA CONFDERATIONS CUP
2013 CONCACAF GOLD CUP

AWAY 2012-14

Design: adidas

White replaced black as the nation's primary change colour in 2012 with a design that replicated the previous year's home kit but in a dazzling white and red combination, accentuated with just a hint of gold.

Worn in: A 2–1 win over Japan, Mexico's only win of the 2013 Confederations Cup.
Worn by: Gerardo Torrado, Jesús Zavala.

2014 FIFA WORLD CUP

HOME 2014

Design: adidas

A dynamic 'lightning bolt' chest design in red and white dominated Mexico's shirt for the 2014 World Cup. Two tones of green, white shoulder bands and a thin shadow design adorned the lightweight adizero fabric shirt.

Worn in: A 3–1 victory over Croatia in the 2014 World Cup where it was worn with the away kit's shorts and socks, creating an unsettling combination.
Worn by: Rafael Márquez, Paul Aguilar.

2014 FIFA WORLD CUP

AWAY 2014-16

Design: adidas

'Show your colours, or fade away' screamed the marketing material to promote this bright red Mexico away kit. The Climacool shirt continued the zig-zag 'power pattern' theme established on the home jersey but in a new design. A thin strip of green, white and red ran across the back of the shirt.

Worn in: A 0–0 draw with Brazil in the group stages of the 2014 World Cup.
Worn by: Héctor Moreno, Francisco Rodriguez.

2015 COPA AMERICA / 2015 CONCACAF GOLD CUP

★

HOME 2015-16

Design: adidas

One of the most controversial of all Mexican home strips (promoted by a 'There will be haters' marketing campaign) was this black and lime green home Climacool fabric outfit. The traditional red, white and green colour scheme was only featured on the hem and on the socks.

Worn in: Mexico's convincing 3–1 win over Jamaica in the final of the 2015 Gold Cup.
Worn by: Jesús Corona, Oribe Peralta.

2015 COPA AMERICA / 2015, 2017 CONCACAF GOLD CUP
2016 COPA AMERICA / 2017 FIFA CONFEDERATIONS CUP

AWAY 2015-17

Design: adidas

The side's next away kit, launched in readiness for the 2015 Copa America (and also worn in the 2016 tournament), complemented the home design perfectly. The strip featured a button-up grandad collar and black and lime green trim. The national flag was hinted at in the hem and sock design.

Worn in: The devastating 7–0 loss to Chile in the quarter-finals of the 2016 Copa America.
Worn by: Andrés Guardado, Héctor Herrera.

2016 COPA AMERICA / 2017 FIFA CONFEDERATIONS CUP
2017 CONCACAF GOLD CUP

HOME 2016-17

Design: adidas

Following the black home experiment the Mexican Football Federation reverted to tradition with a green, white and red home kit. A simple strip that benefited from its lack of over design with just the three-stripe trim placed on each side of the shirt and a restrained shadow stripe providing visual focus.

Worn in: The 4–1 defeat by Germany in the semi-finals of the 2017 Confederations Cup.
Worn by: Javier Hernández, Giovani dos Santos.

2018 FIFA WORLD CUP

HOME 2017-18

Design: adidas

Adidas went for a much darker green again for Mexico's next World Cup kit. The design followed the ethos adidas adopted for the tournament, namely seeking inspiration from past, iconic strips. In Mexico's case it was the early '90s 'adidas equipment' shirts that provided a reference point, with thin lines in a lighter green creating the side colour panels.

Worn in: A 2017 3–3 friendly draw vs Belgium.
Worn by: Carlos Vela, Carlos Salcedo.

1986 FIFA WORLD CUP

A glorious tournament for kits – here the USSR's Oleg Blokhin in the nation's adidas Climalite away kit takes on Paul James of Canada (minus one boot) in their unmistakable adidas home strip.

1986 FIFA WORLD CUP

Shadow striped adidas templates were massively popular in the finals. This was eveident in the game between Iraq and Belgium that saw both sides in their home strips.

NETHERLANDS

One of the most impressive sights is the wave of orange that reaches around the stadium whenever the Netherlands play an international fixture.

Very few nations own a colour in quite the same way as the Netherlands own orange. The reason for the colour choice is simple. Though it does not feature in the country's flag (which is also true for Italy), orange is the colour of the Dutch Royal Family, who descend from the House of Orange, and is beloved throughout the whole country.

For the nation's first ever match in 1905, though, the team played Belgium sporting a white shirt with a diagonal sash depicting the colours of the flag. It was a design that was to be resurrected by Nike in 2006 and created a new theme for away strips, which continued for several years and provided a refreshing break from plain white reversals of the home kit that had been favoured previously.

Nike have kitted out the Dutch since 1996, taking over from Lotto. Prior to that, adidas were technical partners and for many the golden era of the Netherlands' football history – the Total Football philosophy of the '70s – is forever associated with adidas.

It is from this period that one of the most best-known pieces of football kit lore emerges. Namely, Johan Cruyff's rebellious removal of one of adidas' three stripes on his shirt so as to remain loyal to his personal sponsor, Puma – arch rivals, of course!

The Netherlands line up during the 1974 World Cup sporting their beautiful adidas kit of the time – including Cruyff's 'altered' version.

HOME 1966–70

Design: Umbro

The Netherlands' last appearance in a World Cup had been in 1938 so by the '60s the team had been in the doldrums for some time. In 1966 Georg Keßler's side were wearing a simple long sleeved crew-neck jersey that replaced an earlier collared shirt. Also worn with the white away shorts.

Worn in: A 4–0 win over Luxembourg in a 1969 qualifier for the 1970 World Cup.
Worn by: Theo Pahlplatz, Dick van Dijk.

AWAY 1966–70

Design: Umbro

If the home kit was of its time – simple and functional – the away kit did feature a nice touch in the shape of the coloured turnover of the socks; designed to replicate the Dutch flag (albeit with orange replacing the red!) The '60s shirt was adorned with a blue and gold Royal Dutch Football Association heraldic crest.

Worn in: The unsuccessful 1970 World Cup qualifying campaign.
Worn by: Wim Suurbier, Henk Groot.

HOME 1970–74

Design: Umbro

With the Netherlands again missing out on a World Cup the side regrouped and, thanks to the introduction of a new, large, monochromatic crest, began to sport a strip that was edging closer to the classic outfit of the '70s.

Worn in: Two 1973 high-scoring wins over Iceland, 5–0 and 8–1, part of the impressive Dutch 1974 World Cup qualifying campaign.
Worn by: Dick Schneider, Wim Van Hanegem.

AWAY 1970–74

Design: Umbro

An all-white change version of the new strip was also worn which sadly ditched the neat coloured socks turnover. František Fadrhonc took over the management of the Netherlands in 1970 and much to the joy of the nation led his team to qualification for the 1974 World Cup.

Worn in: A 2–1 triumph in Norway in a 1974 World Cup qualifier (1973).
Worn by: Gerrit Muhren, Barry Hulshoff.

HOME 1974–75

Design: adidas

Following their superb World Cup qualifying campaign and with their 'Total Football' philosophy gathering pace, a new kit supplier, adidas, took on the Dutch contract and dressed the side in a jersey that featured a self-coloured wrapover crew neck and cuffs, and three-stripe trim. Also worn with the away kit's white shorts.

Worn in: A 0–0 draw with Sweden in the 1974 World Cup.
Worn by: Johan Cruyff, Piet Keizer.

HOME 1974–75

Design: adidas

A v-neck featured on the Netherlands short sleeved version of their first adidas kit. These strips gained notoriety when Johan Cruyff, who enjoyed a personal sponsorship with Puma, removed one of the trademark three stripes in order to stay loyal to Puma.

Worn in: The 1974 World Cup Final (with white shorts) that sadly ended in a 2–1 defeat against West Germany.
Worn by: Arie Haan, Ruud Krol.

AWAY 1974–75

Design: adidas

The long sleeved version of the strips reflected the design of the home. Interestingly the crew neck wrapped in the opposite direction of most similar designs since. As with all Netherlands kits all elements of the outfits were able to mix and match perfectly.

Worn in: The unforgettable 2–0 triumph over current World Champions Brazil (the Dutch wore orange socks in this game).
Worn by: Wim Rijsbergen, Rinus Israel.

AWAY 1974–75

Design: adidas

The last of the outfits that accompanied Rinus Michels' revolutionary Dutch side unsurprisingly mirrored the home design but wasn't actually worn in the tournament. These (unbranded) adidas kits have entered football iconography as symbolic of this magnificent Netherlands team, although it is unclear if this short sleeved away strip was ever worn.

HOME 1975–77

Design: adidas

It's unclear why the KNVB crest switched to the other side of the chest on the next batch of strips (although some 1975 outings saw the badge on the traditional left). The kit remained the same except that the crew neck and cuffs were now black. Occasionally the away white shorts were favoured over the black pairs.

Worn in: The astonishing 5–0 demolition of Belgium in the Euro 76 qualifiers.
Worn by: Wim Suurbier, Adri van Kraay.

AWAY 1975–77

Design: adidas

The design changes on the home kit were also rolled out onto the away, meaning that now the shirt featured black neck and cuffs and the badge on the right hand side. Curiously, the shirts were still unbranded – perhaps the badge was moved to cover the adidas trefoil logo? It is uncertain whether this strip was actually ever required on the field of play.

HOME 1976

Design: adidas

A one-off short sleeved shirt was worn for the 1976 European Championship. The self coloured crew-necked shirt continued the 'back to front' placement of the team badge. Curiously it also featured an additional crest on the shorts.

Worn in: A 3–1 defeat by Czechoslovakia in the semi-finals of Euro 76. Also worn in the 3–2 win over Yugoslavia in the third place match.
Worn by: Johan Neeskens, Rob Rensenbrink.

HOME 1978

Design: adidas

As the side prepared for the 1978 World Cup in Argentina this short-lived long sleeved shirt made a handful of appearances. It was the first Dutch shirt since the early '60s to feature a collar and was paired with white shorts with black trim.

Worn in: A 1–0 friendly win over Austria.
Worn by: Willy van der Kerkhof, Arie Haan.

HOME 1978–81

Design: adidas

White shorts were now preferred with the home kit by the time the World Cup arrived (although the change orange pairs were worn in two games during the group stages and a black pair in 1979). The shirt was the classic adidas 'Worldcup Dress' template complete with its logo positioned high on the chest.

Worn in: The disappointing 3–1 defeat against Argentina in the 1978 World Cup Final.
Worn by: Johnny Rep, Wim Jansen.

AWAY 1978–81

Design: adidas

Orange replaced black to great effect on the strip unveiled for the World Cup. The adidas logo and team crest remained in black (although, orange variants were worn later in its lifespan). Paired with orange shorts that allowed the team to switch home and away elements with ease.

Worn in: An impressive 2–1 win over Italy in the second group stage that sent Oranje through to the final.
Worn by: René van de Kerkhof, Ruud Krol.

HOME 1979–81

Design: adidas

A simple short sleeved version of the Worldcup Dress design began to be worn more frequently from 1979. The cuffless shirt featured the same neck and 'unbalanced' positioning of the adidas logo and KNVB crest as the home.

Worn in: A 1–0 win over Greece in the Netherlands' opening game of Euro 80 – it was to prove a disappointing tournament.
Worn by: Kees Kist, Martien Vreijsen.

AWAY 1979–83

Design: adidas

A straightforward white and orange short sleeved version of the next adidas kit was launched for Euro 80, where it made one appearance. Due to a sponsorship row all manufacturers' logos were blocked out during the tournament. Long sleeved versions of this shirt were worn into early 1983.

Worn in: A 1–1 draw with Czechoslovakia in Euro 80 (worn with white shorts).
Worn by: Michel van de Korput, Dick Nanninga

AWAY 1980

Design: adidas

Curiously the basic design available as an away choice from 1975–77 was resurrected for one game against the French in 1980. The shirt now featured the adidas trefoil logo that followed the placement on its other outfits at the time. Quite why the standard away shirt was not worn is a mystery.

Worn in: A 0–0 draw with France.
Worn by: Frans Thijssen, Pierre Vermeulen.

HOME 1981

Design: adidas

Worn in both long and short sleeved versions the new, rather short lived, Dutch kit reintroduced a collar and incorporated raglan sleeves and black piping that extended down each side of the shirt.

Worn in: A 1–0 win over France in a 1981 qualifying match for the 1982 World Cup.
Worn by: Arnold Muhren, Epo Ophof.

HOME 1981–84

Design: adidas

The magnificent 'Santiago' adidas template made its debut in Dutch colours in late 1981 and was designed to provide a long sleeved pinstripe complement to the 'La Paz' short sleeved template. A self-coloured collar and black v-insert helped cement this design as a real international classic.

Worn in: A superb 6–0 thrashing of Denmark in March 1984 – a fine farewell to this kit.
Worn by: Peter Houtman, André Hoekstra.

HOME 1981–83

Design: adidas

That most '80s of all football apparel decoration – the pinstripes – arrived in the Netherlands in 1981. The short sleeved shirt (using adidas' 'La Paz' template) didn't make its full debut until 1982 but was a real design stalwart with its simple v-neck and cuffs.

Worn in: A 1983 3–0 win over Iceland in a Euro 84 qualifier.
Worn by: Erwin Koeman, Ronald Koeman.

AWAY 1981–83

Design: adidas

The away version of the 'Santiago' template was every bit as good as the home, with the adidas trefoil logo rendered in black (nearly always the case when placed on white fabric) standing out well. It's just a pity that, as far records show, it was never worn by the first team.

AWAY 1981–84

Design: adidas

The white version of the 'La Paz' strip featured orange v-neck and cuffs and orange pinstripes with the shorts and socks, as usual, designed to mix and match with the home kit. As with so many Dutch kits of the era, it is unclear whether this was ever worn in action. After the impressive 1978 World Cup, the side, now managed by Kees Rijvers, fell into some decline, failing to qualify for the 1982 World Cup.

THIRD 1983

Design: adidas

Although the white version of the long sleeved, pinstriped 'Santiago' shirt was never called into active service, this sublime two-tone blue did get worn, in a single game against Belgium. It was the first time a colour other than orange, white or black had played such a major role in a Dutch kit for many years.

Worn in: A friendly 1–1 draw with Belgium.
Worn by: Peter Boeve, Michel Valke.

HOME 1984–87

Design: adidas

As the new year dawned, it really felt like a fresh start in the Netherlands kitbag with the unveiling of new designs that focused solely on orange and white. The cuffless shirt with wrapover v-neck and horizontal shadow stripes became known as the 'Aberdeen' template.

Worn in: The heartbreaking 2–1 win vs Belgium in a 1985 World Cup play-off that was just not good enough to send the Dutch to Mexico.
Worn by: Frank Rijkaard, Rob de Wit.

AWAY 1984–87

Design: adidas

After the relative lows of the early '80s, the Netherlands side, under returning manager Rinus Michels, were hoping for a change of fortune in their smart new outfits. The 'Aberdeen' template was another adidas classic that found its way into many international dressing rooms in the mid-'80s.

Worn in: The 1–0 defeat by Belgium in the first leg of the World Cup qualifier play-off (1985).
Worn by: Bennie Wijnstekers, Wim Kieft.

HOME 1987–89

Design: adidas

Early into 1987 the Oranje switched to a new adidas design that at first glance was remarkably similar to the previous. The difference came from the introduction of a diagonal 'brickwork' shadow pattern. Not worn in Euro 88 but reinstated after the tournament.

Worn in: Two superb wins over Cyprus in the Euro 88 qualifiers, 8–0 and 4–0 (1987).
Worn by: Sonny Silooy, Wilbert Suvrijn.

1988 UEFA EUROPEAN CHAMPIONSHIP

AWAY 1987–89

Design: adidas

It's interesting to note that by the late '80s it was no longer a given that the away strip for a side would follow the design of the home. Such was the case with the Netherlands in 1987 where an alternative adidas design, featuring octagonal block shadow prints, was opted for. It was the official away kit for Euro 88 but not needed in the tournament.

Worn in: A vital 2–1 win against Wales in 1989.
Worn by: Graeme Rutjes, Jan Wouters.

1988 UEFA EUROPEAN CHAMPIONSHIP

HOME 1988

Design: adidas

A first major tournament qualification for eight years was clearly worth celebrating and adidas did just that with the introduction of one of the most iconic football shirts ever. With its all-over geometric print it was outrageous for the time but it is now regarded as a classic.

Worn in: The incredible Euro 88 tournament – culminating in an all-orange 2–0 victory over the USSR in the final!
Worn by: Ruud Gullit, Marco van Basten.

THIRD 1988–89

Design: adidas

This beautiful sky blue version of the much revered 1988 adidas design seems to have been another Dutch kit destined never to have been worn. In all likelihood this was a third strip design to accompany the home and away outfits first launched in early 1987.

HOME 1989

Design: adidas

A temporary new crest was included on this plain and simple Netherlands kit in 1989 to mark the centenary of the Royal Dutch Football Association. Two versions of the shirt seem to exist: one with a wrapover v-neck as illustrated here and a replica version with a collar.

Worn in: The Italia 90 qualifying campaign, including a great 3–0 win over Finland.
Worn by: Johnny van't Schip, Berry van Aerle.

1990 FIFA WORLD CUP

HOME 1989–90

Design: adidas

This next Netherlands strip featured in the 1990 World Cup and was the last to be produced by adidas. It took a sensible and sober approach to design with a neat wrapover neck and trim collar adorning the plain raglan sleeved jersey. The shorts and socks remained identical to those of the previous outfit.

Worn in: A 2–1 defeat against West Germany in the knockout stage of Italia 90.
Worn by: Adri van Tiggelen, Jan Wouters.

1990 FIFA WORLD CUP

AWAY 1989–90

Design: adidas

First worn in 1990, adidas' away kit farewell played it safe and went for a straightforward reversal of the home kit. The team, now managed by Leo Beenhakker, entered the tournament with optimism but failed to make an impact.

Worn in: A 1–1 draw with Egypt in the World Cup group stages.
Worn by: Graeme Rutjes, Gerald Vanenburg.

HOME 1991–93

Design: Lotto

After almost 20 years with adidas, the Netherlands signed a new apparel deal with Italian sportswear firm Lotto in 1991. Lotto brought a fresh look to the richer orange coloured uniform with the introduction of a red and royal blue trim (replicating the Dutch flag) and an abstract, 'painterly' shadow pattern.

Worn in: The 5–4 defeat on penalties to Denmark in the semi-final of Euro 92.
Worn by: Bryan Roy.

AWAY 1991–93

Design: Lotto

Lotto went for the tried and tested reversal of the home kit for their first change outfit for the Oranje. The only difference coming with the choice of fabric; in this case they opted for a repeat shadow pattern of the Lotto logo in preference to the abstract design on the home.

Worn in: A 2–1 defeat against Norway in a 1992 qualifier for the 1994 World Cup.
Worn by: Rob Witschge.

THIRD 1991–93

Design: Lotto

With the added presence of blue on the Lotto kits it was no surprise that a third outfit, comprising that colour, was unveiled. The design was identical to the home strip, including the abstract shadow pattern. Evidence suggests, though, that the design was never actually required by the first team.

HOME 1994–96

Design: Lotto

It was clear that a new kit philosophy of just minor changes from strip to strip was employed during the early '90s as the next Dutch kit varied little from the previous design; the only difference coming from the shadow print of the fabric. In this case a repeat pattern of the KNVB crest was incorporated.

Worn in: A 2–0 win over a plucky Republic of Ireland side in the second round of USA 94.
Worn by: Wim Jonk, Frank de Boer.

AWAY 1994–96

Design: Lotto

Another straightforward mirroring of the home design but in reversed colours was sported as Dick Advocaat's team prepared for the 1994 World Cup in the USA.

Worn in: The thrilling 3–2 defeat by Brazil in the quarter-finals of the 1994 World Cup. Also worn in the 1995 2–0 win over the Republic of Ireland in a qualifying play-off for Euro 96.
Worn by: Stan Valckx, Danny Blind.

HOME 1996

Design: Lotto

One of the more adventurous kits in recent years was this last Dutch hurrah from Lotto that was worn in Euro 96. The shirt was the same as the previous, except it now also included a shadow print of Dutch players celebrating a goal, while actually wearing the basic design of this shirt! Confused?

Worn in: The 5–4 defeat on penalties to France that put the Dutch out of the tournament.
Worn by: Dennis Bergkamp, Jordi Cruyff.

AWAY 1996

Design: Lotto

Lotto's last away kit for the Netherlands brought a bit of '90s flair to the previously plain white shirt by adding a graduated orange band across the chest and on each sleeve – a clever way to reinforce the sense of 'orange' on the change outfit.

Worn by: A 2–0 win over Switzerland in the group stages of Euro 96 – the only time this kit was worn.
Worn by: Edgar Davids, Clarence Seedorf.

HOME 1996–97

Design: Nike

Given that Nike's main European office is in Holland it was only fitting they took over the Dutch contract as the team prepared for the 1998 World Cup qualifiers. The flourishes of the Lotto strips were gone and in their place came this smart but simple strip. The kit also saw the launch of a new team badge

Worn by: A crushing 7–1 demolition of Wales en route to France 1998.
Worn by: Frank de Boer, Patrick Kluivert.

AWAY 1996-97

Design: Nike

With an agenda to refresh the Dutch wardrobe, Nike introduced a blue version of the home kit as their first change outfit to form a strikingly fresh colour combination. Blue had formed an integral part of early Dutch kits. Socks and shorts reflected the functional simplicity of the home strips.

Worn in: A superb 3–0 win away at Belgium in the 1998 World Cup qualifying campaign.
Worn by: Wim Jonk, Aron Winter.

THIRD 1996-97

Design: Nike

A first for the Netherlands – an official third kit! Again the design reflected that of both of their other kits of the time, including tidy collar and side panels in breathable fabric. Interestingly, Nike plumped for blue to trim the white shirt rather than the more predictable orange.

Worn in: A 2–1 defeat against France in a 1997 friendly.
Worn by: Arthur Numan, Phillip Cocu.

1998 FIFA WORLD CUP

HOME 1998-99

Design: Nike

Nike really hit its stride with this set of Dutch strips and took the opportunity to reintroduce black to the side's palette – the first time it had been included in a Netherlands shirt since 1988. Angled stripes gave a menacing look to the shirt and accompanied Guus Hiddink's side in a tremendous World Cup tournament.

Worn in: The disappointing 4–2 defeat on penalties to Brazil in the France 98 semi-final.
Worn by: Marc van Hintum, Jeffrey Talan.

1998 FIFA WORLD CUP

AWAY 1998-99

Design: Nike

Blue was kept on as the Netherlands' change colour in 1998 and again became part of a design that replicated that of the home. The shorts were now also blue. In a strange move the socks were the same basic colour as the home pairs, albeit with new trim.

Worn in: A 0–0 draw with Belgium in the World Cup group stages – oddly the Belgians also wore their away kit.
Worn by: Marc Overmars, Ronald de Boer.

2000 UEFA EUROPEAN CHAMPIONSHIP

HOME 2000-02

Design: Nike

Black played an even more prominent role in the next Netherlands kit that was to feature in Euro 2000 – a tournament which the Dutch were to co-host. A simple v-neck was the only main adornment on a very basic outfit that nevertheless carried some menace.

Worn in: Another European Championship semi-final penalties defeat – this time to Italy who triumphed 3–1.
Worn by: Paul Bosvelt, Bolo Zenden.

2000 UEFA EUROPEAN CHAMPIONSHIP

AWAY 2000-02

Design: Nike

Nike persevered with a blue change kit as Frank Rijkaard's men prepared for the Euro 2000 tournament. The black that had played such a key role in the new home kit was also utilised here, combining with a delicate orange trim to create a stylishly effective outfit. The collar design was standard Nike issue.

Worn in: An impressive group stage 3–0 win over Denmark in Euro 2000.
Worn by: Giovanni van Bronckhorst.

HOME 2002-03

Design: Nike

Worn originally in the side's Euro 2004 qualifiers with black shorts, following three impressive wins where the orange away shorts had been sported, the team switched kits and instead opted for all orange (in a more fluorescent hue) for the rest of this strip's lifespan.

Worn in: A superb 6–1 thrashing of Scotland in the play-offs that sealed Euro 2004 qualification.
Worn by: Wesley Sneijder, Rafael van der Vaart.

AWAY 2002-03

Design: Nike

The team's first black away shirt (that mirrored the dynamic and angular approach of Nike at the time) followed the same fate as the home; it started with its original shorts before changing to a powerful all-black combo. Both sets of Dutch shirts were dual layered – a new innovation intended to regulate moisture loss.

Worn in: A 1–1 friendly draw vs Belgium (2003).
Worn by: Andre Ooijer, Mark van Bommel.

2004 UEFA EUROPEAN CHAMPIONSHIP

HOME 2004-06

Design: Nike

The first fixtures of the year saw a rich new Netherlands kit unveiled that followed Nike's Total 90 range (signified by the huge circle around the squad number on the front of the jersey). The shirt featured a high-placed Nike swoosh and curved white piping. Latterly worn with the away strip's orange shorts.

Worn in: An opening 1-1 draw with Germany in the Euro 2004 group stages.
Worn by: Wilfred Bouma, Ruud van Nistlerooy.

2004 UEFA EUROPEAN CHAMPIONSHIP

AWAY 2004-06

Design: Nike

After the opening game, much of Euro 2004 saw Dick Advocaat's Dutch team perform an about-face again and opt for either all-orange or all-white kits, mixing and matching between the two outfits. The away simply reversed the design of the home.

Worn in: Two crucial games in Euro 2004 – the penalties win over Sweden and the unfortunate 2-1 defeat against Portugal in the semi-final.
Worn by: Pierre van Hooijdonk, Arjen Robben.

THIRD 2004-06

Design: Nike

With no black appearing in either of the team's first two strips, it appears it was all saved up for this fine third kit (that again replicated the Total 90 template). Its introduction arguably creates one of the Netherlands' greatest ever sets of strips. Just a shame this was never worn in action! All three designs featured a variation of the Nike swoosh placed enlarged and asymmetrically on the left sleeve.

SPECIAL 2005

Design: Nike

For a series of friendlies in 2005 Nike launched a new campaign to raise awareness of and make a stand against the growing issue of racism in football. It issued a special one-off design for several teams in its roster that featured a bold and symbolic black and white halved shirt.

Worn in: A 0-0 draw with England in February 2005.
Worn by: Denny Landzaat, Romeo Castelen.

HOME 2006-08

Design: Nike

2006 saw a complete revamp of the traditional Dutch strip. Gone was the sole reliance on orange and white, and blue was re-introduced as a bold new sock colour to create a stunning ensemble – complete with an old-fashioned collar. The KNVB crest was now housed within an additional shield similar to that worn in 1938.

Worn in: An impressive 4-1 win over Russia in a 2007 friendly.
Worn by: Dirk Kuyt, Robin van Persie.

2006 FIFA WORLD CUP

AWAY 2006-07

Design: Nike

Those Oranje fans with a keen interest in history would have spotted immediately the inspiration behind Nike's next change kit. With its diagonal representation of the Dutch flag on a simple white shirt it was a tribute to the first ever Netherlands kit, worn in 1905 vs Belgium.

Worn in: An ill-tempered 1-0 defeat by Portugal in the second round of the 2006 World Cup – a match later known as 'The battle for Nürnberg'.
Worn by: Jan Vennegoor of Hesselink.

2006 FIFA WORLD CUP

HOME 2006

Design: Nike

As with the previous two home kits, Marco van Basten's Netherlands decided to go all-orange for the tournament. As the away outfit didn't feature any orange, a brand new pair of shorts and socks in the traditional Dutch colour was worn. After the World Cup the side reverted to the orange/white/blue of the main 2006 kit.

Worn in: Wins over Serbia & Montenegro (1-0) and Côte d'Ivoire (2-1) in the World Cup.
Worn by: Johnny Heitinga, Joris Mathijsen.

2008 UEFA EUROPEAN CHAMPIONSHIP

HOME 2008-09

Design: Nike

Another fascinating and rich design emerged from the Nike creative studio in the shape of this kit. It retained the blue socks theme from the previous home outfit and incorporated the Dutch flag within a neat, angular wrapover v-neck construction. Orange change shorts and socks were also worn when a clash occurred.

Worn in: Superb wins over Italy (3-0) and France (4-1) in the group stages of Euro 2008.
Worn by: Nigel De Jong, Orlando Engelaar.

AWAY 2007–09

Design: Nike

Blue became the first choice change colour for the World Cup and it was first worn in the last game of 2007, although sadly this fine outfit was not required in the tournament. The Dutch flag colours stretched across the chest and this exquisite design was topped off with royal blue shorts and white socks. A small flag appeared above the angular crest design.

Worn in: A 3–0 friendly win over Croatia (1998).
Worn by: Ryan Babel, Klaas Jan Huntelaar.

HOME 2010–11

Design: Nike

Experimentations with the colours of the national flag were abandoned in 2010 with the launch of a new strip that proudly reinstated black as a key participant in the team's visual identity. A flash of white featured on each side

Worn in: An all-orange 1–0 defeat against Spain in the 2010 World Cup Final. Also worn in the Netherlands' record victory: 11–0 vs San Marino in September 2011.
Worn by: Gregory Van Der Wiel, Eljero Elia.

AWAY 2010–11

Design: Nike

This crisp change kit again sought inspiration from early Netherlands strips and was crafted from the established, away colour theme of white, blue and red. Dynamic and menacing chevrons framed the logos. All Nike jerseys from 2010 were produced entirely from recycled polyester. Also worn with white shorts.

Worn in: The good 2–1 win over Cameroon in the 2010 World Cup group stage.
Worn by: Khalid Boulahrouz, Ron Vlaar.

HOME 2012–13

Design: Nike

With inspiration apparently taken again from that first Netherlands jersey, this design plumped for a simple single colour approach from the off. Laser-cut ventilation holes on the side of the shirt aimed to help keep players cool. Also worn with the away black shorts.

Worn in: A disappointing Euro 2012 tournament including group stage defeats to Denmark (1–0) and Germany (2–1).
Worn by: Jetro Willems, Ibrahim Afellay.

AWAY 2012

Design: Nike

Surprisingly debuted in a friendly match against England in February 2012, this wonderful all-black outfit fitted perfectly into the Dutch kit canon. A stylish and arrogantly placed single flash of orange housed the Nike logo on the right-hand side. Like the equivalent home, the recycling credentials of this kit were emphasised in the strip's marketing and promotion.

Worn in: A 2–1 defeat by Portugal in Euro 2012.
Worn by: Erik Pieters, Urby Emanuelson.

AWAY 2013

Design: Nike

After just one year the black change strip was replaced by a new ensemble that mirrored the design of the home in white, red and blue to create a memorable and brave design. Each kit was made from recycling approximately 13 plastic bottles and featured the ventilation holes common on all Nike designs of the time.

Worn in: A 1–1 draw with Italy on the kit's first outing in February 2013.
Worn by: Kevin Strootman, Adam Maher.

HOME 2014–15

Design: Nike

Worn for the first time in March 2014 this kit returned to a pure and classic orange and white aesthetic. It featured an elegant retro-style crest to commemorate the 125th anniversary of the KNVB. The inside of the shirt's cuffs were white and could be folded back to reveal the inner colour if desired.

Worn in: The devastating penalties defeat by Argentina in the 2014 World Cup semi-final.
Worn by: Georginio Wijnaldum, Daley Blind.

AWAY 2014

Design: Nike

Louis van Gaal's fine Dutch side sported this stunning and sophisticated blue change strip in the Brazil 2014 World Cup. The fabric incorporated a beautifully constructed array of gradated tonal shapes offset with bright orange applications.

Worn in: The rampant 5–1 thrashing of then World Champions, Spain, in the opening game of the 2014 World Cup.
Worn by: Stefan De Vrij, Bruno Martins Indi.

AWAY 2015

Design: Nike

With a one-year away kit cycle established, a fresh white kit was unveiled to complement the clean stylings of the home. The shirt was economical with its visual flair – this was reserved for the shorts, which featured a wonderful array of thin tonal orange and white bands (hints of these were included on the sides of the shirt).

Worn in: A 2–0 friendly win over Spain.
Worn by: Memphis Depay, Daryl Janmaat.

HOME 2016–17

Design: Nike

Surprisingly, the Netherlands failed to qualify for the 2016 European Championship and therefore the wider audience was robbed of this impressive home strip. Created within Nike's uniform Vapor template, the shirt saw orange and blue solely on a home kit for the first time.

Worn in: The strong 2017 5–0 thrashing of Luxembourg in a 2018 World Cup qualifier.
Worn by: Joël Veltman, Wesley Hoedt.

AWAY 2016–17

Design: Nike

A key feature of the 2016 Vapor strips was the contrasting sock colour in comparison to the shirts and shorts. This created a visual 'flicker' effect on the pitch that helped players identify their teammates. This all-blue strip was a suitable partner for its home equivalent.

Worn in: A 2–1 win over Poland in 2016.
Worn by: Quincy Promes, Vincent Janssen.

An ecstatic Robin van Persie celebrates scoring against the Ivory Coast in the 2006 World Cup while sporting the all-orange version of the classic 2006–08 Nike home kit.

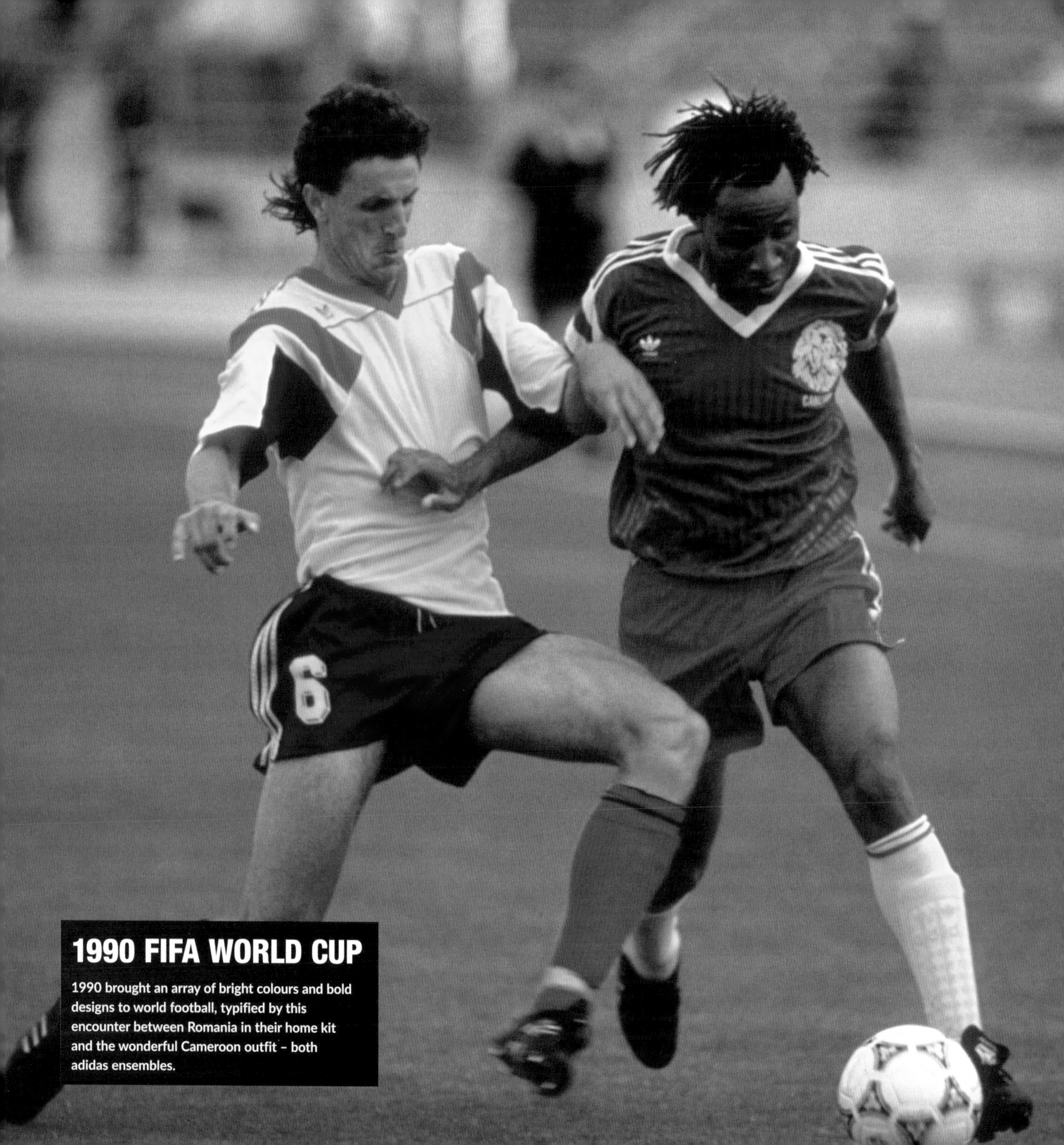

1990 FIFA WORLD CUP

1990 brought an array of bright colours and bold designs to world football, typified by this encounter between Romania in their home kit and the wonderful Cameroon outfit – both adidas ensembles.

1990 FIFA WORLD CUP

Colombia's Carlos Estrada clashes with Yugoslavia's Vujadin Stanojkovic in their Group D match. Both teams sported their adidas away kits.

NORTHERN IRELAND

Until 1931, the established colour of the Northern Ireland football team was not the familiar green that supporters know today, but blue.

The official reason for the conversion to green was apparently to avoid the constant colour clashes with Scotland who, of course, play in navy. But there may have been more complex, political reasons behind the switch, involving cross-border rivalry with the Free State of Ireland (later to be renamed the Republic of Ireland).

Whatever the reason, green has been the colour of the side ever since, although blue makes frequent reappearances in the Northern Ireland kit cupboard. Generally it is used as an away colour, but for a short period during the mid-'90s it was an integral part of the home kit, giving the outfit its own unique feel in comparison to the similarly clad Republic.

The recent kit history of the team has been fairly consistent, with remarkably few different strips worn by the side. In the country's halcyon days of the '80s, adidas decked the team out in a series of elegant strips – green (for home) and white (away). In fact, away kits played a large part in the side's plucky performances in both the 1982 and 1986 World Cup finals, including the superb win over hosts Spain in 1982.

Umbro took over the kit contract in 1990 and were followed by Asics and later Olympic Sport before Umbro returned in 2004 with a series of classy outfits, including a memorable lace-up, collared, anniversary shirt in olive green with a heritage harp badge.

In 2012, adidas signed again with the Irish Football Association, and since then have dressed the team in a series of strong designs that have often looked back to the glory days of the early '80s for their inspiration.

SPECIAL THANKS TO LINDEN MACK

Northern Ireland line up in their adidas away kit before the glorious 1–0 win over hosts Spain in the 1982 World Cup finals.

HOME 1966-67

Design: Umbro

As with all the home international sides, the Irish entered the second half of the '60s in a *de rigueur* Umbro Aztec shirt, familiar of for its crew-necked long sleeve design. The team crest at this time appeared on a large white patch.

Worn in: The 1967 1–0 win over Scotland in a Euro 68 qualifier – a game remembered today as 'The George Best Match' thanks to his superlative performance on the day.
Worn by: Walter Bruce

AWAY 1966-74

Design: Umbro

A straightforward reversal of the home shirt acted as Bertie Peacock's team's change strip. However, due to the relative lack of teams who play in green (and far fewer fixtures than are played today) it is unlikely the strip ever saw competitive duty during its long lifespan. The side failed to qualify for the 1970 and 1974 World Cups despite some undeniable talent in the team.

HOME 1967-74

Design: Umbro

In 1967 the team crest began to be embroidered directly onto the fabric rather than as part of a white patch, adding a much more professional look to the team strip. Green change shorts were also worn with this kit on occasion. Billy Bingham took over as team manager in 1967.

Worn in: A 4–1 victory over Turkey in a 1968 qualifier for the 1970 World Cup.
Worn by: George Best, Derek Dougan.

HOME 1974

Design: Umbro

Wing collars were everywhere in football in the 1970s and they were introduced to the Northern Ireland kit in 1974 while Terry Neill was team manager. The shorts and socks remained simple and classic.

Worn in: An all-green 1–0 win over Scotland in the 1974 Home Internationals.
Worn by: Dave Clements, Tommy Cassidy.

AWAY 1974

Design: Umbro

Naturally the white away kit was also updated and modernised in 1974, but again it is unclear whether it was ever actually required. It's interesting to note that prior to tougher rules on shorts clashes, international away shirts were often worn with the home kit's shorts alongside change socks.

HOME 1975-76

Design: Umbro

With Dave Clements now manager, the Umbro kit was updated with the inclusion of their mid-'70s small diamond logo on the right breast and the shorts. Originally worn with plain green socks, diamond-trimmed pairs were introduced in 1976.

Worn in: A 3–0 win over Norway in a 1975 qualifier for Euro 76.
Worn by: Sammy Morgan, Chris Nicholl.

AWAY 1975-76

Design: Umbro

Long sleeves were the standard choice for football apparel in the late '60s and early '70s with short sleeved options not becoming more common until later in the decade. The next away kit went through the same modifications as the home with the addition of visible Umbro branding throughout.

HOME 1977

Design: Umbro

One of the more eyebrow-raising kits from the era was this final Umbro outfit. The shirt was dominated by a centrally placed oversized Celtic cross crest. An Umbro logo appeared on each lapel and restrained trim featured on the shorts and socks. Alternative black change shorts were also worn with this kit.

Worn in: Defeats to England (2–1) and Scotland (3–0) in this year's Home Internationals.
Worn by: Pat Rice, Allan Hunter.

AWAY 1977

Design: Umbro

These unforgettable 'Celtic cross' kits lasted only until June 1977 and the end of the Umbro deal. The away design mirrored that of the home, although of course in the familiar white. Due to the relative lack of green-clad teams, however, it is unlikely this strip ever saw match action.

HOME 1977–79, 1980–82

Design: adidas

Adidas replaced Umbro as kit suppliers in September 1977. They immediately introduced a silky version of their classic '70s three-stripe, collar shirt. This first version of the adidas home shirt featured a green neck and was reintroduced after a six month break at the end of 1979.

Worn in: The 2–2 draw with Austria in the group stages of the 1982 World Cup.
Worn by: Bryan Hamilton, Martin O'Neill.

AWAY 1977–81

Design: adidas

A standard white reversal of the home strip became adidas' first change kit for Danny Blanchflower's team. The green shorts and white socks were designed to be seamlessly mixed and matched between this and the home outfit.

Worn in: The superb 1–0 win over the Republic of Ireland in the 1979 Euro 80 qualifier clash at Windsor Park.
Worn by: Derek Spence, Sammy Nelson.

HOME 1979–80

Design: adidas

For some reason the team's home shirt was tweaked from late 1979 to Spring 1980 with the green neck of the collar switched to a contrasting white. Other than that, the kit remained the same.

Worn in: 1–0 wins over Scotland and Wales in the 1980 Home Internationals that helped the Irish clinch their first Home International title in 66 years.
Worn by: Jimmy Nicholl, Noel Brotherston.

AWAY 1982–85

Design: adidas

To celebrate Northern Ireland's magnificent qualification for the World Cup finals for the first time since 1958 the away shirt was modernised with the addition of fashionable pinstripes. However, retaining the collar gave the strip a slightly old-fashioned look during the tournament.

Worn in: The epic 1–0 win over hosts Spain in the group stage of the 1982 World Cup.
Worn by: Gerry Armstrong, Norman Whiteside.

HOME 1983–85

Design: adidas

By 1983 the wing-collared Irish home kit was crying out to be revamped. Adidas obliged with this stunningly sophisticated shadow striped jersey. The shorts and socks remained essentially the same as the previous kit's although logo placement did vary.

Worn in: The 2–0 win over Scotland on the way to claiming the last ever Home Internationals trophy.
Worn by: Mal Donaghy, Sammy McIlroy.

AWAY 1985–86

Design: adidas

The pinstriped change shirt went through a minor modification in 1985 with the removal of the collar and the introduction of a much more contemporary v-neck. The new shirt wasn't required during this period, however. The kit coincided with a golden era for Northern Irish football as Billy Bingham's side enjoyed the momentum created during the 1982 World Cup.

HOME 1986–90

Design: adidas

A few months prior to the start of the 1986 World Cup finals – the Irish's second consecutive appearance in the tournament – another alluring home kit was launched. Using a standard template, the fabric featured a diagonal brickwork shadow pattern and multi-trimmed wrapover v-neck.

Worn in: The 3–0 defeat against Brazil in the Irish's last game of the 1986 World Cup.
Worn by: Colin Clarke, Nigel Worthington.

1986 FIFA WORLD CUP

AWAY 1986–90

Design: adidas

Another white reversal of the home kit was selected for the next Northern Ireland away strip. It featured all the trappings of the home – the only difference came from the inclusion of non-contrasting, wrapover v-neck and cuffs. By the end of these kits' long lifespan the side's football fortunes had slumped dramatically.

Worn in: The 2–1 defeat against Spain in the 1986 World Cup (worn with white shorts).
Worn by: Jimmy Quinn, Alan McDonald.

HOME 1990–92

Design: Umbro

After a 13 year gap Umbro returned to Belfast bringing with them an outrageous new style of strip. The fabric comprised a complex geometric array of green and white triangles alongside very fine pinstripes. A little navy blue featured on the trim – the colour's first Irish appearance for many years.

Worn in: A 2–1 win over Austria in a Euro 92 qualifier (1991).
Worn by: Iain Dowie, Kingsley Black.

AWAY 1990–93

Design: Umbro

After years of simple white away kits, Umbro really rocked the boat with the introduction of this stunning navy blue concoction in 1990. The design followed that of the home strip (officially entitled 'St Etienne' in the Umbro catalogue) and was retained for a year longer than the green equivalent to allow Umbro to stagger the issue of new Northern Ireland strips. Despite its extended lifespan the kit was never used by the first team.

HOME 1992–94

Design: Umbro

After the excesses of their previous Northern Ireland strips, Umbro took a more elegant approach with this timeless outfit. The design was a standard Umbro template and featured a delicate white pinstripe, a 1920s style button-up collar and very long, baggy shorts.

Worn in: 2–1 wins over Latvia and Albania during the team's unsuccessful 1994 World Cup qualifying campaign.
Worn by: Gerry Taggart, Steve Morrow.

AWAY 1993–94

Design: Umbro

Navy blue remained for Umbro's second and last (for the time being) change kit. With retro fashions commonplace, Umbro unveiled another traditionally styled shirt – enhanced with a fresh array of white and green stripes and horizontal trim across the shorts' hem.

Worn in: A 1993 3–0 drubbing at the hands of the Republic of Ireland in a 1994 World Cup qualifier.
Worn by: Michael O'Neill, Jim Magilton.

HOME 1994–96

Design: Asics

This attractive new strip adorned the backs of Bryan Hamilton's men courtesy of Japanese sportswear firm Asics. Featuring a minimalist design, the only nod to extravagance was an intricate ribbed collar that featured a navy blue inset and button-up neck. Very restrained trim decorated the shorts and socks.

Worn in: The thrilling 5–3 goalfest against Austria in a 1995 qualifier for Euro 96.
Worn by: Keith Gillespie, Gerry McMahon.

AWAY 1994–96

Design: Asics

For the first time since the 1986–90 strips, Northern Ireland sported a simple reversal of their home colours as Asics clearly decided to tread a familiar path with their first outfits for the side – an attitude that was to change with their next kits! The nation were still struggling to qualify for a major tournament at this time.

Worn in: A 2–0 home friendly defeat against Norway in 1996.
Worn by: Steve Lomas, Nigel Worthington.

HOME 1996–98

Design: Asics

Asics may have played it safe with their first Irish kits but they certainly stuck their necks out with this bold and adventurous design. Navy blue was given much more prominence as part of this extraordinary quartered shirt. The shorts also featured asymmetrical coloured trim, with green on one leg and blue on the other.

Worn in: An impressive 1–1 draw with Germany in a 1996 friendly.
Worn by: Ian Nolan, Neil Lennon.

AWAY 1996–98

Design: Asics

More surprises were in store for Norn Iron fans with the introduction of this red and white quartered strip. Due to the nation's complicated political history, Northern Ireland are one of those relatively few sides whose kit colours do not match those of the flag. This confident outfit clearly attempted to rectify the matter!

Worn in: A 1997 2–0 friendly defeat by Italy.
Worn by: Kevin Horlock, James Quinn.

HOME 1998–99

Design: Olympic Sportswear

With the Asics contract at an end, the IFA switched to Olympic Sportswear and their kit brand 'OS' for their next strips, launched to coincide with the start of the Euro 2000 qualifiers. Navy blue still featured strongly in an outrageous design made up of painterly curved marks on the right-hand side of the shirt.

Worn in: Two poor draws with Moldova during another failed qualifying campaign.
Worn by: Aaron Hughes, Stephen Robinson.

AWAY 1998–99

Design: Olympic Sportswear

Olympic carried on with the red and white theme from the last Asics kit in a design that replicated the unorthodox flair of the home outfit – with the addition of a new silvery-grey hue. Lawrie McMenemy took over the reigns of the Northern Ireland side in 1998 following the team's failure to reach the 1998 World Cup.

Worn in: The 1–0 charity friendly win against the Republic of Ireland in 1999.
Worn by: Barry Hunter, Adrian Coote.

HOME 1999–2001

Design: Patrick

After the abstract expressionist lustre of the previous home outfit, a more familiar, if not slightly pedestrian, two-colour design arrived at Windsor Park courtesy of Patrick (an apt name for an Ireland kit supplier!) A simple collar was introduced along with Patrick's familiar dual-striped trim on the shoulders.

Worn in: A 3–0 win over Iceland in a 2001 qualifier for the 2002 World Cup.
Worn by: Mark Williams, Peter Kennedy.

AWAY 1999–2001

Design: Patrick

Following the red experiments of the previous two away strips it was back to blue for Sammy McIlroy's team with this attractive Patrick change kit. The strip balanced the blue nicely with white and green sleeves and dual stripe trim. The navy shorts were worn with the home shirt on at least one occasion.

Worn in: The friendly 3–0 win over Malta in 2000.
Worn by: Colin Murdock, Danny Sonner.

HOME 2002–04

Design: Patrick

Previewed in December 2001 and worn for the first time the following February, is very contemporary home kit saw the reintroduction of navy as an integral element of the first choice outfit. The colour was included as part of the slick v-neck and the white-trimmed side panels that also continued on the shorts.

Worn in: A dreadful 1–0 defeat against Armenia in the Euro 2004 qualifiers.
Worn by: Andy Smith, David Healy.

AWAY 2002–04

Design: Patrick

After disappearing from the British game for much of the late '80s/early '90s, Patrick kits became more widespread as the 2000s progressed. Their final away strip for the Irish reverted to a smart white and green – the first time in six years that this once familiar change combination had been worn by the team.

Worn in: A 5–0 humiliation at the hands of Spain in a 2002 Belfast friendly.
Worn by: George McCartney, Pat McCourt.

HOME 2004–06

Design: Umbro

After 10 years apart Umbro returned as the national side's kit supplier as the side prepared to kick off their 2006 World Cup qualifying campaign. Their first design was well received and featured dynamic navy and white flashes on each shoulder. The shirt was manufactured using Umbro's 'X-Static' hi-tech fabric.

Worn in: The unforgettable 1–0 win over England in a 2005 qualifier for the World Cup.
Worn by: Jeff Whitley, Paul McVeigh.

AWAY 2004–06

Design: Umbro

The favoured white and green away colourway was retained by Umbro within this classy outfit. The lightweight shirt featured similar stylings to that of the home, including a minimalist neck and sleeve flashes. The shorts and socks were interchangeable with the home pairs. Lawrie Sanchez was appointed manager in 2004.

Worn in: A hard-fought 2004 2–2 draw with Wales in a 2006 World Cup qualifier.
Worn by: Damien Johnson, Tony Capaldi.

SPECIAL 2005

Design: Umbro

To commemorate the 125th anniversary of the Irish Football Association, a unique one-off design was released to co-exist with the existing home and away designs. The special shirt attempted to recreate the team's kit design from its early days including a darker green, 'harp' IFA badge and a lace-up collar.

Worn in: A 4–1 defeat by Germany and a 1–1 draw with Portugal – the strip's only outings.
Worn by: Warren Feeney, Gareth McAuley.

HOME 2006–08

Design: Umbro

A sophisticated asymmetrical new home kit appeared ready for the Euro 2008 qualifiers. Visually sparse, a navy flash on the right shoulder and high-placed Umbro logo (leaving space for a squad number below) were the main focuses. White socks became first choice.

Worn in: The stunning 3–2 win over Spain in a 2006 qualifier for Euro 2008 thanks to a David Healy hat trick.
Worn by: Keith Gillespie, Sammy Clingan.

AWAY 2006–07

Design: Umbro

Blue returned to the Northern Ireland palette in 2006 – although now in a much lighter shade than previously. The cut was similar to the home design and included broad white panels on each sleeve and a modern neck design. The strip was launched at a June 2006 fashion show along with the home kit.

Worn in: A 2006 0–0 draw with Denmark in a Euro 2008 qualifier.
Worn by: Stephen Craigan, Chris Baird.

AWAY 2007–09

Design: Umbro

Like its new home companion, the new away kit featured all the intricate bells and whistles you could expect from an Umbro kit of this time. Shoulder diamond icons were joined by green underarm flashes and dual green and navy pinstripes inspired by Northern Ireland's exciting adventures in the 1982 World Cup.

Worn in: An awful 1–0 defeat in Latvia that helped derail the team's Euro 2008 camapign.
Worn by: Michael Duff, Jonny Evans.

HOME 2008–10

Design: Umbro

Umbro entered a phase of increasingly complex kits as the first decade of the millennium drew to a close. This kit featured curved white seam flashes (trimmed with navy), a fine shadow diagonal pinstripe weave and small diamond icons on each sleeve.

Worn in: An impressive 3–2 triumph over Poland in a 2009 qualifier for the 2010 World Cup.
Worn by: Michael O'Connor, Andy Little.

AWAY 2009–11

Design: Umbro

Although white still formed the core of this strip, it was now complemented with navy rather than white to create an interesting new look for Nigel Worthington's team. Subtle shadow stripes decorated the fabric. The kit's navy shorts were worn with the 2008–10 and the 2010–12 home strips on occasion.

Worn in: A dismal friendly 1–0 defeat against Albania in 2010.
Worn by: Ryan McGivern, Rory Patterson.

HOME 2010–12

Design: Umbro

Umbro's 'Tailored by...' campaign shook up the football kit world with stunning results by eschewing all the superfluous trimmings of its recent designs and reverting to visually simple, classic kit production. A white crew neck was joined by shadow stripes in this wonderful strip.

Worn in: A 1–0 win over Slovenia (2010) and a 4–0 thrashing of the Faroe Islands – the only two Irish victories in this kit.
Worn by: Corry Evans, Grant McCann.

AWAY 2011-12

Design: Umbro

It was a shame that the beauty of the 'Tailored by Umbro' ethos coincided with the end of the company's deal with the IFA. Still, the brand went out with a bang with this arrogant strip, dominated by bold green and navy dual chevrons and gold logo accents. The shorts and socks were also worn with the home kit.

Worn in: The shocking 5–0 defeat by the Republic of Ireland in the 2011 Nations Cup.
Worn by: Johnny Gorman, Adam Thompson.

HOME 2012-13

Design: adidas

The prodigal adidas returned with a strip that brought back fond memories of their first stint with the Northern Ireland side in the 1980s (although of course pinstripes only appeared on their white away kit at that time). A mini white inset neck completed this strong ensemble.

Worn in: A 1–0 win over Russia in a 2013 qualifier for the 2014 World Cup – incredibly the side's only victory in this shirt.
Worn by: Martin Paterson, Craig Cathcart.

AWAY 2012-13

Design: adidas

Black is always a winner with replica shirt wearers and the colour made its first Northern Ireland appearance with this enigmatic strip. Green trim and neck design provided a welcome freshness to the strip. The black colour accurately reflected the mood during a poor period on the pitch for the Irish.

Worn in: A worrying 0–0 draw with minnows Malta in a 2013 friendly.
Worn by: Chris Brunt, Alex Bruce.

HOME 2014

Design: adidas

Adidas took a brave stance with their next Irish home kit with the unveiling of a new dark green shirt accompanied by light green accents and trim. The jersey was adidas' popular Condivo 14 teamwear template and was joined by white shorts, with dark green trim. Also worn with the away kit's green shorts.

Worn in: The important (all-green) 2–0 away win in Greece in a Euro 2016 qualifier.
Worn by: Jamie Ward, Shane Ferguson.

AWAY 2014

Design: adidas

This simple but strong change design reverted to white but paired it with the darker green introduced on its partner home kit. The shirt was formed from adidas' Climacool fabric and featured a basic crew neck, joined by green shoulder flashes in a design reminiscent of some of adidas' late '80s strips.

Worn in: A great 2–1 win over Hungary in a Euro 2016 qualifier.
Worn by: Kyle Lafferty, Niall McGinn.

HOME 2015

Design: adidas

The basic aesthetic of adidas kits at this time continued with the 2015 home strip (the IFA and adidas had now introduced a single year kit cycle). An innovative mesh-like trim adorned the crew neck, cuffs and hem of the emerald green shirt.

Worn in: The wonderful 3–1 win over Greece that marked qualification for Euro 2016 – the nation's first ever European Championship.
Worn by: Danny Lafferty, Steven Davis.

AWAY 2015

Design: adidas

Another courageous change kit design was launched by adidas as Michael O'Neill's side attempted to qualify for Euro 2016. The two tone blue shirt was a beautiful design, trimmed elegantly with the mesh-like white stylings of the home kit and a self-coloured v-neck.

Worn in: A 1–0 friendly defeat against Scotland (who also wore their away kit despite playing at home!)
Worn by: Will Grigg, Oliver Norwood.

2016 UEFA EUROPEAN CHAMPIONSHIP

HOME 2016-17

Design: adidas

With the country's first major tournament for 30 years looming, a new home Climacool kit featuring large quantities of navy thanks to the sleeves and gradated chest band was unveiled. Initially unpopular with supporters thanks to the contrasting sleeves, the design will always be remembered for the return to the big stage.

Worn in: The 2–0 win over the Ukraine in Euro 2017 – the team's sole victory in the tournament.
Worn by: Stuart Dallas, Conor Washington.

2016 UEFA EUROPEAN CHAMPIONSHIP

AWAY 2016-17

Design: adidas

The new white away kit for Euro 2016 essentially followed the same style as the home including Climacool fabric and the neat chest band in two tones of green. The shorts and socks of this undeniably smart strip were able to be interchanged with those of the home kit if necessary.

Worn in: The 1-0 defeat against Wales in the second stage of Euro 2016.
Worn by: Paddy McNair, Conor McLaughlin.

HOME 2017-18

Design: adidas

Sadly qualification for the 2018 World Cup eluded Michael O'Neill's team. Had they succeeded they would have worn this exquisite new adidas home strip that reverted to a solid emerald green, adorned with faint shadow pinstripes.

Worn in: The 1-0 defeat in the first leg of the 2018 World Cup play-offs against Switzerland on the kit's debut in 2017.
Worn by: George Saville, Josh Magennis.

James Ward celebrates his goal against Greece in a Euro 2016 qualifier in 2014. The darker green adidas kit brought a fresh look to the Irish palette.

Northern Ireland players in the 2016-17 adidas home kit after the 2-0 defeat against Germany in a November 2016 World Cup qualifier.

1994 FIFA WORLD CUP

Mexico's goalkeeper Jorge Campos in one of his many infamous Umbro jerseys in the 1994 FIFA World Cup match against the Republic of Ireland, who are sporting their adidas away strip.

1994 FIFA WORLD CUP

Big and brash was the kit message for the 1994 FIFA World Cup. Bulgaria's Tzvetanov in his team's adidas away kit gets past Germany's Thomas Hassler in this quarter-final match.

PORTUGAL

Euro 2016 at last saw Portugal fulfil the potential they had been nurturing for some years thanks to the 1–0 win over France in the final.

The final saw Portugal sporting Nike's universal Vapor template in the deep red that the side currently prefers. From the team's first major tournament in 1966, Portugal's rich and lively kit history has proved to be one of individuality.

The Portuguese colour scheme comes straight from the red and green of the national flag: even the greater expanse of red on the shirts compared to the green of the shorts mirrors nicely the unbalanced colour proportions of the flag. White provides light relief as a trim colour.

Until 1978 the Portuguese shield that features on the flag doubled as the national crest, before it was replaced by a design linked to the Portuguese Football Federation.

White has often been the natural away colour choice, and was paired up with blue in the '60s and '70s (blue forming a part of the Portugal kit in the '30s) before settling into the established Portuguese football colour palette.

Since 1997 the side has been kitted out by Nike, but for much of the '70s and '80s it was the international stalwart adidas that was the technical supplier. This ensured the Portugal team sported the very latest designs – all crafted into the national red and green. Local company Olympic Sportswear was also a technical sponsor for a short period in the mid '90s.

Nike has experimented with the exact shade of the team jersey, and in recent years has plumped for a deeper, more maroon-like red, often trimmed with an opulent golden yellow, which has added a real touch of class and individuality to the team kit.

SPECIAL THANKS TO GUSTAVO TOMÁS

An adidas-clad Portugal players celebrate qualifying for the 1984 European Championship after beating the USSR 1–0 in a 1983 qualifier in Lisbon.

HOME 1966–73

Design: Marlec

The 1966 World Cup was Portugal's first ever major tournament – and they graced the English venues in this simple but classic, long sleeved crew-necked jersey. Despite Umbro pitching for the deal pre-tournament, the team opted for a version by local suppliers Marlec.

Worn in: The dramatic 4–3 win over North Korea in the 1966 World Cup quarter-finals.
Worn by: José Augusto, Eusebio – top scorer in the tournament with nine goals.

AWAY 1966–73

Design: Marlec

Following the design of the home, the away strip added a little extra flair by incorporating a two-colour crew neck and three-colour cuffs. The shirt re-appeared in 1976 when it was worn with white shorts and socks. The shirts weren't used in the 1966 World Cup but the blue shorts featured in two group games.

Worn in: The 2–1 win over the USSR in the 1966 World Cup third place play-off.
Worn by: Festa, José Torres.

HOME 1969–72

Design: Marlec

The short sleeved version of the Portuguese kit during this period was another smart but standard design. The shirts and shorts remained the same as the long sleeved incarnation. Despite the success of the 1966 World Cup the side, now managed by José Maria Antunes, failed to qualify for the 1970 tournament.

Worn in: Wins over France (2–1) and England (3–1).
Worn by: Klaus Allofs, Hans Dorfner.

AWAY 1969–72

Design: Marlec

Employing the same principles as the long sleeved version, the short sleeved Portugal away shirt proudly sported embellished collar and cuffs. A long sleeved version of the shirt was also worn earlier in the decade. The kit also occasionally featured the home white shorts or red shorts.

Worn in: The 4–1 victory over Chile in the 1972 Brazil Independence Cup.
Worn by: Joaquim Dinis, Timula Messias.

HOME 1972–73

Design: Unknown

An alternative short-sleeved home shirt was introduced for a brief period in 1972. Worn with the same shorts and socks as the long sleeved version, the jersey featured a white, green and red-trimmed v-neck and cuffs.

Worn in: José Augusto's side's unsuccessful 1974 World Cup qualifying campaign.
Worn by: Fernando Peres, Calisto Adolfo.

HOME 1973–76

Design: Unknown

A splash of white to the home shirt really freshened up the strip of José Augusto's Portugal side. In essence the multi-trimmed jersey was a natural successor to the previous away outfit. An alternate jersey switched the colours around on the cuffs.

Worn in: A 1–0 win over Cyprus in a 1975 qualifier for Euro 76.
Worn by: Joao Jacinto, Humberto Coelho.

AWAY 1973–76

Design: Unknown

White made its way into the trim of the next Portugal away shirt and those with a keen eye will notice how the order of colours on the cuffs varied from those on the previous change outfit. An alternate jersey removed white from the neck and switched the colours on the cuffs. Worn primarily with white shorts and socks.

Worn in: A 2–0 friendly triumph over France in 1975.
Worn by: Marinho, Francisco Rebelo.

HOME 1976–79

Design: adidas

Unusually no branding, apart from the three stripes of course, was visible on this standard adidas self-coloured, v-neck template that was used by many of its roster in the mid-'70s. The shirt was also often worn with the white socks from the change kit or just plain white socks.

Worn in: A 4–0 win over Cyprus in a 1978 World Cup qualifier (1977).
Worn by: Francisco Vital, Alfredo Murca.

AWAY 1976–79

Design: adidas

adidas followed the design of the home for its first Portuguese away kit but thanks to the green and red adaptation of the three-stripes it created surely one of the all-time classic Portugal away shirts! The jersey was paired with the regular home shorts and socks and was worn with both long and short sleeves.

Worn in: An impressive 4–2 win in Denmark in a 1977 qualifier for the 1978 World Cup.
Worn by: Machado Octavio, Manuel Fernandes.

AWAY 1978

Design: adidas

This classic adidas template was used as an alternate long sleeved change strip for at least one game in 1978. The shirt and socks were straightforward reversals of the home outfit and were joined by the home white shorts. Like the home strip, it featured no green within its design. Versions of the shirt exist with the new team crest housed within a patch.

Worn in: A 2–0 defeat by France in a friendly.
Worn by: Joao Cardoso, Celso de Matos.

HOME 1979–83

Design: adidas

Green took a larger role in the 1979 Portugal home strip, replacing the white shorts of previous strips and creating a classy and more unique ensemble. A collar was introduced to the cuffless shirt and white piping trimmed the raglan sleeves and the sides of the body. Also worn with trimmed socks and on occasion the away kit's white shorts.

Worn in: A 1–0 win over the USSR in 1983.
Worn by: Carlos Manuel, Jordao.

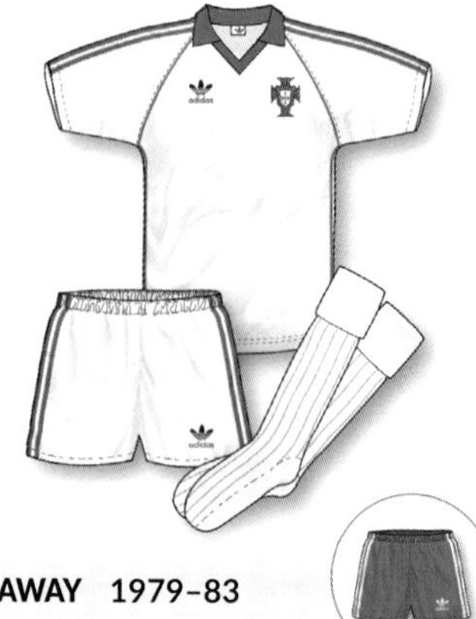

AWAY 1979–83

Design: adidas

Following on from the alternate long sleeved away shirt from 1978, the next regular Portugal away kit stuck with the simple two-colour approach of white and red in a style that reflected that of the home. It was also worn with green change shorts.

Worn in: A 3–0 friendly defeat against France in 1983.
Worn by: Lopes Virgilio, Eurico Gomes.

HOME 1980

Design: adidas

One of the most iconic of '70s football kit designs was this particular adidas template that found its way into the kitbag of pretty all its teams at the time. A relatively rare addition to the Portuguese canon, it was worn in at least one game.

Worn in: A 0–0 draw with Scotland in a 1980 World Cup qualifier. Again the Portugal side failed to make it through to the finals.
Worn by: Joao Laranjeira, Sheu Han.

THIRD 1981–83

Design: adidas

Green formed the core of a Portugal shirt for the first time in 1981. However, this smart jersey (crafted from a standard issue adidas pinstriped design that cropped up as a third kit for several teams at the time) was never worn by the full side.

HOME 1983

Design: adidas

A brave new Portugal shirt saw the introduction of a neat green insert collar and green three-stripe trim – no white in sight (apart from the adidas logo!) An elegant looking strip, it will be forever associated, though, with a disastrous result against the USSR, after which the previous home kit was reinstated.

Worn in: A crushing 5–0 thrashing at the hands of the USSR.
Worn by: Antonio Bastos Lopes, Nene.

AWAY 1983

Design: adidas

A straightforward reversal of the new home strip found green again pushed to the fore as it had been with the previous third kit. And, like that kit, this shirt was never worn by the first team. One can only presume this whole set of outfits was ditched following the defeat against the USSR.

HOME 1984

Design: adidas

One of adidas' more functional, but no less classic, templates of the '70s and '80s was its short sleeved, cuffless crew-necked shirt. Portugal wore a plain red and white version for a handful of games in 1984 prior to that year's European Championship.

Worn in: A 2–1 victory over Luxembourg.
Worn by: Eurico, Alvaro.

AWAY 1984

Design: adidas

A white and red version of the short-lived 1984 design was also produced but never worn by the first team. Fernando Cabrita had taken over from Glória as team manager in 1983 and led a technical commission that also included José Augusto, António Morais and Toni.

1984 EUROPEAN CHAMPIONSHIP

HOME 1984

Design: adidas

Dual-colour diagonal pinstripes were the order of the day for the next set of kits, which took over from the short-lived insert collar design. This was worn as Fernando Cabrita's side took part in Euro 1984 – Portugal's first major tournament for 18 years. The shirt was also worn with shadow striped shorts.

Worn in: Draws with West Germany (0–0) and Spain (1–1) in Euro 1984.
Worn by: Chalana, Antonio Sousa.

1984 EUROPEAN CHAMPIONSHIP

AWAY 1984–86

Design: adidas

Reflecting the design of the home, this all-white strip was a real beauty, predominantly trimmed with red but with the alternating green pinstripes adding interest. The placement of the adidas logo on this sets of kits tended to vary, sometimes appearing very high on the shoulder and occasionally lower down.

Worn in: The thrilling 3–2 defeat against France in the semi-finals of Euro 84.
Worn by: Diamantino, Frasco.

HOME 1985–86

Design: adidas

Following the side's impressive Euro 84 the home shirt went through a minor alteration with a white wrapover crew neck replacing the green and the colours of the three stripes reversed. The shorts initially featured pinstripes before shadow stripes were introduced.

Worn in: The unforgettable 1–0 triumph over West Germany in 1985 that sealed qualification for the following year's World Cup finals.
Worn by: Frederico Rosa, Pedro Venancio.

1986 FIFA WORLD CUP

HOME 1986

Design: adidas

A Selecção das Quinas got off to a superb start in the 1986 World Cup in their new outfit – complete with the green shadow striped shorts that had first appeared with the previous kit. The shirt featured a subtle gradated zig-zag pattern with just the merest touch of green on the wrapover v-neck.

Worn in: A superb 1–0 win over England in their opening game of the World Cup.
Worn by: Barglela José Antonio, Antonio André.

1986 FIFA WORLD CUP

AWAY 1986–87

Design: adidas

Unusually for the time, the Portuguese away kit for the World Cup did not reflect the design of the home and instead incorporated the standard adidas diagonal 'brickwork' shadow pattern that was then popular. Sadly the team's tournament was blighted by a player dispute and ended in disappointment. A red v-neck version also existed but was never worn.

Worn in: The dismal 3–1 defeat by Morocco.
Worn by: Paulo Futre, Jaime Pacheco.

HOME 1986

Design: adidas

As Torres' side regrouped after their eventful World Cup a new design of shirt was introduced for the two remaining games that year (both Euro 88 qualifiers). The strips were a basic adidas design (entitled 'Aberdeen') for the time, and featured horizontal shadow stripes and a red-trimmed wrapover v-neck. This home version was worn just once.

Worn in: A 1–1 draw with Sweden.
Worn by: José Coelho, Jaime das Merces.

AWAY 1986

Design: adidas

A white change version of the horizontal shadow striped adidas stop gap kit was also worn following the World Cup and simply followed the design of the home. Like the home outfit it was worn just once.

Worn in: A 1986 1–1 draw with Switzerland in a Euro 88 qualifier.
Worn by: Alberto da Fonseca, Ze Beto.

HOME 1987

Design: adidas

With new manager Ruy Seabra attempting to steady the ship, Portugal embarked on the Euro 88 qualifying campaign with a new home shirt that reverted to just red and white, and adopted the diagonal brickwork pattern that featured on the World Cup's away strip. Worn just three times.

Worn in: A 1–0 win against Belgium in a friendly.
Worn by: Antonio Jesus, Nascimento.

HOME 1987

Design: adidas

Another one-off Portugal shirt curiosity popped up in 1987. Worn with the same shorts and socks as the regular strip, this jersey took the subtle zig-zag pattern from the recent World Cup strip and topped it off with a simple white crew neck. Worn in both long and short sleeves.

Worn in: A 1–0 defeat against Italy in 1987.
Worn by: Frasco, Adão.

HOME 1987–90

Design: adidas

A new era of kit design began to emerge in th late '80s with the introduction of a new hi-tec fabric, 'Climalite', designed to keep players coc on the pitch. The next Portugal home kit (introduced late 1987) also featured additiona seams that ran down from the white 'spears' that appeared on either side.

Worn in: A 1988 1–0 triumph over Luxembou in an Italia 90 qualifier,
Worn by: Jaime Magalhaes, Fernando Gomes.

HOME 1987–90

Design: adidas

For much of the '80s Portugal's kit had been identical in both short and long sleeved versions. However, with the launch of the new Climalite kits the short sleeved shirt opted for a simple v-neck rather than a collar. In latter games the white shorts and green socks of the subsequent 1990–91 strip were worn.

Worn in: A narrow 1–0 win over the Netherlands in a Euro 92 qualifier (1990).
Worn by: Galo, Pedro Venancio.

AWAY 1987–90

Design: adidas

After a couple of years in mismatched home and away outfits parity returned in 1987 with the unveiling of a new away kit that simply copied the design of the home.

Worn in: A 2–1 victory against Greece (1989)
Worn by: Jorge Placido, Rui Barros.

AWAY 1987–90

Design: adidas

Again, the short sleeved version of the away kit opted for a v-neck rather than the collar of the long sleeved version. The '80s proved another fallow spell for Portugal with qualification for both Euro 88 and Italia 90 beyond their grasp.

Worn in: A 2–1 win over Switzerland in an Italia 90 World Cup qualifier (1989).
Worn by: Paneira, Luis Sobrinho.

HOME 1990–92

Design: adidas

After the relative simplicity of the late '80s outfits a new kit was launched in 1990 for jus a handful of games. It featured dynamic angul white panels across the shoulders and under the arms – a taster for the upcoming adidas equipment re-brand perhaps? Also worn with plain green shorts.

Worn in: A 3–2 defeat against Greece in a European Championship qualifier (1991).
Worn by: Leal, Rui Aguas.

AWAY 1990-92

Design: adidas

The white version of this latest strip was a real gem; the red and green shoulder flashes leaping out from the pure white fabric. The shirt was worn with the white shorts that were first choice with the 1990 kit but looked just as good on the occasions when the shirt was paired with the green home change shorts.

Worn in: A 1-0 defeat against the Netherlands in a 1991 qualifier for Euro 92.
Worn by: Emilio Peixe, César Brito.

HOME 1991-92

Design: adidas

Shoulder flashes were still the order of the day with the next kit for Carlos Queiroz's side in a design that followed that of the 1990 away strip. A diagonal shadow pattern was also incorporated alongside two different shorts designs. Squad numbers were introduced on the front of the shirt in 1992.

Worn in: A 2-0 friendly win over the Netherlands in 1992.
Worn by: Helder.

HOME 1992-94

Design: adidas

A new colour entered the Portuguese palette in 1992 – yellow! Replacing white, it bought a real touch of freshness to the next set of kits which unusually sported the traditional trefoil adidas logo, despite being fashioned from the new 'adidas equipment' re-branded templates. Two different sock designs were worn.

Worn in: Big 1994 World Cup qualifier wins over Scotland (5-0) and Malta (4-0) in 1993.
Worn by: José Semedo, Antonio Veloso.

AWAY 1992-94

Design: adidas

The adidas era ended in 1994 (despite some bold prototypes prepared for the subsequent set of strips) with this stunning away kit. Curiously, both this and the home kit featured the same diagonal shadow pattern as the 1991-92 outfits.

Worn in: A 1-0 win in Malta in a 1993 qualifier for the 1994 World Cup.
Worn by: José Rui Lopes Aguas, Joao Domingos Silva Pinto.

HOME 1995

Design: Olympic Sportswear

It was quite a coup for the small Portuguese sportswear manufacturer Olympic Sportswear when it clinched the national team contract in 1995. Its first home kit dismissed the bold colour panels of the late adidas designs and instead went for elegance and sophistication.

Worn in: The 1-0 win over Denmark in the 1995 Skydome tournament – Portugal's first trophy triumph.
Worn by: Carlos Secretario, Nelo.

AWAY 1995

Design: Olympic Sportswear

The white change version of the new strip reflected the design of the home (including the deep green neck style and painterly horizontal shadow stripes that also incorporated the Olympic Sportswear logo). It was worn for just one game only.

Worn in: A 1-1 draw with Canada in the 1995 Skydome tournament.
Worn by: Caetano, Vado.

HOME 1995-96

Design: Olympic Sportswear

Just eight months after the launch of the first Olympic Sportswear strip a second set was unveiled. The differences were minor; raglan sleeves, a new shadow pattern based around the country crest, and red and yellow bands on the shorts.

Worn in: A good 3-0 victory over the Republic of Ireland in a Euro 96 qualifier.
Worn by: Jorge Cadete, Pedro Barbosa.

AWAY 1995-96

Design: Olympic Sportswear

This classy white strip was actually the first of the second batch of strips to be worn on the pitch – and it made an explosive start! As with the home, the move on from the previous kit was minimal and did include the same socks as previously worn.

Worn in: The 7-0 drubbing of Liechtenstein in 1995 on the kit's debut.
Worn by: Oliveira Domingos, Antonio Folha.

HOME 1996

Design: Olympic Sportswear

A new set of kits were worn by António Oliveira's team in Euro 96 (Portugal's first major tournament in 10 years). The design brought in more green to the jersey in the form of a single stripe down each arm. A rich navy blue was also introduced as additional trim. Later versions of the shirt omitted the shadow print.

Worn in: An impressive unbeaten run in the Euro 96 group games.
Worn by: Fernando Couto, Luis Figo.

AWAY 1996

Design: Olympic Sportswear

Another splendid Portugal kit that was surplus to requirements in a major tournament (although the white socks were worn with the home kit against Croatia). Like the home, the shirt featured a large shadow print of the national shield that once, of course, acted as the Portuguese crest on the team shirts.

Worn in: A 3-0 triumph over Albania.
Worn by: Paulinho Santos, Oceano.

HOME 1997-98

Design: Nike

After two years (and six kits) with Olympic, Portugal switched to global sportswear giant Nike. Its first kit was a magnificent affair, comprising muted tones (including an almost claret-like red) and delicate yellow piping. It was first worn in a friendly against France where a sponsor's logo (promoting the Portuguese Expo 98 event) featured on the jersey.

Worn in: A 3-1 win over Armenia (1997).
Worn by: Joao Vieira Pinto, Paulo Sousa.

AWAY 1997-1999

Design: Nike

Nike was striving for a higher profile in the mid-'90s and part of its masterplan was to rejuvenate and seek new inspiration for its teams' away kits. In Portugal's case they expanded on the introduction of navy in the previous strips and made it a fundamental part of the new change outfit.

Worn in: The 1999 3-0 win over Hungary (in Lisbon) in the Euro 2000 qualifiers.
Worn by: Paulo Sergio Madeira, Pauleta.

THIRD 1997-2000

Design: Nike

Nike launched this sumptuous royal blue third kit to complete its initial set of strips for Portugal (although like the away, this third kit also straddled the subsequent home outfit). The design was the same as that of the home strip and included large contrasting colour panels trimmed with piping. Although never worn by the first team, it did see action with junior sides.

HOME 1998-99

Design: Nike

In a curious move, the next Portuguese home shirt simply replicated the stylings of the away that had been introduced in 1997, complete with contrasting sleeves and arched neck design. The only difference came in the shape of bold yellow trim across the sleeves and down each side of the shorts.

Worn in: A 3-1 win over Hungary in 1998.
Worn by: Ricardo Sa Pinto, Dimas.

HOME 2000-01

Design: Nike

Portugal, now under the managerial reign of Humberto Coelho, graced the Euro 2000 tournament with this classic, simple ensemble. Just like the team, it exuded confidence and class. The green was restricted to simply the shorts and yellow trim was implemented throughout.

Worn in: The superb Euro 2000 group victories over England (3-2) and Germany (3-0).
Worn by: Nuno Gomes, Dani.

AWAY 2000-02

Design: Nike

The understated elegance of the new template introduced for the home shirt also worked beautifully for the away. With no green or red it relied totally on the white and blue of historical Portuguese change uniforms, Dual colour trim adorned the shorts and socks with breathable fabric panels introduced under the arms and down the sides of the jersey.

Worn in: A 5-1 thrashing of Angola in 2001.
Worn by: Nuno Frechaut, José Luis Vidigal.

HOME 2002-03

Design: Nike

Fabric and garment technology began to dominate apparel design by the time the 2002 World Cup kicked off. Nike launched a series of dual-layered 'Cool Motion' shirts in a new initiative to regulate player temperature. The minimalist neck design was complemented by sharp angular side panels and yellow trim.

Worn in: A poor World Cup including defeats to the USA (3-2) and South Korea (1-0).
Worn by: Sérgio Conceição, Rui Jorge.

AWAY 2002-03

Design: Nike

The construction of this shirt was the same as the home, but in standard Nike style for the era some differences were introduced such as a collar and coloured shoulder inserts. Again, navy (in a slightly more muted shade than usual) and white were used to provide a stark alternative to the richness of the home kit.

Worn in: A 1-0 win over Kazakhstan (2003).
Worn by: Cristiano Ronaldo, who made his international debut in the above match.

HOME 2004-06

Design: Nike

Another fabric innovation from Nike's design studio was its 'Total 90' range - clothing designed to provide dryness and comfort for the full 90 minutes. Arched golden trim curved down each side of the slightly lighter red shirt and asymmetrical placing of Nike's swoosh logo and the Portuguese crest added visual interest.

Worn in: A superb Euro 2004 tournament that ended with a 1-0 defeat by Greece in the final.
Worn by: Jorge Andrade, Costinha.

AWAY 2004-06

Design: Nike

Away from home, white and navy was again the order of the day, fashioned into a shirt with a slightly different neck construction to the home. As with the home shirt, the fabric incorporated a delicate shadow pattern. The Total 90 range was easily identifiable thanks to the large circle surrounding the squad number on the front of the shirt.

Worn in: A 4-1 win over Canada (2005).
Worn by: Fernando Meira, Luis Boa Morte.

SPECIAL 2005

Design: Nike

In an innovative move, Nike launched an anti-racism campaign in 2005 entitled 'Stand Up, Speak Up' in which its roster of international sides ditched their traditional colours and adopted a symbolic black and white halved jersey - a powerful gesture that highlighted the universal power of the football shirt.

Worn in: A 1-0 defeat against the Republic of Ireland in February 2005.
Worn by: Simao, Tiago.

HOME 2006-08

Design: Nike

2006 saw a return to more of a maroon hue for the base colour of Portugal's new shirt. There were rumours of a move to encourage teams to sport single-colour kits that led to some sides, including Portugal, going down that avenue.

Worn in: The 1-0 semi-final defeat by France in the 2006 World Cup and the infamous 'Battle of Nuremberg' match against the Netherlands.
Worn by: Nuno Valente, Miguel.

AWAY 2006-07

Design: Nike

The 2006 World Cup proved to be yet another tournament that Portugal managed to avoid wearing a change strip! This meant no one got to see this enigmatic all-black outfit in Germany. Following the home design, it featured the merest hint of colour as part of the trim.

Worn in: A 2006 3-0 win vs Luxembourg.
Worn by: Nuno Maniche, Deco.

THIRD 2006-07

Design: Nike

In order to properly confirm with the light vs dark rule in major tournaments an all-white third kit was also prepared for the 2006 World Cup. Conceptual designs became more common at this time; the gold trim on all three of Portugal's shirts was based on the rigging ropes used by historical Portuguese explorers.

Worn in: A 2-1 victory over Belgium in a 2007 European Championship qualifier.
Worn by: Petit, Jorge Andrade.

AWAY 2007

Design: Nike

Another all white shirt was unveiled in 2007 with just the merest hint of a blue trim on the shorts. The shirt featured an old-fashioned collar complete with a small placket. It was a very basic design that lacked some of the visual appeal of the previous white strip.

Worn in: A 1–1 draw with Armenia in a European Championship qualifier.
Worn by: Helder Postiga, Fernando Meira.

2008 UEFA EUROPEAN CHAMPIONSHIP

HOME 2008–09

Design: Nike

Although Luiz Felipe Scolari's team stuck with the single colour approach first introduced in 2006, with their next kit it was now a much lighter and brighter red than the previous maroon shade. A mandarin neck and green flashes down each side of the shirt completed the design.

Worn in: The tense 3–2 defeat against Germany in the Euro 2008 semi-finals.
Worn by: Pepe, Raul Meireles.

2008 UEFA EUROPEAN CHAMPIONSHIP

AWAY 2008–09

Design: Nike

It was a return to a more traditional away colour combination for Euro 2008: an all-white kit with colour provided simply by red and green. And for once a Portuguese away kit was required in a major tournament! The design reflected that of the home, with the exception of the inclusion of a classic v-neck.

Worn in: A 3–1 win over the Czech Republic in the group stages of Euro 2008.
Worn by: José Bosingwa, Ricardo Carvalho.

2010 FIFA WORLD CUP

HOME 2010–12

Design: Nike

Never one to rest on its design laurels, Nike opted for an arrogant and rather in-your-face shirt for Portugal's 2010 World Cup adventure. The shirt featured a broad green chest band with a red dot pattern and was paired with white (or red) shorts and green socks.

Worn in: A 7–0 humiliation of North Korea in the 2010 World Cup group stages – a re-run of the famous 1966 match.
Worn by: Liedson, Miguel Veloso.

2010 FIFA WORLD CUP

AWAY 2010–12

Design: Nike

If the home kit had a certain swagger about it, the away had even more! A bold dual-colour stripe ran vertically down the front of the shirt – an effective way to incorporate the country's national colours within the strip. The shorts and socks reflected the design of the home pairs.

Worn in: The 1–0 defeat against Spain in the second round of the World Cup that sent Carlos Queiroz' side home.
Worn by: Danny, Hugo Almeida.

2012 UEFA EUROPEAN CHAMPIONSHIP

HOME 2012–13

Design: Nike

Although rather plain aesthetically, this Portuguese home shirt was packed with technological advancements. The shorts were made from 100% recycled polyester and the shirt from 96%. It was also 23% lighter than four years earlier AND utilised Nike's Dri-FIT hi-tech advancement to keep players cool.

Worn in: A superb 2–1 win over the Netherlands in Euro 2012.
Worn by: Joao Pereira, Nélson Oliveira.

2012 UEFA EUROPEAN CHAMPIONSHIP

AWAY 2012

Design: Nike

As with the 2006 set of kits, the Nike design team sought inspiration from Portugal's famous historical explorers for the next change strip, borrowing the iconic cross symbol used on the sails of their ships. And as with the home kit, laser-cut ventilation holes featured on each side.

Worn in: A thrilling 3–2 triumph over Denmark in Euro 2012 thanks to a last gasp winner. Also worn in the semi-final penalties defeat by Spain.
Worn by: Silvestre Varela, João Moutinho.

AWAY 2013

Design: Nike

A new all-black strip appeared in 2013, full of menace and inspired apparently by the volcanic basalt rock associated with Portugal. In a nice touch the design retained the impressive cross motif of the previous away, now represented in tonal form across the front of the shirt to create a beautiful ensemble.

Worn in: A 3–2 defeat against Ecuador on the kit's debut.
Worn by: Bruno Alves, Neto.

HOME 2014–15

Design: Nike

This striking shirt was unveiled as Paulo Bento's side prepared for the 2014 World Cup. The shirt featured an exciting two-tone red striped combination blending with maroon shorts and socks. The shirt was designed to mark 100 years of the Portuguese Football Federation.

Worn in: A poor World Cup campaign that saw Portugal fail to make the second round.
Worn by: Ricardo Costa, Eder.

AWAY 2014–15

Design: Nike

After eight years blue was back in a prominent role – to mark the centenary of the Portuguese Football Association. This gorgeous shirt, with it's unique stand-up crew neck combined with long placket, brought back memories of the side's '60s outfits. A new pattern of laser-cut ventilation holes were present on each side.

Worn in: A 1–0 friendly win over Mexico in 2014.
Worn by: Fábio Coentrão, Vieirinha.

AWAY 2015

Design: Nike

Black returned as the central colour of the next A Selecção das Quinas outfit, although it now included a spectacular and rather bold red and green gradated and painterly abstract design across the front. The shirt also featured a streamlined v-neck design and red inner.

Worn in: A 2–0 friendly triumph over Luxembourg.
Worn by: Danilo Pereira, Lucas João.

★

HOME 2016–17

Design: Nike

2016 saw the unveiling of Nike's Vapor template with Aeroswift fabric technology. Rolled out across its roster, most strips featured the same colour shirts and shorts but different colour socks, to exploit the 'flicker' effect caused when players run, enabling teammates to pick them out more easily.

Worn in: The glorious and unforgettable 1–0 win over France in the final of Euro 2016.
Worn by: William Carvalho, Adrien Silva.

AWAY 2016–17

Design: Nike

Nike freshened up the Portuguese colour palette again in 2016 with the introduction of this bright, mint green kit, again in the Vapor template. As with all of these strips, the jersey featured raglan sleeves in a complementary shade and contrasting socks (these included red flashes on the reverse).

Worn in: Important Euro 2016 wins: 1–0 vs Croatia and 2–0 over Wales in the semi-final.
Worn by: Raphael Guerreiro, Renato Sanches.

THIRD 2016

Design: adidas

Eyebrows were raised in September 2016 when Portugal played Switzerland in a World Cup qualifier sporting this alternate version of their mint green away kit that dispensed with the darker sleeve colour. Whether a FIFA rule prompted this can only be speculated. The regular away kit was back in action the following year.

Worn in: A 2–0 defeat against Switzerland.
Worn by: Cédric Soares, Bernardo Silva.

Christiano Ronaldo in the distinctive 2012 Nike away shirt in the Euro 2012 quarter-final match against the Czech Republic.

1998 FIFA WORLD CUP

Heavily patterned and decorated strips were a feature of this tournament. Here we see South Africa's Quinton Fortune in the team's Kappa kit and France's Lilian Thuram wearing adidas.

1998 FIFA WORLD CUP

Kappa also kitted out Jamaica in 1998 FIFA tournament, and the result is seen here in this shot from their Group H tie against an Asics-clad Japan side. Both strips exude flair and confidence.

REPUBLIC OF IRELAND

One of the longest kit relationships in football came to a surprising end in 2017 when New Balance took over the contract to supply apparel for the Republic of Ireland from Umbro.

The sheer consistency and quality produced by Umbro for the boys in green was truly impressive, and the company managed continually to provide the side with imaginative, innovative and beautiful strips in the famous emerald green. The green has been accompanied by the orange of the Irish tricolour at times, although navy blue has also sometimes been used to freshen up the Irish strip.

Ireland's first period of success came under the revolutionary guidance of Jack Charlton and was accompanied by adidas, who dressed the team as they rose to prominence on the world stage.

One of the more interesting aspects of Ireland's relationship with adidas is that it followed close on the heels of the deal made by the Football Association of Ireland (FAI) with Irish sportswear legends O'Neills. The two companies had actually spent some time in legal discussions concerning O'Neills' use of three-stripe trim on their kits – the three-stripe trim is universally associated with adidas and in the early '80s was registered as a trademark.

O'Neills and adidas ended up settling their dispute, with the result that the Irish firm were allowed to decorate their kits with the trim provided that they were only on sale in Ireland.

Away from home, green is the traditional Irish away colour, although the Umbro years brought in orange, grey and black options, all designs that really livened up the Irish kitbag.

SPECIAL THANKS TO DENIS HURLEY

Simple but strong; the 'Tailored by Umbro' 2010–11 home strip, modelled here by Robbie Keane and Liam Lawrence during the Euro 2012 qualifier against Andorra in 2010.

HOME 1966–69

Design: Unknown

Rather snazzy hooped socks had been in favour with the Irish for some years by the time the '60s drew to a close, adding a unique touch to the standard long sleeved, crew-necked jersey. The shirt was also worn at least once with the plain white socks of the away kit.

Worn in: A 2–1 win over Turkey in a 1966 qualifier for Euro 68.
Worn by: Andy McEvoy, Frank O'Neill.

HOME 1966–69

Design: Unknown

A late '50s style short sleeved v-neck shirt was also worn throughout the '60s, predominantly in the first half of the decade but also in the latter half as an alternative to the long sleeved jersey. It was a simple design with contrasting neck and cuffs, and was worn with the regular shorts and socks from the long sleeved version.

AWAY 1966–72

Design: Unknown

A straightforward reversal of the home kit served as a (seldom worn!) change strip for Johnny Carey's team. As was the norm for many nations at the time, the change shirt and socks were worn with the regular home shorts. The Irish suffered a torrid time results-wise in the '60s, failing to qualify for the 1966 World Cup and Euro 68.

HOME 1969–72

Design: Unknown

With football fashions becoming a little more sober as the '70s dawned, the hooped socks were abandoned, to be replaced by plain green pairs (although an alternative white pair with green turnovers was also worn).

Worn in: Disappointing qualifying campaigns for the 1970 World Cup and Euro 72 tournaments.
Worn by: Al Finucane, Paddy Dunning.

HOME 1972

Design: Unknown

Crew-necked shirts, although still popular in certain countries, were losing popularity in Europe and in 1972 the Irish updated the strip to include a collar with v-neck combination. Liam Tuohy had been appointed manager in 1971 and attempted to lead his team to the 1974 World Cup.

Worn in: A 3–2 win over Ecuador.
Worn by: Tommy McConville, Johnny Giles.

HOME 1972–75

Design: Unknown

Another kit upgrade occurred in 1973 with the addition of the most ubiquitous of all '70s football fashions – the wing inset collar. Twin stripes were also added to the sides of the shorts and the sock turnovers, helping to ensure the kit was right up to date.

Worn in: A 3–0 win over the USSR in a 1974 qualifier for Euro 76.
Worn by: Ray Treacy, Joe Kinnear.

AWAY 1973–75

Design: Unknown

Although it seems that an away kit was never required during this period (not many teams play in green!) it's safe to assume that the away kit would have been a straightforward reversal of the home strip. The early '70s still found the boys in green struggling on the world football stage, although results did improve slightly with the arrival of Liam Tuohy.

HOME 1973

Design: adidas

Legend says that the team kit was not put on the plane when Liam Tuohy's side travelled to France in May 1973 for a 1974 World Cup qualifier. Fortunately their hosts lent them an all-green adidas strip, complete with wrapover crew neck and resplendent with three-stripe trim. The match proved to be Tuohy's last.

Worn in: The above-mentioned game in Paris vs France that ended in a 1–1 draw.
Worn by: Mick Martin, Don Givens.

HOME 1974

Design: Athleta

With Johnny Giles now in charge, Ireland took part in a three-game South American tour in Spring 1974. Brazilian sportswear brand Athleta kitted out the side in a lightweight, short sleeved crew-neck shirt. Unlike many strips at the time the badge was placed centrally.

Worn in: Defeats by Brazil (2–1) and Uruguay (2–0) alongside a 2–1 victory over Chile.
Worn by: Eoin Hand, Jimmy Conway.

HOME 1976–78

Design: O'Neills

1976 saw the beginning of a fruitful and creative partnership between Irish sportswear firm O'Neills and the Irish side. Its standard designs brought the addition of striped trim which caught the eye of adidas' lawyers at the time! Around 1977 the badge was updated to include just three shamrocks.

Worn in: A 1977 1–0 win vs France in a 1978 World Cup qualifier.
Worn by: Liam Brady, Steve Heighway.

HOME 1976

Design: O'Neills

One of the more unusual Irish kits from the O'Neills era was this alternate short sleeved home shirt. Aside from the use of a plain collar the other main difference was the addition of black in the sleeve taping, forming a design of four white stripes and three black.

Worn in: A 3–3 draw with Turkey in a friendly match.
Worn by: Terry Conroy, Joe Waters.

AWAY 1976–78

Design: O'Neills

This attractive all-white ensemble became O'Neills' first branded away shirt for Johnny Giles' team as they narrowly missed out on 1978 World Cup qualification. The shirt featured contrasting collar and cuffs and was worn with the home shorts. Like many other Ireland change shirts at the time, there wasn't a great need for an away kit and it's unclear this shirt was ever actually worn.

HOME 1978–83

Design: O'Neills

Dual-colour trim on kits in the '70s was still not commonplace so it was a surprise to see O'Neills launch this beautifully flamboyant new design for the Green Army that now included yellow. An alternate version with green cuffs and neck is also believed to have been worn.

Worn in: The brilliant 1980 2–1 win over the Netherlands in a qualifier for the 1982 World Cup.
Worn by: Gerry Daly, Tony Grealish.

AWAY 1978–83

Design: O'Neills

The third colour was also introduced to the away kit which now, following stricter rules on clashes, had its own unique green shorts. Alternative white socks with green-only trim were also worn, as was a long sleeved version with self-coloured collar and cuffs. In 1980 Eoin Hand took over the managerial reins.

Worn in: A 1979 1–0 defeat against Northern Ireland in the Euro 80 qualifiers.
Worn by: Ashley Grimes, John Devine.

HOME 1983–84

Design: O'Neills

The first fixture of 1983, against Malta, saw the Irish side sport an updated version of their kit. More or less the same as the previous design, the only differences came from the addition of stylish white and yellow pinstripes, and piping that trimmed the raglan sleeves. Initially worn with a short-lived alternate badge design.

Worn in: An 8–0 drubbing of Malta in a 1983 Euro 84 qualifier – Ireland's record victory.
Worn by: Mark Lawrenson, Mick Martin.

AWAY 1983–85

Design: O'Neills

As usual a basic reversal of the new home kit formed the next Irish change outfit – with one exception, in that the collar was now a wrapover v-neck and both it and the cuffs were a non-contrasting white. As with all Ireland kits at the time, the shorts and socks were able to be mixed and matched between the two outfits.

Worn in: A 1984 3–0 defeat in Denmark during the 1986 World Cup qualifying campaign.
Worn by: Frank Stapleton, Jim Beglin.

AWAY 1984

Design: O'Neills

The Irish kit went through plenty of minor variations and anomalies in the O'Neills years with this alternative change kit a prime example. The raglan sleeves were replaced by a more standard design, which were now pinstriped and had their trim removed. A new sock design was also introduced.

Worn in: A 1–0 defeat against Norway in a 1984 qualifier for the 1986 World Cup.
Worn by: Mickey Walsh, Kevin O'Callaghan.

HOME 1985

Design: O'Neills

The Irish kit went through plenty of minor variations and anomalies in the O'Neills years and towards the end of the pinstriped outfit's lifespan a version of the shirt with a modern v-neck was briefly worn (the v-neck also made appearances in long sleeves). The rest of the strip remained unchanged.

Worn in: A 2–1 friendly defeat against England in 1985.
Worn by: Chris Hughton, Ronnie Whelan.

HOME 1985

Design: O'Neills

Prior to the launch of the next official home strip this enigmatic design appeared – for just one game. The FAI secretary asked O'Neills to create a bright and dynamic new strip in the hope of inspiring the Irish team, However, a lacklustre performance in its sole outing mothballed the design.

Worn in: A 0–0 draw with Norway in a 1985 qualifier for the 1986 World Cup.
Worn by: Michael Robinson, Tony Galvin.

HOME 1985

Design: O'Neills

After the extravagance of the shortlived amber kit, a more sedate and classy green and white outfit emerged. Minimalist in design, a trimmed v-neck was complemented by shoulder stripes and a new simple badge. An alternate version of the shirt featured the round FAI badge, along with a small shamrock motif on the right sleeve.

Worn in: A 1985 3–0 win over Switzerland in a 1986 World Cup qualifier.
Worn by: Kevin Sheedy, Kevin Moran.

AWAY 1985

Design: O'Neills

A reversed version of this simple design was worn as the team's next away kit, the removal of the stripes on the sock turnover being the only difference. In 1983 O'Neills and adidas settled their long-running dispute over the three stripes, with O'Neills permitted to use them on products sold only in Ireland.

Worn in: A 0–0 draw in Switzerland in a qualifier for the 1986 World Cup.
Worn by: Mick McCarthy, Tony Cascarino.

AWAY 1985

Design: O'Neills

A second version of this last change kit to be produced by O'Neills for the FAI was worn for just one game against the USSR. The design was identical to the regular jersey except that the central stripe on the shoulder trim was now yellow. These final O'Neills kits also marked the end of Hand's time in charge of the team.

Worn in: A 2–0 defeat against the USSR in a 1986 World Cup qualifier.
Worn by: Gary Waddock, David O'Leary.

HOME 1986–87

Design: adidas

New year, new manager and new kit supplier – 1986 was a milestone year for the FAI. Adidas' first strip for the Republic of Ireland was a basic v-necked jersey adorned with adidas' three stripes. In its first year of use, the kit sported the current badge, before the familiar orange FAI badge was launched in 1987.

Worn in: A 1–0 defeat against Wales in 1986 – Jack Charlton's first game in charge.
Worn by: John Aldridge, Dave Langan.

AWAY 1986–87

Design: adidas

The away followed the simple but classic design of the home with the exception of a non-contrasting set of v-neck and cuffs. The FAI signed a deal with Opel this year and although FIFA rules forbade them from wearing the new shirts in games, all Irish replica jerseys henceforth bore their logo. It seems this strip was never called into action during its lifetime.

HOME 1987

Design: adidas

Jack Charlton's rejuvenation of the Irish team was gathering pace rapidly and the team achieved qualification for their first major tournament – Euro 88. In the last game of 1987 the team wore a shirt that, with the addition of orange trim on the v-neck, was almost a hybrid between the standard jersey and the collared shirt that was to follow.

Worn in: A 5–0 friendly win over Israel.
Worn by: David Kelly, John Byrne.

1988 UEFA EUROPEAN CHAMPIONSHIP

HOME 1988–90

Design: adidas

Ever the trendsetters, adidas' next Ireland shirt included a white mesh fabric band on each sleeve to help players cope with the temperature in hotter climates. After three years of fairly basic kits, orange was introduced to the strip as a third colour, giving the entire outfit a fresh appearance.

Worn in: The plucky displays at Euro 88, including a 1–0 victory over England.
Worn by: Ray Houghton, Andy Townsend.

1988 UEFA EUROPEAN CHAMPIONSHIP

AWAY 1988–90

Design: adidas

Ireland's fine continental-style away kit for the Euro 88 finals (although it wasn't required in the tournament) and 1990 World Cup qualifying campaign again simply reversed the design of the home – with the exception of the contrasting collar and cuffs.

Worn in: The glorious 2–0 win over Malta in 1989 that sealed Ireland's qualification for their first ever World Cup.
Worn by: Steve Staunton, Chris Morris.

1990 FIFA WORLD CUP

HOME 1990–92

Design: adidas

Accompanying Big Jack's side in the 1990 World Cup was a new adidas outfit (worn for the first time in a 1–0 friendly win over the USSR) that featured a cuffless shirt with a simple orange-trimmed wrapover v-neck and a repeated V shaped shadow pattern.

Worn in: The epic 5–4 penalty shootout against Romania in the second stage of the 1990 World Cup.
Worn by: Alan McLoughlin, Paul McGrath.

1990 FIFA WORLD CUP

AWAY 1990–92

Design: adidas

Historically Irish away kits were seldom required. However, during major tournaments rules made sure that people watching on black and white TVs could separate the sides through one team wearing a 'dark' strip and the other 'light'. This led to this white strip seeing lots of use in Italia 90. A new team badge was launched in 1991.

Worn in: The unlucky 1–0 defeat against Italy in the 1990 World Cup quarter-finals.
Worn by: Niall Quinn, John Sheridan.

HOME 1992–94

Design: adidas

adidas undertook a radical re-branding project in the early '90s. Gone was the famed trefoil logo and three stripe mark, and in came 'adidas equipment' accompanied by large bold graphics. This design was launched with the help of a 4–0 thrashing of Latvia in September 1992.

Worn in: The impressive USA 94 World Cup qualifiers, including vital 1992 draws against Spain (0–0) and Denmark (0–0).
Worn by: Dennis Irwin.

AWAY 1992–94

Design: adidas

No surprises with the design of the next away kit as it once again replicated the design of the home, in white. Orange was restricted to the merest of trims on the new neck design on both of these strips and a striped vertical shadow pattern was also incorporated into the fabric.

Worn in: The joyous 1–1 draw with Northern Ireland in 1993 that ensured Irish qualification to a second consecutive World Cup!
Worn by: Alan Kernaghan, Terry Phelan.

1994 FIFA WORLD CUP

HOME 1994

Design: adidas

This kit, the final home design to be produced for Ireland by adidas, was first worn in Spring of 1994 but lasted for no more than a few months before the deal with the FAI ended. The main adornment on the shirt came from an intricate abstract shadow design.

Worn in: The incredible 1–0 win over Italy in the 1994 World Cup – a kit mix-up meant that both sides nearly took to the pitch in white!
Worn by: Jason McAteer, Tommy Coyne.

1994 FIFA WORLD CUP

AWAY 1994

Design: adidas

As was the case with the previous World Cup, Ireland's white away kit was often called upon in USA 94 four years later. In fact, it appeared in all but one of the side's matches. For the first time the design did not reflect the style of the home and instead included a confident array of fading speckled green stripes with orange trim.

Worn in: The heartbreaking 2–0 defeat by the Netherlands that ended Ireland's World Cup.
Worn by: Roy Keane, Phil Babb.

HOME 1994–95

Design: Umbro

The eight-year deal between the Republic of Ireland and adidas accompanied one of the most celebrated periods in Irish football. Umbro arrived just as the hangover was beginning to kick in. Umbro's first, very baggy, kit saw the introduction of two distinct shades of green – a recurring theme with its Irish kits.

Worn in: A 2–0 defeat against the Netherlands in a Euro 96 qualifying play-off.
Worn by: Jeff Kenna, Eddie McGoldrick.

AWAY 1994–96

Design: Umbro

Umbro replicated the lavish curved decoration of the home shirt for this seldom-worn away jersey, but rendered it in a bold combination of orange and green. An alternative collar design to the home kit was joined by a diagonally pinstriped shadow fabric. This first set of Umbro kits marked the end of the Jack Charlton era.

Worn in: A 4–0 triumph over Northern Ireland in a 1995 Euro 1996 qualifier.
Worn by: Garry Kelly, Mark Kennedy.

HOME 1996–98

Design: Umbro

The first fixture of 1996, with new manager Mick McCarthy at the helm, saw the launch of Umbro's second Irish home kit. An unorthodox and complex design, it introduced sleeve and shorts trim based around a rather cryptic 'FAI' logotype.

Worn in: The 1997 2–1 defeat against Belgium in the second leg of the 1998 World Cup play-off that meant the Irish failed to qualify.
Worn by: Ian Harte, Keith O'Neill.

AWAY 1997–98

Design: Umbro

Orange had begun to make more and more of an impact in Ireland's kits over the past few years, so it was perhaps no surprise when, along with black and splashes of green, it was used to form the most vibrant Irish strip to date. Fashioned from a standard template, the shirt featured a crisp button-up collar/neck design.

Worn in: A tense 3–2 defeat against Macedonia in a 1998 World Cup qualifier (1997).
Worn by: Jon Goodman, Gary Breen.

HOME 1998–2000

Design: Umbro

This extravagantly decorated home strip was unveiled for Ireland's first match of the Euro 2000 qualifiers. Orange was notable by its absence from this strip with navy blue taking its place. The jersey included a neat collar design and the fabric featured an elaborate shadow design based around the FAI crest.

Worn in: Another qualifying play-off exit, this time to Turkey in 1999 for Euro 2000.
Worn by: Rory Delap, Mark Kinsella.

AWAY 1998–99

Design: Umbro

Another interesting strip in the Irish kit canon was this all-black affair. Nothing unusual in the choice of colour; black was (and in fact still is) highly popular when it comes to intimidating away colour alternatives. What made this shirt different was the fact that it was never actually worn by the senior squad – qualifying campaigns seldom give an opportunity to don away strips – especially if you play in green.

HOME 2000–01

Design: Umbro

After the intricacies of its previous three kits, Umbro played it nice and simple with its next strip. A classic, retro two-colour design, it featured an old-fashioned button-up white collar (giving it a rugby feel), ample cut, restrained use of trim and a subtle textured fabric.

Worn in: A great 2–2 draw in Holland in a 2002 World Cup qualifier (2000).
Worn by: Richard Dunne, Kevin Kilbane.

AWAY 2000-01

Design: Umbro

The late '90s saw a batch of Umbro designs supplied to all of its roster that were marketed as 'training kits', but also often worn as change outfits. This smart design featured a distinctive set of coloured shoulder panels and reversed stitching accompanied by ribbed hi-tech fabric side panels.

Worn in: A 2001 4–0 thrashing of Cyprus in the 2002 World Cup qualifying campaign.
Worn by: David Connolly, Damian Duff.

HOME 2001-03

Design: Umbro

The short-lived previous set of kits were updated in the summer of 2001. Until 2000 Ireland had sported bespoke home kits that did not follow a standard Umbro template. However, this design, like the previous, was also worn by other Umbro-supplied sides. It featured a simple crew neck and reversed white stitching.

Worn in: A strong 1–1 draw with Germany in the 2002 World Cup finals.
Worn by: Steven Reid, Matt Holland.

AWAY 2001-02

Design: Umbro

Ireland's next away kit again featured navy blue in a prominent role. The design was constructed from Umbro's new Sportswool fabric – designed to help manage moisture and temperature. The strip was only worn once during the successful World Cup qualifiers where it was paired not with its designated blue shorts, but the white change shorts of the 00-01 away kit.

Worn in: The 2001 2–0 win in Estonia.
Worn by: Stephen Carr, Gary O'Brien.

AWAY 2002-03

Design: Umbro

Prior to the side's departure for the World Cup a new away strip was launched – Ireland's third consecutive white and navy change kit. An elegant design, the shirt included a contemporary v-neck and navy blue underarm panels, accentuated by green reversed stitching. The kit was also worn with green shorts.

Worn in: The 3–2 penalties defeat by Spain in the second stage of the 2002 World Cup.
Worn by: Kenny Cunningham, Steve Finnan.

HOME 2003-04

Design: Umbro

This home kit was one of the most blatantly contemporary the side had worn – both in terms of aesthetics and construction. Umbro's lightweight 'Vapatech' fabric (which seemed a slightly bluer shade of green than previously worn) included a series of horizontal white pinstripes combined with a suave shaded effect.

Worn in: A patchy Euro 2004 campaign including a 2–1 win over Albania in 2003.
Worn by: Lee Carsley, Gary Doherty.

AWAY 2003-05

Design: Umbro

After the modernist approach of the home strip, a slightly more traditional angle was adopted for the Irish away kit. Modern flair still existed though in the shape of breathable fabric underarm panels and a green sleeve trim that included a subtle representation of the Ireland flag. Brian Kerr was appointed manager in 2003.

Worn in: A 2003 2–0 defeat against Switzerland in a Euro 2004 qualifying match.
Worn by: Clinton Morrison, John O'Shea.

HOME 2004-06

Design: Umbro

Having failed to qualify for Euro 2004, Kerr's men kicked off their 2006 World Cup qualifiers with this home kit. A restrained outfit, it featured white underarm panels and delicate orange and white trim, teamed with Umbro's latest fabric technology. A restyled FAI crest was introduced with this kit.

Worn in: The shock 2005 2–2 draw with Israel during the unsuccessful World Cup qualifiers.
Worn by: Andy Reid, Graham Kavanagh.

AWAY 2005-07

Design: Umbro

The redesigned FAI badge also featured a darker, olive green within its design and it was this shade that became an integral part of the next Umbro away kit. The lightweight jersey featured dynamic shards of the two shades of green across the shoulders along with side panels that regulated moisture.

Worn in: A 1–0 win over Cyprus in a 2005 qualifier for the 2006 World Cup.
Worn by: Stephen Elliott, Robbie Keane.

HOME 2006-08

Design: Umbro

This suave and sophisticated home strip coincided with the arrival of Steve Staunton as manager following another poor qualifying campaign. A subtle blend of fabrics was adorned with the merest suggestion of white and orange. Initially worn with green socks, soon unfamiliar white pairs were preferred.

Worn in: The humiliating 5-2 defeat against Cyprus in 2006 (Euro 2008 qualifier).
Worn by: Alan Lee.

AWAY 2007

Design: Umbro

A slate grey away kit emerged in 2007 that typified Umbro's design ethos at the time, namely asymmetrical elements and small, intricate flashes of trim and colour. The strip was worn once (at home!) with the shirt and shorts joined by the, rather mismatched, home white socks.

Worn in: A 1-0 victory over Wales in a Euro 2008 qualifying match.
Worn by: Stephen Ireland, Paul McShane.

HOME 2008-09

Design: Umbro

This stunning strip was the latest Umbro outfit to feature its new lightweight 'X-static' fabric which was more effective at regulating body temperature. Graceful orange and white decorations were joined by a new interpretation of Umbro's diamond trim. Giovanni Trapattoni replaced Staunton as manager in 2008.

Worn in: The controversial 2010 World Cup qualifying 1-0 play-off defeat by France (2009).
Worn by: Glenn Whelan, Kevin Doyle.

AWAY 2008-09

Design: Umbro

A suitable partner to its home equivalent, the next Green Army change strip featured more of the arching and dynamic trim and fabric textures that were part of Umbro's design toolbox. Umbro's logo was placed high on the chest, allowing space for the squad number.

Worn in: A 0-0 draw with Montenegro in a 2008 qualifier for the 2010 World Cup where the home white shorts were worn with the kit.
Worn by: Aiden McGeady, Stephen Hunt.

AWAY 2009-10

Design: Umbro

Dark green was brought back to the Irish palette in 2009 in the shape of this strip that included fine horizontal pinstripes and shadow hoops alongside underam panels that reached down the sides of the jersey. Two small Umbro diamonds were also included on each sleeve.

Worn in: An impressive 1-1 draw with Italy in a 2009 qualifier for the 2010 World Cup – another tournament the Irish missed out on.
Worn by: Keith Andrews, Andy Keogh.

THIRD 2009-10

Design: Umbro

Umbro relaunched its complete football apparel offering in 2009 with its 'Tailored by Umbro' range, attempting to inject a touch of class and finesse to the kit world. Ireland's first-ever third outfit was released before the range was launched but has touches of the new direction. Sadly the kit was never worn by the first team. In 2010 the FAI signed a sponsorship deal with mobile phone network Three.

HOME 2010-11

Design: Umbro

The first 'Tailored by Umbro' Irish home kit was an absolute classic. Fashioned in a darker 'St Patricks Green' the fine strip included an elegant gold trim that accompanied simple white decoration. 1950s-style hooped socks completed the outfit. Also worn with the green shorts and socks from the away kit.

Worn in: The fabulous 5-0 win over neighbours Northern Ireland in the 2011 Nations Cup.
Worn by: Liam Lawrence, Damien Delaney.

AWAY 2010-11

Design: Umbro

This next away kit proved to be a perfect accompaniment to the simple but strong home outfit. It essentially followed the same design, although the shirt was given its own uniqueness thanks to the inclusion of a crew neck. The hoops motif of the home socks were echoed on the turnovers.

Worn in: The wonderful 4-0 win over Estonia in the first leg of the Euro 2012 play-offs.
Worn by: Sean St Ledger-Hall, Keith Fahey.

HOME 2011-12

Design: Umbro

Another stunning home shirt emerged in Summer 2011. The collared shirt featured an intricate shadow hatched stripe design, trimmed beautifully with gold. The previous home kit was a hard act to follow but this strip, again under the 'Tailored by Umbro' banner, more than held its own.

Worn in: Two defeats in the group stage of Euro 2012: 3-1 to Croatia and 4-0 to Spain.
Worn by: James McClean, Darron Gibson.

THIRD 2011-12

Design: Umbro

Black was chosen to form a new Ireland third outfit in a template design also used by many of Umbro's roster. The shirt featured a striking green band that reached across the chest and arms along with a 'Henley' button-up neck, designed to look good as casualwear, or as marketed by Umbro, during the 1350 minutes a day you spend not playing football!

Worn in: A superb 2–0 friendly win over Italy.
Worn by: Seamus Coleman, Keith Treacy.

AWAY 2012-13

Design: Umbro

The early part of the 2010s saw a kit resurgence in bold, simple colour blocks in the form of stripes, hoops and sashes. This fine away strip is a perfect example, featuring an asymmetrical arrangement of two-tone green stripes that, like the previous away strip, was echoed on the socks.

Worn in: A 2–0 defeat against Italy in the Irish's very tough Euro 2012 group.
Worn by: Stephen Ward, Simon Cox.

HOME 2012-13

Design: Umbro

After the extravagance of the previous home shirt a new, plainer kit was launched, which featured a cotton-like marl effect. A tonal neck was joined by white panels. Following the failure to qualify for the World Cup Martin O'Neill replaced Trapattoni as manager.

Worn in: The 2012 6–1 defeat against Germany in a 2014 World Cup qualifier – Ireland's biggest ever home loss.
Worn by: James McCarthy, Darren O'Dea.

AWAY 2013-14

Design: Umbro

A mean and menacing black and charcoal striped affair became Ireland's new change kit in March 2013, launched under a 'Symbol of a New Dawn' marketing campaign. Subtle white and green trim were used as highlights. Delicate stitching at the base of the placket recreated the Irish tricolour flag.

Worn in: A 0-0 friendly draw with Wales in 2013.
Worn by: Wes Hoolahan, Ciaran Clark.

HOME 2014-15

Design: Umbro

Single-colour strips were all the rage at this time, inspired perhaps by interpretations of FIFA rulings. Another great Umbro home shirt saw a minimal design adorned with fine tonal hoops, a functional white polo shirt collar alongside thin hoops on the socks.

Worn in: Quite possibly the greatest result in Irish football history: the 1–0 win over Germany in a 2015 qualifier for Euro 2016.
Worn by: Shane Long, Jon Walters.

AWAY 2014-15

Design: Umbro

White returned as Martin O'Neill's men embarked on a successful Euro 2016 qualifying campaign. It resurrected the colour palette of the team's early 2000s change strips, with navy playing a dominant role. The jersey also featured the same polo collar as the home kit. Also worn with the home strip's green shorts.

Worn in: A 1–1 draw with Bosnia in the Euro 2016 play-off first leg.
Worn by: Jeff Hendrick, Robbie Brady.

AWAY 2015-16

Design: Umbro

One of the more controversial Ireland away kits was launched in 2015 and saw a grey colourway introduced with white sleeves and side panels, complemented by a light green band. The chest featured a gorgeous Celtic pattern – surprisingly the first time this classic Irish iconic device had made an appearance on the team kit in such a major way. This kit was never required in its short lifespan.

2016 UEFA EUROPEAN CHAMPIONSHIP

2016 UEFA EUROPEAN CHAMPIONSHIP

HOME 2016–17

Design: Umbro

Umbro again looked to the past for inspiration for what was to be its final home shirt for the Irish. The design had more than just a hint of the classic late '80s/early '90s home outfits with its rich orange trim. Underarm and side panels echoed the feel of the 2014 away kit. Diagonal shadow stripes completed the design.

Worn in: A 1–1 draw with Sweden in the in first Euro 2016 match for the boys in green.
Worn by: Cyrus Christie, David McGoldrick.

AWAY 2016–17

Design: Umbro

2017 was to be the last year of Umbro's long and successful relationship with the Green Army. It went out with a bang with a unique white change design, decorated with a series of green bands on each sleeve and featuring a simple, dual-coloured crew neck.

Worn in: A great 1–0 win vs Italy in Euro 2016 followed by the 2–1 defeat against France in the knockout stage.
Worn by: Daryl Murphy, Shane Duffy.

HOME 2017–18

Design: New Balance

The first home kit in the New Balance Irish deal was a solid affair that again leaned heavily on the inclusion of a deep orange to provide a contrast to the green and white. A neat and tidy button-up crew neck was joined by vertical shadow stripes.

Worn in: The crushing 5–1 defeat by Denmark in the second leg of the play-off for the 2018 World Cup that meant the Irish failed to qualify.
Worn by: David Meyler, Harry Arter.

AWAY 2017–18

Design: New Balance

A darker green (officially named 'Eden Green') was used to accompany the white of New Balance's first away kit for the Irish. A more traditional collared approach was adopted with restrained tricolour trim throughout including the inside of the cuffs which could be folded to display the national colours if desired.

Worn in: A 0–0 draw with Denmark in the first leg of the ill-fated World Cup play-off.
Worn by: Callum O'Dowda, Conor Hourihane.

The Republic of Ireland line up in their adidas home strip before facing Italy in the 1994 World Cup finals.

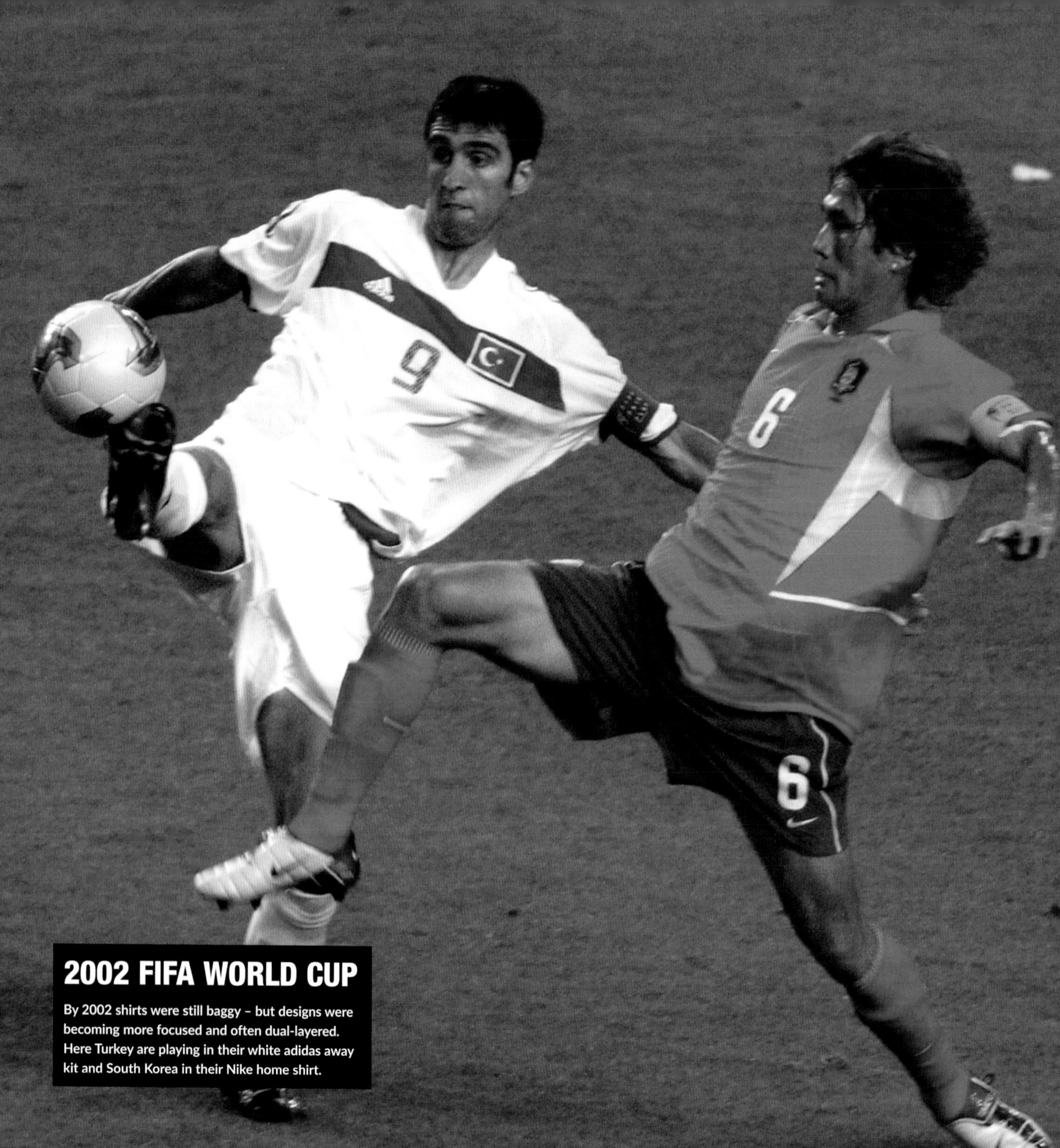

2002 FIFA WORLD CUP

By 2002 shirts were still baggy – but designs were becoming more focused and often dual-layered. Here Turkey are playing in their white adidas away kit and South Korea in their Nike home shirt.

2002 FIFA WORLD CUP

China's Chen Yang is in their own version of the latest dual-layered adidas design, while Gilberto Martinez of Costa Rica is sporting the team's Joma home strip.

RUSSIA / USSR

The kit history of Russia and the USSR is one of the most perplexing of all the world football nations. To the untrained eye, the strip is either red or white, though the sheer number of combinations, variations and anomalies is mind-blowing!

Unlike most nations, who introduce a single design of kit and stick with it through a prescribed period before updating to a new design, the USSR drew upon a huge variety of strip styles. It seemed that they selected whichever one caught their eye on the day!

The unpredictable kit choices even extended beyond basic football fashion niceties. Such was the regularity with which they wore away outfits, even at home, that their choice of white, their regular away colour, seemed to have become their first choice.

For many older fans who witnessed the USSR team in full flow during the '70s and '80s, it was always the enigmatic CCCP text, blazoned across the chests of the players' that caught the eye – especially in those pre-sponsorship days.

The CCCP stood for Союз Советских Социалистических Республик – Russian for Union of Soviet Socialist Republics – and helped add to the mystique of the USSR side.

Kit selection seems to have been a moveable feast until the arrival of Nike in the late 1990s.

The USSR dissolved in 1991 and the Russian side emerged via the short-lived CIS (Commonwealth of Independent States) team. Russia was quick to establish their own visual identity with a colour scheme taken from the nation's white, red and blue flag.

However, recent years have seen adidas forge a new look for the Russian Football Union by reverting to the dynamic and intimidating red of the previous Soviet days, often in a new dark maroon or burgundy shade.

The USSR pose for a team photo during the 1986 World Cup finals in Mexico. The side are wearing their short-lived Climalite adidas home kit.

HOME 1966–70

Design: Umbro (assumed)

The USSR took part in the 1966 World Cup wearing an alternate long sleeved, crew-neck jersey – the height of football fashion at the time. The shirt was also worn with two other alternative sock styles: two white stripes and a white turnover.

Worn in: A superb World Cup – Russia finishing in fourth place with wins over Italy (1–0) and Hungary (2–1) along the way.
Worn by: Igor Chislenko, Valeri Porkujan.

AWAY 1966

Design: Unknown

Nikolai Morozov's team's regular collared away shirt (a style worn since the '50s) made one appearance at the 1966 World Cup where it was paired with light blue shorts to avoid a clash.

Worn in: A good 3–0 win over South Korea in the 1966 World Cup.
Worn by: Eduard Malofeyev, Anatoli Banishevski.

HOME 1966–72

Design: Unknown

This red collared shirt, with open neck, had been the Soviet's first choice kit since the '50s. Available in both long and short sleeved versions, over its many years of use it was also paired on several occasions with single-striped red socks and in 1968 mainly with white socks – indicative of USSR's inconsistent kit selection.

Worn in: The 2–0 defeat against England in the third place play-off of Euro 1968.
Worn by: Murtaz Khurtzilava.

AWAY 1966–73

Design: Unknown

The USSR's traditional away kit in the late '60s was an all white affair, with either single- or double-striped socks being favoured. For a period in 1968 it's possible the USSR switched to white as first choice kit as the outfit was donned in many games, often at home. Worn in both long and short sleeved options.

Worn in: A 0–0 draw with Italy in the semi-finals of Euro 1968 – Italy won on the toss of a coin!
Worn by: Anatoli Byshovetz, Aleksandr Lenev.

HOME 1970

Design: Unknown

For the 1970 World Cup Gavril Kaczalin's team sported their standard home kit but opted for a new curved and contemporary rendering of their iconic CCCP text. The shirt was worn with the newly introduced contrasting turnover socks and, for one match, navy change shorts.

Worn in: The superb 4–1 win over Belgium in the 1970 World Cup, followed by the 1–0 defeat against Uruguay in the semi-finals.
Worn by: Kakhi Asatiani, Viatly Khmelnitzky.

HOME 1970–75

Design: Unknown

Contrasting turnover socks were introduced at the start of 1970 and were worn (initially only with the short sleeved version of this shirt) alongside the single- and double-striped pairs until 1973. Even more confusingly, white socks were also occasionally favoured as first choice! The rest of the kit remained unchanged.

Worn in: The sad 3–0 defeat against West Germany in the Euro 72 final.
Worn by: Vladimir Onishchenko, Viktor Kolotov.

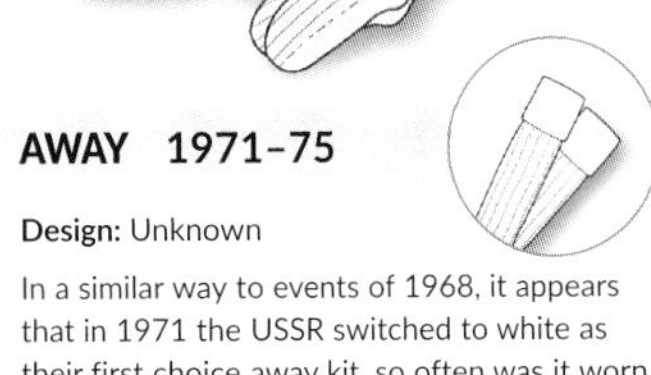

AWAY 1971–75

Design: Unknown

In a similar way to events of 1968, it appears that in 1971 the USSR switched to white as their first choice away kit, so often was it worn that year. Alternative all-white socks were also worn alongside the previous striped pairs. The shirt was produced in both long and short sleeved versions.

Worn in: The 1–0 win over Hungary in the semi-finals of Euro 72.
Worn by: Vladimir Troshkin, Yuri Istomin.

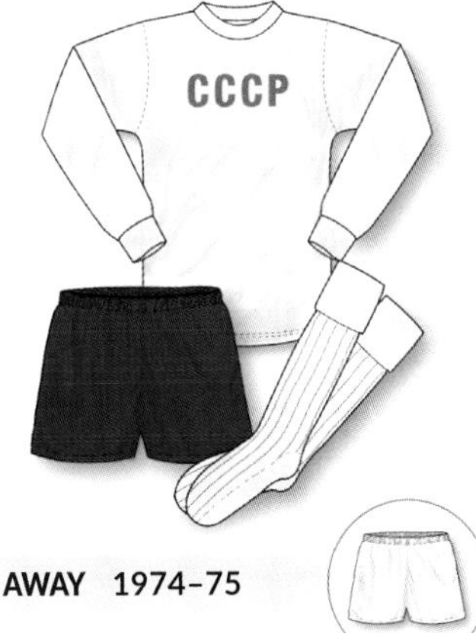

AWAY 1974–75

Design: Unknown

An alternative crew-necked white away shirt was also worn at this time in both long and short sleeved versions. It appeared with either navy blue or white shorts.

Worn in: A 4–1 win victory against Switzerland in a 1975 qualifier for Euro 76.
Worn by: Viktor Ziagintzev, Mikhail Fomenko.

HOME 1974–76

Design: Unknown

For a handful of friendly games over a three-year period a v-necked jersey was also worn. Available in both long and short sleeves it was also paired with red socks with white turnover and plain white socks.

Worn in: A 2–0 friendly defeat against Brazil in 1976 where the kit featured additional red stripes on the shorts.
Worn by: Peter Slobodian, Aleksandr Tarkhanov.

HOME 1976

Design: Unknown

A home red crew-neck shirt emerged in 1976. Unlike the '60s version, the design was updated to include contrasting white trim. In its two known outings (both friendlies), it was worn with the away kit's white socks. The '70s proved a bleak time for the Soviet team.

Worn in: A 2–2 draw with Czechoslovakia in a friendly match.
Worn by: Stefan Reshko, Evgeny Lovchev.

AWAY 1976

Design: Unknown

The next Russian away kit consisted of a simple white reversal of the home outfit, complete with contrasting crew neck and cuffs, and worn with the home shorts and away white socks that, at least for one game, were adorned with adidas three-stripe trim.

Worn in: A 2–0 defeat against Czechoslovakia in a qualifier for Euro 76.
Worn by: Viktor Matvienko, Leonid Nazarenko.

HOME 1976

Design: adidas

adidas apparel began to creep into the Soviet kit cupboard in the mid '70s. This particular short sleeved shirt featured the company's familiar crew neck and three-stripe trim combination, and was joined by a frankly massive rendering of the CCCP text, high across the chest.

Worn in: A 0–0 friendly draw with Argentina.
Worn by: Nazar Petrosian, Vladimir Suchilin.

HOME 1977–84

Design: adidas

In the ever-changing world of Soviet kits this classic crew-neck adidas shirt and its away partner were the cornerstone of the USSR kitbag for many years. It came in short and long sleeved versions and was initially worn only with an adidas logo on the right-hand side.

Worn in: Wins over Iceland (5–0) and Turkey (3–0) en route to qualification for the 1982 World Cup finals.
Worn by: Valeri Gazzaev, Oleg Romantzev.

AWAY 1977–85

Design: adidas

As with the home shirt, this white change outfit is clearly THE definitive USSR away kit from this period (especially in its long sleeved 'Worldcup Dress' incarnation). As with the home strip, an earlier version featured only an adidas logo on the shirt and in 1985 the new outlined CCCP text was introduced.

Worn in: A 1977 4–2 win over Yugoslavia.
Worn by: Aleksandr Maksimenkov, Vladimir Astapovski.

HOME 1978

Design: adidas

In the latter part of the year another set of adidas strips appeared. Worn only briefly, possibly for just one or two matches at most, the long sleeved jerseys featured self-coloured crew neck and cuffs and a trefoil logo, minus 'adidas' text.

Worn in: A 1–0 friendly defeat against West Germany.
Worn by: Sergei Prigoda, Vladimir Veremeyev.

AWAY 1978

Design: adidas

A white away version of the alternate long sleeved design also featured in just one game that year. The design reversed that of the home, with the addition of plain red shorts, minus the adidas three-stripe trim. The CCCP text appeared larger on these shirts than on others from the era.

Worn in: A 2–0 triumph over Turkey.
Worn by: Vladimir Gutzayev, Aleksandr Makhovikov.

HOME 1978–79

Design: adidas

Towards the end of 1978 Nikita Simonyan's men took part in a series of three friendlies in Japan. During the games they wore an alternative set of kits. The design was plain with a white crew neck. It was also worn with long sleeves, complete with a curious additional logo on the left-hand side.

Worn in: A 4–1 win in the first of the three friendlies against Japan.
Worn by: Tamaz Kostava, David Kipiani.

AWAY 1978–79

Design: adidas

A white version of the alternative shirt for the Japanese tour was also produced. It was worn in the second of the fixtures with red shorts, but later reappeared in a match against Hungary where it was worn with the standard white home shorts.

Worn in: A 2–0 defeat against Hungary in a 1978 qualifier for Euro 80.
Worn by: Vasile Zhupikov, Anatoli Konikov.

HOME 1981–83

Design: adidas

Introduced in the autumn of 1981 was this new set of kits that, with their inset collar, were reminiscent of a '70s design. Although the sleeves were proudly adorned with their three-stripe trim, the adidas logo was missing from the shirts – presumably covered again with the team crest.

Worn in: 1982 World Cup qualifier wins over Turkey (4–0) and Wales (3–0) – both 1981.
Worn by: Vitaly Daraselia, Vladimir Lozinski.

AWAY 1981–83

Design: adidas

The inset collar jerseys became the team's regular long sleeved option throughout 1981 and much of 1982. By 1983, when curiously white seemed to be preferred over red as USSR home choice colour, a short sleeved version of the jersey was also worn.

Worn in: A remarkable 5–0 humiliation of Portugal in a 1983 qualifier for Euro 84.
Worn by: Nikolai Larionov, Leonid Buriak.

1982 FIFA WORLD CUP

HOME 1982–84

Design: adidas

The USSR's first World Cup for 12 years brought with it a superb set of fashionable pinstriped adidas outfits that featured contrasting v-neck and cuffs. A neat touch was small CCCP text on the left cuff. Primarily introduced for the World Cup, these shirts made only the odd appearance in later years.

Worn in: The 2–2 draw vs Scotland that meant the USSR progressed in the 1982 World Cup.
Worn by: Ramaz Shengelia, Sergei Borovski.

1982 FIFA WORLD CUP

AWAY 1982–85

Design: adidas

A reversal of the new pinstriped glory was also produced and worn with the home white shorts and white socks. As with the home jersey, the adidas logo appeared, unusually, on the left-hand side, although from 1983 onwards the usual slightly random badge/logo placement situation arose again.

Worn in: A 1–0 win over Belgium in the second round of the 1982 World Cup.
Worn by: Anatoli Demianenko, Vitaly Daraselia.

HOME 1985–88

Design: adidas

Worn primarily as a long sleeved only shirt on its launch in 1985, this fine shirt (known as 'Aberdeen' in the adidas catalogue) was a magnificent stalwart of the company's kit portfolio at the time. A short sleeved version of the horizontally shadow striped jersey also made one appearance in 1987.

Worn in: A 2–0 win over the Republic of Ireland in a 1985 qualifier for the 1986 World Cup.
Worn by: Oleg Blokhin.

AWAY 1985–88

Design: adidas

A short sleeved version of this strip also appeared after the World Cup, which, like the home kit, added an adidas logo and swapped sides with the team crest. The shirt occasionally featured the outlined CCCP text introduced in 1985 and was later paired with the hem-trimmed shorts as worn in Euro 88.

Worn in: A 4–0 win over Norway in a 1986 qualifier for Euro 88.
Worn by: Sergei Baltacha, Sergei Gotzmanov.

HOME 1985

Design: adidas

Worn with both long and short sleeves, this shirt introduced a new outlined version of the CCCP text that was also to pop up occasionally on other contemporary Soviet kits. White piping trimmed the raglan sleeves and ran down each side of the jersey. Eduard Malofeyev's team were unbeaten in this particular design.

Worn in: A 4–0 win over Switzerland en route to qualification for the 1986 World Cup.
Worn by: Georgi Kondratiev, Yuri Gavrilov.

AWAY 1985–86

Design: adidas

As with its home partner, the white shirt was also introduced in 1985 and incorporated its piping and collar/v-neck combination along with the new CCCP font. Unlike the home strip though, this shirt was also worn the following year in a single match.

Worn in: A 2–0 victory over Romania in a 1985 friendly match.
Worn by: Fedor Cherenkov, Oleg Protasov.

HOME 1986

Design: adidas

The Red Army played two low-key friendlies against club sides in early 1986 during which they donned an alternative, short sleeved home shirt. The design was reminiscent of the 1982 World Cup jersey, with a slightly different silhouette, minus the pinstripes and with the inclusion of a thinner v-neck.

Worn in: A 2–0 friendly win against Mexican side Irapuato prior to the World Cup.
Worn by: Volodymyr Bezsonov.

HOME 1986

Design: adidas

Contrary to popular belief, in the 1986 World Cup Valeriy Lobanovskyi's USSR side did not sport the 'diagonal brickwork' shirt that's often attributed to the tournament, but instead wore this plainer jersey featuring adidas' new Climalite 2000 temperature regulating fabric.

Worn in: A 1–1 draw with France – this strip's only outing in the World Cup.
Worn by: Ivan Yaremchuk.

AWAY 1986

Design: adidas

The innovative Climalite 2000 fabric that comprised the Soviet strip for the 1986 World Cup wasn't able to include a shadow (jacquard) pattern, meaning that the fabric was left plain. A small Climalite 2000 logo appeared on the left sleeve of these simple outfits. The shirt made at least one appearance after the World Cup.

Worn in: The close 4–3 defeat by Belgium that sent the Soviet Union out of the World Cup.
Worn by: Vadym Yevtushenko, Andrei Bal.

HOME 1986–89

Design: adidas

Early in 1986 the USSR long sleeved kits were refreshed with a new design that would have been familiar to all adidas fans at the time. The overriding aesthetic focus was a series of dual-colour diagonal pinstripes with navy blue now added to the Soviet kit palette. Also worn in a badgeless version with adidas logo.

Worn in: A Euro 88 qualifying 2–0 victory over East Germany (1987).
Worn by: Anatoli Demianenko, Sergei Rodionov.

AWAY 1986

Design: adidas

This strip, unlike its red compatriot, was only worn once and again illustrates the rather haphazard Soviet approach to kit selection with numerous designs happily co-existing with each other. Both this and the home outfit also featured very delicate pinstripes on the shorts and by 1989 the new hem-trimmed shorts of Euro 88 were worn with these kits.

Worn in: A 1986 2–0 friendly defeat by Spain.
Worn by: Fedor Cherenkov, Aleksandr Chivadze.

AWAY 1987

Design: adidas

Another one-off shirt emerged in 1987 in a match against Norway. The shirt was a standard adidas design, often worn by junior international teams, and was produced using a new version of the hi-tech Climalite fabric.

Worn in: The 1–0 win over Norway in a 1987 Euro 88 qualifying match.
Worn by: Aleksandr Zavarov.

HOME 1988–89

Design: adidas

Introduced just prior to Euro 88 (but not worn in the tournament itself) was this classic adidas 'diagonal brickwork' shadow pattern shirt (the design many erroneously believe the team wore in the 1986 World Cup). Like so many Soviet strips these shirts co-existed simultaneously with other designs.

Worn in: A 2–1 win over Poland in a 1988 friendly.
Worn by: Vagiz Khidiatullin, Ivan Vishnevski.

AWAY 1989–90

Design: adidas

Unveiled a year after the red version, the white 'diagonal brickwork' strip was worn with either long or short sleeves and featured the new arched representation of the CCCP text. It was also occasionally paired with plain white, three-striped shorts.

Worn in: A 1989 2–0 friendly win over Turkey.
Worn by: Ivan Yaremchuk.

1988 UEFA EUROPEAN CHAMPIONSHIP

HOME 1988–90

Design: adidas

One of the most iconic adidas designs of the '80s (made famous by the Netherlands), complete with gradated colour and outlined geometric shapes, also found a home in the Soviet Union dressing-room. The shirt also made at least one brief reappearance in 1990 where it sported the new arched CCCP text.

Worn in: A great 3–1 victory over England in Euro 88.
Worn by: Alexi Mikhailichenko, Viktor Pasulko.

1988 UEFA EUROPEAN CHAMPIONSHIP

AWAY 1988–90

Design: adidas

Another less known adidas template became Valeriy Lobanovskyi's team's away kit as they enjoyed a superb Euro 88. It saw plenty of action not only in the tournament itself but also in subsequent years. The design featured a wrapover crew neck and was decorated with a tonal repeated octagon print.

Worn in: The bitterly disappointing 2–0 defeat by the Netherlands in the final of Euro 88.
Worn by: Igor Belanov, Tengiz Sulakvelidze.

HOME 1989–90

Design: adidas

Primarily worn with short sleeves although a long sleeved version did appear twice, this wrapover crew-neck jersey was the reversal of the popular Euro 88 away shirt launched a season earlier. Complete with striking octagon pattern the shirt was the preferred home design during this period.

Worn in: The 2–1 triumph over Bulgaria in a 1989 friendly match.
Worn by: Aleksandr Borodyuk, Sergei Aleinikov.

HOME 1990

Design: Score

A rather unusual addition to the Soviet kit canon dates from the team's participation in the USA Marlboro Cup in 1990. For some reason the side didn't sport kits from their regular apparel partners, adidas, and instead took to the field in attractive new outfits produced by Score.

Worn in: A penalties win over Colombia in the Marlboro Cup after the game ended 0–0.
Worn by: Sergei Rodionov, Vasili Rats.

AWAY 1990

Design: Score

White versions of the Score design were also worn by Valeriy Lobanovskyi's team, although perversely these were sported only in long sleeves, and the red worn solely in short! The jersey featured a high cycling jersey-style neck and bold Score vertical branding on the socks.

Worn in: A 2–1 victory over Costa Rica in the Marlboro Cup.
Worn by: Gennadi Litovchenko, Fedor Cherenkov.

1990 FIFA WORLD CUP

HOME 1990

Design: adidas

For their third consecutive major tournament, the USSR decided to take part in a new kit. A 'painterly' red shirt with abstract white splashes was heavily promoted pre-World Cup, but in the end the side donned a different jersey that instead leaned on a dynamic chest pattern of small triangular shapes in white and grey.

Worn in: A 2–0 defeat by Argentina that eliminated the USSR from the 1990 World Cup.
Worn by: Oleg Protasov.

AWAY 1990

Design: adidas

A white version of the unorthodox and somewhat challenging World Cup strip also made appearances in the tournament and reflected the design of the home version. As usual with the Soviet strip, it was worn with the home kit's white shorts.

Worn in: A 4–0 thrashing of Cameroon in the group stages of the 1990 World Cup.
Worn by: Andrei Zygmantovich, Igor Dobrovolski.

HOME 1990–91

Design: adidas

Worn for only a few months towards the end of 1990 this shirt utilised another familiar adidas template that featured broad white panels on both shoulders and sleeves in a design that foretold the coming of the adidas equipment designs a year or so later. Also worn with short sleeves.

Worn in: A 1990 3–0 friendly win against Israel.
Worn by: Sergei Yuran, Khoren Oganesian.

AWAY 1990–91

Design: adidas

As usual a white version of this short-lived strip was also worn in a design that mirrored the home outfit, including the simple wrapover v-neck. The shirt was also worn with plain white shorts with three-stripe trim. Adidas logos appeared on the socks.

Worn in: A 2–0 victory over Norway in a 1990 qualifier for Euro 92.
Worn by: Oleg Kuznetzov, Andrei Kanchelskis.

HOME 1991–93

Design: adidas

One can speculate that Russian abstract painter Kandinsky may have influenced these shirts – the last to be worn by the USSR before its dissolution. Dynamic patterns of black and grey shapes adorned the fabric, all held together with a single white band. Also worn by the CIS and Russian sides.

Worn in: The 4–0 victory over Cyprus en route to Euro 92.
Worn by: Andrej Chernishov, Dmitri Galiamin.

AWAY 1991–92

Design: adidas

The white version of the last USSR kit was also used pre-Euro 92 by the CIS and then later in the year for two games by the new Russia side, one of which was accompanied by blue shorts.

Worn in: The last match to be played by the USSR: a 3–0 win over Cyprus in a 1991 qualifier for Euro 92. Also, the first match to be played by Russia the following year, in a 2–0 friendly victory against Mexico.
Worn by: Sergei Kolotovkin, Dmitri Popov.

HOME 1992

Design: adidas

Following the breakup of the Soviet Union in 1991 a temporary team from the subsequent alliance, the Commonwealth of Independent States (CIS), took the place of the USSR in Euro 92. The team strip was still produced by adidas under their new 'adidas equipment' brand that relied on large bold slabs of colour.

Worn in: A 3–0 defeat against Scotland in Euro 92 – the CIS's last international fixture.
Worn by: Kakhaber Tskhadadze, Igor Shalimov.

AWAY 1992

Design: adidas

The CIS (who were later to transform into Russia) also wore a reversed version of their adidas equipment strip that featured the same large slabs of colour on each shoulder. These kits were introduced just prior to Euro 92 but immediately after the tournament the team reverted to the previous design.

Worn in: A 0–0 draw with the Netherlands in the Euro 92 group stage.
Worn by: Oleg Kuznetsov, Igor Korneev.

HOME 1992

Design: adidas

For the last game of 1992 the newly created Russian team turned out in this stop-gap adidas strip, the first to be worn featuring the new national colour scheme of white, blue and red. Worn long sleeved with a wrapover crew neck, it made just one appearance.

Worn in: A 2–0 win over Luxembourg in a qualifier for the 1994 World Cup.
Worn by: Aleksandr Borodyuk, Vladimir Tatarchuk.

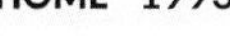

HOME 1993–95

Design: Reebok

The start of 1993 saw Pavel Sadyrin's team emerge in their first proper Russia kit. Produced by US firm Reebok, the design was dominated by an extraordinary large, two-colour version of their logo spread across the shoulders and chest and the right leg of the shorts. Also worn with plain white and red socks.

Worn in: A 3–0 1994 World Cup qualifier in 1993 against Hungary.
Worn by: Igor Kolyvanov, Andrei Ivanov.

AWAY 1993–95

Design: Reebok

The Russian Football Union wanted a complete break from the previous red and white palette of the USSR and reinforced the new colour scheme with three kits. Extraordinarily, though, despite the new Reebok deal, the last red USSR kit was also called back into active service in March 1993 vs Israel. This blue strip didn't see action until January 1994.

Worn in: The 3–0 friendly win in Austria.
Worn by: Ramiz Mamedov, Omari Tetradze.

THIRD 1993–94

Design: Reebok

The final strip in Reebok's first set of Russian outfits was naturally in red, the final colour from the country's new flag. As with its home and away equivalents, the strip was trimmed with the remaining of the three colours, creating a very strong combination of kits with elements that could be mixed and matched when required.

Worn in: The 1–0 friendly win in the USA.
Worn by: Oleg Sergeyev, Andrei Chernishov.

HOME 1993

Design: Reebok

Just six months after the unveiling of the first Reebok kits a new home design was worn in the June match vs Iceland. An asymmetrical blue sleeve with red flash was the core of the design. The white kit was only worn twice before the side reverted to the previous outfits – it seems old Russian kit habits die hard!

Worn in: A 1–1 draw with Iceland in a 1994 World Cup qualifier.
Worn by: Sergei Gorlukovich, Igor Korneyev.

AWAY 1993

Design: Reebok

An attractive blue away version of the latest Reebok design also emerged and, like the home strip, was only worn twice before the first Reebok kits were reinstated. The shorts from the previous strips were worn although a new array of plain socks in red, white and blue were produced and worn as part of all these kits.

Worn in: The 3–1 away win in Hungary en route to qualification for the 1994 World Cup.
Worn by: Youri Nikiforov, Viktor Onopko.

HOME 1994

Design: Reebok

Memories of USSR's kit selection philosophy must have come flooding back with another one-off home kit that appeared in the side's last match before the 1994 World Cup. It essentially followed the bold Reebok branding of the first set of kits, except now the secondary colour was all red, with the blue removed.

Worn in: A 2–1 friendly win against Slovakia.
Worn by: Andrei Piatnitski.

HOME 1994–96

Design: Reebok

Traditionally the USSR donned special kits for a major tournament, and Russia followed that tradition with this dynamic and warlike home shirt, including chequerboard red and blue sleeve tribal markings. The kit became first choice in April 1995 with all manner of shorts and socks colour combinations then worn.

Worn in: A 6–1 thrashing of Cameroon in the Russians' last game of the 1994 World Cup.
Worn by: Oleg Salenko, Igor Lediakov.

AWAY 1994–96

Design: Reebok

The new tribal design, complete with contemporary neck design, in this instance coloured red, adapted superbly to the blue away palette. Like the home shirt, Spring 1995 saw the kits come back into use with a variety of 'mix and match' shorts and socks concoctions worn.

Worn in: A 2–0 defeat against Brazil in the group stages of the 1994 World Cup.
Worn by: Vladislav Ternavski, Dmitri Khlestov.

THIRD 1995

Design: Reebok

Based on the design of the impressive first set of Reebok kits, this new red third jersey dismissed the blue element of the enlarged Reebok logo and stuck to a simple two-colour palette. It was worn with plain white shorts.

Worn in: A great 6–0 away win for Oleg Romantsev's team against Finland in a 1995 qualifier for Euro 96.
Worn by: Vasili Kulkov, Valery Karpin.

THIRD 1996

Design: Reebok

A new, and some might argue somewhat superfluous, red third kit was produced in 1996. Worn long sleeved, it featured a similar contemporary neck design to the kits worn in the 1994 World Cup and included broad three-quarter length white stripes on each sleeve. A chequerboard band featured on the socks.

Worn in: A 2–0 win in Malta in the Four Nation Tournament – the only outing for this strip.
Worn by: Vladimir Beschastnykh.

HOME 1996

Design: Reebok

Reebok had one last random kit tucked away in the back of the kit cupboard in the shape of this white and blue version of the first Reebok home kit. It was also a close relative of the white and red incarnation worn against Slovakia in 1994 and, like that strip, the reasons for its selection are a mystery.

Worn in: A 2–0 friendly triumph against the Republic of Ireland.
Worn by: Alexandr Mostovoi, Sergei Kiriakov.

1996 UEFA EUROPEAN CHAMPIONSHIP

HOME 1996

Design: Reebok

The final collection of Reebok kits were in marked contrast to their earlier outfits. Much more sober in appearance, they were simple, but classy, with a repeated shadow pattern of the team badge. The white shirt was worn four times this year in total, with a different shorts and socks combination in every game!

Worn in: A 3–3 draw with the Czech Republic in Euro 96.
Worn by: Igor Yanovski, Dmitri Khokhlov.

1996 UEFA EUROPEAN CHAMPIONSHIP

AWAY 1996

Design: Reebok

A red version of this latest attractive Reebok design became the side's primary change colour in Euro 96. It was paired with white shorts and the same red socks as the home kit.

Worn in: A 3–0 defeat against Germany in the group stage of Euro 96.
Worn by: Yuri Kovtun, Igor Simutenkov.

1996 UEFA EUROPEAN CHAMPIONSHIP

THIRD 1996

Design: Reebok

Finally, the last Reebok kit was this blue ensemble that completed the, by now established, trio of Russia strips. The smart blue jersey was paired with red or plain blue shorts and white or red socks.

Worn in: A 1–1 draw with Israel in a 1998 World Cup qualifier. Also worn (with blue shorts and red socks) in 2–2 friendly draw with Brazil.
Worn by: Valeriy Minko, Yevgenii Bushmanov.

HOME 1997

Design: Nike

As the new year dawned it was farewell Reebok and hello Nike. The first kits produced by the American sportswear giant for Boris Ignatyev's team were only temporary outfits and would have been familiar to any Arsenal fans.

Worn in: Just two games: a friendly 0–0 draw with Yugoslavia and a 1–1 draw with Cyprus in a 1998 World Cup qualifier where the white shirt was paired with blue shorts and red socks.
Worn by: Igor Chugainov, Aleksei Gerasimenko.

AWAY 1997

Design: Nike

The short-term Nike long sleeved kits introduced at the start of the year were also produced in blue. Unusually, the blue shorts were unbranded.

Worn in: A 2–1 win over Switzerland in the final of the Carlsberg Cup – this blue kit's only outing. The Carlsberg Cup was a four-team tournament that took place in Hong Kong over Chinese New Year.
Worn by: Igor Simutenkov, Ilia Tsymbalar.

THIRD 1997

Design: Nike

To complete the set of strips an all red-version also existed. The shirt reversed the colours of the home to create a replica of the Arsenal shirt from 1994 to 1996. The shorts featured an extremely large Nike swoosh logo on the left-hand side.

Worn in: A 1–1 draw with Yugoslavia in the Carlsberg Cup – Russia ending up 6–5 winners on penalties.
Worn by: Andrei Tikhonov, Oleg Veretennikov.

HOME 1997–98

Design: Nike

Nike's first longer term Russian kits emerged in April 1997 and brought a fresh look to the strip. Broad red panels arched under each arm and down the shirt sides with collar and shorts in a new, lighter shade of blue. The shirt was occasionally worn with the away kit's shorts and change socks to create an all-white look.

Worn in: The 1998 World Cup qualifier play-off 1–0 defeat against Italy.
Worn by: Dmitri Alenichev, Yuri Kovtun.

AWAY 1997–98

Design: Nike

A new approach to the Russian away outfit emerged as Boris Ignatyev's team tried – in vain – to qualify for the 1998 World Cup. Using the same template as the home shirt, two shades of blue worked beautifully together with a delicate red trim as the finishing touch. A new badge design was also introduced this year.

Worn in: Just one game – a 1–0 defeat by Bulgaria in a 1998 World Cup qualifier (1997).
Worn by: Akhrik Tsveiba, Aleksei Kosolapov.

HOME 1998–2000

Design: Nike

Still sticking with the familiar colour palette the next Russian strip reduced red to a minor role, and instead promoted the lighter shade of blue to sleeve trim. Just a few months after the kit was launched the RFU switched to an all-white outfit, often worn with the previous kit's socks.

Worn in: The 1–1 Euro 2000 qualifier in 1999 vs the Ukraine that meant the Russians would miss out on another major tournament.
Worn by: Alexei Smertin, Yuri Drozdov.

AWAY 1998–2000

Design: Nike

The two-tone blue approach was kept on for this change strip, as Anatoliy Byshovets attempted to lead the team to Euro 2000 qualification. A poor start to the campaign, however, saw Oleg Romantsev reappointed. As well as being worn once with the home kit's blue shorts and change blue socks, red change shorts also made a single appearance.

Worn in: A 1–1 friendly with Slovakia in 2000.
Worn by: Maxim Demenko.

HOME 2001–02

Design: Nike

A classic Nike template was brought into use for this kit which followed the trend set with the previous outfit and opted for an all-white approach. Breathable mesh fabric panels were incorporated into the jersey. The socks remained the same as those from the previous kit.

Worn in: The 4–0 triumph over Switzerland in a 2001 qualifying match for the 2002 World Cup.
Worn by: Yegor Titov, Rolan Gusev.

AWAY 2001–02

Design: Nike

The same template as the home strip was used for the away with navy mesh panels complementing the lighter blue shirt. As with the home kit, a slight dash of red was used on the collar placket. The kit was worn three times during Oleg Romantsev's successful World Cup qualifying campaign.

Worn in: A 3–0 away win at the Faroe Islands in a 2001 qualifier for the 2002 World Cup.
Worn by: Sergei Semak, Marat Izmailov.

2002 FIFA WORLD CUP

HOME 2002–03

Design: Nike

This strip featured Nike's dual-layer shirt design, designed to improve sweat and temperature control. Lighter blue mesh panels angled dramatically on each side of the shirt. As often happens with Russian kits, a shorts colour switch occurred with the away blue pairs preferred from August 2003 onwards.

Worn in: The tense 3–2 defeat by Belgium that sent the Russians home from the World Cup.
Worn by: Dmitry Sychev, Andrei Solomatin.

2002 FIFA WORLD CUP

AWAY 2002–03

Design: Nike

The angular dual-layered style of the home kit dominated the 2002 World Cup and was also rolled out with the Russian away strip, although an inset collar replaced the minimalist neck of the first choice. A nice touch saw red introduced on the two stripes at the bottom of the jersey. 'Russia' text was added under the team badge.

Worn in: A 1–0 defeat against Georgia in a Euro 2004 qualifier in 2003.
Worn by: Evgeny Aldonin, Sergei Ignashevich.

2004 UEFA EUROPEAN CHAMPIONSHIP

HOME 2004–05

Design: Nike

Nike's 'Total 90' template formed the basis for the kit worn as Valery Gazzaev's side prepared for Euro 2004. A combination of hi-tech Dri-fit fabrics with blue piping, a centrally placed badge, enlarged Nike swoosh logo on the left-hand sleeve and broad contrasting back panel helped create a fine looking outfit.

Worn in: All three of the team's Euro 2004 games – the best result, a 2–1 win over Greece.
Worn by: Dmitry Bulykin, Dmitri Kirichenko.

2004 UEFA EUROPEAN CHAMPIONSHIP

AWAY 2004–05

Design: Nike

The blue version of the 'Total 90' Russian kit, which, like the home shirt, was worn from the start of the year and featured a frankly huge circle with squad number on the front of the jersey. The design was an almost perfect reversal of the home, except for the lack of red trim on the socks and a self-coloured neck.

Worn in: A thrilling 4–3 victory over Lithuania in a 2004 friendly.
Worn by: Andrey Karyaka, Andrei Arshavin.

SPECIAL 2005

Design: Nike

A brave and powerful initiative from Nike entitled 'Stand Up, Speak Up' saw many of its national sides, including Portugal and the Netherlands, don the same black and white halved shirt to symbolise the fight against racism. Russia wore theirs, paired with black shorts and white socks, just once against Italy.

Worn in: The 2–0 friendly defeat against Italy in 2005.
Worn by: Aleksej Bugaev, Dmitri Loskov.

HOME 2006–07

Design: Nike

Following the failure to qualify for the 2006 World Cup Nike and the RFU re-evaluated the team kit and opted for a return to the red shirts from the USSR era. However, white shorts and blue socks retained the national Russian colourway. The relatively plain design was enlivened by the introduction of a new crest.

Worn in: Good wins over Estonia (2–0) and Andorra (4–0) on the way to Euro 2008.
Worn by: Pavel Pogrebnyak, Vladimir Bystrov.

AWAY 2006–07

Design: Nike

White – the colour of all Russian home shirts to date – was now second choice and paired up with simple blue shorts and red standard Nike socks. After the flamboyant ideas and statements of the previous uniforms these kits were relatively sober and plain affairs. Guus Hiddink took over as national manager in 2006.

Worn in: A 2–0 win over Macedonia in a 2006 qualifier for Euro 2008 (white socks worn).
Worn by: Vassili Berezutskiy, Alexei Berezutskiy.

2008 UEFA EUROPEAN CHAMPIONSHIP

HOME 2008

Design: Nike

After their brief sojourn in red, a rejuvenated Russia were back in all white in time for Euro 2008. This stunning home kit saw the national flag re-configured as chest bands across the front of the shirt, trimmed with gold. The shirt featured a tighter, more dynamic fit and was made of Nike's hi-tech Dri-Fit fabric.

Worn in: A superb 3–1 win over the Netherlands at Euro 2008.
Worn by: Ivan Saenko, Dmitri Torbinsky.

2008 UEFA EUROPEAN CHAMPIONSHIP

AWAY 2008

Design: Nike

The away version of the last Nike kit for Hiddink's side worked beautifully in a powerful all red. Squad numbers were housed in a small panel in the centre of the chest bands and mesh fabric ran down each shirt side. A gold pattern inside the neck symbolised architecture found in Russia's underground system.

Worn in: The crushing 3–0 defeat against Spain in the Euro 2008 semi-finals.
Worn by: Alexander Anyukov, Igor Semshov.

HOME 2008

Design: adidas

The RFU announced its new kit deal with adidas in September 2008, with the new design first worn in a World Cup qualifier against Wales that month. The first adidas shirt, which saw a return to USSR-style red, was a standard template, stop-gap adidas design that unusually featured three-quarter length sleeves.

Worn in: Just three games – wins over Wales and Finland and a 2–1 defeat by Germany.
Worn by: Vladimir Bystrov, Alan Dzagoev.

AWAY 2008

Design: adidas

A straightforward reversal of the home shirt was called into action as adidas' debut away kit and, like the home shirt, was really only a temporary measure before the first bespoke set of Russia kits were launched the following year. Although in the end, the kit was never required for active use by the first team although it was worn by the U21s.

HOME 2009

Design: adidas

March 2009 saw adidas introduce its first major set of kits for the RFU and flex its design muscles by installing a radical new colour palette of a deep maroon and gold – traditional Russian colours. The shirt featured a high, cycling jersey neck and a shadow print of an eagle on the front.

Worn in: The 3–0 away victory over Finland in a 2009 qualifier for the 2010 World Cup.
Worn by: Roman Pavlyuchenko.

AWAY 2009

Design: adidas

The RFU plumped for an all-white away approach this year, trimmed with restraint with red and blue. Like the home design, the away shirt utilised sweat-wicking Climacool fabric and reversed stitching. Although based on a standard adidas template, a shadow eagle print added a bespoke touch.

Worn in: A fine 3–1 triumph over Wales in the 2010 World Cup qualifying campaign.
Worn by: Alexei Rebko.

HOME 2009–10

Design: adidas

First worn towards the end of 2009 just eight months after the previous strip, Russian art and icons influenced this stunning strip, which retained the maroon and gold theme introduced earlier in the year. The jersey featured a shadow print eagle inspired by traditional Russian art.

Worn in: Both legs of the 2010 World Cup play-off against Slovenia who, despite a Russian win in the first leg, qualified on the away goals rule.
Worn by: Diniyar Bilyaletdinov, Renat Yanbaev.

AWAY 2010

Design: adidas

The away kit continued the highly patriotic feel of the home outfit by incorporating the colours of the national flag (with the maroon of the home strip introduced as the red shade). The tightly cropped eagle shadow print also featured. Both new kits were available in Techfit compression style or the looser Formotion fit.

Worn in: A 1–1 friendly draw with Hungary.
Worn by: Denis Kolodin.

HOME 2011

Design: adidas

A more familiar shade of red returned to the Russia kit in 2011 in a well considered and attractive design. Graceful curves in national colours were accompanied by white trim and a clever shadow pattern of small stars on the right side of the chest.

Worn in: An impressive 6–0 thrashing of Andorra on the way to qualification for Euro 2012.
Worn by: Alan Dzagoev, Denis Glushakov.

AWAY 2011

Design: adidas

Reversing the design of the home, this change outfit featured an extra touch of innovation by retaining a red panel that housed the shadow star print on the chest and accentuated the colours of the flag that arched across the jersey. Dick Advocaat led the team through a Euro 2012 qualifying campaign.

Worn in: A 0–0 draw with Armenia in this strip's first outing (Euro 2012 qualifier).
Worn by: Konstantin Zyryonov, Roman Shishkin.

2012 UEFA EUROPEAN CHAMPIONSHIP

HOME 2011-13

Design: adidas

Sashes came back into football kit fashion in the 2010s and found their way to this shirt that cleverly blended the patriotic feel of the early Russian strips with the rich red and gold of earlier designs. The Climacool shirt was available in either Techfit or Formotion style.

Worn in: All three Russian games in Euro 2012, including the wonderful 4–1 victory over the Czech Republic in their opening game.
Worn by: Roman Shirokov, Yuri Zhirkov.

2012 UEFA EUROPEAN CHAMPIONSHIP

AWAY 2012-13

Design: adidas

Unveiled a couple of months after the home design, the away followed the design of its red compatriot, including the Russian flag sash and subtle shadow pattern on the fabric. Due to the side's surprising early exit from Euro 2012 the strip didn't make any appearances in the tournament itself.

Worn in: A 1–1 draw with Uruguay in a 2012 friendly.
Worn by: Alexander Kerzhakov, Igor Denisov.

2014 FIFA WORLD CUP

HOME 2014-15

Design: adidas

Fabio Capello had been appointed Russian manager in 2012 and led the team to the 2014 World Cup where they sported this impressive deep red/maroon combination. A watermark print made reference to the Monument to the Conquerors of Space in Moscow.

Worn in: Disappointing draws with South Korea and Algeria in the 2014 World Cup.
Worn by: Aleksandr Kokorin, Aleksei Kozlov.

2014 FIFA WORLD CUP

AWAY 2014-15

Design: adidas

The space theme continued with this attractive change kit, which was influenced by the view of Earth from space, including beautiful gradated shades of blue. This latest set of Russian strips were available in adidas' latest hi-tech, lightweight fabric, adizero. A new team crest was also introduced this year.

Worn in: A tight 1–0 defeat by Belgium in the group stages of a dismal World Cup for Russia.
Worn by: Maxim Kanunnikov, Oleg Shatov.

2016 UEFA EUROPEAN CHAMPIONSHIP

HOME 2015-16

Design: adidas

It was another classy outfit for the Russians as they prepared for Euro 2016. Adidas moved its three stripes to the sides of the shirts and the adizero fabric featured a repeated shadow pattern of the Russian crest. Adidas' standard shorts and sock designs completed the kit.

Worn in: The 1–1 draw with England, followed by the 2–1 defeat against Slovakia in a poor tournament for Leonid Slutsky's team.
Worn by: Vassili Berezutskiy, Igor Smolnikov.

2016 UEFA EUROPEAN CHAMPIONSHIP
2017 FIFA CONFEDERATIONS CUP

AWAY 2015-17

Design: adidas

Memories of the Russian side from a decade earlier came flooding back with the introduction of this next away strip, which recreated the white/lighter blue/red combination so favoured back in the Reebok and Nike eras. A large eagle shadow print, in a painterly style, featured on the chest.

Worn in: The poor 3–0 defeat against Wales in the group stages of Euro 2016.
Worn by: Fedor Smolov, Artem Dzyuba.

2017 FIFA CONFEDERATIONS CUP

HOME 2016-17

Design: adidas

Adidas designers clearly had an interest in their kit back catalogue when they created this strip. With a lighter shade of red and secondary colour of white, the classic USSR kits of the '70s came to mind. The zig-zag shadow pattern was a standard adidas style from the late '80s, although interestingly the USSR never wore it.

Worn in: A 2–0 victory over New Zealand in the Confederations Cup – Russia's sole win.
Worn by: Aleksandr Erokhin, Dmitriy Poloz.

2018 FIFA WORLD CUP

HOME 2017-18

Design: adidas

As Russia prepared to host the 2018 World Cup they unveiled their kit for the tournament which formed part of adidas' impressive array of retro-themed designs. The style was commonly worn by adidas' teams in the late '80s and featured angular white panels across each shoulder. The choice of this design to be resurrected is relatively unorthodox, though, as the USSR only wore it in the 1988 Olympics.

Since taking over the Russia contract adidas have opted for shades of red as their primary base colour. This sublime maroon outfit dates from 2009–10.

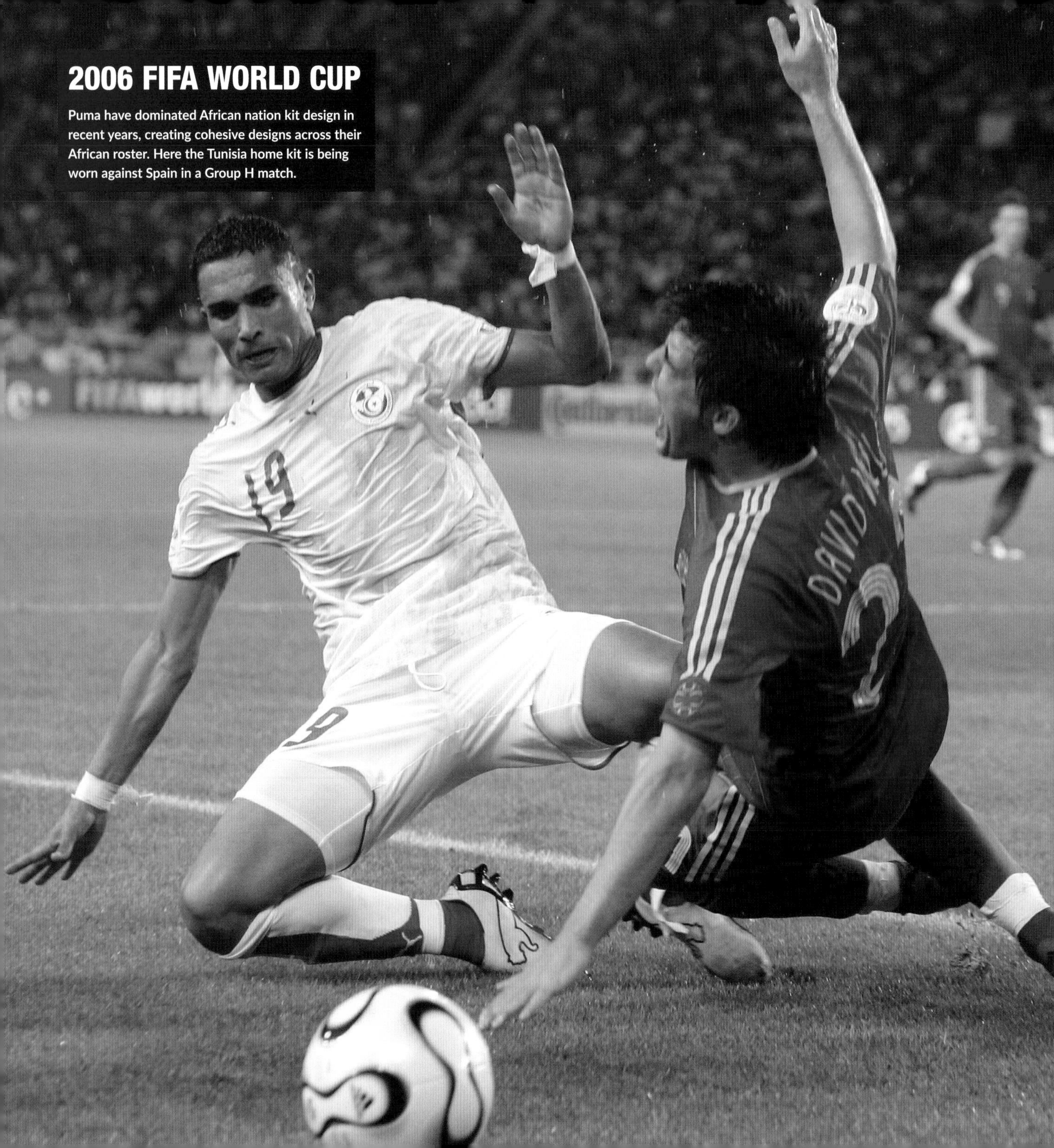

2006 FIFA WORLD CUP

Puma have dominated African nation kit design in recent years, creating cohesive designs across their African roster. Here the Tunisia home kit is being worn against Spain in a Group H match.

2006 FIFA WORLD CUP

Croatia in their familiar chequerboard Nike home kit compete against an adidas-clad Japan in the group stages. By 2006 shirts were becoming more fitted.

SCOTLAND

Since 1998 major tournaments have missed out on the navy blue of Scotland – and of course the colourful Tartan Army support.

The blue of the team strip is, naturally, taken from the saltire – the country's national flag, although in a much darker shade and there is much debate as to the origins of this selection.

Traditionally the shirt is paired with white shorts and socks that, in some form or other, are red themed. However the team have turned out in primrose and pink – the racing colours of Lord Rosebery, an early patron of the game in Scotland. Taking influence from those kits, pink has re-emerged several times in the Scottish away strip kitbag over the years in a variety of different shades, most recently the adidas kit that the Scots were controversially forced to wear against the Auld Enemy, England, due to FIFA's decision that the white sleeves on the Scots' home jersey caused a clash with England's shirts.

It's difficult to pin down a stable away colour for Scotland. For years white was the first choice, but since the '80s a whole array of hues have been worn including red, amber and, of course, pink. The designs of some of these strips have also at times been challenging, with some fans even questioning whether Scotland were guinea pigs for kit designers to try out some of their more daring ideas.

Adidas are currently Scotland's technical sponsor, but previous to that the team enjoyed a long and fruitful relationship with Umbro until Fila took over in 2000, closely followed by Diadora three years later.

Few countries in the world have such a distinctive and unique visual icon as Scotland's tartan designs. The fact that tartan is available in a wide variety of colours AND that it's fabric based poses the question why the Scots haven't incorporated tartan into their kits on a more frequent basis?

Scotland line up before their 1978 World Cup match against Peru in the classic late 70s Umbro home kit (worn here with change shorts).

HOME 1966–71

Design: Umbro

The Scots missed out on the England World Cup party in 1966 but got revenge a year later in one of the nation's most fondly remembered matches while wearing this fine '60s long sleeved, crew-neck Aztec jersey. Despite its simplicity, it's rightly regarded as a classic.

Worn in: The 3–2 win over England in 1967 – when Scotland became unofficial World Champions!
Worn by: Denis Law, Jim McCalliog.

HOME 1966

Design: Umbro

Scotland met Celtic neighbours Wales at Ninian Park in a Euro 68 qualifier in 1966 and turned out in this one-off variation of their home kit. Although the shorts and navy socks (with red turnover) were consistent with the regular home kit, the jersey now featured non-contrasting crew neck and cuffs.

Worn in: The 1–1 draw with Wales in the 1966 European Championship qualifier.
Worn by: Jimmy Johnstone, Jim Baxter.

AWAY 1965–71

Design: Umbro

White had been the Scots' traditional away colours for many years and in the mid-'60s the design was updated to reflect the fashionable long sleeved/crew-neck style. Scotland didn't manage to qualify for any major tournament throughout the '60s and Bobby Brown took over as manager in 1967.

Worn in: A superb 5–0 win over Cyprus in a 1970 World Cup qualifier (1968).
Worn by: Alan Gilzean, Bobby Murdoch.

HOME 1972

Design: Umbro

With '70s flamboyant trends in full swing Umbro updated the Scotland shirt with the addition of a wing collar with white insert. The rest of the outfit remained the same as it had been towards the end of the '60s. Change red socks were also worn.

Worn in: A 2–0 victory for Tommy Docherty's side over Northern Ireland in the 1972 Home Internationals.
Worn by: George Graham, Billy McNeil.

AWAY 1972–76

Design: Umbro

The *de rigueur* '70s wing collar naturally found its way to the away kit. As with the previous strip, the shirt (which was worn in both long and short sleeved versions) featured self-coloured collar and cuffs. In 1973 a small Umbro logo was added to the shorts.

Worn in: A fantastic 4–1 win in Denmark in a 1972 qualifier for the 1974 World Cup.
Worn by: Peter Lorimer, Joe Harper.

HOME 1973–76

Design: Umbro

The home kit was updated slightly in 1973 with red socks becoming a permanent fixture and the first sign of visible branding with the presence of an Umbro logo on the shorts – it was also added to the shirts in 1974. Willie Ormond took over as manager in 1973 and led his team to the 1974 World Cup finals.

Worn in: An embarrassing 5–0 defeat by England in Ormond's first match in charge.
Worn by: Lou Macari, Sandy Jardine.

1974 FIFA WORLD CUP

HOME 1974

Design: Umbro

Short sleeves began to be favoured by the time the 1974 World Cup arrived, as did manufacturers' logos, and an Umbro diamond was added to the jersey that was first worn in the 1974 Home Internationals. Rather gimmicky sock tags also featured with this kit.

Worn in: An unbeaten 1974 World Cup tournament including a 2–0 win over Zaire and a 0–0 draw with the mighty Brazil.
Worn by: Billy Bremner, Danny McGrain.

1974 FIFA WORLD CUP

AWAY 1974

Design: Umbro

The beautiful all-white away strip was updated with the Umbro logo and sock tags in time for the Germany World Cup – Scotland's first major tournament for 16 years. Self-coloured collar and cuffs were still favoured. Both World Cup shirts were made from mesh-like airtex fabric.

Worn in: A 1–1 draw with Yugoslavia in the 1974 World Cup – sadly not enough for Scotland to progress to the next stage.
Worn by: Joe Jordan, David Hay.

HOME 1976–80

Design: Umbro

A real favourite with many Scotland fans was this classic Umbro strip that was launched at the 1976 Home Internationals. The wing collar/inset combination remained, but now it was joined throughout by Umbro's diamond taping – a result of increased kit branding at the time.

Worn in: The 3–2 win over the Netherlands in the 1978 World Cup (preceded by a dismal defeat against Peru and a draw with Iran).
Worn by: Archie Gemmill – scorer of THAT goal.

AWAY 1976–80

Design: Umbro

Diamond taping also made it to Ally McLeod's Scotland away jersey. Navy or white shorts were worn and the socks' red trim meant that each element could be seamlessly interchanged. The kit was not used in the disappointing 1978 World Cup although the shorts were worn with the home kit on two occasions.

Worn in: A marvellous (all white) 4–0 triumph over Norway.
Worn by: John Robertson, Gordon McQueen.

HOME 1980–82

Design: Umbro

In 1980, with the Scots now managed by Jock Stein, the design was given the merest of revamps. The white inset collar was replaced by a simpler and far less clumsy neck. Due to international regulations the taping remained 'solid' rather than the more familiar 'double diamond' style used in domestic leagues.

Worn in: A superb 2–1 win over Sweden in 1981 in a 1982 World Cup qualifier.
Worn by: Kenny Dalglish, Asa Hartford.

AWAY 1980–82

Design: Umbro

Although the Scots had worn white away strips for much of the '70s, Umbro decided to switch to a rich red to coincide with the updated home kit. The strip was only ever worn twice, once with red socks and once with white, but both times in airtex fabric. Both 1980 shirts pioneered the use of player names on the reverse.

Worn in: A 1982 World Cup qualifier 1–0 win over Israel (1981).
Worn by: Graeme Souness, Kenny Burns.

HOME 1982–85

Design: Umbro

The early '80s kit design renaissance hit Scotland just in time for the 1982 Spain World Cup with the introduction of this silky new outfit. The elaborate collar and trim of the '70s was banished in favour of minimal white piping and a modern v-neck.

Worn in: A 5–2 win over New Zealand, and a 4–1 defeat by Brazil in the 1982 World Cup.
Worn by: David Narey, scorer of a wonder goal against Brazil, Alan Brazil.

AWAY 1982–85

Design: Umbro

Red and navy remained the Scots' away colours of choice in the early '80s. Rather than simply mirroring the home strip, however, this time the side sported a classic pinstriped shirt. As with the home kit, the only form of trim on the shorts was a single red stripe down each leg – a far cry from the extravagant stylings of the '70s.

Worn in: 1985's 1–0 victory over Iceland in the 1986 World Cup qualifying campaign.
Worn by: Roy Aitken, Jim Bett.

HOME 1985–88

Design: Umbro

Although this modernistic shirt was a nice enough design, the rather experimental 'horror-zontal' shorts that accompanied it are still remembered with a shudder by the Tartan Army. Umbro logos were added to the socks towards the end of this kit's lifespan.

Worn in: Defeats to Denmark (1–0) and West Germany (2–1) in the 1986 World Cup.
Worn by: Gordon Strachan, Maurice Malpas.

AWAY 1985–88

Design: Umbro

A fresh colour arrived in the Scotland kit cupboard in the shape of this lemon-yellow away strip. The design followed the style of the home, complete with wrapover round neck and broad horizontal shadow hoops. The shirt also featured the rather gothic SFA logo on the right sleeve. Andy Roxburgh was appointed manager following Jock Stein's tragic death in 1986.

Worn in: A 1–0 friendly win vs Israel in 1986.
Worn by: Paul McStay, Willie Miller.

1990 FIFA WORLD CUP

HOME 1988–91

Design: Umbro

Certainly one of the most sophisticated strips the Scots have ever worn, this shirt featured a slightly larger cut, an updated crest design, elegant shadow pinstripe, and a button-down collar and long placket with just a hint of tartan. The design was inspired and totally bespoke.

Worn in: The great 2–1 win over Sweden followed by the unlucky 1–0 defeat against Brazil in the 1990 World Cup.
Worn by: Mo Johnston, Ally McCoist.

1990 FIFA WORLD CUP

AWAY 1988–91

Design: Umbro

In the most radical reworking of a Scotland away strip to date, Umbro reverted to white for the first time since 1979. The jersey (officially named 'Roma' in the Umbro catalogue) was embellished with bold navy and yellow horizontal bands topped off with a diagonal shadow stripe pattern and the two SFA logos.

Worn in: A dire 1–0 defeat by Costa Rica in the 1990 World Cup for Andy Roxburgh's team.
Worn by: Alex McLeish, Murdo MacLeod.

1992 UEFA EUROPEAN CHAMPIONSHIP

HOME 1991–94

Design: Umbro

Umbro were the first company to revive the ancient tradition of long shorts in the early '90s and this Scotland kit was one of its earliest ventures into the once-forgotten fashion. The shirt was baggier and featured a cryptic design on the right sleeve. Squad numbers featured on the front of the shirts for the first time.

Worn in: A great 3–0 win over CIS in Euro 92 – Scotland's first European Championship.
Worn by: Richard Gough, Dave McPherson.

1992 UEFA EUROPEAN CHAMPIONSHIP

AWAY 1991–93

Design: Umbro

Without doubt this white kit (a design named 'Hampden') was one of the most outrageous outfits the Scots had worn to date. Although the early '90s saw traditional values return to home kits, away strips tended to mutate into increasingly unconventional designs. The shirt was also worn with change white shorts.

Worn in: A 2–0 triumph vs San Marino in the Euro 92 qualifiers (1991).
Worn by: Gordon Durie, Stuart McCall.

AWAY 1993–94

Design: Umbro

Salmon pink (a popular Umbro mid-'90s hue) was introduced as the country's next away strip colour midway through the 1994 World Cup qualifiers. The jersey saw a retro '20s collar introduced (complete with a small version of the Scotland crest in the neck) accompanied by thin purple and white stripes.

Worn in: The 3–1 defeat by Italy that meant the Scots would not qualify for the 1994 World Cup.
Worn by: Eoin Jess, Tom Boyd.

1996 UEFA EUROPEAN CHAMPIONSHIP

HOME 1994–96

Design: Umbro

With 'Braveheart' stirring the hearts of Scots everywhere surely one of the most patriotic strips ever worn by the side emerged in 1994. The courageous all-navy design featured an SFA-commissioned green and purple tartan paired with purple and pale yellow. The diamond taping was removed in Euro 96.

Worn in: The heartbreaking 2–0 defeat against England in Euro 96.
Worn by: Gary McAllister, Colin Hendry.

1996 UEFA EUROPEAN CHAMPIONSHIP

AWAY 1994–96

Design: Umbro

Umbro's purple patch came to an end with this outrageous and highly decorative strip that divided opinion among supporters. Purple had also featured in the previous two away designs, but now it was combined with two shades of green to form a dynamic but rather abstract arrangement of angular geometric shapes.

Worn in: A 2–0 win over San Marino in 1995 during the Euro 96 qualifiers.
Worn by: Pat Nevin, Colin Calderwood.

HOME 1996–98

Design: Umbro

A much more familiar colour scheme greeted the Tartan Army when Craig Brown's side stepped out to play Austria in 1996 at the start of the World Cup qualifiers. The design itself took a flamboyant approach with white sleeve panels, trimmed with red piping.

Worn in: The successful 1998 World Cup qualifiers including the infamous 'match' against a no-show Estonia in 1996.
Worn by: Billy McKinlay, John McGinlay.

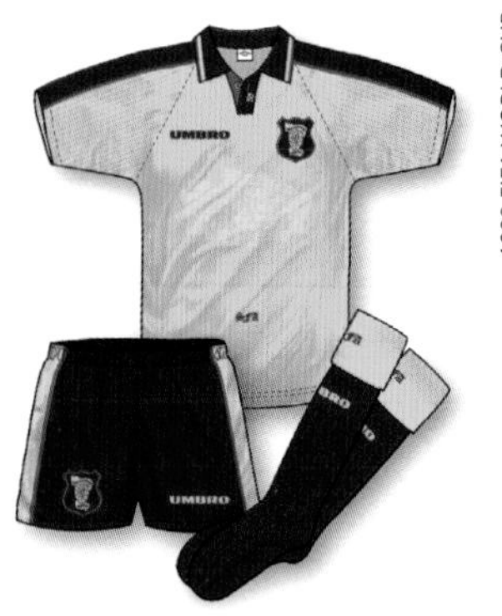

1998 FIFA WORLD CUP

AWAY 1996–98

Design: Umbro

Although it lacked the dynamic feel of the previous change kit, Scotland's next outfit was no less energetic due to its vivid combination of a deep yellow, trimmed with a striking red and navy combination. The incredibly baggy kit incorporated a watermark-style montage based on the Scottish crest.

Worn in: The crushing 3–0 defeat by Morocco in Scotland's last game at the 1998 World Cup.
Worn by: Scot Gemmill, John Collins.

1998 FIFA WORLD CUP

HOME 1998–2000

Design: Umbro

This new strip was introduced just in time for the World Cup. A simpler design than the previous, the shirt featured thin horizontal shadow stripes and a new collar design, complete with just a hint of tartan. It proved to be the last Scotland home shirt to be produced by long-term kit partners Umbro.

Worn in: The disappointing 2–1 defeat by Brazil in the opening game of the 1998 World Cup.
Worn by: Craig Burley, Paul Lambert.

AWAY 1999–2000

Design: Umbro

Launched with the help of a full squad team photo, this strip saw a return of salmon pink, albeit in a more muted shade. It was elegantly combined with navy blue and trimmed with white. A bold chest band housed the Umbro logo, squad number and crest. A new version of Umbro's diamond trim adorned each sleeve.

Worn in: The memorable 1–0 win over mighty Germany in a 1999 friendly – the kit's debut.
Worn by: Don Hutchison, David Weir.

HOME 2000–02

Design: Fila

Italian sportswear company Fila brought a touch of continental chic when it arrived at Hampden with this excellent strip in 2000. Collars were history and instead a discreetly trimmed v-neck was introduced alongside a breathable fabric, multi-panel combination – all held together with reversed stitching.

Worn in: A 2001 2–1 victory over Latvia during a poor 2002 World Cup qualifying campaign.
Worn by: Matt Elliott, Dougie Freedman.

AWAY 2000–02

Design: Fila

Fila's first Scotland away kit was a solid combination of simplicity and flair with the white shirt enhanced by navy side and underarm panels, trimmed with yellow piping. The v-neck featured an asymmetrical navy and yellow flash. As with the home kit, the Scotland crest was simplified and an SFA monogram added.

Worn in: A 5–0 thrashing by France in a 2002 friendly – Berti Vogts' first match in charge.
Worn by: Gary Caldwell, Christian Dailly.

HOME 2002–03

Design: Fila

A distinctly retro feel was adopted for Fila's last Scottish home strip for the new era under their first-ever foreign coach. It was an ingenious design: although it did not directly copy a previous Scotland strip, it gave the impression that it had. The debonair jersey featured a '70s inset white collar combined with '80s pinstripes.

Worn in: A hard-fought 1–1 draw with Germany in the Euro 2004 qualifiers (2003).
Worn by: Jackie McNamara, Dominic Matteo.

AWAY 2002–03

Design: Fila

The 1986 World Cup away kit was clear inspiration with this elegant strip, launched shortly after the home kit. The jersey featured a streamlined crew neck and a navy chest band. 2003 marked the end of the SFA's three-year deal with Fila, which had produced consistently solid designs in its short tenure.

Worn in: A 2–0 win over Iceland in a Euro 2004 qualifier (2002).
Worn by: Gary Naysmith, Stevie Crawford.

HOME 2003–05

Design: Diadora

It was all change on the Scotland kit front in 2003. Not only was there a new home and away strip from new kit supplier Diadora, but a redesigned version of the Scottish crest was also launched. Diadora's first home kit featured a double-layered neck and white panels, with the socks reverting to navy with a maroon trim.

Worn in: The great 2003 1–0 win vs the Netherlands in the Euro 2004 play-off first leg.
Worn by: Darren Fletcher, James McFadden.

AWAY 2003-05

Design: Diadora

Diadora kept it simple with its first away strip. Formed from a workmanlike white and navy, a touch of sophistication was added with the inclusion of reversed seams that curved anatomically down the jersey. Berti Vogts left the Scotland post in 2004.

Worn in: The not so great 6–0 defeat against the Netherlands in the second leg of the Euro 2004 play-off.
Worn by: Steven Pressley, Neil McCann.

THIRD 2004-06

Design: Diadora

This fine amber jersey was the first-ever third shirt worn by a Scottish side. Consisting of a standard Diadora template, the lightweight, tight-fitting shirt featured angled navy mesh inset strips and Diadora's hi-tech 'One of Eleven' shoulder flashes that changed colour depending on body temperature.

Worn in: A 3–0 defeat by Hungary in 2004 – the biggest Scots Hampden defeat since 1973.
Worn by: Nigel Quashie, Steven Caldwell.

HOME 2005-07

Design: Diadora

This home kit has to be one of the most contemporary worn by the Scots to date. It was packed with asymmetrical features: a curved white flash and trim on the right shirt sleeve, horizontal trim on the right leg of the shorts and an innovative sock design that included a white stripe just on the right leg.

Worn in: The 5–1 win over Bulgaria en route to winning the 2006 Kirin Cup!
Worn by: Kris Boyd, Lee McCulloch.

AWAY 2005-07

Design: Diadora

The latest in a long line of radical Scotland away kits appeared in 2005. Its extreme nature, however, came not from garish patterns, but from the choice of colour; sky blue. This unorthodox selection was fashioned into a stylish outfit which, when grouped with the home and third strips, made a formidable set.

Worn in: A superb 2–1 away win vs Norway in a 2005 qualifier for the 2006 World Cup.
Worn by: Kenny Miller, Paul Hartley.

HOME 2007-08

Design: Diadora

A totally new approach to a Scottish kit came in the form of this all-dark navy strip. Elegant and arrogant, the strip was trimmed throughout with gold and incorporated an abbreviated shadow pattern of the saltire on the front. Lightweight and slim-fitting, the jersey still included Diadora's 'One of Eleven' logos.

Worn in: The classic 1–0 win against France in the Euro 2008 qualifiers (2006).
Worn by: Graham Alexander, Gary Teale.

AWAY 2007-09

Design: Diadora

A favourite with the fans, this enigmatic away kit followed the same basic template as the home but crafted it into a slick white and sky blue concoction, trimmed opulently with gold and featuring a full. It was a good period for the Scots who earned a placed in the top 20 of FIFA's world rankings.

Worn in: The astonishing 2007 1–0 away victory in France (Euro 2008 qualifiers).
Worn by: Scott Brown, Barry Ferguson.

HOME 2008-09

Design: Diadora

It was a return to a more traditional colour palette in this last Diadora home strip. Pointed white panels on either side of the neck gave an impression of a wing collar with red piping used as an accent. Despite two earlier wins over France, Scotland failed to qualify for Euro 2008 and endured an awful World Cup qualifying campaign under new manager George Burley.

Worn in: A 2–1 win over Iceland (2009).
Worn by: James Morrison, Ross McCormack.

THIRD 2007-09

Design: Diadora

A beautiful maroon (officially 'cherry red') and gold combination helped create this stunning strip for Alex McLeish's side as they prepared to take on Georgia in a Euro 2008 qualifier. Despite its undisputed attractiveness, many supporters felt a third kit was unnecessary.

Worn in: The 2–0 defeat against Georgia in the 2007 qualifier for Euro 2008, after which the kit was never seen again.
Worn by: Stephen McManus, Shaun Maloney.

AWAY 2009

Design: Diadora

The final Diadora outfit brought in the very latest fabric technology of breathable mesh panels in order to wick sweat from the body more quickly and regulate temperature. Trimmed heavily with navy and just a hint of sky blue, the reverse of the shirt featured the text 'ALBA' – the Gaelic name for Scotland.

Worn in: A 4–0 drubbing at the hands of Norway in a 2010 World Cup qualifier.
Worn by: Callum Davidson, Kris Commons.

HOME 2010–11

Design: adidas

After seven years with Diadora, the SFA signed a new kit deal with the mighty adidas – the famous three stripes were to appear on a Scotland shirt for the first time. The shirt was a good start to the relationship; it used adidas' standard 'Condivo' template with the addition of a watermark of the Scotland crest on the front.

Worn in: A 1–0 triumph over the Czech Republic on the kit's debut in 2010.
Worn by: Christophe Berra, James McArthur.

AWAY 2010–11

Design: adidas

A bright yellow and navy version of the Condivo template was selected as the first adidas change strip for the SFA. The shirt was constructed from adidas' Climacool hi-tech fabric in a Formotion fit which was designed to optimise performance and comfort while a player was in motion. Craig Levein was appointed manager.

Worn in: The fine 3–1 win against Wales in the 2010 Nations Cup.
Worn by: Charlie Adam, Steven Naismith.

HOME 2011–13

Design: adidas

One of the best recent Scotland strips was unveiled in a November 2011 friendly against Cyprus. A broad white collar and new round badge brought back memories of the '70s, but it was the beautiful embossed montage featuring the saltire blended with key moments in Scottish football history that added a touch of class.

Worn in: Two victories over Croatia (1–0 and 2–0) in the 2014 World Cup qualifiers (2013).
Worn by: Robert Snodgrass, Charlie Mulgrew.

AWAY 2012–14

Design: adidas

Launched a few months after its home partner, the away saw a return to a white kit in this practical but considered design. A v-neck was joined by a horizontal shadow pattern that adorned the Climacool fabric. The shirt also used adidas' TechFit compression technology designed to improve performance on the pitch.

Worn in: A 2–0 defeat against Belgium in a 2012 qualifier for the 2014 World Cup.
Worn by: Jamie Mackie, Alan Hutton.

HOME 2013–15

Design: adidas

With Gordon Strachan now manager a new strip emerged towards the end of the year. It was a slick and masterful ensemble with navy complemented silver trim, a tonal badge and discreet tartan panels. A small embroidered spider on the back of the shirt represented the famous Scottish story of Robert the Bruce.

Worn in: The unfortunate 1–0 defeat by Poland in the 2006 World Cup qualifying campaign.
Worn by: James Collins, David Partridge.

AWAY 2014–15

Design: adidas

Memories of the famous primrose and pink Lord Rosebery Scotland shirt came flooding back with this new away design that took these colours and employed them on a white shirt, complete with button-up grandad neck. It was a shirt that divided opinion among the Tartan Army, however!

Worn in: A 1–1 draw with the Republic of Ireland (2015) in a Euro 2016 qualifier.
Worn by: Grant Hanley, Ikechi Anya.

HOME 2015–17

Design: adidas

Not afraid to take risks, adidas introduced white raglan sleeves to this fresh home strip where they were joined by a shadow tartan pattern. The design was not unique to Scotland, though, and was also included in the Bosnia and Herzegovina away kit at the time.

Worn in: Another frustrating World Cup qualifying campaign, including a thrilling 2–2 draw with England in 2017.
Worn by: Leigh Griffiths, Stuart Armstrong.

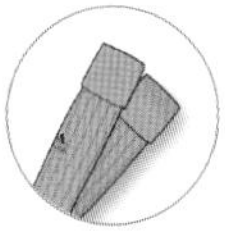

AWAY 2015–17

Design: adidas

Pink was retained as a key Scotland colour for this Climacool outfit – but now in a bright neon shade. The jersey, which saw plenty of match action, was trimmed with black and featured a tonal badge. Also worn with pink socks.

Worn in: The 3–0 2018 World Cup qualifier defeat by England in 2016 where this strip controversially had to be worn as FIFA claimed the Scots' home strip clashed with England's.
Worn by: James Forrest, Lee Wallace.

HOME 2017–18

Design: adidas

It was a much more traditional look for Scotland with their next kit – the one they would have worn in the 2018 World Cup had they qualified – with a return to the iconic navy/white/red combination. Echoes of the Mexico 1986 kit were present with the trimmed collar, and the front of the shirt was decorated with a subtle retelling of the classic adidas geometric pattern of the late '80s as made famous by the Netherlands.

Graeme Souness wearing the controversial hooped shorts of the Umbro home kit in the 1986 FIFA World Cup finals in Mexico.

Adidas' bold primrose and pink 'Rosebery' inspired away kit from 2014–15, here worn before a friendly game against Northern Ireland in 2015.

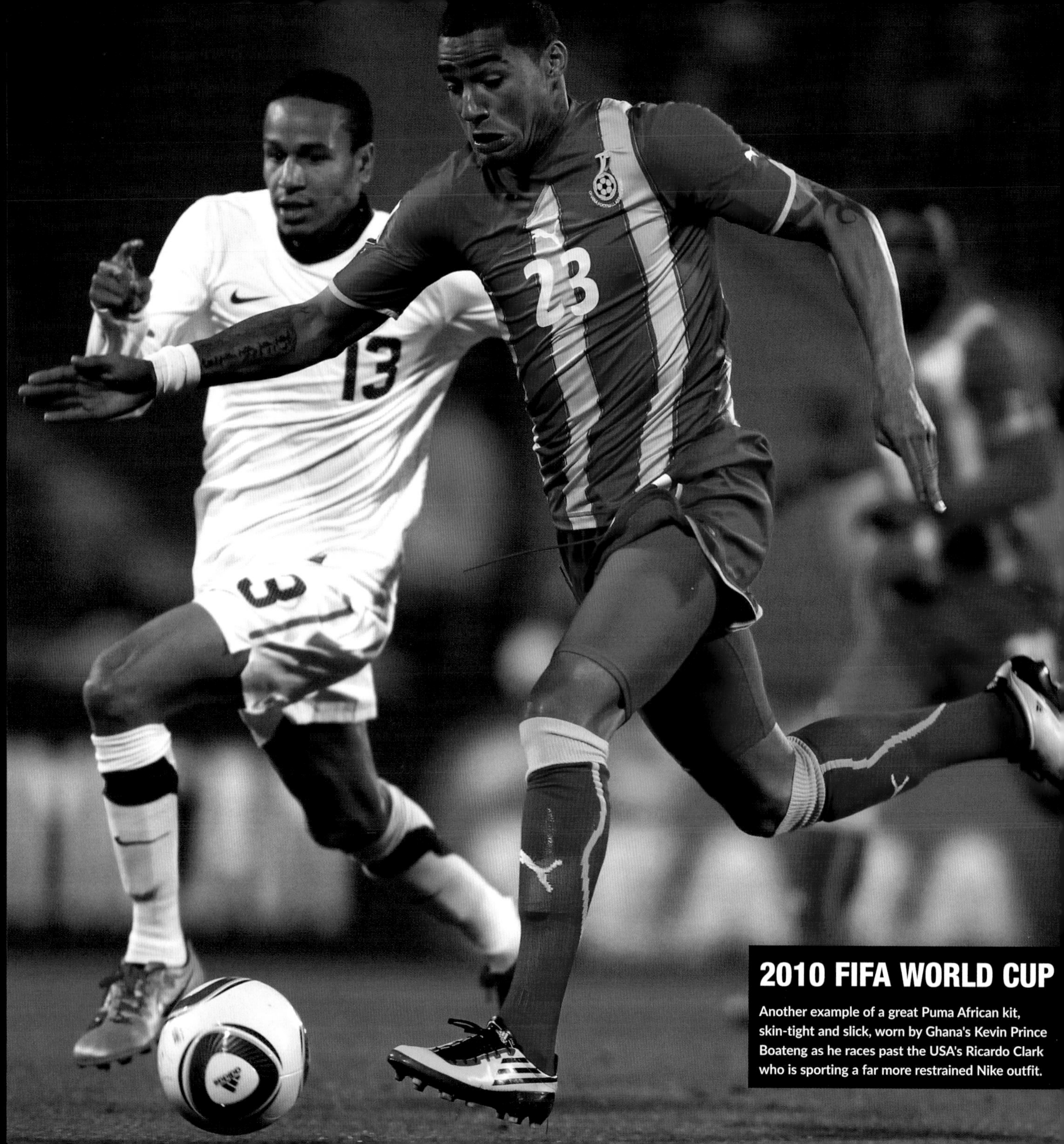

2010 FIFA WORLD CUP

Another example of a great Puma African kit, skin-tight and slick, worn by Ghana's Kevin Prince Boateng as he races past the USA's Ricardo Clark who is sporting a far more restrained Nike outfit.

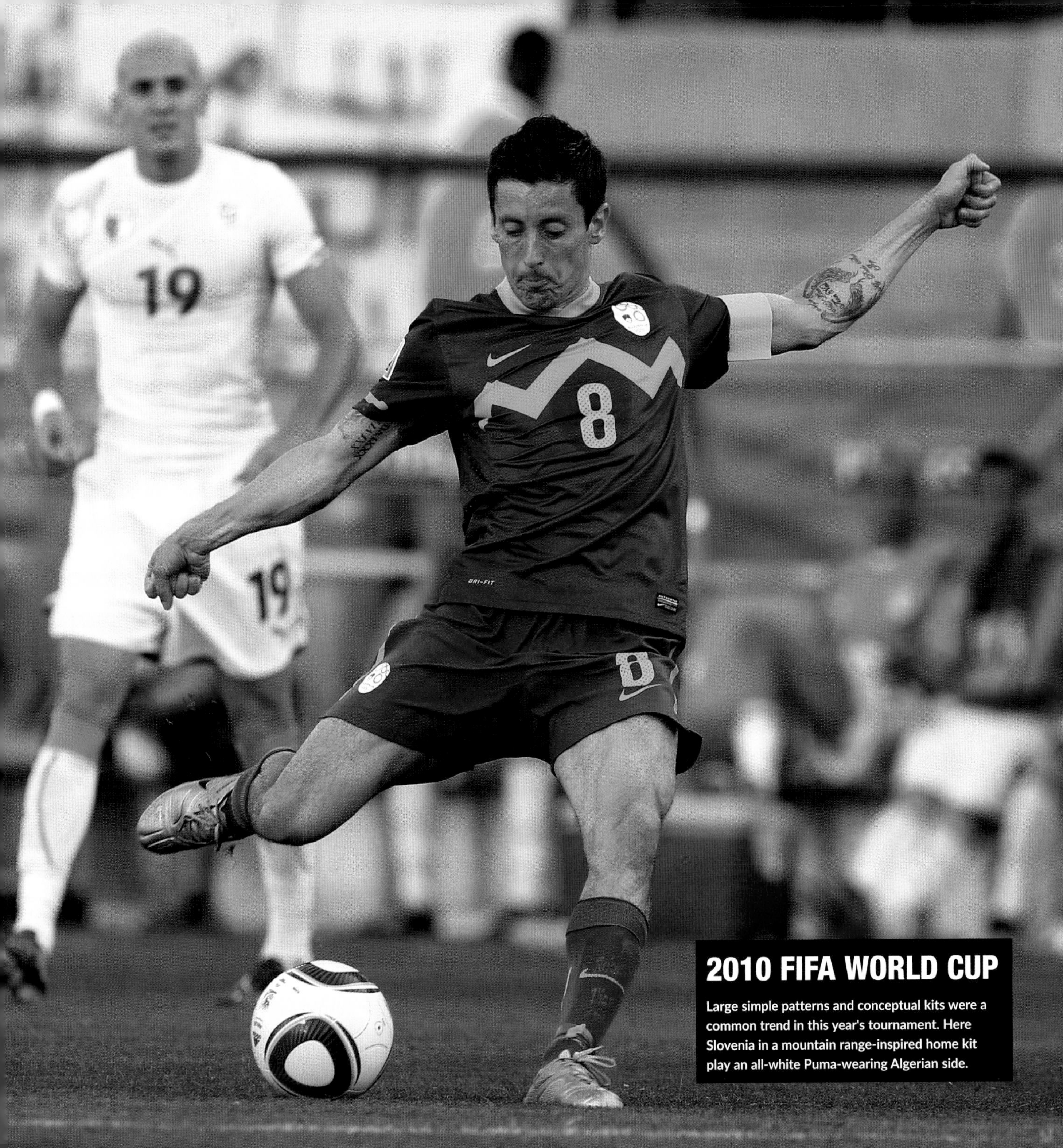

2010 FIFA WORLD CUP

Large simple patterns and conceptual kits were a common trend in this year's tournament. Here Slovenia in a mountain range-inspired home kit play an all-white Puma-wearing Algerian side.

SPAIN

Surely one of the most glorious of international kits is Spain's. The unique balance of red and yellow, often accentuated via the clever use of black or navy blue, is instantly recognisable across the world.

Go back a few decades, and the Spanish kit record was very stable and formulaic: red shirts, blue shorts and black socks (with a red and yellow turnover that cleverly replicated the country's flag). As an away kit all they needed was a blue shirt – everything else remained the same.

Blue had, in fact, played a key role in many of the side's strips in the first half of the 20th century and continues to be a key ingredient in the unique Spanish football colour palette.

As the kit world became more sophisticated and brighter colours went out of favour, a dark navy shade replaced the blue. White also became a more favoured away colour, although blue was never far behind in the kit cupboard; Spain were one of the few nations who took part in tournaments regularly equipped with three kits.

Since adidas took over the contract from Le Coq Sportif in 1991, a vibrant array of designs have fully exploited the majesty of Spain's unique colour scheme.

Later designs experimented further, using different tonal variations of colour, but it's when the side are in red, yellow and royal blue that they encapsulate the spirit of their footballing heritage perfectly.

The Spain squad celebrate beating the Netherlands 1–0 in the 2010 World Cup final. The Spanish actually wore their away kit in the match itself but switched to their traditional red to receive the trophy.

HOME 1966–78

Design: Umbro

Spain wore this classic, crew-neck home shirt, pretty much unchanged, for almost 20 years (it was actually first worn circa 1959). So rigid was their kit tradition that short-sleeved versions didn't exist; generally players simply rolled up their sleeves. The kit coincided with a real low point in the side's football fortunes – the '70s.

Worn in: Spain's only 1966 World Cup win: a 2–1 victory over Switzerland.
Worn by: Manuel Sanchis, Amancio.

AWAY 1966–78

Design: Umbro

Spain's away strip during this period sets out their basic kit philosophy right up until the early '90s – i.e. don a blue shirt and wear it with the home blue shorts and black, red and yellow socks. It was an uncomplicated strategy but, thanks to the country's unique colour scheme, it was one that worked incredibly well.

Worn in: A 2–1 win over Denmark in a 1974 qualifier for Euro 76.
Worn by: Roberto Martinez, José Claramunt.

HOME 1978–80

Design: adidas

In came adidas, ready for the 1978 World Cup finals and brought with them a new silkier fabric and a high fitting wrapover crew neck and even the occasional short-sleeved version. Other than that, the basic strip remained the same – including the rather clever way the sock turnover replicated the Spanish flag.

Worn in: An honourable 0–0 draw with Brazil and a 1–0 victory over Sweden in Argentina 78.
Worn by: Eugenio Leal, Santillana.

AWAY 1978–80

Design: adidas

As was the norm, Ladislao Kubala's side retained the same basic and very practical kit premise: that a blue shirt was all that was required to provide an adequate change alternative. As before the team crest appeared with a red border.

Worn in: A 1–0 friendly win over the Netherlands (1980).
Worn by: Juanito, Dani.

HOME 1980

Design: adidas

A brand new style greeted Spanish supporters as they cheered on their side in Italy's Euro 80 tournament. Shorts and socks remained the same but in came a cool short sleeved, v-neck version of the famous all-red jersey. The team sadly failed to win a single game throughout the tournament.

Worn in: 2–1 defeats to Belgium and England in Euro 80.
Worn by: Antonio Olmo, Saura.

AWAY 1980

Design: adidas

It is fair to assume that a blue version of the new v-neck short sleeved shirt was match-prepared for Euro 80, but was never required in the tournament, after which Spain reverted to the previous wrapover crew-neck strip.

HOME 1981

Design: adidas

Another fresh look arrived as 1981 dawned, which saw the introduction of a collar onto the Spanish shirt that was worn in both short and long sleeved versions. The rest of the design remained the same, including the non-contrasting colour scheme of the jersey.

Worn in: A friendly 2–1 win over England.
Worn by: Joaquín, Marcos.

AWAY 1981

Design: adidas

Naturally a simple blue away shirt was produced for José Emilio Santamaria's team. It's curious to note that the adidas branding wasn't present on these shirts, as by the time the '80s gathered pace manufacturers' logos were commonplace.

Worn in: A 2–0 defeat against Portugal.
Worn by: Victor Munoz, Satrustegui.

HOME 1981

Design: adidas

For their last game of 1981 José Santamaría's team donned a one-off kit that featured adidas branding in the shape of its famous trefoil logo and three-stripe trim for the first time. However, interestingly white was chosen rather than perhaps the more obvious yellow. It's possible then that this was simply a generic adidas outfit that was badged up for Spain.

Worn in: A 2–0 friendly win over Belgium.
Worn by: Quini, Satrustegui.

HOME 1982–83

Design: adidas

Arguably the first true Spanish strip of the modern era was this stunning adidas ensemble. The shiny, silky shirt still featured a self-coloured collar but now had rich yellow three-stripe taping, including on the shorts (with the addition of red stripes in between).

Worn in: A 2–1 defeat by West Germany and a goalless draw with England in the 1982 World Cup that saw the Spanish eliminated.
Worn by: Miguel Angel Alonso, Gordillo.

AWAY 1982–83

Design: adidas

The blue away version of this strip was arguably even better than the home; it retained the self-coloured collar but added to it with red and yellow taping to help craft a superb outfit. The Spanish coat of arms was introduced as the new badge. These kits accompanied the side as they hosted the 1982 World Cup, although this blue strip wasn't used in the tournament.

Worn in: A 1983 2–1 defeat by the Netherlands.
Worn by: José Camacho, Francisco Guerri.

THIRD 1982–83

Design: adidas

As a forerunner of the white Spanish change strips that were to appear later in the decade, an all-white version with simple red trim was produced in the last years of the adidas contract. However, it appears this cuffless, collared jersey with raglan sleeves and red piping was never actually worn.

HOME 1984–86

Design: Le Coq Sportif

French supplier Le Coq Sportif arrived in Spain in 1984 and was to kit out the side for the rest of the decade. In essence its first set of strips continued the established non-contrasting collar tradition but dispensed with additional colour and trim, the shirts decorated only with elegant shadow stripes.

Worn in: The disappointing 2–0 defeat against France in the Euro 84 final.
Worn by: Senor, José Camacho.

AWAY 1984–86

Design: Le Coq Sportif

A break from recent tradition found Miguel Muñoz and his team decked out in heroic all white for their regular change strip. Simple and stylish, it's interesting to note that the flag representation still existed on the white socks.

Worn in: A 1–1 draw with neighbours Portugal in the group stages of Euro 84.
Worn by: Gallego, Julio Alberto.

THIRD 1984–86

Design: Le Coq Sportif

Setting the pattern for the rest of the decade, a blue change strip was also in the Spanish kitbag and began to be preferred to the white away kit following Euro 84. It followed the design of the home including the stylish shadow stripes on both the shirts and shorts, accompanied by the patriotic socks.

Worn in: The 3–0 defeat against Wales in a 1985 qualifier for the 1986 World Cup.
Worn by: Maceda, Juan Carlos Rojo.

HOME 1986

Design: Le Coq Sportif

Launched midway through 1986 in preparation for that year's World Cup, the new Spanish shirt took the tried and tested existing model and added the merest touch of decoration in the form of two contrasting thin stripes on each sleeve and asymmetrically on the shorts.

Worn in: The superb 5–1 win over Denmark in the knockout stage of the World Cup followed by the semi-final penalty defeat by Belgium.
Worn by: Butragueno, Goiko.

AWAY 1986–87

Design: Le Coq Sportif

White remained as first choice away outfit for this next set of strips, and again the design mirrored that of the home with the integrity of the Spanish football colour scheme maintained thanks to the nice addition of blue Le Coq Sportif logos. The kit wasn't required in the 1986 World Cup.

Worn in: A 1986 2–1 win over Albania in a Euro 88 qualifier.
Worn by: Hipolito Rincon, Eloy.

THIRD 1986–87

Design: Le Coq Sportif

Although a blue third version of this second set of Le Coq Sportif Spain kits existed, complete with the swish piping trim, thanks to the luck of the colour draw, it was never worn on the pitch as Miguel Muñoz's side embarked on qualification for Euro 88.

HOME 1988–91

Design: Le Coq Sportif

The third and last set of Le Coq Sportif uniforms again retained the basic design structure that Spain had become accustomed to, but also added visual interest with an intricate shadow pattern of Le Coq Sportif logos and thin stripes and a dash of yellow on the neck and cuffs.

Worn in: A single win for Spain in a frustrating Euro 88; a 3–2 triumph over Denmark.
Worn by: Andrinua, Tomas.

AWAY 1988–91

Design: Le Coq Sportif

The addition of yellow to the red cuffs and neck of this next all-white away kit managed to cleverly replicate the Spanish flag on every element of the uniform. This set of strips lasted until the 1990 World Cup and although the shirt wasn't worn in either tournament, the shorts and socks were sported in Spain's Italia 90 match against Uruguay.

Worn in: A 1990 3–2 defeat by Czechoslovakia.
Worn by: Goikoetxea, Michel.

THIRD 1988–91

Design: Le Coq Sportif

The *de rigueur* blue version of the Spain kit appeared in the same stylings as the home and away, but unlike the previous blue outfit this did see some action. In a move reminiscent of the '60s and '70s the shirt was worn with the home shorts and socks.

Worn in: A 1989 2–0 win vs Malta in an Italia 90 World Cup qualifier.
Worn by: Manolo, Beguiristain.

HOME 1991–92

Design: adidas

Towards the end of 1991 adidas returned to kit out the Spanish side, now managed by Vicente Miera. This was just prior to the adidas equipment re-branding of 1992 so a stopgap set of kits were worn for just a few games. The home dispensed with yellow trim, preferring white.

Worn in: Two defeats in this kit's first two outings: 2–0 to Iceland and 2–1 to France.
Worn by: Juan Vizcaino, Sanchis.

AWAY 1991–92

Design: adidas

Adidas reinstated blue as La Furia's regular change strip. Just like the old days, the kit retained the shorts and socks of the home strip (oddly the socks were identical to the ones from the last Le Coq Sportif outfit) although the lack of yellow gave the kit an oddly unfamiliar feel. The shirt featured a repeated shadow adidas logo pattern.

Worn in: A 1992 0–0 draw with Portugal.
Worn by: Guillermo Amor, Fernando Giner.

THIRD 1991–92

Design: adidas

In order, no doubt, to retain a healthy light/dark kit option a white version of the short-lived new adidas strips was produced but never worn. It was a shame as, again, the integration of red and yellow stripes proved a very effective way of incorporating the Spanish flag into a change outfit.

HOME 1992–94

Design: adidas

Spain had failed to qualify for Euro 92, meaning that this fine outfit didn't make it to a major tournament. The new 'adidas equipment' brand brought in a new logo and bold colour panels in preference to the famous three stripes. Shadow stripes added a touch of additional flair to this magnificent ensemble.

Worn in: Impressive World Cup qualifier 5–0 wins over Latvia (1992) and Lithuania (1993).
Worn by: José Bakero, Roberto Solozabal.

AWAY 1992–94

Design: adidas

As with the previous adidas kit, it was decided that a blue shirt was all that was needed to create a suitable change kit. In a stroke of design genius the bold shoulder panels were coloured to replicate the Spanish flag.

Worn in: A 1–0 defeat by Denmark in a 1993 qualifier for the 1994 World Cup.
Worn by: Alkorta, Salinas.

THIRD 1992–94

Design: adidas

A very smart all-white version of the adidas equipment kits was also produced that, like the regular blue away, also included the Spanish flag colour sequence on the shoulders. Although the strip was never worn by the first team it did make an appearance at the 1992 FIFA Futsal World Championship in Hong Kong.

HOME 1994–95

Design: adidas

One of the biggest shake-ups in recent Spain kit history came in early 1994 when adidas reintroduced the navy blue, which had formed a part of the Spanish colour palette up until the '50s, throughout the strip. A bold set of three stripes, comprising a series of diamonds, provided visual decoration.

Worn in: A USA 94 1–1 draw with Germany followed by a good 3–0 win vs Switzerland.
Worn by: Luis Enrique, Nadal.

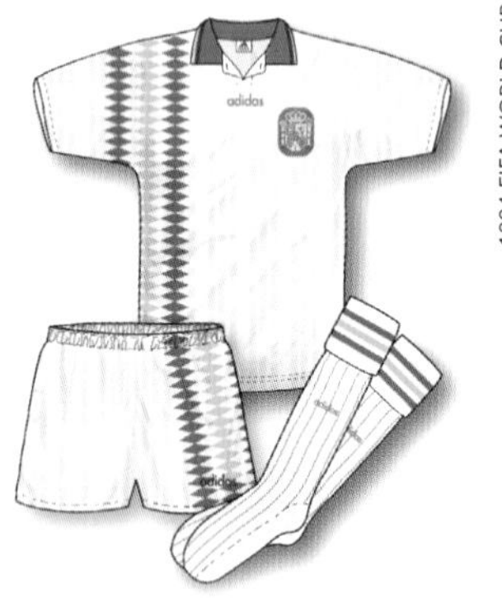

1994 FIFA WORLD CUP

AWAY 1994–95

Design: adidas

Javier Clemente's side donned this wondrous white third strip in USA 94. The design reflected that of the home, but instead used simply red and yellow to trim the outfit. A more old-fashioned collar was introduced and adidas' logo was reduced to a simple wordmarque.

Worn in: The bitterly disappointing last-minute 2–1 defeat by Italy in the USA 94 quarter-final.
Worn by: Jaime Magalhaes, Fernando Gomes.

1994 FIFA WORLD CUP

THIRD 1994–95

Design: adidas

A sophisticated navy version of this dynamic set of Spain kits was launched, with the dark hue providing a suitable canvas for the Spanish red and yellow to really shine. All three kits moved the trim on the shirts to the alternate side of the shorts to great effect.

Worn in: A 1994 4–1 thrashing of Belgium in a Euro 96 qualifier.
Worn by: Guerrero, Alberto Belsue.

1996 UEFA EUROPEAN CHAMPIONSHIP

HOME 1996–97

Design: adidas

With Spain's Euro 96 qualification secured, a new set of strips was launched that included even more navy than the previous, using the colour for the left sleeve and side. The adidas three stripes in red and yellow provided a striking adornment, along with a shadow print of the Royal Spanish Football Federation logo.

Worn in: The tense quarter-final 0–0 draw with Euro 96 hosts England, who won on penalties.
Worn by: Javier Manjarin Pereda, Sergi.

1996 UEFA EUROPEAN CHAMPIONSHIP

AWAY 1996–97

Design: adidas

Navy became the side's regular change strip with this next adidas range. The shirts featured a neat grandad-style neck with three-button placket. New truncated arrangements of the adidas trademark three stripes decorated each side of the shorts and a small Spanish flag was added to the socks and the left sleeve.

Worn in: A 0–0 friendly draw with Norway on this kit's debut.
Worn by: Francisco 'Kiko' Narvaez, Abelardo.

1996 UEFA EUROPEAN CHAMPIONSHIP

THIRD 1996–97

Design: adidas

Spain's next third strip was a standard adidas template for the time, but one that worked incredibly well in white with the red and yellow again forming representations of the Spanish flag throughout the ensemble.

Worn in: The 2–1 win over Slovakia in a 1997 qualifier for the 1998 World Cup.
Worn by: Roberto Rios, Alkorta.

1998 FIFA WORLD CUP

HOME 1998–99

Design: adidas

It was an optimistic Spanish side who qualified for the 1998 World Cup. Their new strip, which was debuted in the first game of 1998 against France, featured a dynamic navy v-neck, trimmed with red and yellow and a Royal Spanish Football Federation motif.

Worn in: The 6–1 win over Bulgaria that, thanks to other results, wasn't enough to keep Spain from being eliminated from France 98.
Worn by: Raúl, Carlos Aguilera.

1998 FIFA WORLD CUP

AWAY 1998–99

Design: adidas

Another break from tradition occurred with the unveiling of the Spanish away kit for 1998 that decided to complement the white strip with navy, rather than a perhaps more predictable red and yellow. It was a very striking outfit, that mirrored the design of the home, although it did lack a traditional Spanish feel.

Worn in: The famous, although disappointing for Spain, 3–2 defeat by Nigeria at France 98.
Worn by: Andoni Zubizarreta, Hierro.

1998 FIFA WORLD CUP

THIRD 1998–99

Design: adidas

A new adidas design was packed for the 1998 World Cup but was never required on the pitch. The strip featured a royal blue colour scheme, trimmed with white and light touches of red and yellow. A collar with button-up placket was included rather than the v-neck of the home and away outfits.

2000 UEFA EUROPEAN CHAMPIONSHIP

HOME 1999–2001

Design: adidas

A fresher and lighter strip appeared towards the end of 1999. Featuring a slightly lighter red core, the increased yellow presence saw a return to a more familiar Spanish colour combination. Piping curved under each arm and the socks reproduced the Spanish flag on the turnovers. José Antonio Camacho was now team coach.

Worn in: The sad 2–1 loss to France in the Euro 2000 quarter-final.
Worn by: Gaizka Mendieta, Pedro Munitis.

2000 UEFA EUROPEAN CHAMPIONSHIP

AWAY 1999–2001

Design: adidas

Navy returned as La Furia's away strip for the Euro 2000 tournament. The shirt was a standard adidas template that worked well with the carefully considered red and yellow decorations. The home shorts and socks also featured in this outfit, bringing back memories again of the '70s and '80s. By a curious twist of fate this kit was never worn, and Spain managed to sport their home kit in every match during this period.

2000 UEFA EUROPEAN CHAMPIONSHIP

THIRD 1999–2001

Design: adidas

This basic, understated but highly effective all-white strip was also produced and was trimmed with red and yellow giving it a traditional Spanish vibe. Like its navy counterpart it was never worn in action (although the shorts did make an appearance with the home kit vs England in 2001). Essentially the same design as the away, the main difference came in the shape of a functional collar/v-neck combination.

2002 FIFA WORLD CUP

HOME 2001–03

Design: adidas

Although visually simple yet stylish, from a construction point of view, thanks to its dual layers (designed to wick sweat from the body) this was one of the most complex worn by a Spanish side. Perforated side panels allowed the inner yellow layer to show through.

Worn in: Yet another quarter-final defeat in 2002, this time to South Korea who won on penalties after a controversial 0–0 draw.
Worn by: Javier De Pedro, Ruben Baraja.

AWAY 2001-03

Design: adidas

History repeated itself in 2002 as the team's smart white change strip wasn't required on the field of play during the World Cup. The design followed that of the home, including the addition of 'ESPANA' text above the team crest. A one-off version of the shirt was worn in 2003 with red cuffs and full length three-stripe trim.

Worn in: A 1–0 friendly defeat against the Netherlands in 2001.
Worn by: Ivan Helguera, Carlos Puyol.

THIRD 2001-03

Design: adidas

Following the dual-layered design of the home and away strips, a new navy third kit was unveiled. Basic replica versions of these jerseys were not dual-layered and instead only included a visual approximation of how the perforated side panels revealed the inner layer colour. This fine uniform was never worn in action during its lifespan.

HOME 2004-05

Design: adidas

The next Spanish home kit edged closer to the classic look and feel of Spain's '80s strips. The shirt, which featured dainty collar and updated dual-layer construction, was comprised of just red and yellow and adidas included a new pointed three-stripe style.

Worn in: A 1–0 win over Russia, followed by a 1–1 draw against Greece during a difficult Euro 2004 campaign.
Worn by: Juanito, Fernando Torres.

AWAY 2004-05

Design: adidas

The three-stripe trim on the team's next away kit was dual-coloured which, in conjunction with the navy adidas logo, managed to ensure all elements of Spain's palette were present and correct (although the navy turnovers on the socks did stand out perhaps a little too much!).

Worn in: The 1–0 defeat by Portugal in a make-or-break group stage game in Euro 2004 that saw Inaki Sáez's squad sent home.
Worn by: Raul Bravo, Míchel Salgado.

THIRD 2004-05

Design: adidas

In what proved to be the last navy third kit for a while, adidas launched a new strip that was based on the design of the home and away versions. Like the away outfit it featured a fresh dual-coloured three-stripe trim throughout. The backs of this set of strips all featured prominent contrasting angular panels on the sleeves.

Worn in: A 0–0 draw with Lithuania in a 2004 Germany 2006 World Cup qualifier.
Worn by: Victor, David Albelda.

HOME 2005-07

Design: adidas

If the previous home strip had taken a small step towards a more classic Spain outfit, this next home shirt, unveiled late in 2005, took a whole leap forward! Gone was the secondary navy colour, to be replaced by a bright royal blue. Suave pinstripes and a minimalist neck design completed the ensemble.

Worn in: Three group stage wins in the World Cup against Ukraine, Tunisia and Saudi Arabia.
Worn by: Cesc Fabregas, Joan Capdevila.

AWAY 2005-07

Design: adidas

A standard adidas template was selected for the Germany 2006 away strip that featured graceful, curved panels on each side. Although taken to the World Cup that year, the strip was not required. These latest kits saw a new design initiative with the adidas logo included on the reverse of the shorts rather than the front.

Worn in: A good 2–1 triumph over Denmark (2007) in a European Championship qualifier.
Worn by: David Silva, Angel.

★

HOME 2007-09

Design: adidas

In a design that didn't really progress much from the previous, navy made a bold return replacing the summery royal shade of the last kit. Glamorous gold replaced the country's familiar yellow to create an elegant and sophisticated look for Luis Aragonés' team.

Worn in: The glorious 1–0 win vs Germany in the Euro 2008 final! Spain's first major tournament since 1964.
Worn by: David Villa, Marcos Senna.

AWAY 2007-09

Design: adidas

The golden theme was extended to the away kit, creating a jersey quite unlike anything worn by the team before. The visual appearance was restrained with navy trim complementing the lush gold. The shirt was often worn with the home kit's shorts and socks, although it was officially launched with white pairs.

Worn in: The stunning 3–0 win over Russia in the Euro 2008 semi-final.
Worn by: Carlos Marchena, Xavi.

HOME 2009

Design: adidas

Buoyed by the Euro 2008 success, a confident Spain side, now led by Vicente del Bosque, entered the 2009 FIFA Confederations Cup in a dynamic new strip that again leaned heavily on gold and navy as secondary colours. The kit was to last for just eight months.

Worn in: A 2–0 win over South Africa in the Confederations Cup that set a world record 15 consecutive straight international wins.
Worn by: Sergio Busquets, Gerard Piqué.

HOME 2009-10

Design: adidas

Previewed in a late 2009 friendly against Argentina, the new Spain strip that was to feature in the 2010 World Cup finals saw a return of the royal blue shorts of earlier strips. The shirt was available to players in either tight Techfit (worn tight with compression taping) or a more relaxed Formotion fit.

Worn in: The 1–0 win over Germany in the 2010 World Cup semi-final.
Worn by: Xabi Alonso, Sergio Ramos.

AWAY 2010-11

Design: adidas

Navy was reinstated as the main Spanish change colour for South Africa 2010 in a design that will be forever remembered as the strip worn when Spain won the World Cup! The shadow striped shirt was also worn with change white shorts and socks.

Worn in: The tense 1–0 victory over the Netherlands in the World Cup Final.
Worn by: Andrés Iniesta – the scorer of the winning goal in the final.

HOME 2010-11

Design: adidas

For Spaniards around the world the most important design features of this shirt were the small star above the badge and the special gold shield – commemorating the World Cup win earlier in 2010. Royal blue played a larger role on this jersey (available in both Techfit and Formotion).

Worn in: A good 3–1 win over Scotland in a 2011 qualifying match for Euro 2012.
Worn by: Santi Cazorla, Pedro.

AWAY 2011

Design: adidas

A clean, bright and simply beautiful white strip that, as with the home strip, came in both Techfit and Formotion versions and featured the commemorative extra features to mark the 2010 World Cup win. From a construction point of view this was very similar to the style worn the previous year.

Worn in: A 2–2 draw with Costa Rica (2012).
Worn by: Nacho Monreal, Jesús Navas.

HOME 2011-12

Design: adidas

First worn late in 2011 as Spain prepared themselves for Euro 2012. The shirt was a variation on adidas' Condivo 12 template and incorporated a reintroduction of navy and dual diagonal shadow stripes on the jersey. Available in either Techfit or Formotion versions.

Worn in: The stunning 4–0 thrashing of Italy in the Euro 2012 final – Spain's third consecutive major trophy triumph!
Worn by: Álvaro Arbeloa, Juan Mata.

AWAY 2012

Design: adidas

Vicente del Bosque's team opened 2012 with a brave Techfit/Formotion kit design that introduced a light blue colour into the Spanish palette. It was trimmed with black alongside just a splash of red and yellow on the socks. A gradated black sash provided the main visual element. Black change shorts were also worn.

Worn in: A last minute 1–0 win over Croatia in the group stages of Euro 2012.
Worn by: Álvaro Negredo, Jordi Alba.

HOME 2012–13

Design: adidas

With the 2013 Confederations Cup looming Spain unveiled their next kit. Inspired by the Spanish strip of 1924 the overriding decoration came in the form of a yellow 'V' stretching from the neck to the chest. The design was later to be produced as the Campeon 13 jersey. The World Cup winners' shield also featured.

Worn in: The 3–0 defeat against Brazil in the Confederations Cup final.
Worn by: Fernando Meira, Isco.

HOME 2013–14

Design: adidas

Spain defended their World Cup title in a design that again dismissed tradition and instead opted for a fashionable one-colour ensemble. A more muted two-tone combination of reds were trimmed with an appropriate gold that also lent itself to the tonal badge.

Worn in: The dreadful 2–0 defeat against Chile that ensured Spain's World Cup was to end in bitter disappointment.
Worn by: Koke, Javi Martinez.

AWAY 2014

Design: adidas

A kit first for Spain came in the shape of this all-black strip that was to prove problematic in the tournament. It was trimmed with a bright 'electricity' yellow and a horizontal band with gradated stripes reached across the chest. Adidas' 2014 kits were made from 'adizero' fabric that was 40% lighter than previous strips.

Worn in: Spain's solitary win in the 2014 World Cup: a 3–0 victory over Australia.
Worn by: Juanfran, Raul Albiol.

THIRD 2014

Design: adidas

FIFA were unhappy with Spain's red home strip and black away (their preference being that all teams came to the World Cup equipped with a light and dark kit) and ordered the side to produce a one-off all white version of the home outfit for the team's opening match against the Netherlands, who also wore their change kit.

Worn in: The match against the Netherlands in the 2014 World Cup that ended in a 5–1 defeat.
Worn by: César Azpilicueta, Diego Costa.

HOME 2015–17

Design: adidas

After the disastrous World Cup a wounded Spain regrouped and sought inspiration from this splendid outfit that, thanks to its royal blue shorts and black socks, saw the classic old Spanish kit colours return for the first time in over 20 years. The adidas stripes moved from the shoulders to the sides of the adizero shirt.

Worn in: Wins over the Czech Republic (1–0) and Turkey (3–0) in Euro 2016.
Worn by: Álvaro Morata, Nolito.

AWAY 2015–16

Design: adidas

This vibrant (and divisive!) outfit featured a large abstract pattern made up of several shades of yellow and red. There was method to the madness, though; the pattern represented a heat map of Torres' winning goal in the Euro 2012 final with the triangles symbolising the team's 'tiki-taka' style of play.

Worn in: A 2–1 defeat against Croatia (who also wore their away kit!) in Euro 2016.
Worn by: Aritz Aduriz, Lucas Vázquez.

AWAY 2016–17

Design: adidas

It has to be said that despite its beauty, the controversial Euro 2016 away kit didn't tick everyone's boxes. So, after just 11 months, and to the surprise of supporters, a new and much more sober new white kit was launched. It featured the same shorts and socks as the previous outfit.

Worn in: A 2–0 World Cup qualifier against Albania in 2016.
Worn by: Vitolo, Thiago Alcántara.

HOME 2017–18

Design: adidas

Adidas took a distinctly retro approach to their entire kit roster in 2017 in preparation for the Russia World Cup the following year. Spain's new strip, of course, harked back to the 1994 World Cup for its inspiration. The shirt caused some political controversy, however, as thanks to the presence of thin red lines, the blue diamonds took on a rather purplish tint and therefore, unintentionally, suggested the colour scheme of The Second Spanish Republic.

Xabi Alonso, Jordi Alba and Alvaro Arbeola in Spain's beautiful 2011–12 adidas home kit, worn here in the 4–0 thrashing of Italy in the final of Euro 2012.

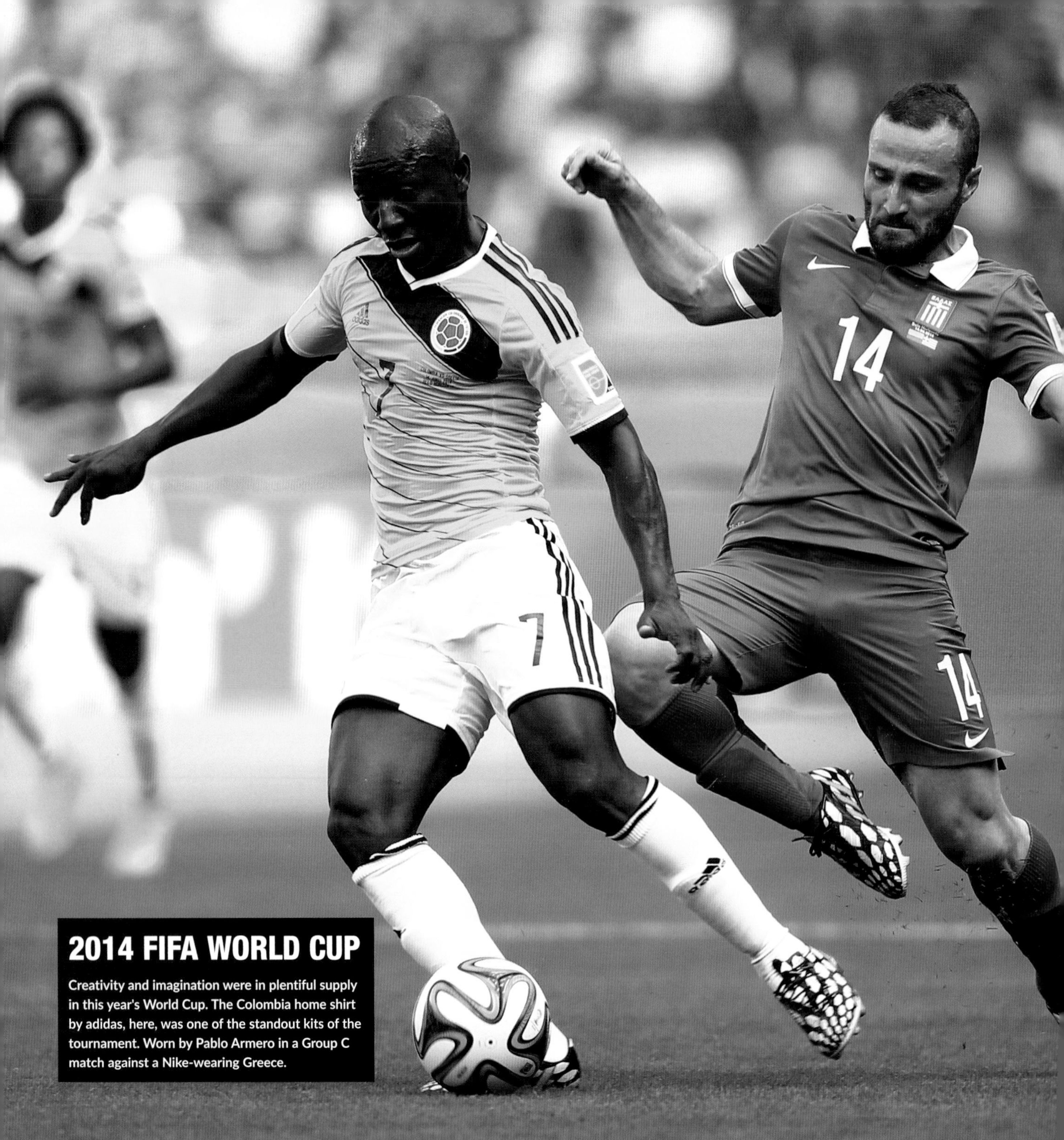

2014 FIFA WORLD CUP

Creativity and imagination were in plentiful supply in this year's World Cup. The Colombia home shirt by adidas, here, was one of the standout kits of the tournament. Worn by Pablo Armero in a Group C match against a Nike-wearing Greece.

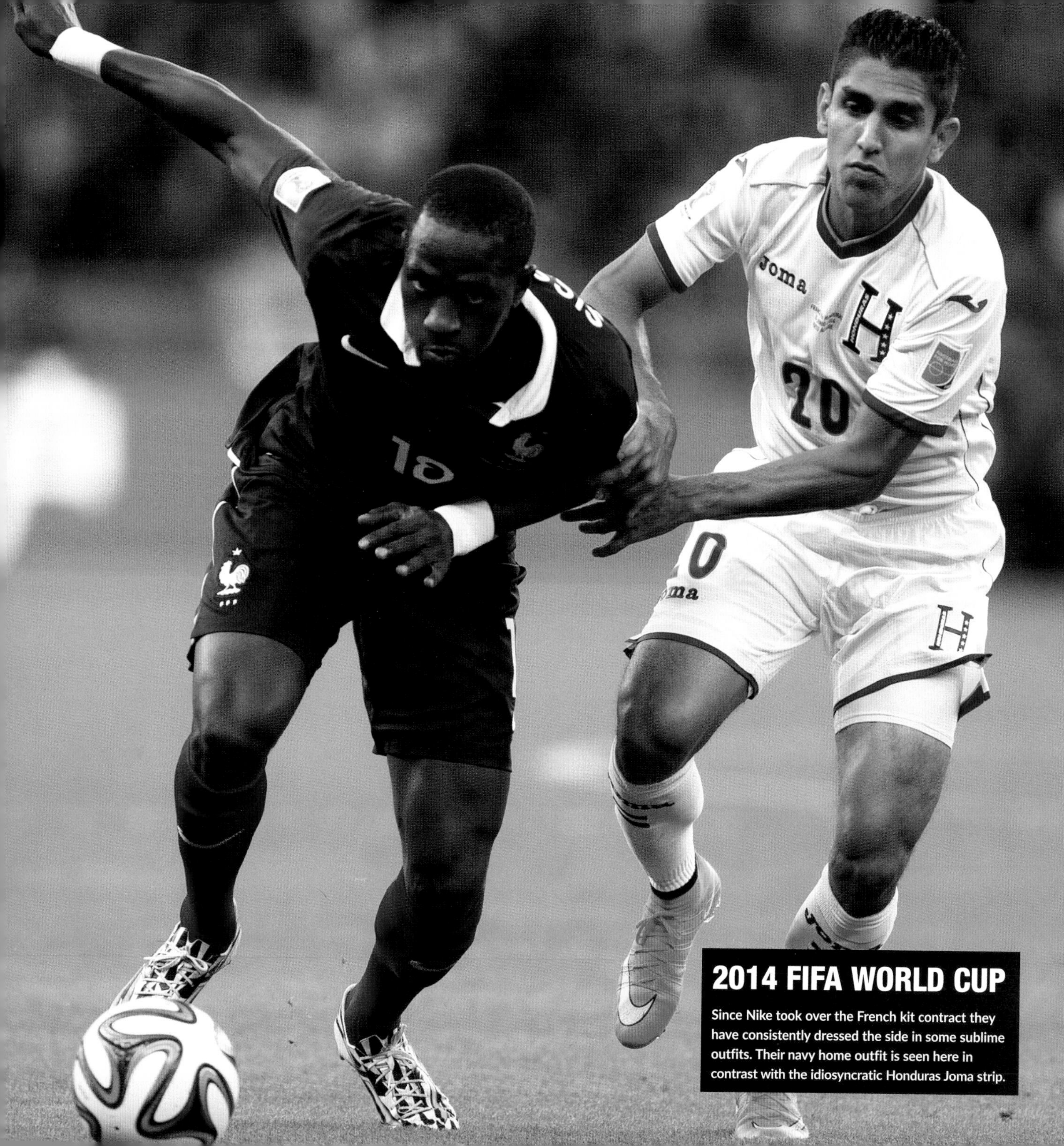

2014 FIFA WORLD CUP

Since Nike took over the French kit contract they have consistently dressed the side in some sublime outfits. Their navy home outfit is seen here in contrast with the idiosyncratic Honduras Joma strip.

SWEDEN

The yellow and blue of Sweden is another of those highly distinctive international kits, based on the colours of the national flag and instantly recognisable.

As Sweden aren't one of those countries who don a change kit at the drop of the hat, their almost unique colour scheme means the home outfit has accompanied most of the nation's most exciting moments on a football pitch.

When an away kit has been required, various shades of blue have featured over the years, although white has also been popular.

Umbro produced the team strip in the late '60s and early '70s before adidas took over in 1974 and embarked on a long and fruitful relationship, concocting various designs in yellow and blue. Some of their more successful moments in Swedish colours came from the 'adidas equipment' years of the early 1990s. Then, thanks to the broad shirt panels on the design, blue gained extra prominence.

Umbro returned in 2003 with a wide array of more restrained designs, full of style and confidence. They also produced two commemorative shirts for the team, which were stunning but had very few outings on the pitch.

After 10 years, the Swedish Football Association again turned to adidas for their apparel, and once again the three stripes adorn the Swedes' kit.

Joyful Swedish players celebrate in their adidas equipment home kit following the 4–0 thrashing of Bulgaria in the 1994 World Cup.

HOME 1966–68

Design: Umbro

A typical late '60s crew-neck jersey replaced the previous collared shirt early in 1966. It was generally worn with long sleeves but a short sleeved version was also available. The team crest was simply the Sweden flag. Orvar Bergmark's team failed to qualify for the 1966 World Cup.

Worn in: A 2–1 win over near neighbours Denmark in a 1966 friendly.
Worn by: Tom Turesson, Roland Lundblad.

AWAY 1966–68

Design: Umbro

For some teams back in the '60s and '70s simply changing the jersey was enough to create an effective away kit and such was the case with Sweden, who sported this straight reversal of their home shirt (available in long and short sleeves) when a colour clash occurred.

Worn in: The exciting 3–2 defeat against the mighty Brazil in a 1966 friendly.
Worn by: Ove Kindvall, Agne Simonsson.

HOME 1968–73

Design: Umbro

Sweden's strips were updated in 1968 to include a specially designed team badge rather than simply the flag. The rest of the strip remained the same. A short sleeved version was worn frequently during this period.

Worn in: The incredible 5–2 win in Norway followed by the important 2–0 win over France – both 1969 qualifiers for the 1970 World Cup.
Worn by: Roland Grip, Orjan Persson.

AWAY 1968–73

Design: Umbro

Naturally, the new badge also appeared on the blue change shirt. Worn with the home kit's shorts and socks, change pairs in yellow (with a blue stripe on each leg) and blue respectively were also sported. However, unless the team was competing in a World Cup there was little opportunity for a Sweden change kit!

Worn in: A 3–1 friendly defeat against England in 1968.
Worn by: Rolf Andersson, Inge Ejderstedt.

1970 FIFA WORLD CUP

HOME 1970–73

Design: Umbro

A new design of short sleeved shirt was launched in preparation for the 1970 World Cup. It was a simple v-neck fashioned from airtex fabric, designed to keep players cooler in the fierce Mexico heat. The shirt made occasional appearances in subsequent years.

Worn in: A 1–1 draw with Israel followed by a 1–0 win over Uruguay in the 1970 World Cup.
Worn by: Tommy Svensson, Ove Grahn.

1970 FIFA WORLD CUP

AWAY 1970–73

Design: Umbro

This smart change version of the team's new v-neck short sleeved shirt was not used in the 1970 World Cup finals – in fact it is unclear if this version of the Sweden away kit ever saw action during its three-year tenure.

HOME 1974–77

Design: adidas

In common with so many countries at that time, Sweden signed an apparel deal with adidas in readiness for the 1974 World Cup. The long sleeved strip was a standard issue unbranded template with a reversed wrapover crew neck and three-stripe trim throughout. Also worn with short sleeves.

Worn in: The qualifying campaign for Euro 76.
Worn by: Thomas Sjoberg, Bjorn Nordqvist.

AWAY 1974

Design: adidas

This kit curiosity was worn for at least one game at the start of 1974 against West Germany. It featured a lighter than usual blue shirt with yellow collar and cuffs, paired with considerably darker blue shorts and the regular home yellow socks.

Worn in: A 2–0 defeat against West Germany in a 1974 friendly match.
Worn by: Jan Olsson II, Bo Larsson.

HOME 1974–78

Design: adidas

A v-neck short sleeved shirt was again adopted in time for the 1974 World Cup. It was a classic early '70s adidas design, unbranded on the jersey but with a three-stripe trim leaving no doubt who the manufacturer was. A long sleeved version was also worn on occasion.

Worn in: A 2–1 victory over Yugoslavia in the second stage of the 1974 World Cup – sadly not enough for the Swedes to progress.
Worn by: Conny Torstensson, Ralf Edstrom.

AWAY 1974–82

Design: adidas

This brand new away short sleeved shirt featured a non-contrasting v-neck and cuffs and white-stripe trim (although yellow appeared on the socks). Although the shirts featured no logo, a small adidas trefoil marque did feature on the shorts.

Worn in: A 0–0 draw with the Netherlands in the 1974 World Cup.
Worn by: Roland Sandberg, Staffan Tapper.

HOME 1977–82

Design: adidas

The classic adidas 'Worldcup Dress' template was ubiquitous at the 1978 World Cup. Simple but functional, the high trefoil logo and low team crest add to its style. It was worn in both long and short sleeved versions throughout this period, and in later years with the occasional sponsor, such as Stena Line and Sparbanken.

Worn in: Defeats to Austria and Spain (both 1–0) in the 1978 World Cup group stage.
Worn by: Anders Linderoth, Benny Wendt.

AWAY 1977–83

Design: adidas

The Swedes, now managed by Georg Ericsson, also wore this endearing away version of the Worldcup Dress adidas shirt. It was trimmed now with yellow and paired up with white shorts. The shirt caused controversy when worn with a sponsor's logo in a 1983 friendly against the Netherlands.

Worn in: An honourable 1–1 draw with Brazil in the group stage of the 1978 World Cup.
Worn by: Lennart Larsson, Hasse Borg.

HOME 1978–79

Design: adidas

It wasn't uncommon among adidas' roster for the odd 'one-off' shirt to feature in a game. This collared jersey is a prime example. The shirt was worn with the same shorts and socks as the regular kit at the time, but an adidas logo now also appeared on the jersey. Worn in both long and short sleeved versions.

Worn in: A 2–2 draw with France in a Euro 80 qualifier.
Worn by: Anders Gronhagen, Mats Nordgren.

HOME 1980–82

Design: adidas

A new variation of the side's regular short sleeved shirt emerged in 1980 (although the crew-neck short sleeved jersey was also still worn during this period). Essentially the same as the previous version except that now the v-neck and cuffs were self-coloured, giving a very different overall look to the shirt.

Worn in: A good 3–0 win over Portugal in a 1982 World Cup qualifier (1981).
Worn by: Stig Fredriksson, Jan Svensson.

HOME 1982–84

Design: adidas

It was a new look Sweden side that emerged in 1982 wearing the football fashion that most sums up the '80s – pinstripes! This smart looking outfit (adidas' 'La Paz' template) saw the v-neck and cuffs switch back to a contrasting blue.

Worn in: A 4–0 thrashing of Malta in a 1984 qualifier for the 1986 World Cup.
Worn by: Ingemar Erlandsson, Thomas Sunesson.

AWAY 1982–84

Design: adidas

Adidas took a radical step with its next change kit for the Swedes. Rather than following the traditional blue shirt approach, it opted for a white shirt with black trim and pinstripes. Sweden were one of very few countries whose kits displayed a sponsor, and for the only match in which this was worn Sparbanken's logo featured on the shirts.

Worn in: A 3–3 friendly draw with Brazil in 1983.
Worn by: Dan Corneliusson, Ulf Eriksson.

THIRD 1982–84

Design: adidas

Unusually, given the relative lack of airings a Swedish away strip gets, a third kit was also launched that followed the same pinstriped design as the team's other two strips, but in a more familiar blue, trimmed with white.

Worn in: The 1984 2–0 defeat by West Germany in a 1986 World Cup qualifier.
Worn by: Glenn Stromberg, Mats Gren.

HOME 1985–86

Design: adidas

A real favourite adidas template of the mid '80s was this crew-necked shirt with its dynamic diagonal pinstripes – a design that didn't get a lot of exposure in domestic football. Occasionally worn with the logo of team sponsors Sparbanken on the front AND the back of the shirts.

Worn in: A good 2–2 draw with West Germany in a 1986 World Cup qualifier (1985).
Worn by: Andreas Ravelli, Mats Magnusson.

AWAY 1985–86

Design: adidas

It can be safely assumed that a straight reversal of the home strip was adopted for the next Swedish away outfit, although it seems a change strip was not required during this period. Shadow stripes now featured on the shorts. Olle Nordin took over as manager following the failure to qualify for the 1986 World Cup.

HOME 1985

Design: adidas

Another familiar adidas template (officially named 'Aberdeen') made at least one appearance in 1985, possibly as a long sleeved version of the regular diagonally pinstriped home kit was not available. The shirt featured a wrapover v-neck and horizontal shadow stripes.

Worn in: A 3–0 win against Denmark in 1985 in a friendly match.
Worn by: Sven Dahlkvist, Robert Prytz.

HOME 1987–88

Design: adidas

A lesser known adidas design began to be worn by the Swedes at the start of 1987. A cuffless shirt, topped with a crew neck, was adorned with a gradated zig-zag shadow pattern. A new style of shorts with broad yellow bands at the hems was also unveiled. Available in both long and short sleeves.

Worn in: An impressive 1–0 victory over Italy in a 1987 qualifier for Euro 88.
Worn by: Peter Larsson, Lennart Nilsson.

AWAY 1987–88

Design: adidas

The zig-zag pattern that decorated these latest Swedish shirts worked extremely well in the blue colour of the change shirts. The shirt was worn with blue shorts and socks and was used during the side's attempts to qualify for the 1988 European Championship.

Worn in: A 1–1 draw with West Germany in a 1987 friendly game.
Worn by: Glenn Hysen, Johnny Ekstrom.

1990 FIFA WORLD CUP

HOME 1988–91

Design: adidas

Sweden prepared for their World Cup qualifying campaign with a brand new strip featuring a standard adidas shadow pattern resembling diagonal brickwork. Initially worn with the shorts from the previous kit, midway through 1989 the away blue shorts were favoured. Change yellow shorts were also worn.

Worn in: A poor 1990 World Cup including 2–1 defeats to Scotland and Costa Rica.
Worn by: Tomas Brolin, Jonas Thern.

1990 FIFA WORLD CUP

AWAY 1988–91

Design: adidas

A reversal of the home design formed the next Swedish away kit and accompanied the side through their successful Italia 90 World Cup qualifying campaign. Both kits at this time were also available in long sleeves.

Worn in: The 2–1 defeat by Brazil in the Swedes' opening 1990 World Cup match.
Worn by: Anders Limpar, Stefan Schwarz.

1992 UEFA EUROPEAN CHAMPIONSHIP

HOME 1991–92

Design: adidas

The June 1991 friendly against Colombia was selected as the match in which to debut the next Sweden home kit. Retaining the same shadow striped shorts as the previous ensemble, the baggy fitting shirt featured a new diagonal shadow print and dual blue bands on each shoulder/sleeve.

Worn in: The marvellous 4–0 drubbing of Denmark in a 1991 friendly.
Worn by: Martin Dahlin, Kennet Andersson.

AWAY 1991–92

Design: adidas

Once again the home colours were reversed for this away strip. The shadow print also included a pattern of small adidas trefoil logos. As hosts of the forthcoming 1992 European Championship Tommy Svensson's team embarked on a lengthy series of friendlies.

Worn in: A 1–0 defeat against Australia (one of the few nations that cause a colour clash for Sweden!) in a 1992 friendly.
Worn by: Mikael Martinsson, Jan Jansson.

HOME 1992–93

Design: adidas

Sweden proudly took to the pitch on their home soil for Euro 92 wearing this stunning outfit, part of the radical overhaul of kit design during adidas' rebrand as 'adidas equipment'. Three broad stripes sat on the right sleeve. Squad numbers were included on the front of shirts for the first time.

Worn in: A great 2–1 win over England and the 3–2 semi-final defeat by Germany (Euro 92).
Worn by: Joakim Nilsson, Roger Ljung.

AWAY 1992–93

Design: adidas

From a kit perspective Euro 92 was dominated by the big, bold branding of the new-look adidas – a design aesthetic that really shook up the football kit world. Sweden's away strip simply reversed the colours of the home and included the centrally placed badge and adidas equipment logo. However, this fine strip was never worn in action.

1994 FIFA WORLD CUP

1994 FIFA WORLD CUP

HOME 1994–96

Design: adidas

Another impressive qualifying campaign saw Sweden through to the 1994 World Cup in the USA. The next set of adidas strips moved the broad stripes to either side of the shirt and introduced two fine strips of red on the truncated v-neck – red of course a colour component of the team badge.

Worn in: An impressive 4–0 win vs Bulgaria in the 1996 World Cup third place match.
Worn by: Henrik Larsson, Patrik Andersson.

AWAY 1994–96

Design: adidas

The heat of the USA World Cup may have inspired adidas to issue a white away kit, rather than the traditional blue – the first time in 10 years that Sweden had worn white. Thanks to a great World Cup (where the Swedes were top scorers) they reached second place in the FIFA rankings in November 1994.

Worn in: The 1–0 defeat against Brazil in the semi-final of the 1994 World Cup.
Worn by: Jesper Blomqvist, Roland Nilsson.

HOME 1996–97

Design: adidas

Buoyed by their superb World Cup Sweden were confident of making it to Euro 96. Sadly this was not to be, but if they had qualified they would have sported this bold, arrogant design with its large curved panels on each side and an increase of red. It was a design also worn by several other teams in adidas' roster.

Worn in: The 2–1 win over Scotland in a 1997 qualifier for the 1998 World Cup.
Worn by: Andreas Andersson, Pontus Kaamark.

AWAY 1996–97

Design: adidas

The blue away version of Sweden's latest strip appeared arguably even more brash and in your face than the home incarnation. This splendid outfit featured white trim with just a dash of yellow. These jerseys, with their lack of sewn-on sleeves, were known as 'batwing' shirts. The shorts were the same as the home but with white side panels rather than yellow. It appears this kit was never required during its lifespan.

HOME 1998–99

Design: adidas

After six years of rather 'larger than life' strips adidas entered a period of relative calm, producing kits of sophistication and elegance that mixed modern and historical influences. The latest loose-fitting home shirt was no exception and featured a shadow print coupled with a retro lace-up collar and blue insert.

Worn in: An unbeaten Euro 2000 qualifying campaign including a 2–1 win over England.
Worn by: Johan Mjallby, Jorgen Pettersson.

AWAY 1998–99

Design: adidas

Tommy Söderberg took over as manager and led the side through a magnificent Euro 2000 qualifying campaign where they won every game bar one. White returned as the away strip in the shape of this exciting v-necked concoction. Broad blue and yellow bands ran under each arm and down the sides.

Worn in: A 1999 friendly defeat against South Africa.
Worn by: Marcus Allback, Hakan Mild.

2000 UEFA EUROPEAN CHAMPIONSHIP

HOME 2000–02

Design: adidas

A confident Swedish side entered 2000 with a new design that featured more blue on the home shirt than ever before. Blue raglan sleeves were joined by a simple, trimmed collar and exquisite white piping. The familiar yellow appeared slightly 'warmer' than usual.

Worn in: 2–1 defeats to Belgium and Italy in a bitterly disappointing Euro 2000.
Worn by: Freddie Ljungberg, Tomas Gustafsson.

2000 UEFA EUROPEAN CHAMPIONSHIP

AWAY 2000–02

Design: adidas

White remained as the away colour of choice this year in a design that replicated the same basic template as the home but with different colour panelling (with an added emphasis on yellow) and cuffs. The kit wasn't required in the 2000 European Championship and it seems didn't make any appearances on the pitch at any point during its tenure.

2002 FIFA WORLD CUP

HOME 2002

Design: adidas

The 2002 World Cup in Korea and Japan provided a perfect shop front for adidas' latest innovation – dual-layered shirts, designed to wick sweat and regulate temperature. Perforated side panels allowed the inner blue layer to show through.

Worn in: The shock 2–1 defeat against Senegal (thanks to a Golden Goal) in the second round of the 2002 World Cup.
Worn by: Magnus Svensson, Olof Mellberg.

2002 FIFA WORLD CUP

AWAY 2002

Design: adidas

Adidas' last set of kits went for three designs in each of Sweden's main strip colours. The white away featured distinctive raglan sleeves and the same dual-layer construction as the home. Basic replica versions of these shirts were single-layered and included a 'fake' visual effect of the perforated side panels. All three of these strips were available for just one year and it seems this white strip wasn't required at all during this time.

2002 FIFA WORLD CUP

THIRD 2002

Design: adidas

This blue third shirt (only the second 'official' such kit the Swedes had worn) featured the same dual-layer 'Climacool' fabric as the other two outfits and thanks to its self-colour collar bore a passing resemblance to the team's mid '70s away strip.

Worn in: Two important games at the 2002 World Cup: a 1–1 draw with England followed by a 2–1 win against Nigeria.
Worn by: Niclas Alexandersson, Teddy Lucic.

2004 UEFA EUROPEAN CHAMPIONSHIP

HOME 2003–05

Design: Umbro

After Sweden's 30-odd years with adidas, UK kit manufacturer Umbro announced that it had secured the Sweden kit contract in July 2002. It hit the ground running with its first outfit for the side – simple, slick, yet smart.

Worn in: The 5–0 win over Bulgaria in Euro 2004. Also worn in the defeat on penalties to the Netherlands in the quarter-finals.
Worn by: Zlatan Ibrahimović, Mattias Jonson.

2004 UEFA EUROPEAN CHAMPIONSHIP

AWAY 2003–04

Design: Umbro

Umbro took a brand new approach with its first change kit for the Swedish Football Association by adopting a rich navy blue as its core colour. Replica versions of the shirt were reversible, with a royal blue alternate design on the inside. Although packed and ready, it was not required for the Euro 2004 tournament and research shows it may not ever have been worn on the pitch at all during its tenure.

2006 FIFA WORLD CUP

SPECIAL 2004

Design: Umbro

2004 marked the 100th anniversary of the Swedish Football Association and to commemorate the occasion Umbro produced a special one-off gold shirt. Crafted from a new template (that was also to feature in the forthcoming away strip) the jersey featured a specially designed badge and was worn in selected matches

Worn in: A 1–0 friendly win over England.
Worn by: Johann Elmander, Mikael Nilsson.

AWAY 2005

Design: Umbro

Lars Lagerback's side stuck with blue for the next away kit but returned to a shade more familiar to the team strip. The lightweight and breathable fabric design followed that of the 2004 commemorative strip and, like so many previous Sweden strips, due to favourable colour conditions it appears it was never required.

2006 FIFA WORLD CUP

HOME 2005–07

Design: Umbro

A new year brought some new kits from Umbro. In a design constructed from a combination of lightweight fabrics (and similar to the England kit at the time), a rendering of the Swedish cross appeared asymmetrically on the shoulder. Worn with yellow and, on one occasion against Iceland, white change shorts.

Worn in: A 2–2 draw with England and a 2–0 defeat by Germany in the 2006 World Cup.
Worn by: Kim Kallstrom, Tobias Linderoth.

2006 FIFA WORLD CUP

AWAY 2006–07

Design: Umbro

In preparation for the forthcoming World Cup a new blue change kit was unveiled. It followed the design aesthetic Umbro rolled out across its roster at this time including varying fabric compositions, a high-positioned Umbro logo and asymmetrical elements. The kit was taken to the 2006 World Cup but not required.

Worn in: A 2–1 friendly defeat against Ecuador in 2007.
Worn by: Rade Prica, Pontus Wernbloom.

2008 UEFA EUROPEAN CHAMPIONSHIP

HOME 2007–09

Design: Umbro

Premiered towards the end of 2007, the next home shirt was a highly contemporary and complex affair, full of subtle design flourishes and fashionable asymmetrical decoration. A small rendering of Umbro's classic diamond taping appeared on the right shoulder.

Worn in: A 2–0 victory over Greece – the Swedes' only victory in the 2008 European Championship.
Worn by: Christian Wilhelmsson, Fredrik Stoor.

2008 UEFA EUROPEAN CHAMPIONSHIP

AWAY 2008–09

Design: Umbro

Featuring all the complexities you would expect from an Umbro kit of this era, this navy strip incorporated striking curved flashes of yellow that combined with delicate blue applications. The high-positioned Umbro logo allowed squad numbers to be placed beneath it. The kit was not required in Euro 2008.

Worn in: The 3–1 defeat against the Netherlands in a 2008 friendly match.
Worn by: Behrang Safari, Samuel Holmen.

SPECIAL 2008

Design: Umbro

Another special commemorative shirt was issued in 2008 to mark the 50th anniversary of Sweden hosting the World Cup in 1958. The shirt included an old-fashioned collar and cuffs and the traditional Swedish shirt crest of the '50s: the national flag. Plain blue shorts and socks completed the strip.

Worn in: A 3–2 friendly defeat against France – the only time this kit was worn.
Worn by: Petter Hansson, Marcus Berg.

HOME 2009–10

Design: Umbro

A non-contrasting collar/neck is not something normally associated with Sweden, meaning that this latest home shirt (which had a very short lifespan) fostered a very different look to previous kits. Contrasting trim was kept to a minimum. A disastrous qualifying campaign meant no World Cup for Sweden in 2010.

Worn in: A 4–1 win over Albania in the last 2010 World Cup qualifying match.
Worn by: Rasmus Elm, Markus Rosenberg.

HOME 2010–12

Design: Umbro

Umbro re-wrote the kit rule books with the emergence of 'Tailored by Umbro' in 2009. The company now focused on simple but beautiful designs without the complexities that had dominated its recent designs. This new shirt featured comfortable and lightweight fabric, adorned with a striking blue stripe on the sides.

Worn in: A 5–0 demolition of Finland in a Euro 2012 qualifying match (2011).
Worn by: Emir Bajrami, Daniel Majstorovic.

AWAY 2010–11

Design: Umbro

This Swedish away kit is a prime example of the 'Tailored by Umbro' apparel philosophy that shook up football design at this time. With its delicately trimmed crew neck and cuffs, it was stunningly simple, but stunningly effective. The shorts and socks mirrored the design of the home pairs.

Worn in: A crushing 4–1 defeat at the hands of the Dutch in a Euro 2012 qualifier.
Worn by: Andreas Granqvist, Seb Larsson.

2012 UEFA EUROPEAN CHAMPIONSHIP

AWAY 2011–13

Design: Umbro

Sashes were back in a big way midway through the 2010s and Umbro produced this fine version for Sweden in early 2011. It was a dynamic and confident strip, with the yellow sash providing great contrast to the dark navy core colour of the shirt. Also worn with yellow change shorts.

Worn in: A 2–1 defeat against Ukraine in the group stage of Euro 2012.
Worn by: Tobias Hysen, Alexander Gerndt.

2012 UEFA EUROPEAN CHAMPIONSHIP

HOME 2012–13

Design: Umbro

With qualification for Erik Hamrén's team in the bag a new home kit was unveiled for the tournament – the last to be produced for Sweden by Umbro. A tidy neck design was joined by closely placed pairs of blue pinstripes in this decorative design.

Worn in: The 2–0 win over France in Euro 2012 – sadly Sweden were already eliminated.
Worn by: Martin Olsson, Jonas Olsson.

HOME 2013

Design: adidas

Adidas returned to the Swedish Football Association with this short-lived new kit worn against Argentina in the first game of 2013. It was a straightforward adidas design complete with diagonal textured Climacool fabric – designed to be lightweight and temperature-controlling. Also worn with yellow shorts.

Worn in: A 2–1 victory over Austria in a 2014 World Cup qualifier.
Worn by: Mikael Lustig, Alex Kacaniklic.

AWAY 2013–14

Design: adidas

Navy was retained as the Swedes' change colour and was joined by three bold stripes, bright yellow trim and blue applications. The fabric featured a diamond shadow pattern which incorporated the Swedish cross.

Worn in: A 2–1 win over Moldova in a 2014 friendly match.
Worn by: Erton Fejzullahu, Oscar Lewicki.

HOME 2013–15

Design: adidas

A lighter blue than usual was used to add a bright and fresh touch to this Climacool fabric kit. An interesting combination of blue, yellow and red (taking a major role in a Swedish kit for the first time since 1997) formed a chest band alongside blue side panels.

Worn in: The two defeats to Portugal in the 2014 World Cup qualifying play-offs (2013) when the kit was worn for the first time.
Worn by: Mikael Antonsson, Jimmy Durmaz.

AWAY 2014–15

Design: adidas

The Swedish flag became the key design element in this latest change outfit, fashioned from a black shirt for the first time. The yellow cross, trimmed with blue, featured off centre on the shirt and on the socks. The reverse of the shorts featured a yellow hem. Also worn with the white change shorts from the home kit.

Worn in: A 2–1 defeat against Turkey in a friendly match.
Worn by: Ola Toivonen, Albin Ekdal.

2016 UEFA EUROPEAN CHAMPIONSHIP

HOME 2015–17

Design: adidas

Beautiful in its simplicity, this kit moved the trademark adidas three stripes to each side of the Climacool shirt and featured horizontal shadow stripes and a basic blue crew neck. The blue also appeared lighter than usual. Standard issue adidas socks were worn.

Worn in: 1–0 defeats to Italy and Belgium in Euro 2016. Also worn in the earlier 1–1 draw with the Republic of Ireland.
Worn by: Victor Lindelöf, Emil Forsberg.

2016 UEFA EUROPEAN CHAMPIONSHIP

AWAY 2015–17

Design: adidas

Adidas was enjoying a period of rich creativity at this time with brave and adventurous designs – such as this wonderful away kit. Featuring tones of grey and blue and given an almost cotton-like printed texture, it was quite unlike anything worn by Sweden previously. The strip was not required for use in the 2016 European Championship.

Worn in: A 0–0 draw with Slovenia in 2016.
Worn by: John Guidetti, Isaac Kiese Thelin.

2018 FIFA WORLD CUP

HOME 2017-18

Design: adidas

As with all adidas teams, in 2017 Sweden were dressed in a retro-influenced strip. In the Swedes' case inspiration came from two sources: the diagonally pinstriped jersey worn in 1985 and the diagonal 'brickwork' pattern used three years later. The design was toned down a little and brought up to date with shadow stripes, in two thicknesses, used to decorate the less saturated coloured fabric.

Tomas Brolin races past Brazil's Mozer in their 1990 World Cup match. Brolin is sporting a fine adidas away kit.

The unique 2015–17 adidas away kit (with change light grey shorts) – worn here by John Guidetti in a 2016 friendly against Slovenia in Malmo.

URUGUAY

During Uruguay's early appearances on the international stage, the side appear in all manner of kits and colours, including green, white and a sashed royal blue kit.

In 1910, the side chose sky blue shirts in tribute to domestic side River Plate FC, which had been wearing their away kit of sky blue when they became the first Uruguayan side to beat the legendary Argentinian team Alumni. The colour subsequently remained in the team's kitbag, giving the side the nickname of La Celeste (The Sky Blue). The exact shade of blue has varied over the years – including a very pale hue in the 1986 World Cup and a brief dalliance with royal blue in the early '90s courtesy of NR – but it is always accompanied by black shorts and socks.

The team's away colour is traditionally white, trimmed elegantly with sky blue, although red was reintroduced in 1991 for the first time since 1962. Puma broke with tradition in 2010 and unveiled a stunning all-gold third kit for the Uruguayan Football Association.

Uruguay have been kitted out by a wide range of suppliers since the '60s, including adidas, NR, Enerre, Meta and L-Sporto.

The early '80s found the team wearing Le Coq Sportif strips that were sophisticated yet traditional. In contrast, Uhlsport's designs in the 2000s were strong and athletic looking, with bold panelling and trim.

Puma produced the team strip in the late '80s and then returned to the Uruguay fold in 2006. Since then, they have supplied the side with an array of consistently exquisite designs that often incorporate a shadow watermark pattern of the Sun of May (the traditional symbol that features in the country's flag), including the strip that will be worn in the 2018 World Cup.

The Uruguay side in their L-Sporto home kit prior to the game against Senegal in Group A of the 2002 World Cup finals.

HOME 1966–70

Design: Unknown

For much of their footballing life Uruguay have been recognisable due in part to their love of a v-neck shirt. In fact the team wore them for the entire '60s, '70s and '80s. The 1966 model was badgeless but did include mysterious small white fabric inserts under each arm.

Worn in: A 2–1 victory over France in the group stage of the 1966 World Cup.
Worn by: Pedro Rocha, Julio Cortes.

AWAY 1966–70

Design: Unknown

The late '60s saw La Celeste (The Sky Blue) still sporting red change kits when a clash occurred. The design mirrored that of the home strip and was worn with black shorts and colour matched socks. Although packed for the 1966 World Cup the kit wasn't required during the tournament.

HOME 1966–70

Design: Unknown

As was so often the case in the 1960s, to allow for both cold and warm weather, a long-sleeved crew-neck jersey was often in the kit cupboard alongside a short-sleeved v-neck. Uruguay's version featured contrasting neck and cuffs and was worn with the regular shorts and socks.

Worn in: A 2–0 victory over Chile in a 1969 qualifier for the 1970 World Cup.
Worn by: Ruben Bareno, Omar Caetano.

HOME 1970–74

Design: Unknown

The Uruguay shirt was updated in time for the 1970 World Cup with the addition of an AUF crest on the left-hand side. The rest of the strip remained the same. Juan Hohberg was in charge of the team for the tournament.

Worn in: The 1–0 (aet) victory over the USSR in the quarter-final of the 1970 World Cup followed by the 3–1 defeat by near neighbours Brazil in the semi-final.
Worn by: Luis Cubilla, Julio Morales.

AWAY 1970–74

Design: Unknown

The team opted for a white change kit as they prepared for the Mexico World Cup. The v-neck shirt featured non-contrasting neck and cuffs and the newly added team badge. The shirt was worn with the home kit's black shorts and socks.

Worn in: A 0–0 draw with Italy in the group stages of the 1970 World Cup.
Worn by: Denis Milar, Hector Santos.

HOME 1974–76

Design: adidas

Adidas began to make big inroads into the football apparel market in the mid-'70s and the 1974 World Cup was the first to feature the brand's kits in bulk. Uruguay stuck with the familiar white v-neck and cuffs shirt but now the famous trefoil logo was added to the left

Worn in: All three of the team's 1974 World Cup games including defeats by the Netherlands (2–0) and Sweden (3–0).
Worn by: Walter Mantegazza, Juan Masnik.

AWAY 1974–76

Design: adidas

An all-white version of the Uruguay away kit was introduced in 1974. Unlike the previous design the v-neck and cuffs were formed from a contrasting sky blue. The shorts and socks were able to be worn with the home kit (and vice versa) should a clash occur and made two appearances with the home shirt in the World Cup.

HOME 1976–82

Design: adidas

The famous three stripes of adidas were added to the Uruguay kit in 1976 and lasted until the arrival of Le Coq Sportif in 1983. Original versions of the shirt included a white trefoil logo. Sky blue trim was chosen for the socks and shorts.

Worn in: A 1977 2–0 win against Venezuela – a rare triumph in an unsuccessful 1978 World Cup qualifying campaign.
Worn by: Ildo Maneiro, Di Bartolomeo.

AWAY 1976-82

Design: adidas

All white remained as Uruguay's change kit but the shirt featured a classic adidas crew neck as opposed to the v-neck favoured on the home jersey. The white shorts and socks were also worn with the first choice sky blue strip on occasion.

HOME 1983

Design: Le Coq Sportif

French company Le Coq Sportif took over the AUF contract from adidas in 1983. They dressed the team in a neat pinstriped jersey with a wrapover v-neck. The shirt was cuffless and, unusually, badgeless.

Worn in: The 1983 Copa America final against Brazil: Uruguay won the first leg 2–0 and drew the second game 1–1 to claim the title on aggregate.
Worn by: Carlos Aguilera, Luis Acosta.

HOME 1983

Design: Le Coq Sportif

An alternate long-sleeved option was also worn by Omar Borrás's side. Paired with the same black shorts and socks as the regular home kit, the long-sleeved (but badgeless) shirt retained the pinstripes but added a wrapover crew neck.

Worn in: A 2–1 win over Chile in the 1983 Copa America.
Worn by: Eduardo Acevedo, Nelson Agresta.

HOME 1984-85

Design: Le Coq Sportif

The team strip was updated in 1984 with elegant shadow stripes replacing the pinstripes of the first Le Coq Sportif outfit. The bands on the socks now switched to sky blue. An alternate collared shirt was worn in the 1985 Kirin Cup tournament.

Worn in: Wins over Ecuador (2–0) and Chile (2–1) on the way to qualification for the 1986 World Cup in Mexico.
Worn by: Venancio Ramos, Amaro Nadal.

AWAY 1984-85

Design: Le Coq Sportif

An all-white away kit was used throughout the 1980s. This design mirrored that of the home strip including the cuffless shirt and shadow striped fabric. The white shorts and socks could be interchanged with the home pairs if necessary.

Worn in: The 2–0 defeat by France in the 1985 Intercontinental Championship.
Worn by: Venancio Ramos, Dario Pereyra.

HOME 1986

Design: Le Coq Sportif

The team strip went through a minor modification in 1985 with the removal of the shadow stripes (presumably to a 'cooler' fabric), but other than that the strip remained identical to the previous Le Coq Sportif outfit.

Worn in: A 1–1 draw with West Germany in the 1986 World Cup – the only time the home kit was required in the tournament.
Worn by: Antonio Alzamendi, José Batista.

AWAY 1986

Design: Le Coq Sportif

The side's heroic all-white strip went through the same fabric modification as the home in readiness for the Mexico 1986 World Cup.

Worn in: Three of La Celeste's World Cup matches including a 6–1 humiliation at the hands of Denmark and a 1–0 defeat by Argentina in the knockout stages that sent Uruguay home.
Worn by: Enzo Francescoli, Víctor Diogo.

HOME 1987-90

Design: Puma

After Le Coq Sportif's four year spell Puma arrived in Uruguay in the first of their two spells with La Celeste. Their first strips were way ahead of their time and wouldn't look out of place in the 2010s. The shirt featured broad white sleeve trim and a wrapover v-neck. Broad sky blue side panels adorned the shorts.

Worn in: 1989 2–0 wins over Bolivia and Peru during a great World Cup qualifying campaign.
Worn by: Santiago Ostolaza, Eduardo Pereyra.

1987 COPA AMERICA / 1989 COPA AMERICA

AWAY 1987–90

Design: Puma

Puma's trim philosophy suited the Uruguay away kit perfectly with the white and sky blue combining to beautiful effect. Initial versions of both this and the home shorts were minus the side trim panels.

Worn in: Two matches against Argentina (who also wore their away kit) in the 1989 Copa America: the first ended in a 1–0 defeat, the second a 2–0 victory.
Worn by: Antonio Alzamendi, Ruben Sosa.

1990 FIFA WORLD CUP

HOME 1990–91

Design: Puma

Puma's next design that was due to be worn in the 1990 World Cup echoed the early '80s Le Coq Sportif kits with their shadow stripes that, to be honest, by 1990 were beginning to look a little old-fashioned. The distinctive white sleeve stripes of the previous outfits were discarded to create a plainer strip.

Worn in: A 0–0 draw with Spain in the 1990 World Cup.
Worn by: Daniel Fonseca, José Herrera.

1990 FIFA WORLD CUP

AWAY 1990–91

Design: Puma

The tried and tested white and sky blue version of the team's home kit was employed by Puma for Uruguay's 1990 World Cup strip.

Worn in: A 1–0 victory over the Korea Republic in the group stages followed by a 2–0 loss to Italy in the knockout stages that eliminated Uruguay.
Worn by: Jose Perdomo, Nelson Gutierrez.

1991 COPA AMERICA

HOME 1990–91

Design: Puma

A special long-sleeved shirt was also produced by Puma at this time. Similar to the Le Coq Sportif long-sleeved option of the early '80s, this badgeless (although later versions did include the AUF crest) design featured a wrapover crew neck. Shadow stripes decorated the fabric. Alternative hem-trimmed shorts were worn with this ensemble.

Worn in: A 1990 2–1 defeat by Mexico.
Worn by: Enrique Vaca, Ricardo Pelaez.

HOME 1992

Design: Enerre

Japanese sportswear company Enerre began supplying the AUF strip in 1992. Their first, short-lived, outfit wasn't a million miles away in terms of design from the previous Puma kit – the big difference though came with the controversial replacing of black with royal blue.

Worn in: A great 1–0 win over Brazil in a friendly match – the kit's first outing. In fact the team enjoyed a 100% win ratio in this kit!
Worn by: Fernando Kanapkis, Adrain Paz.

1993 COPA AMERICA

HOME 1992–95

Design: Enerre

The 1990s brought with them an era of bold and brash, heavily patterned football apparel as typified by this new Enerre strip, launched just a few months after this first Uruguay kit. The royal blue theme continued and a pattern of dynamic, abstract triangles and chequerboard effect decorated the right sleeve.

Worn in: A 1–0 win for Luis Cubilla's team against the USA in the 1993 Copa America.
Worn by: Santiago Ostolaza, Marcelo Saralegui.

1993 COPA AMERICA

AWAY 1992–95

Design: Enerre

After over 20 years of white change strips, Enerre brought back red as a Uruguay change colour – supposedly due to white being considered unlucky. The design, including its shadow striped fabric and asymmetrical abstract embellishments, copied the design of the home outfit. Four stars, symbolising La Celeste's Olympics and World Cup titles, were placed above the AUF crest.

1995 COPA AMERICA

★

HOME 1995–96

Design: Enerre

Enerre's second set of Uruguay strips retained the sky blue/royal blue ethos but brought the colours together in a more balanced and measured new design. Broad colour panels angled inwards on each side of the shirt and the theme continued on the shorts.

Worn in: The glorious 1995 Copa America final win on penalties over Brazil. The game had ended 1–1 in normal time.
Worn by: Pablo Bengoechea, Gus Poyet.

AWAY 1995-98

Design: Enerre

The latest Enerre design was produced in a red, royal blue and white version and was worn for three major tournaments. The fabric on this second set of Enerre strips included an elongated diamond shadow pattern.

Worn in: A 5-3 defeat by Japan in a 1996 friendly match.
Worn by: Alvaro Recoba, Robert Siboldi.

HOME 1997-98

Design: Enerre

In a move that pleased the traditionalists, it was decided that after five years it was time to end the royal blue experiment and return to black as the secondary colour on the Uruguay strip. So Enerre updated the design and debuted it in a 0-0 draw with Argentina at the start of the year. Victor Pua Sosa was now team manager.

Worn in: A 4-3 win over South Africa in the 2007 Confederations Cup.
Worn by: César Pellegrin, Martin Rivas.

HOME 1999-2000

Design: Tenfield

The AUF signed a deal with Tenfield and it was in their incredibly shiny strips that Uruguay competed in the 1999 Copa America. The strip was modest in design, with just a white collar and sky blue insert (complete with 'Uruguay' text), small Uruguay flags and the team crest adorning the jersey.

Worn in: The 3-0 defeat by Brazil in the final of the 1999 Copa America.
Worn by: Federico Magallanes, Fernando Picun.

AWAY 1999-2001

Design: Tenfield

Red versions of both Tenfield kits were produced although the first was never worn. The second version featured the new shadow striped fabric and the AUF crest that was now embroidered directly onto the shirt itself, rather than appearing as part of a patch. Jerseys at this time were still very baggy in fit.

Worn in: A 2-1 defeat by Argentina in a 2000 qualifier for the 2002 World Cup.
Worn by: Gabriel Cedres, Gonzalo Sorondo.

HOME 2000-01

Design: Tenfield

The first set of Tenfield kits went through a slight modification in 2000 with the silky fabric replaced by shadow striped design and trim added to the collar. The shadow stripes switched orientation on the sleeves in an unorthodox but effective style. Blue piping now also ran down each side of the shorts.

Worn in: The 2-1 defeat by Mexico in the semi-final of the 2001 Copa America.
Worn by: Richard Morales, Rodrigo Lemos.

HOME 2001-02

Design: L-Sporto

Following the 2001 Copa America, Uruguay adopted a new set of kits, supplied by L-Sporto. The new approach was minimalist, featuring only sky blue and black with piping decorating the raglan sleeves and shirt sides. The strips carried no visible manufacturer branding.

Worn in: The 3-0 win over Australia in the 2002 World Cup play-off that secured a place in the tournament for Alvaro Recoba's team.
Worn by: Gianni Guigou, Dario Silva.

AWAY 2001-03

Design: L-Sporto

No surprises with the first La Celeste away kit as supplied by US sportswear company L-Sporto: a straightforward red rendering of the home design, complete with a small graphic of the national flag on the right-hand sleeve and trimmed, athletic cut shorts. Later versions of this shirt carried a L-Sporto logo.

Worn in: A 1-1 friendly draw with Italy in 2002.
Worn by: Pablo Garcia, Fabian O'Neill.

HOME 2002-04

Design: L-Sporto

First worn in a friendly against the USA, Uruguay's 2002 World Cup strip looked to the team's 1930 World Cup winning shirt for inspiration. The shirt featured an old-fashioned lace-up collar, breathable fabric panels and a subtle L-Sporto logo on the left sleeve.

Worn in: All three of the side's World Cup matches including a 0-0 draw with France. The team failed to win a game in the tournament.
Worn by: Gustavo Varela, Paolo Montero.

AWAY 2002–04

Design: L-Sporto

The by now established red incarnation of the home kit formed La Celeste's change outfit for the 2002 World Cup. The shirts continued the theme of including a flag graphic on the right sleeve. Although in Víctor Púa's kitbag this fine strip was not required in the tournament itself. Oddly, the previous crew-neck away design was resurrected later in 2003.

Worn in: A friendly 2003 2–2 draw with Japan.
Worn by: Alejandro Lembo, Bruno Silva.

THIRD 2002–04

Design: L-Sporto

If the away strip followed the easy route of simply replicating the home design in red, this wonderful third kit took the opposite route, opting for a highly creative and exciting design that included an asymmetrical placement of the Uruguay flag on the left shoulder. It appears though that the shirt was never worn by the first team in a major fixture although it did make an appearance in a low-key match.

HOME 2004–05

Design: Uhlsport

Eschewing the post-modern approach of the L-Sporto strips, new kit suppliers Uhlsport brought the Uruguay kit up to date with a highly contemporary and athletic-looking design, with curved black panels and white piping creating a very different look for the team.

Worn in: A 3–1 win over Paraguay in the 2004 Copa America. Also worn in the following penalties semi-final defeat by Brazil.
Worn by: Marcelo Sosa, Joe Bizera.

AWAY 2004–05

Design: Uhlsport

Uhlsport continued the functional approach of simply reflecting the home strip design in red for their first away kit for Uruguay. Additional Uhlsport branding featured on the lower sides of the shirt and the top of the shorts.

Worn in: Two 2004 4–2 defeats by Argentina: one in the 2004 Copa America and the second a 2006 World Cup qualifier later in the year.
Worn by: Vicente Sanchez, Luis Barbat.

THIRD 2004–05

Design: Uhlsport

An attractive all white with sky blue applications became Uruguay's third shirt in 2004. Naturally, it followed the same design as the home and away strips but, unfortunately, it appears the strip was never required on the pitch.

HOME 2005–06

Design: Uhlsport

Uhlsport continued the multi-panel and very modern look for their next Uruguay home. A crew neck with white flashes and black reversed stitching was joined by round sleeve panels and side panels. Broad colour blocks adorned the shorts.

Worn in: The crushing penalties defeat by minnows Australia in the second leg of the 2005 play-off for the 2006 World Cup.
Worn by: Dario Rodriguez, Richard Morales.

AWAY 2005–06

Design: Uhlsport

A very effective red, white and black option was used for Uhlsport's second Uruguay away kit with a design that copied that of the home strip, including additional Uhlsport logos on each sleeve. Óscar Tabárez was appointed new team manager in 2006 following the team's failure to qualify for that year's World Cup.

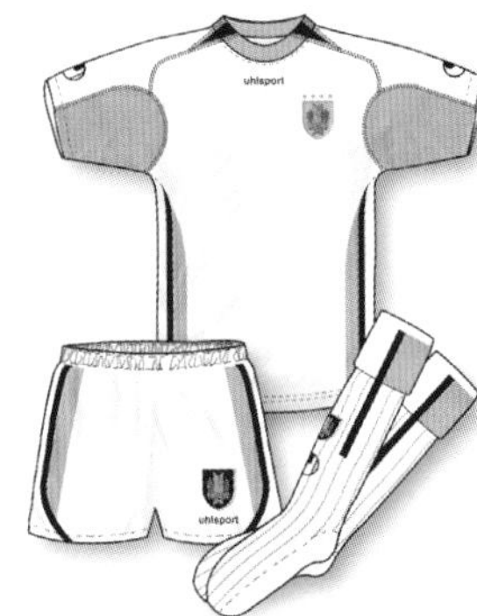

THIRD 2005–06

Design: Uhlsport

The very slick basic template Uhlsport introduced in 2005 worked extremely well in this third choice version of white, with sky blue and black trim. Although not worn by the first team, the shorts and socks did make an appearance with the home shirt in a 2005 friendly match against Spain.

HOME 2006

Design: Uhlsport

Uhlsport's last kit for Uruguay lasted just a matter of months and used the same shorts and socks from the previous kit. The shirt was now simplified with a round neck and suave white piping running down each side of the shirt. Enlarged Uhlsport logos appeared again on each sleeve.

Worn in: A 4–0 friendly win over Venezuela.
Worn by: Vicente Sanchez, Sergio Blanco.

2007 COPA AMERICA

HOME 2007–08

Design: Puma

Puma returned to Uruguay in 2007 to start another creative and vibrant period of kit partnership with the AUF. Their first design was sleek and sophisticated, featuring a basic crew neck (with contrasting inner) and a large off-centre Sun of May shadow print. Secondary Puma logos appeared high on the shoulders.

Worn in: The tense semi-final 5–4 penalties defeat by Brazil in the 2007 Copa America.
Worn by: Diego Forlan, Sebastian Abreu.

2007 COPA AMERICA

AWAY 2007–08

Design: Puma

A red version of the first design in the new sequence of Puma strips was used as the team's next away kit. The outfit mirrored that of the home, including a large arched colour panel on the reverse. The kit was never worn in an official match but did make some appearances in low-key games. Alternative versions of both this and the home shirt placed the AUF crest centrally under the Puma logo.

HOME 2008–09

Design: Puma

Sky blue and black remained the only colour focus for this next kit. The design used a standard Puma template that incorporated a tight v-neck and contrasting underarm panels in a breathable fabric that stretched down on the reverse of the jersey.

Worn in: A highly successful 2010 World Cup qualifying campaign for Oscar Tabarez's team including a 6–0 thrashing of Peru in 2008.
Worn by: Carlos Bueno, Diego Perez.

AWAY 2008–09

Design: Puma

Although it utilised a teamwear design, the next Uruguay change kit opted for a different look to that of the home strip. A collar was added to the shirt and the Puma logo and AUF crest placed together on the left-hand side. Attractive hooped socks made a nice addition to the outfit.

Worn in: A 3–1 triumph over Japan in the 2008 Kirin Challenge Cup.
Worn by: Ignacio Gonzalez, Sebastian Eguren.

2010 FIFA WORLD CUP
2011 COPA AMERICA

HOME 2010–11

Design: Puma

After the simplicity of the previous two home kits Tabarez's side turned out in a more complex outfit, featuring a layered, angular collar, white and gold flashes and a repeated Sun of May shadow pattern.

Worn in: The 3–2 defeat by the Netherlands in the semi-final of the 2010 World Cup. Also worn in the 3–0 victory over Paraguay in the 2011 Copa America final.
Worn by: Luis Suárez, Maxi Pereira.

2010 FIFA WORLD CUP
2011 COPA AMERICA

AWAY 2010–12

Design: Puma

La Celeste brought back white as their primary choice change kit for the first time in 20 years in the form of this sublime outfit. Both 2010 shorts included a badge featuring the national flag in the centre of the waistband.

Worn in: A 3–0 victory against South Africa in the group stages of the 2010 World Cup. Also worn in the thrilling quarter-final penalties win over Argentina in the 2011 Copa America.
Worn by: Alvaro Fernandez, Diego Perez.

2010 FIFA WORLD CUP

THIRD 2010–12

Design: Puma

In a design that echoed that of the white away kit, an extravagant gold third kit was unveiled by Puma in 2010, The strip was trimmed with black and featured the Puma logo and AUF crest placed centrally. The shorts retained the waistband patch from the home and away kits. However, although the strip was available for the 2010 World Cup and 2011 Copa America it was not required in either tournament.

HOME 2012–13

Design: Puma

New year – new kit. The next home strip dispensed with the fripperies of the previous, instead preferring a crew neck, thin shadow stripes and asymmetrical Sun of May panel on the shoulder. Apart from the Confederations Cup the strip was used until the end of 2013.

Worn in: The 2014 World Cup qualifier play-off against Jordan – Uruguay won the first leg 5–0 and drew the second 0–0.
Worn by: Cristian Rodriguez, Nicolas Lodeiro.

AWAY 2012–13

Design: Puma

The asymmetrical approach continued on La Celeste's next away kit with the introduction of a single sky blue panel on the left-hand side of the shirt that housed the AUF crest. The Puma logo was placed high on the right shoulder.

Worn in: A 2–1 defeat by Spain in Uruguay's opening game of the 2013 Confederations Cup. Also worn in a 4–2 friendly win over Japan in 2013.
Worn by: Walter Gargano, Edinson Cavani.

HOME 2013

Design: Puma

A strip inspired by the legendary Uruguay team that won gold at the 1924 Olympics was launched just for the 2013 Confederations Cup. A simple yet stunning design, a smart 'fake' lace-up neck provided the main visual focus for the strip.

Worn in: An 8–0 thrashing of Tahiti in the 2013 Confederations Cup followed by the 2–1 defeat by Brazil in the tournament's semi-final.
Worn by: Álvaro González, Egidio Arévalo.

HOME 2014–16

Design: Puma

Tight fitting shirts were the order of the day as teams prepared for the 2014 World Cup. Uruguay's home shirt for the tournament resurrected the popular gold trim from the last World Cup to decorate each side of the shirt. A tonal Sun of May graphic sat behind the crest.

Worn in: A 2–1 victory against England in the 2014 World Cup followed by the 2–0 defeat by Colombia in the knockout stage.
Worn by: José Giménez, Martín Cáceres.

AWAY 2014–16

Design: Puma

Essentially reflecting the design of the home kit, the new white change outfit replaced the round neck of the home shirt with a v-neck design that also incorporated a sky blue inset panel. A small Uruguayan national flag sat on the waistband of the home and away shorts.

Worn in: A 1–0 win over Italy in the 2014 World Cup group stage that included Suárez's infamous biting incident.
Worn by: Diego Godin, Nicolas Lodeiro.

HOME 2016–17

Design: Puma

First worn in a 2016 qualifier for the 2018 World Cup against Brazil, this shirt brought a bold new look to La Celeste's kit. Large black panels (a standard Puma design) reached across each shoulder with just a hint of gold on the inside of the crew neck. The traditional Sun of May formed part of a large embossed print.

Worn in: A 3–1 loss to Mexico in Uruguay's opening game of the 2016 Copa America.
Worn by: Mathías Vecino, Carlos Sánchez.

AWAY 2016–17

Design: Puma

Puma excelled themselves with this beautiful change kit that incorporated the Uruguay flag iconography at the foot of the shirt in a genius way. The rest of the template reflected that of the home with gold highlights bringing a touch of glamour to the outfit.

Worn in: A 3–0 win over Jamaica in the 2016 Copa America – Uruguay's sole win in a disappointing tournament.
Worn by: Abel Hernández, Mathías Corujo.

HOME 2017–18

Design: Puma

The kit Uruguay will wear in the 2018 World Cup was unveiled towards the end of 2017. Officially in 'silver lake blue', it contained all the elements required to make it a real classic including a traditional v-neck (given a slightly modern twist), a mesh Sun of May graphic and an updated AUF crest. Mesh stripes featured on each sleeve.

USA

The USA's chequered and eventful football past extends past the pitch and continues into the kitbag!

Arguably no team in world football has enjoyed such a wide and inconsistent variety of designs and colour selections as the US side, although their strips (almost) always end up in patriotic red, white or blue.

When the side regrouped in the late '60s, red was selected as first choice kit. During the subsequent decade, a fluid selection of red, white and blue were all worn as home kits at some point or other. In fact, many US kit experts claim that there was in fact no official first choice hue until the late '80s, when white was firmly established as the team's primary colour.

Even during the '80s, kit designs were fluid and, at times, random. Many short-lived uniforms featured a variety of different crests and branding.

By the end of the decade, the US embraced a new focused era of professionalism and the kit followed suit, becoming more stable and consistent. However, the designs were still exciting, lively and varied.

Nike took over from long-term technical suppliers adidas in 1995 and began to look to the past for inspiration, resurrecting the sash style that was favoured by various historical US teams. They also even looked to the infamous Team America strips from 1983, which have clearly influenced the side's 2017 kit.

However, it is adidas that has supplied the USA with possibly their most famous uniforms: in the 1994 World Cup, highly anticipated and hosted in the United States, the patriotic 'stars and stripes' set of kits created a benchmark in international excellence.

SPECIAL THANKS TO NICHOLAS LARIMER, CHRIS OAKLEY

A classic adidas kit sported by the US team pictured before their 1993 2–0 victory against England in the US Cup.

HOME 1968–69

Design: Unknown

After a few years of relative inactivity the national team regrouped under manager Phil Woosnam and started well on their campaign for qualification for the 1970 World Cup. During the qualifiers it seems red was preferred as first choice strip accompanied by muted blue shorts.

Worn in: A 3–3 friendly defeat against Israel in 1968.
Worn by: Willie Roy, Nick Krat.

HOME 1968–74

Design: Unknown

In typical '60s style, a short sleeved alternative shirt accompanied the long sleeved crew-neck version for warmer climes. The unbadged shirt featured contrasting neck and cuffs. The shirt was also later worn with change red shorts and the white pairs from the 1971–74 away kit.

Worn in: The defeats by Haiti (2–0 and 1–0) that thwarted the USA's qualification for the 1970 World Cup.
Worn by: Peter Millar, Dietrich Albrecht.

AWAY 1971–74

Design: Unknown

The national team went into decline again following the World Cup qualifying failure and were dormant until 1971. They emerged wearing a badged, short sleeved white shirt with dual-coloured contrasting v-neck and cuffs. Bob Kehoe took over as manager for the unsuccessful 1974 World Cup qualifiers.

Worn in: A 3–2 defeat against Canada in a 1974 World Cup qualifier (1972).
Worn by: Larry Hausemann, Gary Rensing.

HOME 1974

Design: Unknown

The favourite football fashion statement of the '70s – the wing collar – appeared on the US kit in 1974. The slightly haphazard philosophy between home and change colours continued with red now appearing as first choice. In this year the sport's governing body changed its name to the United States Soccer Federation.

Worn in: A 3–1 defeat against Mexico.
Worn by: Dennis Vaninger, Werner Roth.

AWAY 1974

Design: Unknown

A blue version of the long sleeved, wing-collared shirt also existed at this time. Worn with the same white shorts as the home kit, blue socks completed the uniform. It's unclear in which games this strip was worn. Detmar Cramer was appointed manager.

Worn in: A 1–0 friendly defeat against San José Earthquakes.
Worn by: Bobby Smith, Mike Ivanow.

HOME 1975–81

Design: adidas

The first visible branding appeared on a US kit in 1975, coinciding with the increased interest in the American game. International kit masters adidas took on the deal and supplied the team with its classic 'Worldcup Dress' template. A simple monogram (that was updated slightly in 1979) replaced the previous shield design.

Worn in: A 6–0 friendly defeat against France in 1979.
Worn by: Angelo di Bernado, Glenn Myernick.

HOME 1975–76

Design: adidas

As with many of adidas' mid-'70s roster a v-necked short sleeved alternative shirt was issued for the US team. Curiously, though, this range of outfits across its teams were often minus the adidas trefoil logo (although it did appear on later versions). A simple monogram crest replaced the previous shield design.

Worn in: A 3–0 defeat against Mexico in a 1976 qualifier for the 1978 World Cup.
Worn by: Alex Skotarek, Al Trost.

AWAY 1975–81

Design: adidas

A superb white, blue and red version of the Worldcup Dress kit template was also worn in the latter half of the '70s. It must be remembered here that home and away colour choices were still fluid!

Worn in: A 4–1 defeat by the Soviet Union in a 1979 friendly match.
Worn by: Chris Bahr, Bruce Hudson.

HOME 1976

Design: adidas

America hosted the four-team Bicentennial Tournament in 1976. To accompany 'Team America' (as they were known) adidas supplied updated kit in a fully patriotic palette of colours that included a commemorative badge on the front.

Worn in: The 3–1 defeat against England in the Bicentennial Tournament.
Worn by: Pelé (who for contractual reasons blocked out the three-stripe trim on the shirt!)

AWAY 1976

Design: adidas

A smart white shirt was also produced that mirrored the design of the home and included dual-colour three-stripe trim. Unlike the red shirt, the adidas logo did feature. A host of star players guested for the US side who wore a unique strip in each of their three games in the Bicentennial Tournament.

Worn in: A 4–0 defeat against Italy in Team America's first game of the tournament.
Worn by: Tommy Smith, Bobby Moore.

THIRD 1976

Design: adidas

The blue version of the Team America (not to be confused with the 1983 incarnation) strip reflected the design of the other outfits, including the self-coloured v-neck and cuffs. Like the white shirt, the adidas trefoil logo was included. Red trim featured on the socks and rounded off a superb trio of uniforms.

Worn in: A 2–0 defeat against Brazil in the Bicentennial Tournament.
Worn by: Giorgio Chinaglia, Stewart Scullion.

HOME 1976–80

Design: adidas

The standard Worldcup Dress shirt was also available in a short sleeved version alongside this alternative version that introduced blue to the three-stripe trim on the sleeves. Interest in football stateside grew during this period, in part due to the increased popularity of the NASL.

Worn in: A 2–1 friendly win over El Salvador in 1977.
Worn by: Steve Ralbovsky, Mike Flater.

AWAY 1976–80

Design: adidas

A new red-trimmed cuffless white shirt emerged in 1980. It followed the crew-necked design of the long sleeved jersey. The white shorts and socks were now also trimmed with red.

Worn in: A 5–1 thrashing at the hands of Mexico in a qualifier for the 1982 World Cup.
Worn by: Rick Davies, Colin Fowles.

HOME 1980–81

Design: adidas

As Walt Chyzowych's team prepared for the 1982 World Cup qualifiers their short sleeved home shirt was refreshed with contrasting white v-neck, cuffs and raglan sleeves, trimmed elegantly in white. A new team monogram was introduced and appeared, unusually, on the right-hand side of the shirt.

Worn in: A superb 2–1 victory over Mexico in a 1980 qualifier for the 1982 World Cup.
Worn by: Steve Moyers, Mark Liveric.

AWAY 1980–81

Design: Unknown

The change version of the latest US uniform followed the same design, but introduced a red collar with self-coloured v-neck. Again, there was inconsistency with the style and positioning of the team monogram and adidas logos throughout the kit.

THIRD 1980–81

Design: adidas

An attractive all-blue third choice outfit completed this fine set of strips. As with the away, a collar was featured but included a contrasting v-neck section. The adidas trefoil logo and team monogram also switched sides.

HOME 1983

Design: adidas

With success on the pitch still eluding the country US Soccer decided to enter the national side in the NASL under the rebranded 'Team America' moniker. The strip was full of American extravagance and razzamatazz with the clever representation of the 'Stars and Stripes' flag creating a striking strip. More sedate three-stripe shorts were also worn.

Worn in: A 1-0 win over Tulsa Roughnecks.
Worn by: Perry van der Beck, Tony Crescitelli.

AWAY 1983

Design: adidas

The raglan sleeved shirt design from the last US strips was retained for the seldom worn Team America change kit. The fabric was adorned with beautiful baseball-style red pinstripes to help create a splendid away/road option for Alkis Panagoulias' team. Squad numbers appeared on the front and sleeves of these shirts as well as on the traditional back.

Worn in: A 3–0 defeat by Chicago Sting.
Worn by: Jeff Durgan, Bruce Savage.

HOME 1984

Design: adidas

What appears to be a one-off home white strip was worn against Italy in a 1984 friendly. The secondary colour was a darker, more maroon like red. The shirt featured a collar and three-stripe trim.

Worn in: An honourable 0–0 draw with Italy.
Worn by: Gregg Thompson, Alan Green.

HOME 1984–85

Design: adidas

The Team America experiment had failed and US Soccer went back to the drawing board in an attempt to rebuild the side. White was now chosen as the first choice home kit colour and adidas' well known diagonal pinstripe template was used for the new outfit. Towards the end of the life of this strip (and its blue and red equivalents) an additional crest was added.

AWAY 1984–85

Design: adidas

Blue was promoted as the new away kit in a design that mirrored that of the home outfit, including the new outlined USA monogram. The diagonal pinstriped uniforms were first worn in the 1984 Olympics before being replaced (although this blue kit did make a reappearance against England).

Worn in: Friendly defeats by West Germany (1–0) and England (5–0).
Worn by: Dan Canter, Mike Windischmann.

THIRD 1984–85

Design: adidas

Red completed the trio of uniforms in the patriotic American colours. The kit again reproduced the dual-colour diagonal pinstripes that also featured on its blue and white partners. With all three strips consisting of the same design there was a degree of mixing and matching across the outfits.

HOME 1985–87

Design: adidas

For the final run of World Cup qualifiers Alkis Panagoulias' team donned a variation of the horizontally shadow striped 'Aberdeen' template – a favourite with many of adidas' other teams at the time. The newly designed team crest also appeared on these kits. The team went on sabbatical in 1986 following the disastrous World Cup qualifying failure.

Worn in: A 1–1 draw with Costa Rica in 1985.
Worn by: John Kerr, Ed Radwanski.

AWAY 1985–87

Design: adidas

With the collapse of the NASL in 1984 football found itself in a downward spiral by 1985. US Soccer was placing all the footballing hopes of the nation on qualification for the 1986 World Cup. This blue version of the team kit was to play a major role in this quest.

Worn in: The final 1986 World Cup qualifier against Costa Rica in 1985, with the US just needing a draw – sadly Costa Rica won 1–0.
Worn by: Kevin Crow, Mike Fox.

HOME 1988–91

Design: adidas

An athletic-looking long-sleeved home shirt emerged as the side's new home look in 1988, complete with collar and refreshed crest design. US Soccer aimed to rebuild during this period as they pushed for World Cup qualification. The organisation also introduced a new 'national team as club' structure that attracted back many senior players to the team.

Worn in: A 2–1 defeat against Croatia in 1990.
Worn by: Eric Eichmann, Jimmy Banks.

HOME 1988–89

Design: adidas

The short-sleeved version of the new clean and smart home kit featured a simple v-neck and slightly different blue shoulder flashes. Although this shirt was retired in 1989, its long sleeved close cousin was available until the dawn of the 'adidas equipment' range in 1991.

Worn in: The marvellous 5–1 victory over Jamaica in a 1988 qualifier for the 1990 World Cup.
Worn by: Paul Krumpe, Brian Bliss.

AWAY 1988–90

Design: adidas

A blue version of the brand new long sleeved design also existed and was still being worn in friendlies at the end of 1990. The strip simply reversed the colours of the home kit and included adidas' latest style of shorts that featured a broad hem trim.

Worn in: A 1–0 friendly defeat against Portugal in 1990.
Worn by: Desmond Armstrong, Troy Dayak.

AWAY 1988–89

Design: adidas

One of the most celebrated of adidas designs found its way briefly to the US kitbag in 1988. The shirt featured the geometric, gradated colour pattern that had been made famous by the Netherlands in Euro 88. The shorts and socks were reversals of the home pairs which allowed them to be interchanged when necessary.

HOME 1989–90

Design: adidas

One of the most underrated adidas designs, yet one that was worn by many of its teams, was this wrapover crew-neck shirt, decorated with a repeated shadow octagon pattern. Vertical shadow stripes were included on the shorts.

Worn in: One of the most glorious matches in US football – the 1–0 win over Trinidad that clinched a' place in the 1990 World Cup!
Worn by: Paul Caligiuri – scorer of the winning goal against Trinidad.

HOME 1989–90

Design: adidas

A darker shade of blue was used in this next US away kit that was worn in the latter stages of their 1990 World Cup qualifying campaign as Bob Gansler led his team to the dawn of a new era. The white shorts featured broad blue trim on the hems although the plainer blue home pairs were also worn with the strip.

Worn in: A 3–1 defeat by the USSR in 1990.
Worn by: John Stollmeyer, Peter Vermes.

1990 FIFA WORLD CUP

HOME 1990–91

Design: adidas

The USA celebrated their first World Cup for 40 years with a new strip – a striking adidas design with broad colour panels on each sleeve and a centralised badge which was relatively unusual for the time. The shorts continued the hem trim design in worn the previous two years.

Worn in: Three straight defeats in the 1990 World Cup: 5–1 against Czechoslovakia, 1–0 vs Italy and 2–1 to Austria.
Worn by: John Harkes, Bruce Murray.

1990 FIFA WORLD CUP

AWAY 1990–91

Design: adidas

Another straightforward reversal of the home kit provided the US with their away kit for Italia 90. A nice touch was that the adidas trefoil logo switched sides between the home and away jerseys. Due to the team's early exit this away kit was not required in the tournament.

Worn in: A 1991 friendly match against Bayern Munich that ended in a 4–0 defeat for the Americans.
Worn by: Fernando Clavijo.

HOME 1991

Design: adidas

The adidas equipment rebrand in 1991 brought with it a bold and brave sequence of new kits that, in the main, ditched the familiar three-stripe trim and introduced in-your-face colour panels. Red was brought back to the kit palette with this shirt that was first worn in June 1991. Bora Milutinovic was now team manager.

Worn in: A 1–1 friendly draw with Costa Rica.
Worn by: Dante Washington, Marcelo Balboa.

AWAY 1991

Design: adidas

A rejuvenated US team, buoyant from victory in the US Cup, took part in the inaugural Gold Cup tournament with their state of the art adidas equipment uniforms. The away strip unusually included a contrasting element on the v-neck and stripped the design back to two colours.

Worn in: The glorious 2–0 win over Mexico in the Gold Cup followed by the penalties win over Honduras in the final.
Worn by: Hugo Perez, Chris Henderson.

HOME 1992–94

Design: adidas

A year after the launch of the adidas equipment strips the team badge was updated to a more modern and dynamic design that reflected the run-up to the US-hosted 1994 World Cup with the text 'World Cup Team' placed under the US monogram. The adidas logo switched to black.

Worn in: Fine wins over the Republic of Ireland (3–1) and Portugal (1–0) to claim the US Cup.
Worn by: Roy Wegerle, Brian Quinn.

AWAY 1992–94

Design: adidas

The white contrasting neck disappeared on this updated version of the first adidas equipment away strip. Initially worn with the previous round badge and three-stripe trim socks, it was soon tweaked further with the addition of the new crest.

Worn in: A 3–3 goalfest against Venezuela in the 1993 Copa America.
Worn by: John Doyle, Cle Kooiman.

THIRD 1993–94

Design: adidas

With qualification for the next World Cup assured as hosts, Bora Milutinovic's side prepared for the tournament with a long series of friendlies. A new, stunning blue kit was launched and used as an alternative to the normal blue design. A standard adidas template, red now joined white on the large shoulder panels.

Worn in: A 0–0 friendly draw with Peru.
Worn by: Joe-Max Moore, Dominic Kinnear.

HOME 1994

Design: adidas

With America hosting the 1994 World Cup, the pressure was on adidas to create a strip that captured the glamour of the US team. It did so perfectly with a set of strips that were both extravagant and arrogant, and, thanks to the reappropriation of the national flag, patriotic.

Worn in: A 1–0 defeat by Brazil in the World Cup – the only outing in the tournament for this kit (worn with the away kit's red shorts).
Worn by: Mike Sorber.

AWAY 1994

Design: adidas

This sublime starry shirt, featuring a denim effect that couldn't be more American if it tried, somewhat overshadowed its home equivalent, often leading people to wonder which was the first choice. The elements of both strips were able to be interchanged, creating possibly the greatest set of international kits ever.

Worn in: The 2–1 win over Colombia in the 1994 World Cup – the USA's sole victory.
Worn by: Alexi Lalas, Earnie Stewart.

HOME 1995–98

Design: Nike

After 20 years with adidas it was time for a change and US Soccer turned to fellow countrymen Nike to produce the team strip. Its first outfit was sedate and sophisticated, taking a very different approach to the last adidas strips and focusing on a white uniform with darker red and navy chest panel.

Worn in: A 2–1 triumph over Chile in the 1995 Copa America.
Worn by: Claudio Reyna, Tom Dooley.

1995 COPA AMERICA / 1996 CONCACAF GOLD CUP
1998 CONCACAF GOLD CUP

AWAY 1995–98

Design: Nike

The new darker colour palette worked beautifully with the next away kit. The design replicated that of the home, including a gap in the chest panel designed to house a squad number. A new shield team crest was also launched this year. Steve Sampson took over as manager following the departure of Milutinovic.

Worn in: The jaw-dropping Copa America 3–0 victory over Argentina in 1995.
Worn by: Frank Klopas, Eric Wynalda.

THIRD 1996

Design: Nike

A lighter blue shade was introduced to create a smart third shirt for Sampson's team. The design mirrored that of the baggy fitting home and away designs and was worn with the standard navy change shorts and socks. Replica versions of these kits moved the team crest to the empty space in the chest bands.

Worn in: A 2–2 draw with Mexico in the US Cup.
Worn by: Cobi Jones, Tab Ramos.

THIRD 1997

Design: Nike

One of the more enigmatic shirts in the US kit history is this attractive dual-hooped pinstripe affair. The design featured simple trimmed v-neck and cuffs. Released as a third shirt, it helped start an ethos of US third outfits that did not necessarily provide a different colour option for the side and instead were used for commemorative or heritage reasons. It's unclear whether this strip ever saw action on the pitch.

1998 FIFA WORLD CUP / 1999 FIFA CONFEDERATIONS CUP
2000 CONCACAF GOLD CUP

HOME 1998–2000

Design: Nike

The US had qualified for the 1998 World Cup and after three years with the previous home strip unveiled this wonderful outfit. Featuring a standard Nike collar, the chest/hoop theme continued and was developed to a much simpler and restrained rendering.

Worn in: Dismal defeats to Iran (2–1) and Yugoslavia (1–0) as the US made an early exit from the 1998 World Cup.
Worn by: Brian McBride, David Regis.

1998 FIFA WORLD CUP / 1999 FIFA CONFEDERATIONS CUP
2000 CONCACAF GOLD CUP

AWAY 1998–2000

Design: Nike

Red is always popular with US supporters, and Nike brought back a change kit in the colour for the first time since 1985. Paired with navy shorts and socks that could also be worn with the home kit if necessary.

Worn in: The 2–0 defeat against Germany in the 1998 World Cup. Also worn in a revenge win by the same score against the same team in the 1999 Confederations Cup.
Worn by: Brian Maisonneuve, Earnie Stewart.

2002 CONCACAF GOLD CUP

★

HOME 2000–02

Design: Nike

Visual decoration seemed to reduce in prominence with every subsequent US kit. This latest design, premiered in the US Nike Cup, was constructed from multiple breathable fabric panels and had a minimalist approach with a simple v-neck and cuffs, trimmed discreetly in red.

Worn in: The 2–0 triumph against Costa Rica that clinched the 2002 Gold Cup for the US!
Worn by: Jeff Agoos.

2002 CONCACAF GOLD CUP

AWAY 2000–02

Design: Nike

The rich red that Nike introduced was used to full effect on this second consecutive road uniform in the colour. Red was also reinstated on the socks, which featured an interesting vertical trim. Bruce Arena had replaced Steve Sampson as team manager in 1998.

Worn in: A 2–0 friendly win over Mexico in 2000. Also worn in a superb 4–0 triumph against El Salvador in the 2002 Gold Cup.
Worn by: Richie Williams, Clint Mathis.

2002 FIFA WORLD CUP / 2003 FIFA CONFEDERATIONS CUP
2003 CONCACAF GOLD CUP

HOME 2002–04

Design: Nike

Launched just prior to the 2002 World Cup this latest design fell in line with Nike's universal dual-layer shirt design: the dual layers wicked sweat more quickly and kept the players cool. Angular panels of red and blue provided a fierce look. Blue shorts were now first choice, although white was also often worn.

Worn in: A fantastic 3-2 win over Portugal in the team's' opening match of the World Cup.
Worn by: John O'Brien, Landon Donovan.

2002 FIFA WORLD CUP / 2003 FIFA CONFEDERATIONS CUP
2003 CONCACAF GOLD CUP

AWAY 2002–04

Design: Nike

A menacing navy and white version (with minimalist crew-neck design) of the dual-layered shirt formed the US away kit as they entered the World Cup. Arena's team enjoyed a great tournament and were unfortunate not to progress to the semi-finals.

Worn in: A 3–1 defeat by Poland in the group stages of the 2002 World Cup and the 1–0 defeat against Germany in the quarter-finals.
Worn by: Pablo Mastroeni, Frankie Hejduk.

THIRD 2003

Design: Nike

For the team's next 'heritage' third shirt (remember, these jerseys weren't designed to provide a colour alternative!) Nike produced a close replica of the iconic jersey worn by the nation in the 1950 World Cup. The only difference was that the sash was now blue, rather than the original red. The Nike swoosh logo was neatly tucked away on the left sleeve.

Worn in: A 2–1 friendly win over New Zealand.
Worn by: Chris Klein, Jovan Kirovski.

2005 CONCACAF GOLD CUP

★

HOME 2004–06

Design: Nike

Another Nike template, the 'Total 90' range, made an appearance in the American kit cupboard in 2004. Graceful piping arched down the sides of the shirt accompanied by breathable mesh fabric. Red appeared only in the shape of the Nike logos and flashes on the shorts.

Worn in: The penalties win over Panama in the 2005 Gold Cup final – the USA's third Gold Cup crown.
Worn by: Eddie Johnson, Gregg Berhalter.

2005 CONCACAF GOLD CUP

AWAY 2004–06

Design: Nike

Red played a more prominent role in the Total 90 change kit but the rest of the design simply reversed that of the home. Like the white shirt, a contrasted colour shoulder panel that housed player names was featured on the back of the shirt. The team badge was included on the shorts for the first time.

Worn in: An all-navy 2–1 win against Honduras in the 2005 Gold Cup semi-finals.
Worn by: DaMarcus Beasley, Conor Casey.

THIRD 2004

Design: Nike

The 1950 shirt was replicated more accurately in 2004 thanks to the inclusion of a red sash rather than the blue version on the previous kit. The jersey featured a retro crest and curious three-quarter length sleeves. The Nike swoosh was rendered in red and placed by the left cuff.

Worn in: A 1–1 draw with Jamaica in a qualifier for the 2006 World Cup.
Worn by: Tony Sanneh.

2006 FIFA WORLD CUP
2007 CONCACAF GOLD CUP / 2007 COPA AMERICA

★

HOME 2006–08

Design: Nike

Premiered in a 1–0 win over Poland, this sublime strip kept it simple with non-contrasting crew neck and a confident navy and red stripe on the left-hand side that was echoed on the reverse of the shorts and socks.

Worn in: A 1–1 draw with Italy and a 2–1 defeat by Ghana in a disappointing World Cup. Also worn in the glorious 2–1 win over rivals Mexico in the 2007 Gold Cup final.
Worn by: Ben Olsen, Benny Feilhaber.

2006 FIFA WORLD CUP
2007 CONCACAF GOLD CUP / 2007 COPA AMERICA

AWAY 2006–08

Design: Nike

The new World Cup away kit must have puzzled supporters on its launch as it had more than a passing resemblance to the team's 1995 change outfit. Differences came in the shape of a contrasting v-neck and swish gold trim on the cuffs. Also worn with the navy shorts from the home kit.

Worn in: A grim 3–0 defeat by the Czech Republic in the group stage of the World Cup.
Worn by: Oguchi Onyewu, Bobby Convey.

2006 FIFA WORLD CUP

THIRD 2006

Design: Nike

The next in the heritage range of third strips continued the sash theme, with the sash now included on a practical deep red jersey that was complemented by a snazzy sock design. The collared uniform completed a fine set of kits, that in turn each featured vertical, horizontal and diagonal visual decoration.

Worn in: A 1–0 friendly win over Latvia just prior to the World Cup.
Worn by: Steve Cherundolo, Josh Wolff.

THIRD 2007

Design: Nike

The heritage third shirt took a new approach in 2007 with this attractive baseball-like royal blue shirt, decorated with closely spaced pinstripes. Red provided discreet highlights and the socks continued the multi-striped look of the previous third outfit. Bob Bradley was appointed manager at the end of 2006.

Worn in: A 1–0 win over Guatemala in the 2007 Gold Cup.
Worn by: Michael Bradley, Taylor Twellman.

HOME 2008–09

Design: Nike

The next US home kit was first worn in the second match of 2008 and dispensed with the bold colours of the previous shirts. Instead it opted for a more subdued decorative approach. The design featured pale hoops trimmed with red and topped with a mandarin-style neck.

Worn in: The astonishing 2009 Confederations Cup, including the incredible 2–0 win over Spain and the thrilling 3–2 defeat by Brazil in the final.
Worn by: Sascha Kljestan, Brian Ching.

AWAY 2008–09

Design: Nike

This charcoal grey change kit was such a deviation from the traditional colours of the US it was not surprising that supporters' opinions were divided. Small flashes of red decorated the neck and the cuffs. The shirt was worn with either white or unique charcoal change shorts.

Worn in: A superb debut – a 3–0 drubbing of Poland in a 2008 friendly.
Worn by: Carlos Bocanegra, Eddie Lewis.

HOME 2010–12

Design: Nike

Sashes were big news in the soccer sartorial world in 2010 and they returned to the US uniforms, albeit on the home kit in a very subtle shadow effect. A simple navy neck and red cuffs completed the pragmatic design along with Nike standard issue shorts and socks.

Worn in: A 2–1 defeat by Ghana in the knock-out stage of the 2010 World Cup. Also worn in the 4–2 loss to Mexico in the 2011 Gold Cup.
Worn by: Jozy Altidore, Robbie Findley.

AWAY 2010–12

Design: Nike

Nike issued the perfect accompaniment to the sleek all-white home kit in the shape of this navy strip, adorned with a white sash and enhanced with flashes of red. All of Nike's 2010 jerseys were made entirely from recycled polyester with each one made from up to eight recycled plastic bottles.

Worn in: Draws with England (1–1) and Slovenia (2–2) in the 2010 World Cup.
Worn by: Edson Buddle, Ricardo Clark.

THIRD 2011

Design: Nike

The fans' favourite colour, red, returned as core colour for this third kit, launched a year after its home and away partners with the #RedAllOver campaign. The only real difference came from the fact that this third strip featured just two colours. The kit helped complete a superb set of outfits for USMNT.

Worn in: A 2–0 victory over Jamaica in the 2011 Gold Cup.
Worn by: Juan Agudelo, Jay DeMerit.

HOME 2012

Design: Nike

Fans old enough to remember the 1983 Team America experiment must have enjoyed a wry smile when this strip was announced as it wore its influences plainly on its sleeve! All that was missing was a star or two. The shirt also featured a shadow sash. Jurgen Klinsmann was appointed team manager in 2011.

Worn in: A 5–1 thrashing of Scotland in a 2012 friendly – this kit's first outing.
Worn by: Jermaine Jones, Maurice Edu.

AWAY 2012–14

Design: Nike

There was something very appealing about this away kit with its navy body partnered by white sleeves and topped with a shadow sash. Both this and the home design featured laser-cut ventilation holes on each side. Unveiled with the same navy shorts as the home uniform, although white pairs were also worn.

Worn in: The 1–0 win over Panama in the 2013 Gold Cup final – the US' fifth Gold Cup crown.
Worn by: Brek Shea, Danny Williams.

HOME 2013

Design: Nike

To mark the 100th anniversary of the US Soccer Federation the team donned this retro-influenced white kit. The Dri-Fit fabric shirt featured an enlarged badge that reproduced the crest of the jersey worn in 1913 and was worn with white or navy shorts.

Worn in: The astonishing 4–3 friendly win over Germany – just one of many impressive friendly wins for Klinsmann's side during this period.
Worn by: Fabian Johnson.

HOME 2014–15

Design: Nike

US Soccer and Nike have certainly embraced a wide variety of wildly different kit designs over the years. After the excesses of the 2012 shirt, the following year the team kept it simple with an all-white outfit that included a flat-knit collared shirt, adorned only with shadow horizontal pinstripes and a touch of red trim.

Worn in: A narrow 2–1 defeat by Belgium (after extra time) in the World Cup knockout stage.
Worn by: Julian Green.

AWAY 2014

Design: Nike

Bright and bold colourways were rampant throughout Nike's offering during this era with many teams sporting loud and challenging designs. Red returned to the US colour palette, topped off with a broad white chest panel and blue yoke alongside tonal badges. This shirt featured laser-cut ventilation holes.

Worn in: A 2–1 victory over Ghana in the 2014 World Cup (revenge for the 2010 defeat!).
Worn by: Kyle Beckerman, Geoff Cameron.

AWAY 2015

Design: Nike

2015 brought a striking new theme to Nike's change kits with the introduction of tonal, painterly lines throughout its strips. The US version was crafted from a fading blue colour, trimmed with white and incorporating a small red neck insert.

Worn in: Two stunning consecutive friendly wins: 4–3 over the Netherlands and 2–1 against Germany.
Worn by: Gyasi Zardes, Bobby Wood.

HOME 2016–17, AWAY 2017

Design: Nike

One of the more controversial recent kit movements was Nike's 'Vapor' template. Generally, the Vapor socks featured a different colour to the shirts and shorts but in the US' case all three elements were white. The strip was worn as an away kit for the 2017 Gold Cup.

Worn in: A cruel twist on the 1989 result – the 2017 2–1 defeat by Trinidad and Tobago that meant the US would miss the 2018 World Cup.
Worn by: Chris Wondolowski, Graham Zusi.

AWAY 2016

Design: Nike

This unorthodox black change/road uniform was actually unveiled before its home equivalent to a mixed reaction from US fans. The shirt followed the Vapor template and included mismatched sleeves; one in dark red and one in navy. These kits also saw the introduction of a new modernistic team crest.

Worn in: A 2016 Copa America 4–1 thrashing of Costa Rica.
Worn by: Alejandro Bedoya, DeAndre Yedlin.

AWAY 2017

Design: Nike

Two tones of red formed the next away kit, which was again in the Vapor template featuring Nike's AeroSwift fabric technology. The slimfit and lightweight shirt also featured text on the cuffs of each sleeve: '1 nation' on one and '1 team' on the other. As usual, the environmental credentials of these kits were impeccable.

Worn in: A 1–1 draw with Honduras in a 2018 World Cup qualifier.
Worn by: Christian Pulisic, Matt Besler.

★

HOME 2017–18

Design: Nike

A special new strip was launched for sole use in the 2017 Gold Cup. Despite relying on a red and navy colourway there was a certain air of the famous Team America 1983 strip to this design, thanks to the cool stars on the shoulders and sleeves and the hooped design. Shadow stars also adorned the fabric.

Worn in: The wonderful 2–1 victory over Jamaica in the 2017 Gold Cup final.
Worn by: Jordan Morris, Kellyn Perry-Acosta.

2018 FIFA WORLD CUP

Just two of the adidas kits football fans can look forward to seeing in the 2018 World Cup: the retro-styled Belgian and the samurai-inspired Japanese home strips

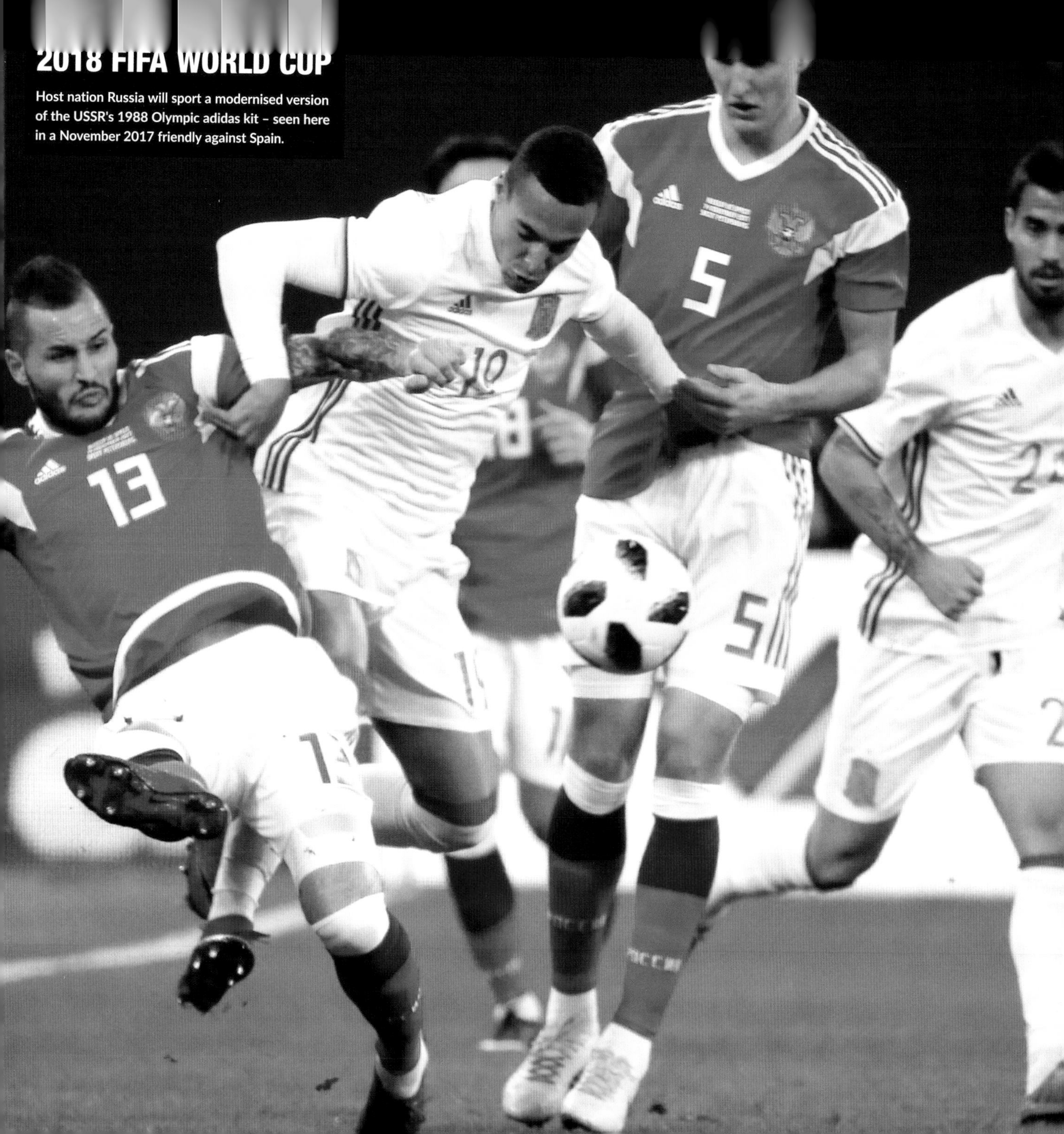

2018 FIFA WORLD CUP

Host nation Russia will sport a modernised version of the USSR's 1988 Olympic adidas kit – seen here in a November 2017 friendly against Spain.

WALES

Sadly the red of Wales has been seen at fewer major tournaments than the nation, and its roll call of fine players, deserve.

Whether it's in a dynamic all-red or a more traditional pairing with white shorts, the Wales kit has traditionally been one of the strongest of the home UK nations. And when it's enhanced with a little yellow and green, taken from the crest of the Football Association of Wales (FAW), it looks even better.

Typical Wales away kits vary from combinations of yellow and green to a plain and simple white. With customary boldness, adidas introduced a slate grey away kit to accompany Chris Coleman's team as Wales finally qualified for a major tournament, Euro 2016, after a gap of nearly 60 years. Unfortunately the side failed to win a game in the unpopular outfit, which was eventually discarded.

Despite their lack of major tournament exposure, there have been many iconic Welsh strips throughout the years. The famous Admiral tramline design from the mid '70s, which first introduced the additional palette of yellow and green, is often considered a favourite among Wales supporters.

The '80s was another golden decade for Wales. The teams were kitted out by adidas and then Hummel, both companies ensuring the side always looked superb. The Hummel era gave birth to one of the rarest of Wales kits: the white shirt worn against the Netherlands in 1990.

Unlike many national sides who remain with the same kit supplier for many years, Wales have partnered with many different companies over the years, including Umbro, in several different phases; Champion; Lotto and Kappa, who employed their groundbreaking range of Kombat kits for the Welsh side in a breathtaking array of colours. Today, the side are back with adidas.

SPECIAL THANKS TO SIMON 'SHAKEY' SHAKESHAFT

Wales line up prior to a 1983 Home International match against Scotland in Swansea. Wales are wearing their 1980–84 adidas home strip.

HOME 1966–67

Design: Umbro

The classic Wales '60s strip saw a typical long sleeved, contrasting crew-neck jersey (Umbro's famous 'Aztec' design) accompanied by red shorts and red socks with white turnover. The team crest was applied as a patch, with match details embroidery above. The '60s proved a dire time for the national side.

Worn in: A 5–1 drubbing at the hands of the World Champions, England, in 1966.
Worn by: Alan Jarvis, Cliff Jones.

AWAY 1966–67

Design: Umbro

Yellow and green were the favoured change colours of Wales during this time. However, an away kit was rarely required so this strip saw very little in the way of pitch action during its tenure. The shorts featured a little additional trim in the way of green stripes on each leg. The same badge patch from the home kit was also used on these jerseys. It is believed that a plain yellow jersey was used from 1967 to 1974

HOME 1967–72

Design: Umbro

The late '60s saw a real trend in single-colour kits that featured no contrasting trim whatsoever and it was to this style that Dave Bowen's men switched as the decade ended. Amazingly, this strip was worn in no fewer than 25 consecutive matches!

Worn in: The 2–0 win over Northern Ireland in a Euro 1968 qualifier – a rare victory during a poor period for the Welsh.
Worn by: Wyn Davies, Ronnie Rees.

HOME 1972

Design: Umbro

A real rarity in the Wales kit canon was this yellow-trimmed Bukta strip, worn just once against England. A local Cardiff sports shop had agreed to sponsor the match and provided a set of Bukta strips, which the team sported instead of their regular Umbro kits. Made from a scratchy, bri-nylon fabric.

Worn in: A 3–0 defeat against England in the Home Internationals.
Worn by: Terry Hennessey, Ron Davies.

HOME 1972–74

Design: Umbro

The Wales kit was refreshed in 1972 to include white shorts, instead of the previous red, which were trimmed in a similar way to the away kit, with a single red stripe on each leg. The jersey remained the same and retained the patch-style team crest.

Worn in: A 2–0 triumph over Poland in a 1974 World Cup qualifier (1973).
Worn by: John Roberts, Trevor Hockey.

AWAY 1973

Design: Umbro

Given the rareness of the Welsh playing in anything other than red at this time, to see them take to the field in Poland in green must have raised a few eyebrows! Essentially a reversal of the previous yellow away strip, the shirt was worn with the white shorts from the home kit and with numbered sock tags.

Worn in: A 1973 3–0 defeat against Poland in a 1974 World Cup qualifier – its only outing.
Worn by: Brian Evans, Mike England.

HOME 1974

Design: Umbro

There were just another tiny couple of tweaks to this strip in the final year of the Umbro deal: a new team crest, no longer as part of a rectangular patch and minus match details, and a tiny Umbro logo – the first manufacturer's logo to appear on a Wales outfield shirt.

Worn in: Wins over Hungary (2–0) and Luxembourg (5–0) in the qualifiers for Euro 76.
Worn by: John Toshack, Gil Reece.

AWAY 1974

Design: Umbro

Yellow was back in the kit cupboard as Mike Smith's Wales team's change colour in a very simple, non-contrasting Aztec jersey, complete with the old-style patch Wales badge. As with many teams the Welsh only wore long sleeved shirts at this time – apart from John Toshack who always preferred short sleeves.

Worn in: A 2–0 defeat against Scotland in the Home Internationals.
Worn by: Malcolm Page, Tony Villars.

HOME 1975

Design: Bukta

To the casual observer this next home strip was no different to the previous, but along with the recently introduced badge style sat the logo of Bukta, who took over the Wales kit deal this year. The shorts, apart from the Bukta logo, remained the same.

Worn in: A close 1–0 victory over Austria in a Euro 76 qualifier.
Worn by: Arfon Griffiths, Brian Flynn.

AWAY 1975

Design: Bukta

Yellow and white are colours that can prove difficult to make work on a team strip, but add a green Bukta logo and you have a distinctive and very Welsh design (especially considering the yellow was described as 'Daffodil Yellow'!). Long sleeves and a crew neck remained on these shirts that were officially named 'Forum'.

Worn in: A 2–1 win in Hungary in a Euro 76 qualifier (1975).
Worn by: Rod Thomas, John Mahoney.

HOME 1976–79

Design: Admiral

Without doubt one of the most popular ever away strips emerged in 1976 courtesy of football kit masters, Admiral, which were dominating football strip innovation in the mid '70s. This famous 'tramline' design in yellow and green was the perfect Welsh complement to the core red colour.

Worn in: A memorable 1–0 win over England in the 1977 Home Internationals.
Worn by: Terry Yorath, Joey Jones.

AWAY 1976–79

Design: Admiral

The yellow Admiral strip replicated the design of the home and completed a superb set of kits for Mike Smith's side. Admiral logos appeared on each lapel and the badge was placed centrally. The yellow socks were worn on occasion with the home outfit.

Worn in: A 1–0 defeat against Czechoslovakia (1977) and a 7–0 thrashing of Malta the following year.
Worn by: Ian Edwards, Leighton Phillips.

HOME 1980–84

Design: adidas

Wales entered the '80s in one of their most iconic jerseys of recent years. Produced by adidas, the shirt introduced white raglan sleeves to the previously all-red shirt, along with a modern v-neck and the ever-present three-stripe mark. The shorts included large red panels on either leg.

Worn in: The stunning 4–1 win over England in the 1980 Home Internationals.
Worn by: Ian Walsh, Mickey Thomas.

AWAY 1980–84

Design: adidas

Adidas' first away strip for Wales mirrored the design of the home in a splendid yellow and green. As with many of their kits at the time, the adidas logo moved from leg to leg throughout the strip's lifespan. Mike England was appointed manager in 1979 in an effort to lift the side to that coveted World Cup qualification.

Worn in: The marvellous 1–0 win in France in a 1982 friendly.
Worn by: Gordon Davies, Jeremy Charles.

THIRD 1982–85

Design: adidas

Many teams in adidas' roster at this time were presented with an additional third kit featuring national colours. However, these strips, worn by junior sides (the Wales U21s donned it against the Dutch), were not often sported by the first teams. This exquisite white shirt with green pinstripes and non-contrasting v-neck and cuffs is a fine example. It is presumed it would have been worn with green shorts and white socks.

HOME 1983

Design: adidas

In the final year of this popular outfit's lifetime the long sleeved version was given a subtle, modernising makeover for just two games. Shadow pinstripes were added along with a plainer style of shorts, minus the additional red panels. Following these games, the side reverted to the standard short sleeved design.

Worn in: A superb 5–0 triumph over Romania and a 1–1 draw with Yugoslavia.
Worn by: Kenny Jackett, Paul Price.

HOME 1984–87

Design: adidas

The home kit was debuted in May 1984 and featured an all-red shirt decorated by three pairs of white bands, each with increasing gaps of darker red between them. The v-neck and cuffs incorporated additional red trim. Also worn with white socks.

Worn in: The famous 3–0 win over Spain and the controversial 1985 1–1 draw with Scotland in a 1986 World Cup qualifier (both 1985).
Worn by: Mark Hughes, Ian Rush.

AWAY 1984–87

Design: adidas

A simple but strong combination of yellow and green formed this seldom worn away kit, decorated naturally with adidas' three-stripe trim. This functional design was worn by a glut of superb players that sadly could still not find the breakthrough to a major tournament.

Worn in: A World Cup qualifier 3–0 defeat against Spain and a thrilling 4–2 defeat against Norway in a friendly match.
Worn by: Alan Curtis, Kevin Ratcliffe.

HOME 1987–90

Design: Hummel

After seven years with adidas, Wales switched to Danish company Hummel, known primarily for its gorgeously daring strips at the time. It launched an attractive silky kit that opted for an all-red approach. White seam piping, shadow patterned fabric and Hummel's distinctive chevron trim featured prominently.

Worn in: A 0–0 draw with Germany in the disappointing 1990 World Cup qualifiers.
Worn by: Glyn Hodges, Clayton Blackmore.

AWAY 1987–90

Design: Hummel

Hummel opted for the same design as the graceful home outfit for this slim fitting change strip but introduced a new colourway. The yellow was now accompanied by black rather than green trim. Mike England's long reign as Welsh manager ended in 1988 after failing to qualify for Euro 88. He was replaced by Terry Yorath.

Worn in: A 1988 1–0 friendly win over Italy.
Worn by: Robbie James, Malcolm Allen.

THIRD 1988–90

Design: Hummel

The 1988 World Cup qualifier against the Netherlands threw up a problem for the FAW as both Welsh strips clashed to some extent with the Netherlands' famous orange. To solve the problem this rare white version of the strip was produced and paired up with the home shorts.

Worn in: The 1990 World Cup qualifying match against the Netherlands that ended in a 1–0 defeat (1988).
Worn by: Alan Davies, Peter Nicholas.

HOME 1990–92

Design: Umbro

From one classy and elegant strip to another... Umbro returned to the Welsh kitbag in 1990 and retained the all-red approach Hummel had introduced three years earlier. However, green was now becoming an integral part of the colour scheme again. An updated version of Umbro's diamond trim adorned the kit.

Worn in: Stunning 1991 1–0 wins over giants of world football, West Germany and Brazil.
Worn by: Mark Aizlewood, Eric Young.

AWAY 1990–93

Design: Umbro

Flamboyant designs were the order of the day as the '90s dawned, but crafted within a traditional structure. A green and red pattern decorated the shoulders and sleeves of this glamorous ensemble. The shorts reflected the design of the home pairs, complete with large trimmed side panels.

Worn in: A poor 2–0 defeat by Belgium in a 1994 World Cup qualifier (1992).
Worn by: Dean Saunders, Paul Bodin.

HOME 1992–94

Design: Umbro

Large all-over prints were the height of fashion in the early '90s and this Wales kit, with its subtle shadow red dragon design and Umbro logo fabric, is typical of the era. The overall cut of the strip was much larger than in recent years and included the revival of long shorts.

Worn in: The 2–1 defeat against Romania that ensured Wales would miss out on the World Cup yet again.
Worn by: Gary Speed, Ryan Giggs.

AWAY 1993-94

Design: Umbro

The previous away kit was retained for a third season ensuring that Umbro could introduce at least one new Welsh kit every year. As well as its lively combination of red and green pinstripes, the shirt also featured a retro '20s style button-up collar. Mike Smith was appointed manager of the side in 1994.

Worn in: A disastrous 3-2 defeat against Moldova in the Euro 96 qualifying campaign.
Worn by: Mark Pembridge, Jeremy Goss.

HOME 1994-96

Design: Umbro

Umbro's last Wales home strip resurrected the green missing from the previous strip with the colour playing a more prominent role in the strip than it had for some time. This standard Umbro design included pairs of green pinstripes along with a diagonal shadow pinstriped fabric.

Worn in: A 3-1 defeat by Norway in a 1994 friendly; the solitary game played under John Toshack in his first spell as Welsh manager.
Worn by: Nathan Blake, Iwan Roberts.

AWAY 1995-96

Design: Umbro

Umbro went out with a bang with this audacious change strip that was introduced at the end of Wales' awful Euro 96 qualifiers. For some, the eccentric away shirts of the mid-'90s were becoming a little too outrageous and fans were certainly bemused by this dark blue strip with its abstract expressionism style print.

Worn in: A 1-0 win over Moldova in 1995 – a rare Euro 96 qualifier victory.
Worn by: Vinnie Jones, Chris Coleman.

HOME 1996-98

Design: Lotto

Italian sportswear company Lotto took over from Umbro in August 1996 as Wales kit suppliers. It made an immediate impact with this confident new strip which, thanks to its central green and white vertical stripes and asymmetrical colour trim, was way ahead of its time.

Worn in: A 6-0 thrashing of San Marino in a 1996 qualifier for the 1998 World Cup.
Worn by: Simon Haworth, Marcus Browning.

AWAY 1996-98

Design: Lotto

Wales went for an aggressive look with this away strip which apparently had some design input from manager Bobby Gould. The shirt reverted to white, but featured a large red 'toothed' pattern on the chest accompanied by green panels on each sleeve with a single enigmatic red stripe on the left.

Worn in: The 7-1 thrashing at the hands of the Netherlands on the kit's debut (1998).
Worn by: John Oster, Gareth Taylor.

THIRD 1996-97

Design: Lotto

The extravagantly embellished green Lotto away shorts made perfect sense when teamed with this green third shirt. Decorated with a broad combination of pinstripes, fading panels and two distinct shades of green, it was an extraordinary design that resembled a leisure polo top more than a football shirt.

Worn in: The astonishing 6-4 defeat by Turkey in a 1997 qualifier for the 1998 World Cup.
Worn by: Karl Ready, Ceri Hughes.

THIRD 1998

Design: Lotto

The plain and simple design proved a palette cleanser after the wild excesses of the previous all-green away kit. It was worn only once, in a friendly against Tunisia, and was a precursor to the next batch of Lotto kits due to be launched later in the year. The shirt featured a basic collar and unobtrusive shadow pattern.

Worn in: A dreadful 4-0 defeat against Tunisia in a 1998 friendly.
Worn by: Robbie Savage, Craig Bellamy.

HOME 1998-2000

Design: Lotto

Wales chose the Euro 2000 qualifier with Italy in 1998 to launch their next kit. The home design featured a simple white collar and cuffs (trimmed with a little red and green) complemented by fine white side piping and a repeated shadow pattern of the Wales crest.

Worn in: A close 3-2 triumph over Belarus in a Euro 2000 qualifier (the only competitive win in this shirt in a dark period for the Welsh).
Worn by: Steve Jenkins, Andy Legg.

AWAY 1998–2000

Design: Lotto

An all-yellow equivalent of the second Lotto home kit was also worn – the first yellow Wales kit for eight years.. The strip replicated the stylings of the home, including the repeated shadow pattern of the Wales crest and the large dragon print. Mark Hughes was appointed manager in 1999 following Gould's departure.

Worn in: The 2–0 defeat by Switzerland in a 1999 Euro 200 qualifier (its only outing).
Worn by: Noel Blake, Mark Delaney.

THIRD 1998–2000

Design: Lotto

A white third kit was also produced to allow for any possible clash eventuality and, like the yellow strip, it was worn only once. The outfit mirrored the design of the home and away kits – the only difference coming from the inclusion of a 'distressed' green dragon graphic rather than the watermarked version on the others.

Worn in: A 1–0 victory over Qatar in a 2000 friendly match.
Worn by: Kit Symons, John Robinson.

FOURTH 1998–2000

Design: Lotto

This all-yellow strip was a real curiosity. Another 'one kit wonder', its only outing was just a month after the standard kits had been unveiled. Quite why the side did not don the regular yellow away strip is a mystery. Interestingly, the Wales B team were known to sport a home-themed version of this kit.

Worn in: The superb 2–1 Euro 2000 qualifier victory over Denmark in 1998.
Worn by: Adrian Williams, Darren Barnard.

HOME 2000

Design: Kappa

Another Italian company, Kappa, took over the supply of Welsh kits and its first outfit for the side was one of the most curious home strips the team have worn as it lasted for just two games before being superseded later in the year. Replica versions were never produced of what was presumably only ever a temporary kit.

Worn in: 3–0 friendly defeats to both Brazil and Portugal.
Worn by: Gareth Roberts, Iwan Roberts.

HOME 2000–02

Design: Kappa

After the previous stop-gap shirt, the Kappa era kicked off in magnificent style with the launch of the Kombat 2000 strips. Developed to thwart the increasing trend of shirt-pulling, the tighter fitting jerseys also featured reversed stitching and sophisticated badge placement with a Kappa logo on each sleeve.

Worn in: A classic 1–0 win for Mark Hughes' Wales over Germany in a 2000 friendly.
Worn by: Jason Koumas, Carl Robinson.

AWAY 2000–02

Design: Kappa

Maintaining its reputation for aesthetically simple yet functional designs, Kappa introduced this reversal of the home outfit for its first Wales away kit. One slight alteration saw red reversed stitching used instead of white. The shorts and socks were designed to mix and match between this and the home outfit.

Worn in: A narrow 3–2 defeat by Norway in 2001 during the 2002 World Cup qualifiers.
Worn by: Steve Jenkins, Simon Davies.

THIRD 2002

Design: Kappa

To a mixed response from the Welsh faithful, this yellow and blue third Kombat 2000 kit was released in 2002 and worn for the only time in a home friendly that year. Kappa explained that the inspiration behind the unusual colour combination came from the yellow and blue included in the Wales crest.

Worn in: The 0–0 draw with the Czech Republic in a 2002 friendly.
Worn by: Andy Melville, John Hartson.

FOURTH 2002

Design: Kappa

One of the rarest kits worn by a Welsh national side was this all pale yellow ensemble, yet another kit that only saw action once. It was presumably created as it was felt that all three Welsh outfits clashed too closely with Croatia's strip at the time, which consisted of a large red and white chequerboard design, amply trimmed with blue. Replica versions were never made.

Worn in: A 1–1 friendly draw with Croatia.
Worn by: Paul Trollope, Robert Earnshaw.

HOME 2002–04

Design: Kappa

Kappa's new template, the Kombat 2002, arrived with Wales enjoying a long-overdue rich vein of form. The shirt featured more white than had been worn in some years, with underarm panels in breathable fabric combining with white reversed stitching. The shorts switched back to red and included broad side panels.

Worn in: The unbelievable Euro 2004 qualifier 2–1 win over Italy in 2002.
Worn by: Robert Page, Rhys Weston.

AWAY 2002–04

Design: Kappa

A plain and simple reversal of the stunning new home kit was launched as Wales' next away choice. The only alteration was the inclusion of a red neck design in preference to a non-contrasting version. However, this strip was never worn. Although these Kappa kits employed the clinging lycra 'second-skin' approach, replica versions were produced in much larger sizes for less athletic Welsh fans.

THIRD 2003–05

Design: Kappa

For the first time a rich shade of blue was chosen for a Wales away kit. Following the Kombat 2003 template, the shirt featured yellow reversed stitching and a similar neck design to that included on the first set of Kappa strips. As was the case with the white away kit, this good-looking blue outfit never made it out of the Wales kit cupboard.

HOME 2004–06

Design: Kappa

There was something unique about Kappa kits at this time. The impression was that they were simply functional items, driven solely by a practical purpose with no unnecessary trim. This Kombat 2004 all-red kit is a great example of this ethos. Very similar to the 2000 kit with the exception of additional ventilation mesh panels.

Worn in: The wonderful 3–2 2005 away win vs Northern Ireland (2006 World Cup qualifier).
Worn by: Ben Thatcher, Paul Parry.

AWAY 2004–06

Design: Kappa

With the new home kit all red, it followed naturally that the new away kit would be a heroic all white that followed the same stylish template as the home. A small embroidered 'Cymru' was included on the reverse. The kits were launched with the advertising tagline: 'Italian style – Welsh passion'.

Worn in: The 2005 2–0 home friendly win over Hungary.
Worn by: Sam Ricketts, Danny Collins.

THIRD 2005–06

Design: Kappa

The FAW and Kappa made a moving tribute to the memory of Wales legend John Charles with the August 2005 launch of this distinctive third kit in his honour. Inspiration for the design came from the various clubs where Charles played his football; the white of Leeds, the stripes of Juventus and, of course, the red of Wales.

Worn in: The unfortunate 1–0 defeat by Poland in the 2006 World Cup qualifying campaign.
Worn by: James Collins, David Partridge.

HOME 2006–07

Design: Kappa

The Welsh kit of 1958, the last time the nation reached a major tournament, was the inspiration for this home strip (launched to celebrate 130 years of the FAW). A broad, plunging v-neck, uncluttered front and the return of white shorts, complete with broad red trim, combined to create a classic, retro-themed strip.

Worn in: A 3–1 triumph over Cyprus in a 2006 qualifier for Euro 2008.
Worn by: Carl Fletcher, Lewin Nyatanga.

AWAY 2006–07

Design: Kappa

Yellow and green returned with some vigour to the Wales palette to recreate the set of classic Wales kits of 1958, complete with slightly looser fitting shirts and VERY long shorts. Mirroring the design of the home, the jersey exuded style.

Worn in: A 2–1 defeat against the Czech Republic in a Euro 2008 qualifier (2006).
Worn by: Gareth Bale, who made his debut in this shirt against Trinidad and Tobago in 2006.

THIRD 2007

Design: Kappa

Another one-off third kit emerged in 2007 to commemorate the 130th anniversary of Wrexham's Racecourse Ground. It reverted back to a predominantly white strip adorned with alternate green and red sleeves. Wales kitman David Griffiths played a large part in the strip's design.

Worn in: A 2–2 friendly home draw with New Zealand.
Worn by: Chris Gunter, Joe Ledley.

HOME 2007–08

Design: Kappa

After just a single season the smart retro-style kit was replaced by a new all-red style, which arguably was the least inspired of all the Kappa Welsh kits. A similar neck design to the 2002 shirt was joined by a faint dragon watermark on the shirt. Match details started to be included on the kit at this time.

Worn in: An impressive 5–2 triumph over Slovakia (2007) in a Euro 2008 qualifier.
Worn by: Danny Gabbidon, Craig Morgan.

AWAY 2007–08

Design: Kappa

Kappa said 'arrivederci' to the Welsh side in 2008 and for its final Welsh kit it unveiled this popular design in yellow and red. The design followed the lead of the home, including the striking pointed flashes on the side. The shirt was just worn twice by the senior side.

Worn in: A 3–0 win at home over Norway in a 2008 friendly.
Worn by: Freddy Eastwood, Jason Koumas.

HOME 2008–10

Design: Champion

The FAW and JJB Sports signed a six-year deal in 2008 with the company's in-house brand, Champion, appointed to supply the team kit. The all-red strip featured contemporary angular white flashes on either side which were complemented by a flash of green on the neck.

Worn in: Wins over Azerbaijan (1–0) and Liechtenstein (2–0) in 2008 qualifiers for the 2010 World Cup.
Worn by: Sam Vokes, Ashley Williams.

AWAY 2009–10

Design: Champion

This sumptuous white strip formed Champion's first change kit. Featuring a different template to the home, curved side panels, delicately trimmed with green, provided the main focus. Following John Hartson's health issues a special one-off version of the shirt was worn as a promotion for cancer charity Checkemlads.com.

Worn in: A home 1–0 friendly win against Estonia in 2009.
Worn by: Joe Cole, Gareth Barry.

THIRD 2008–10

Design: Champion

Bizarrely, this third kit appeared BEFORE the official white away kit, with some fans calling for it to be made the first choice change outfit thanks to its use of the favoured yellow and green colour combination. John Toshack left his position as Welsh manager in 2010.

Worn in: A 1–0 win in Denmark in a 2008 friendly.
Worn by: Jack Collison, Ched Evans.

HOME 2010–11

Design: Umbro

Following the brief sojourn with Champion, the FAW returned to Umbro as part of its deal with JJB. The 'Tailored by Umbro' ethos was in full swing and Wales were supplied with a strong, non-contrasting v-neck shirt (in a light, breathable fabric), plain shorts and perfectly balanced striped socks.

Worn in: A great 5–1 triumph over Luxembourg on the kit's debut in 2010.
Worn by: Andy King, Brian Stock.

AWAY 2010–11

Design: Umbro

A basic, but pragmatic, white change shirt was the first to be produced under the new series of Umbro strips. A neat red collar provided the only contrast and the shirt was worn with red shorts or the white pairs from the home kit.

Worn in: An all-white 4–1 drubbing at the hands of Switzerland in 2010.
Worn by: Andrew Crofts, Christian Ribeiro.

HOME 2011–12

Design: Umbro

September 2011 brought this alluring strip, which reverted to an all-red colourway, trimmed on the neck and cuffs with white. Broad shadow stripes added texture to the shirt. 2011 proved to be a sad year for Welsh football when it was announced team manager Gary Speed passed away in November.

Worn in: A 2–0 victory against Switzerland in a Euro 2012 qualifier (2011).
Worn by: Aaron Ramsey, Simon Church.

AWAY 2011–12

Design: Umbro

Slate grey and red were the order of the day with this kit, crafted in a design also used with the home kit and featuring a unique 'y-neck' collar. Breathable mesh fabric underarm panels were included on this 'Tailored by Umbro' strip. Major tournament qualification was still sadly proving out of reach for the Welsh side.

Worn in: The dreadful 6–1 defeat by Serbia in a 2012 qualifier for the 2014 World Cup.
Worn by: Darcy Blake, Joe Allen.

HOME 2012–13

Design: Umbro

With Chris Coleman's Wales now in a sequence of single-year kits a new design was launched that brought back memories of Admiral's glory days thanks to its prominent inclusion of yellow and green. This stunning outfit managed to encapsulate Wales' visual identity well (even more so when worn with green change socks!).

Worn in: Two 2–1 wins over Scotland in 2014 World Cup qualifiers.
Worn by: Hal Robson-Kanu, Ben Davies.

AWAY 2012–13

Design: Umbro

Umbro's last hurrah for Wales was this adventurous green and white halved affair. The strip featured a sophisticated collar with covered placket and breathable mesh panels. The shorts and socks were plain, with an Umbro logo on the socks (that oddly didn't appear on the home pairs).

Worn in: A 2–0 World Cup qualifier defeat against Croatia in 2012.
Worn by: David Vaughan, Steve Morison.

HOME 2013–14

Design: adidas

After 27 years away a prodigal adidas returned to the FAW. Its first returning strip, which snuck out towards the end of 2013, utilised one of its standard teamwear templates, 'Tabela 14' (featuring diagonal shadow stripes) with the addition of a self-coloured v-neck. The kit was launched with an 'all in or nothing' tagline.

Worn in: The 2–1 triumph vs Cyprus in a 2014 qualifier for Euro 2016.
Worn by: Owain Tudur Jones, Jonny Williams.

AWAY 2013–14

Design: adidas

A not unpleasant, but perhaps slightly pedestrian, all-white strip became the side's new change strip. The shirt used the 'Condivo 14' template, which included shadow horizontal stripes. Shorts and socks were straightforward reversals of the home pairs.

Worn in: A fine 2–1 win against Andorra in 2014 (Euro 2016 qualifier).
Worn by: Emyr Huws, George Williams.

HOME 2014–15

Design: adidas

A bright 'electric' green and red came together beautifully for this new strip with the fabric offset with fine white pinstripes. A mesh-style trim was used on the neck, cuffs and bottom hem of the shirt. This swish shirt featured adidas' hi-tech Climacool fabric.

Worn in: The 2–0 defeat by Bosnia-Herzegovina that, despite the loss, saw Wales at last qualify for a major tournament – Euro 2016!
Worn by: Jazz Richards, Neil Taylor.

AWAY 2014–15

Design: adidas

An optimistic Wales side continued their Euro 2016 qualifying campaign in this bright and bold yellow and red change kit. A defiant band stretched across the chest accompanied, of course, by adidas' trademark three-stripe trim on the shoulders. The shorts and socks mirrored the design of the home pairs.

Worn in: A vital 2014 0–0 draw in Belgium en route to Euro 2016 qualification.
Worn by: Dave Cotterill, James Chester.

HOME 2015–17

Design: adidas

First worn in November 2015, this sharp red and white strip illustrated the no-nonsense approach Wales planned to take to Euro 2016. Functional rather than flashy, the shirt's only main decoration were very subtle shadow pinstripes.

Worn in: The incredible 3–1 victory over Belgium in the quarter-finals of Euro 2016 – the Welsh enjoying a magnificent tournament.
Worn by: Tom Lawrence, Adam Matthews.

AWAY 2016–17

Design: adidas

A two-tone grey Climacool strip was selected to be the Welsh change outfit for Euro 2016. To provide contrast against the sombre uniform a lively green trim was added. The adidas logo now appeared on the reverse of the shorts.

Worn in: The side's two defeats at Euro 2016: 2–1 to England (where arguably the red home kit would have been a better choice) and 2–0 to Portugal in the semi-finals.
Worn by: Adam Henley, Shaun MacDonald.

AWAY 2017

Design: adidas

With the grey away strip gathering a reputation as being unlucky (the team failing to win any of the five matches in which it was worn!), it was announced a new one-off yellow and black change kit (the 'Squadra 17' template) would be worn against Moldova in 2017, much to the relief of players and supporters.

Worn in: A 2–0 win over Moldova in a vital 2018 World Cup qualifier.
Worn by: Ben Woodburn.

HOME 2017–18

Design: adidas

It was a return to all-red for the kit that should have accompanied Chris Coleman's men in the 2018 World Cup – had they qualified. Amidst a flurry of historically influenced designs from adidas this outfit stood out due to its lack of retro stylings, instead featuring a smart and clean look with a single-button crew neck.

Worn in: A 2–0 defeat against France in 2017.
Worn by: Ethan Ampadu, David Brooks.

Gareth Bale celebrates a goal against Scotland in a 2012 qualifier for the 2014 World Cup wearing the stunning Umbro 2012–13 home kit.

The acclaimed adidas USA away kit seen in action here as Cobi Jones takes on Florin Raducioiu of Romania in the 1994 FIFA World Cup.

Dirk Kuyt in a Nike Netherlands kits takes on Sergio Ramos in Spain's adidas away strip during the 2010 FIFA World Cup Final.

CREDITS & ACKNOWLEDGEMENTS

I am indebted to so many people who have helped me make this book happen, I'll try to cover as many people as I can but please forgive me if I miss any of you out!

Firstly, I must say a massive thank you to my wife Julie and daughter Amelie who have been so patient and understanding while I shut myself away in order to get this book finished.

Thank you to Matthew Lowing at Bloomsbury for his unwavering faith and positivity in this project.

Also to my close football kit friends who through their encouragement, inspiration, wisdom and support have helped make this project much easier: Rich Johnson, Chris Oakley and Jay Handley.

Also huge thanks to experts in the subject: Denis Hurley, Joey Smith, Jesse Rabbeljee, Les Motherby, Nicholas Larimer, Gustavo Tomás, Juan José Sánchez, Rob Stokes, Morten Garberg, Mikhail Sipovich, Neal Heard, Austin Long and the legend that is Simon 'Shakey' Shakeshaft.

Thanks also to Juergen Rank and Inigo Turner at adidas for their insights.

And huge thanks to Sean Pankhurst for his help.

Finally a big thank you to all my friends and family who have supported me through some trying times whilst this book was being written, especially: Carl Adams, David Shields, Chris Cachia, Dean Cachia, Elaine Johnson, Laura Hurley-Barrett, Siobhan Stirling, Annabelle Webster, Leon Maidment, Ben Parrish, Nash Kumar, Richard Clarke, Damian Young, Andrea Blurton, Emily & Damon Catt, my inspirational sister Helen and especially the life-saving Caroline Ayers.

Thank you to all the sportswear companies and football federations worldwide who have granted me permission to include them in the book: Jason McDonald (who went above and beyond!), David Seales, Peter Achterman, Jerome Tellier, Andre Delgado, Chris Bakker, Aaron Lavery, Jonathan Hamburger, Gary Dixon, Morten Lund, Mathias Levacq, Hanna Leback, Rowan Hagemann, Nuno Moura, Dave Dekker, Francois Vasseur, Charlotte Hughes, Steven Romeo, Bruno Romeiro, Katja Moesgaard, Mike Gressle, Ian Mallon, Rob Dowling, David Antonietty, Jordi Nolla, Victor M. Alvarado Rodriguez, Heather Wright, Aleksey Savula, Bruno Romeiro, Francesca Casali, Andy Ward, Ebbe Delfs, Kim den Hertog, Maxine Monfries.

Here are just a few of the websites that were referenced for this book.

www.historicalkits.co.uk
www.oldfootballshirts.com
www.switchimageproject.blogspot.co.uk
www.erojkit.com
www.footballshirtculture.com
www.kirefootballkits.blogspot.co.uk
www.project-2010.net
www.classicfootballshirts.co.uk
www.vintagefootballshirts.co.uk
www.socceroverthere.com
www.englandfootballonline.com
www.ussoccer.com
www.chariotsoffire11.blogspot.com
www.futbolmundialkits.blogspot.co.uk
www.colours-of-football.com
www.equiposdefutbol2.blogspot.co.uk
www.cityfootballshirt.blogspot.co.uk
www.camisetasseleccion.es
www.myway.de/matchworn/Match_Worn_Shirts
www.portugalmatchworn.com
www.flickr.com/photos/swedenshirts
www.northernirelandmatchworn.com
www.englandmatchshirts.com
www.walesmatchshirts.com
www.stevensfootballshirts.net
www.irelandsoccershirts.com
www.museumofjerseys.com
www.kitbliss.co.nz

Photo credits

The publishers would like to thank the following sources for their kind permission to reproduce the pictures in this book:

All photographic images courtesy of Getty Images, with the exception of the following:

Alamy 79 (1)

Press Association Images 76, 79 (3)

It was the small 'Observer Book of Football', and it's colour plate section that illustrated the shirts of the entire English Football League that first sparked John's interest in football kits. A seed of a dream was planted and decades later his ambition of producing the world's first comprehensive study of football kit history in England was born in the shape of 'True Colours'.

John was born in Essex and after a decade in the record industry he returned to full time education at the Kent Institute of Art and Design to study for a degree in Graphic Design. As part of his final project he resurrected his love of football kit design and began the research and study that would later emerge as True Colours – a book that received acclaim from kit manufacturers, football clubs, sponsors and fans alike, spearheading a new fascination with football kit design and history.

Since the publication of that groundbreaking book and it's subsequent follow up, 'True Colours Volume 2', John has contributed to many magazines, books and websites along with numerous radio interviews and a leading role in the acclaimed documentary on Admiral Sportswear 'Get Shirty' on ITV. He's also worked in a consultancy role with leading sportswear manufacturers and continues to be immersed in the football kit world.

Today, he runs his own graphic design agency, The Design Practice, based in Maidstone and lives in a small village with his wife and daughter.

www.truecoloursfootballkits.com
www.thedesignpractice.co.uk

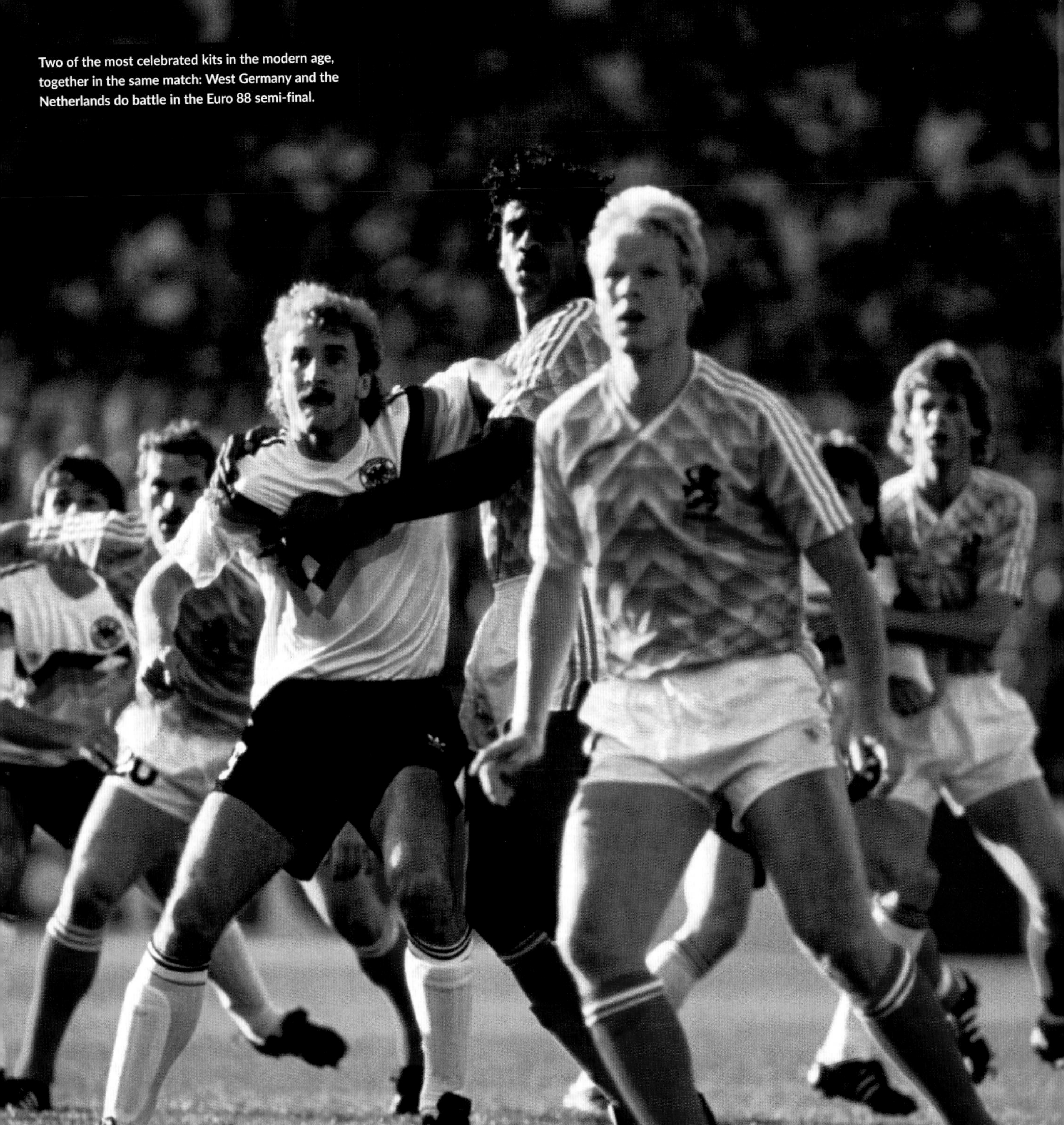

Two of the most celebrated kits in the modern age, together in the same match: West Germany and the Netherlands do battle in the Euro 88 semi-final.

USSR (in adidas) and Brazil (in Topper) compete in a group stage match from the 1982 World Cup finals – Brazil won the game 2–1.